THE
BIRMINGHAM
LAW
SOCIETY

Presented to <u>LOUISE ANN PHEASANT</u>.

<u>PRIZEWINNER 1988</u>.

D. N. Higgs.

<u>D.H.Higgs,</u>   *President*

Law v Business
Business Law Articles from the
Financial Times 1983–1988

BOOK PRIZE.

MISS LOUISE PHEASANT.

Articled to G.D.Blyth of Evershed & Tomkinson.

By the same author

A HISTORY OF THE CZECHS (1975, Allen Lane, Penguin Books)
FAIR TRADING IN EUROPE (with Colin Jones) (1977, Kluwer-Harrap)
CONFLICTS OF NATIONAL LAWS WITH INTERNATIONAL BUSINESS ACTIVITY
  (1982, British-North American Committee)
JUDGES, LAW AND BUSINESSMEN (1983, Kluwer Law and Taxation, Deventer)

LAW v BUSINESS

Business Law Articles from the Financial Times 1983–1988

A. H. Hermann

Dr Jur (Prague), Fellow of the
Chartered Institute of Arbitrators

With twelve cartoons by Joe Cummings

London
Butterworths
1989

United Kingdom	Butterworth & Co (Publishers) Ltd, 88 Kingsway, LONDON WC2B 6AB and 4 Hill Street, EDINBURGH
Australia	Butterworths Pty Ltd, SYDNEY, MELBOURNE, BRISBANE, ADELAIDE, PERTH, CANBERRA and HOBART
Canada	Butterworths Canada Ltd, TORONTO and VANCOUVER
Ireland	Butterworth (Ireland) Ltd, DUBLIN
Malaysia	Malayan Law Journal Sdn Bhd, KUALA LUMPUR
New Zealand	Butterworths of New Zealand Ltd, WELLINGTON and AUCKLAND
Singapore	Butterworth & Co (Asia) Pte Ltd, SINGAPORE
USA	Butterworths Legal Publishers, ST PAUL, Minnesota, SEATTLE, Washington, BOSTON, Massachusetts, AUSTIN, Texas and D & S Publishers, CLEARWATER, Florida

A CIP Catalogue record for this book is available from the British Library.

ISBN 0 406 17701 5

Typeset by Kerrypress, Luton
Printed by Billings, Worcester

Preface

The question I am most frequently asked is: 'How do you select the subjects for your weekly article?' The answer is, I do not.

Current events determine what requires comment in a newspaper. Judgments crying out for legislation or legislation crying out for better judgment. Judgments which are grossly unfair or lacking common sense – often handed down 'with regrets' – or which take much too long and cost too much to arrive at. The reluctance of governments to respect the law when they owe money, their keenness to go to law when it can be abused for some political purpose.

In short, in a newspaper, even such a contemplative one as the *Financial Times*, one writes mainly about the things that go wrong. Over a short period such commentary is hardly a safe basis for generalisations.

However, over the period of 1983–1988, covered in this book, a certain pattern begins to emerge. These were the years when the House of Lords and the Court of Appeal were busy undoing much of the Denning heritage. It is a period when legal principles gave way to observance of precedents often completely out of time or to a literal interpretation to a convoluted statutory text – an interpretation that may be grammatically correct but miles apart from what Parliament really intended.

No account of the six post-Denning years would be complete without referring to such streaks of masochistic madness creeping into the image of English business law, though, I am sure, a more complete account would not create the impression that these features are so dominant as they appear from this book. But, then, this book is not a complete account and I would not have the cheek to try for one.

The resulting picture is all the more lopsided as, to keep the book concise and focused on business law, I could not include in it my running commentary on the slow but steady progress of the reform of civil procedure for which the *Financial Times* consistently pressed over the past decade. An account of these developments would have produced a more optimistic picture.

In the course of editing the articles most repetitions were eliminated but some were left to make each section of the book self-contained.

My thanks are due to Geoffrey Owen, the Editor of the *Financial Times*, first for giving me complete freedom in my column, and second for waiving, on behalf of the company, any copyright claims it had in the articles.

And finally, I would like to acknowledge my indebtedness to the many lawyers all over the world who drew my attention to their problems, discussed them with me and criticised my conclusions; and to the sub-editors of the Features department of the *Financial Times* for their relentless insistence that I clarify whatever did not seem lucid enough in my articles. And to all, thanks for the happy time I had writing them.

A. H. Hermann
October 1988

Contents

1 Law unfit for business

Which law and how to interpret it

Companies and contracts are creatures of law – of a particular national law; but in the case of international business it is not always obvious which national law is applicable. The choice is fairly obvious in the case of company law, more difficult in the case of contracts, and highly controversial when it comes to trade regulations, competition law or product liability.

Moreover, in Europe it is necessary to take into account the supremacy of Community law guaranteeing the free movement of workers and goods, provision of cross-border services, establishment of businesses. The EC rules of competition affect both horizontal and vertical agreements and partly also mergers. They impose severe restrictions on the use of patents, trademarks and copyright. The European Commission and the Court of Justice in Luxembourg see to it that European rules are respected by governments as well as individual judges. They are engaged in a big drive towards harmonisation of the national laws and adoption of additional European rules necessary, in their view, to achieving a 'single European market'.

At first sight the basic rules of substantive law appear to be very much the same everywhere: the differences are in important details and in the possibility of intervention by third parties or governments. Very broadly one can distinguish four systems; civil law, common law, Sharia and the Sino-Japanese law.

All European continental countries have legal systems based on codes adopted at the end of the eighteenth and the first half of the nineteenth century. The best known are the Code Napoleon and the Civil Code of Marie Thérèse, the Austrian Empress and Czech and Hungarian Queen between 1740 and 1780.

These codes, followed after 1850 by special commercial codes, are strongly influenced by the ancient Roman law. In their turn they influenced the legal systems of Turkey and Egypt, and of former French and Italian colonies in Africa and North America, namely Quebec and Louisiana.

Also the Scottish law has been strongly influenced by Roman law, while English law, and with it the law of the US and of the many countries which were part of the British Empire, is based on common law – the law common to the various parts of England and Wales and recorded in the form of judicial decisions by English judges and now overlaid by a mass of statutory law.

This difference between the UK and the rest of the European Community slows down the process of harmonisation of laws between member states which has been energetically though not always successfully, pushed by the European Commission. By contrast, the US seem to live happily with a duality of state and federal laws. Indeed, when doing business with, or in the US, it is important to be aware of the differences which exist between the laws of various states, and between these and the federal law, particularly in jurisdiction over foreign parties, obtaining of evidence from abroad, as well as company law and product liability.

The difference between the UK and the rest of Europe is perhaps greatest when it comes to the interpretation of law. The continental codes and statutes give the citizen and the judge a clear guidance in the form of generally framed principles and rules. The English statutes try to foresee every possible detail but leave out the statement of general principle or aim. By contrast, the common law consisting of binding precedents and principles derived from them gives the judge greater freedom. Some use it to temper law with justice; others insist that they are bound by obsolete and often distorted rules, however unfair or unreasonable is the outcome. This masochistic attitude seems to have been getting the upper hand since the retirement of Lord Denning from the Court of Appeal.

However, the difference between the UK system of binding precedents and the system of the US and continental Europe, where there is no formal obligation on the judges to follow previous decisions of superior courts, must not be overrated. UK judges are often able to select from the several possible, that precedent which suits them best, while the US and continental judges mostly follow the decision of superior courts voluntarily, in order to avoid reversal on appeal.

In some countries law matters more than in others

The difference in the weight which is given to law in different countries is probably of even greater importance than differences in law and its interpretation.

Germany, and most countries of Northern Europe, take law very seriously. In France, the telephone network of higher civil servants, politicians and leading businessmen seems to be more important when great deals are considered. In Italy politics, local as well as national, seem to count more than law in matters big and small.

The 'legalistic' societies of Northern Europe seem to have different methods for loosening up the straight-jacket of legal rules. In Sweden for example, the judge has a very wide discretion; in Germany, his first duty is to help the parties to reach a settlement. In the UK the high cost of litigation keeps most businessmen out of courts.

The US seem to suffer by an unmitigated litigiousness which devours a great part of their gross national product. By contrast, in Japan the penetration of private and business relations by law is small and only of recent date.

Modern Japanese law is mainly derived from the French, German and US legal systems with marked influence of English securities and insurance law. But the traditional codes of conduct and honour survive, making excessive reliance on law and the judicial system unnecessary. Contracts are kept very short and simple and always provide for amicable settlement of disputes by a conciliation system which is part of a judicial process. A professional judge, usually with the help of two assessors appointed by the Supreme Court, acts as a conciliator in some 500 courts of summary jurisdiction. There are two important reasons for avoiding courts: the proceedings can be extremely slow, particularly on appeal, and legal assistance is scarce and expensive. However, while small and medium-sized Japanese companies are still very shy of legal forms and law, the big companies, exposed to international trade move closer to UK and US ways.

The Communist countries of Europe replaced commercial courts by Arbitration Commissions which decide disputes between the state-owned enterprises very much in the style of the courts which they replaced. Disputes between foreign companies and the state trading corporations of Communist Europe can be usually brought before the arbitration service attached to the international chamber of commerce of the country concerned. Some of these countries adopted special laws for international trade, mostly modelled on the Czechoslovakian Law of Foreign Trade of 1963. However, the weight of the legal system, and the method of applying the law differ greatly between the central European countries, East Germany, Czechoslovakia and Hungary on the one hand, and the more Eastern or South-Eastern countries of the Communist block.

Lawyers differ too from country to country

Most businessmen operating in a foreign country will be more concerned with the lawyers available to advise them and assist them than with the legal system itself. Here it is of particular importance not to rely on the experience gained at home.

The English legal profession differs from most not only by being split between the solicitors and barristers but also by a much more narrow concept of its business. Only City solicitors now develop a wide-spectrum service providing assistance not only with contract drafting and litigation or arbitration, but also in negotiations and law compliance – particularly in the field of company and financial services law.

On the continent of Europe, lawyers often keep in close touch with the management even if no conflicts are there to be resolved. As the legal systems of the continential countries are decentralised, good business lawyers are available also in the provincial centres.

The US lawyers' scope is even wider. Their activities embrace law compliance and litigation – this often in an entrepreneurial fashion, as when they organise and finance class actions for a share in the awards – as well as lobbying the executive and legislature.

Though the US contingency fee system is abhorred by English lawyers, their time-based fees often consume a higher proportion of the awards. In Germany, attorneys are paid not time fees but according to the percentage of scale of fees related to the amount in dispute and charged separately for the preparation of trial, presenting of evidence and reaching of settlement. Though this mostly results in lower and predictable costs, foreign clients accustomed to time-based fees are sometimes shocked by an enormous bill for a relatively simple assistance with a contract involving great amounts.

It is, therefore, very important to agree the fees beforehand; budgeting for legal costs is a wise rule and not only in Germany.

UK's missing rights bill

The rejection by the European Court of Human Rights of the claim by UK shipbuilders and aircraft makers for higher compensation for their nationalised enterprises is a forceful reminder of the increasing influence of European courts on the law, and through it on economic policies in the UK.

This influence has often proved beneficial, opening channels of information clogged by the establishment's inclination to secrecy, providing additional protection to inmates of prisons and shielding schoolboys against caning. Above all, it has forced the pace of progress towards the equal treatment of men and women.

The influence of European law is, however, less clearly good when it comes to the solution of economic problems specific to the UK. Equality of the sexes, access to information and treatment of prisoners are human issues, common to the peoples of Europe. Freehold of real estate and nationalisation or re-privatisation of industrial enterprises are specific UK problems for which no help can be expected from foreign courts.

However, nature abhors any void, and European courts tend to fill any space left vacant by national legislation. Compliance with the Strasbourg Court of Human Rights remains voluntary even if the government has so far complied with every one of its decisions. But the European Convention of Human Rights also affects the UK in the guise of mandatory decisions by the Community Court of Justice in Luxembourg. This court is bound to respect principles of law common to all member states, and consequently also the convention on human rights.

Other European Community states can conveniently handle in their own courts many of the issues for which the UK has no domestic tribunal. Administrative courts of these countries deal with complaints against decisions of government departments and constitutional courts scrutinise, on application of those concerned, or of lower courts, whether particular laws and regulations were passed in accordance with constitutional rules and conform with the fundamental rights guaranteed to citizens. If the legislation is found to be incompatible with such fundamental rights, the constitutional court invites the government to submit an amending bill to the legislature.

The review of the constitionality of legislation goes much further in the US where all courts have the power to scrutinise – the last word being reserved, of course, to the Supreme Court, which only recently used its powers to clip a bill proposing a budgetary reform.

Such a wide distribution of the power to declare laws to be incompatible with the constitution is one of the factors contributing to the excessive litigiousness of the US society. Its emulation can hardly be recommended.

But to have no domestic machinery for the screening of legislation is also wrong.

Though the British Parliament did not make the convention a part of UK law, it is in effect being applied in the UK by the two European courts. One must ask whether English and Scottish courts, with their more intimate knowledge of the political, legal and social background, would not apply such a bill of rights faster and more efficiently, particularly when it comes to broad issues of economic and social policy. In their latest decision – as well as in the recent ruling on the claim by the Duke of Westminster – the Strasbourg judges have clearly stated that they do not intend to interfere with the social and economic policies of governments. The convention was designed to protect the dispossessed victims of tyrannical regimes and not to settle competing economic claims by groups, individuals and enterprises within a democratic country.

Thus the long-discussed question, whether the UK should adopt the convention as its own bill of rights, appears to be the wrong question. For most practical purposes the convention is already effective in the UK. The real question is: would it not be better to entrust its operation to UK courts? or, does Parliament fear UK courts more than the European courts in Strasbourg and Luxembourg?

The integration of a bill of rights into the UK system would give a new dimension to judicial review of administrative decisions. This new, fast-growing branch of judicial activity is largely improvised. It would deserve a solid foundation which courts could develop—a system of administrative law.

If adopted as a constitional law which can be changed only by a qualified majority of the parliament, the bill of rights would give a greater stability to ordinary legislation which had to keep within its constitutional framework.

Precedent; the sacred cow of English law

For these reasons, I have regretfully come to the conclusion that the appeal must succeed and the Order of Master Prebble be restored' said Sir John Donaldson, the Master of the Rolls. And Lord Justice Dillon added: 'The learned judge, as it seems to me, has allowed his heart to rule his head. I do not feel able to do that. I would, with reluctance, allow this appeal.[1]

Here you have in a nutshell the judges' dilemma, expressed in their own words. What is not immediately obvious is that the difficulty is of the judges' own making. Instead of treating the doctrine of precedent as a good servant, they have allowed it to become an ugly and oppressive master.

The judgement from which I quote concerned a claim for damages by a young girl rendered paraplegic in a car accident. There was no doubt about the liability of the defendant, who admitted that he had driven carelessly. Cornhill, his insurance company, expected that it would have to pay heavy damages. The company could hardly believe its luck when it learned that the girl lost her claim because her solicitors never served a writ they had issued. Their managing clerk assumed that, as the insurers gave their client £5,000 for a special motor car, liability had been admitted.

In the meantime, the three-year period, within which an action for compensation must be started, had elapsed. However, section 33 of the Limitation Act 1980 gives the court discretion to allow an action to proceed even after three years to avoid hardship, and the solicitors thought that this might provide an emergency exit from their quandary. They started new action, which was thrown out by Master Prebble as out of time, but allowed on appeal by Mr Justice Comyn, about whom Lord Justice Dillon said that he allowed his heart to rule his head.[2]

To most people it would appear that the judge used his head quite properly. If the court has discretion to allow an action out of time to prevent injustice to the injured person because nothing was done within the limitation period, why should it not be able to do the same when at least the first move towards litigation, the issuing of a writ, took place in good time?

It would be wrong to say that judges who do not allow themselves to be guided by their hearts are heartless. It was clear to them that the whole thing was only a tussle between the insurers of the man who caused the accident, and the insurers of the solicitors. Concluding his judgment, Sir John said that should any attempt be made to challenge his judgment, he would hope that some arrangement could be reached between the insurers to enable the girl to get the money quickly. The House of Lords went one step farther. They granted leave to appeal only on condition that £100,000 was paid immediately to the victim. By that time, however, it was more than five years after her accident.

The broader question behind this distressing story of solicitors' negligence and courts' rigidity is whether the binding precedent, this sacred cow of English law, is really so indispensable for law's certainty. It is now often assumed that such respect for precedent is a unique and perennial feature of the English legal system.

It is not unique. All legal systems balance the need for certainty with the need to develop the law in response to new circumstances. In all, legal systems precedents influence the decision of the judge.

Justinian's code, by which Roman law was transmitted for use in modern times, was mainly the result of judge-made law. A civil law judge will respect principles derived from previous decisions of higher courts gladly – it makes his work easier and protects his judgments against reversal. But if he finds that the result will be unfair, or contrary to the fundamental principles of law or the intentions of the legislator, he is duty bound to differ.

Nor was it much different in England until about 100 years ago. Until the beginning of the nineteenth century, previous decisions were referred to in the English courts only as persuasive authority. Whether the House of Lords was bound by its own decisions remained uncertain until 1898.

One wishes that its 1966 decision to give itself greater freedom had started a swing back. As Professor Clive Schmitthoff wrote:

> It would be in the interest of the development of the common law if . . . the decisions in the higher courts were accorded only persuasive, and not binding authority . . . if in an exceptional case, the Court of Appeal or even a High Court judge comes to the conclusion that a principle established by a higher

court is wrong or unworkable or no longer in keeping with the general view of society, the judge in the lower court should be entitled to say so and to decide according to his conscience and conviction.[3]

Most judges think that such a radical change is quite impracticable – but the discontent of those who use the courts may prove stronger. As a first step the Court of Appeal should assume the right to revise its past rulings.[4]

Statutes where one can't see the wood for the trees

A Prime Minister's circular to all departments on the drafting of legislation begins: 'The drafting must be clear, economical of words . . .' and it goes on to ask for a logical chain of ideas in a text broken up into short articles in order to facilitate understanding. Unfortunately, it is not one of Mrs Thatcher's circulars, but that of a French Prime Minister.

The office of the Parliamentary Counsel to the Treasury, which is responsible for drafting UK legislation, still goes by Sir John Rowlatt's law: 'The intelligibility of a Bill is in inverse proportion to its chance of being right.'[5]

The highest judges of the land agree that the office is eminently successful in making statutes unintelligible, particularly when these concern such tremendously important matters as the Employment Act 1980, dealing with blacking and secondary industrial action. As the Act is unintelligible, no one except parliamentary counsel can say whether it is right. Everyone else is free to interpret it in his or her own way.

Every time an Old Bailey judge stops the reporting of a criminal prosecution in order to give a drug addict or prostitute a chance to pick up the wreckage of his or her life, there is a great outcry. 'Justice must be seen to be done', shout the Philistines. But with statutes drafted as they are, no one knows what the law is unless he runs to a solicitor to have them translated into plain English (which the solicitor is not always able to do, often through no fault of his own); and when the law is obscure how can anyone know whether justice is being done, even if he sits through the entire proceedings?

The English style of legislative drafting, was created by Gladstone. He loved long chains of complicated sentences, and sitting across the table with Lord Thring, the first Parliamentary Counsel appointed by him in 1869, he would go through every detail. The next influence was Disraeli. Though he knew better how to make people understand the written word, his primary concern was to have Bills drafted so that they could pass through Parliament. For this purpose it is sometimes better to keep them obscure. Thus Gladstone's style and Disraeli's political instinct contributed to our present nightmare.

WHAT IS TO BE DONE?

Amending legislation which produces a complete revised text instead of the usual references to previous legislation, would, in itself, lead to a great improvement in the readability of statutes. That would also be enhanced by placing the commencement provisions and definition clauses at the beginning of the statute.

It would be a great help if judges could refer to preparatory reports when interpreting legislation, though not to parliamentary debates.

A statement of purpose put in front of a detailed Act drafted for literal interpretation might be of some help when solving situations not foreseen by the parliamentary draftsmen. The real issue, however, is whether statutes should be drafted so as to express the will of Parliament in general terms applicable to a variety of situations, some of which are unforeseeable, or whether they should contain the enumeration of all imaginable situations, burdening the rules with strings of provisos and exceptions.

Some parliamentary draftsmen would be ready to give greater freedom to the judges in legislation concerning the relationship between citizens, but not in public law concerning the relationship between the state and the citizen. They fear that, given the possibility, the judges would always interpret the general rule in favour of the taxpayer or of the criminal.

They could not be more wrong. Detailed tax legislation and its literal interpretation enabled the growth of the tax avoidance industry, but it was Lord Wilberforce's emphasis on the purpose of the law in the *Rossminster* case which brought about the radical reversal of interpretation in favour of the Inland Revenue by eliminating unreal transactions which Chancery judges sustained whenever the draftsmen forgot to eliminate them expressly.

There is obviously a link between the draftsman who thinks that he can foresee the future and the judge who thinks that a grammatical analysis of the text is enough as the Act provides for everything. But what came first – the chicken or the egg? In giving evidence to the Committee on the Preparation of Legislation, Lord Denning said:[6]

> It is because the judges have not felt it right to fill in the gaps and have been giving a literal interpretation for many years that the draftsman has felt he has to try and think of every conceivable thing and put it insofar as he can so that even the person unwilling to understand will follow it. I think the rules of interpretation which the judges have applied have been one of the primary causes why draftsmen have felt that they must have a system of over-detail, over-long sentences, and obscurity.

Lord Denning thinks draftsmen should make a new start:

> If the draftsmen could make acts simpler, the judges could alter their approach to them. . . It could be done by breaking up the form of the statutes, by making them simpler, sticking more to the principles, and not going into so much detail.

Computers can help only a little

Some people hope that computers will help to unravel the making of English common and statute law. But there are limits to artificial intelligence when applied to the interpretation of law. It is highly suitable for following a network of rules, provided this network is logical and not beset by inner contradictions as common law, unfortunately, is. A computer may help to identify the structure of black letter law and unravel some of the lesser intricacies of statutory drafting. It may do a lot of damage in the long run by confirming people in the mistaken belief that law is about little twists and that a good lawyer is the one who finds the twists likely to help your case.

However, from ancient times ordinary people and the best lawyers have known that to observe the law does not mean to follow its twists but to go in the direction in which its strength and power are aimed.[7] England – and gradually since the time of the union, Scotland – became an exception, putting case law before principle.

Only a minority of English judges – Mansfield, Reid and Denning, for example – appreciated the importance of legal principles not only for justice but also for the clarity and consistency of the law. The majority were brainwashed into believing that it is the twists that matter, and that law is necessarily beyond the comprehension of the layman.

Even Shakespeare fell into the trap: no shrewd merchant of Venice would have dreamed of making an obviously invalid contract; and if he was so out of his mind to claim a pound of flesh as a contractual penalty, there would have been no need for Portia's defensive twist. In civil law countries the court is supposed to know the law and contracts which are *contra bonos mores* are invalid from the very beginning.

The view of law as a web of twists and no principle led judges to favour literal interpretation – and this in turn has led to statutes which do not state the intent of parliament and try to provide for every situation. This makes them too long and unintelligible – and fails to provide for every situation as many cannot be foreseen. The English statutes are about two to five times as long as corresponding French, German or Swedish statutes and infinitely less meaningful.

Professor R. M. Goode of Queen Mary College, University of London, a leading expert in English commercial law, wrote:[8] 'All too often our statutes are drafted in turgid and impenetrable prose which leaves the reader unable, without detailed study, even to get a general idea of what is intended.'

It has not always been like this. Sir Henry Thrang who was the first to hold the office of Parliamentary Counsel, instructed the statute draftsmen in 1902 thus: '. . . [the] principle must be enunciated in its most concise form at the very outset of the Act, either in one section or in two or more consecutive sections, as the subject may require.' How far did we get from that? The present-day parliamentary draftsmen seem to be proud of the unintelligibility which, in the words of Sir John Rowlatt, one of their number, they believe to be 'in inverse proportion to (the statutes') chance of being right'.[9]

It is a common experience that only a complete mastery of his subject enables the writer to communicate it simply and clearly. The obscurity of English legislative drafting may be due not so much to the striving for certainty – rarely achieved – as to the draftsman's unfamiliarity with the subject. Such unfamiliarity is often unavoidable if draftsmen are separated from the departments initiating legislation and isolated in a small group given the monopoly of statutory drafting.

There seems to be a good deal of tension between the 'instructing' expert and the parliamentary draftsman. At best, in the words of Mr R. T. Oerton, who recently described his experiences as a member of the Law Commission's staff, the expert feels as if he was operating by remote control a pair of mechanical hands which fail to pick up the materials, keep dropping them, or mix them wrongly; and is frustrated when the product is 'so abstruse that you have to know what (the Parliamentary Counsel) is trying to say before you even begin to see that he may be saying it'.

Sir William Dale, an authority on legislative drafting, suggested that drafting should be de-professionalised to introduce intelligibility and more of the common touch. But there would be no need to *introduce* intelligibility if the drafting was left to departmental lawyers who work side by side with the experts, under the same minister, and have no need to defend a priestly monopoly by weaving a webb of mystery around it.

The drafting of new statutes could be not only more intelligible but also much better if taken out of the hands of expert draftsmen and left to experts in the relevant field of law, attached to the departments initiating the legislation, whose work could be co-ordinated by a legislative division in the Lord Chancellor's Department.

Expert computer systems, like that developed by Professor Capper and Dr Susskind for latent damage, could help a little to unravel the backlog of obscure law. But neither expert lawyers nor expert systems can provide a real and lasting remedy by themselves. That can only be brought about by codification of law. Work on the codification of criminal law is in hand. Codification of business law – not of commercial law in the narrow sense alone – is needed as much, if not more. The Law Commission should be allowed to do it – and given means to do it; it is now pitifully understaffed.

The unpredictable English judges

The usual complaints about the formalism, high costs and inaccessibility of the English judicial process have been overshadowed in the spring of 1988 by the disharmony between judges about some basic principles of UK law and the consequent unpredictability of their decisions.

The rejection by the Court of Appeal of claims against member states of the insolvent International Tin Council is seen as a reversal of the generally accepted view that companies and partnerships can limit their liability towards creditors only when their limited liability is registered and shown on their letterheads.

Another decision, this time by the House of Lords, revealed an alarming instability of their Lordships' views on one of the fundamental features of the arbitration process. The judgment concerned the old problem of whether courts can strike off arbitrations left pending over the head of the defendant, like the sword of Damocles, by a plaintiff who remains inactive, sometimes for more than 10 years.

Some eight years ago, Lord Donaldson, Master of the Rolls, then a High Court judge, held that arbitration should be struck off in the same way as litigation would be under such circumstances. He was confirmed by the Denning Court of Appeal, but to the dismay of the business community this decision was reversed by the Law Lords in 1981.

Seven years later, in *Food Corporation of India*, the Law Lords now say that they were wrong to reverse Lord Denning. They suggest Parliament should undo their misjudgment – though it is difficult to understand why they could not do it themselves and reject the appeal on the facts, if they thought fit.

An alarming hesitation and lack of lucidity in the interpretation of statutory law – itself obscure enough – has been demonstrated by the courts in the industrially important copyright protection of spare parts. This was established by High Court decisions which experts, including leading judges, always considered to be a misunderstanding with absurd consequences. Though provided with an opportunity to correct it in the *Leyland* case, the Law Lords only side-stepped it by inventing the 'right to repairs'.

In the *Lego* case, they have now weakened the spare parts copyright but left it to lower courts to interpret their judgment in a variety of ways. The resulting uncertainty stretches back to the past as the judgment is, of course, retroactive, as are all English judgments.

In the recent 'equal pay' case, the Law Lords imposed stricter requirements on employers than could be assumed to exist either under UK statute or under European Community rules – and they did so again without limiting the retroactive effect of their judgment.

While so radical on equal pay, the Law Lords have proved to be extremely diffident in the *Amstrad* case, where they found it impossible to outlaw assistance to breaches of the Copyright Act by home copying, which, as they said, runs into millions. Instead they appealed to Parliament that 'law which is treated with such contempt should be amended or repealed'.

If other professionals operated in this way, they would expose themselves to malpractice suits. In the case of judges, one must seek remedies on a higher plane.

First, there seems to be an urgent need for a clear statement of the rules of interpretation which would reduce the influence of personal idiosyncrasies.

Second, when judges upset legitimate expectations created by their previous decisions – and this, as the Law Society points out in its 1988 report on tax law, is a frequent occurrence – they should limit the retrospective effect of their judgments, as US courts and the European Court do without hesitation.

And finally, there is obviously need for a much greater and faster legislative intervention in business law. This would be possible if politically uncontroversial matters, as for example arbitration procedure, could be processed by a Select Committee of both Houses of Parliament and treated as a bipartisan legislative project.

Keeping legal costs down

Take a dispute between two medium-sized companies. Each stands to win or lose some £150,000. The lawyers have convinced them both that the law is on their side. The contract from which the dispute arose provides for arbitration, so both sides retain counsel and appoint an arbitrator.

The arbitration takes three weeks, and the claimant company is awarded £75,000 and half of its legal costs. Each party paid about £10,000 to its solicitor; £25,000 to counsel and about £8,000 to his junior. They each paid £3,000 to the arbitrator and another £2,000 for his expenses. The total costs of the arbitration were, therefore, £96,000. Of this amount, the winning party bears £24,000, which reduces the award to £51,000. The losing party has to fork out £147,000.

Both parties feel aggrieved. The claimant got only one-third of what he thought was due to him. The respondent had to pay twice as much as he owed, according to the arbitrator. It will take both parties some time to overcome the feeling of injustice. Only the lawyers are happy. They received £96,000, and will remain good friends.

This is a fictitious case, but typical of hundreds occurring all the time. London's art dealers, for example, shrank from litigation with the auctioneers over the buyers' premium when they found out that the costs would be no less than £500,000.

When big companies and American lawyers are involved, legal expenses rise even higher. Xerox, for example, used to spend $26m annually on fees to outside lawyers – that is, in addition to the salaries of its in-house lawyers. But there is some hope. By assuming greater managerial control over its legal work in 1976, the company succeeded in reducing the fees paid to outside lawyers within five years to about one-fifth – a mere $5m annually.

Three Harvard researchers say that 'success stories like these are still few and far between', but their study[10] on how to cut costs by managing your lawyers contains quite a few interesting pointers.

Managements are often diffident, over-awed by the mysteries of law, and do not apply to lawyers the usual tests of efficiency. They fail to recognise that a legal service, consisting of in-house lawyers, and outside law firms, is not a self-managing institution. It is an executive function to analyse the company's requirements and to provide the best specialist and geographical combination of resources to meet them.

The task of the chief legal executive embraces at least the following three areas:

● the standardisation of routine legal procedures;

- the organisation of law compliance programmes and of a legal prevention service;
- management of litigation services, particularly when these involve outside lawyers.

In organising routine tasks that require minimal or no knowledge of the law, the most important step is to hand these over to non-legal or para-legal personnel. 'Companies have better luck in finding capable people to perform these jobs than law firms because they allow career progression in management, while law firms offer few opportunities for advancement without legal training,' concludes the study.

Some of the routine operations, such as standard contracting, can even be left to word processors as long as operatives know when exceptional treatment is called for and have easy access to a lawyer. Other routine tasks, like the supply of periodic reports and information to government departments and supervisory authorities, are more complicated but even here it is possible to develop charts and systems identifying the chronology of the individual steps and the sources of information.

Law compliance and prevention services require, by contrast, lawyers which have imagination and familiarity with the company's business prospects and ambitions. To be able to do their work properly, these lawyers will have to keep in touch with the operating divisions, as well as to be able to anticipate problems of which the management may not yet be aware.

One of their main tasks is to ensure continuous legal education and information of management and supervisory staffs. Such an educational programme will be tailored to suit the needs of the various divisions. It can be more or less formal, according to the size and needs of the company, but there must always be some procedure to ensure that the lessons have been learned and are applied in practice.

The other task of the compliance and prevention service is to help to avoid major dangers to which the company is exposed because of its financial situation or its operation. The task may be to protect the company against a hostile takeover, to avoid patent infringement, or transgressions of competition rules, for example. Product liability would always be an important subject in manufacturing or marketing organisations.

The co-operation between in-house lawyers and outside law firms can take different shapes: sometimes the in-house lawyer will be in charge of the negotiations or litigation, while in other situations, particularly in connection with legal business abroad, the law firm will be in charge and in-house lawyers will provide support.

Whatever the arrangement is, it should be clearly defined. If fees are to be kept down any legal problem referred to an outside firm should be defined as narrowly as possible. Even so, it is advisable to request estimates and to insist on a detailed breakdown of legal bills, supported, if necessary, by time sheets showing the work done by individual lawyers.

Though planning and supervision can reduce the costs of legal services, and sometimes even improve their quality, radical savings can also be achieved by stepping out of the traditional patterns of litigation and arbitration and trying what is now often called 'methods of alternative dispute resolution.'

The escalation of lawyers' involvement in business has necessarily put an end to the 'spare no costs – just win the case' attitude. Some victories are just too costly.

The obstacles to legal reform

The idea that the English machinery of justice is the best in the world survives somehow alongside the complaints, hardly contested, that it is deficient in three major aspects: the drafting of statutes makes them unintelligible, the method of interpretation of precedent and legislation is uncertain, and the procedure of courts is too slow, too technical and too costly. Although these weaknesses have been acknowledged by eminent committees and Royal Commissions several times over, reform has never got off the ground.

In view of this experience one must ask whether reform is not perhaps blocked by the peculiar constitutional arrangements dividing responsibility for the administration of justice between the Lord Chancellor and Home Secretary, while the drafting of legislation is the monopoly of the Office of the Parliamentary Counsel attached to the Treasury. In short, there is no Ministry of Justice to co-ordinate reform on all three fronts.

A powerful attack on the shortcomings of civil court procedure has been made by Sir John Donaldson, the Master of the Rolls. On assuming his office he took immediate steps to speed up the working of the Court of Appeal.

The Master of the Rolls would like to see opening speeches and pleadings cut to size in all civil courts.

Frivolous litigants should be frightened off by fining those who bring cases in bad faith. Courts should be made accessible to persons of moderate means by making legal aid dependent on the ratio of means to costs instead of a means test as at present. Cases should be assigned to higher courts not according to the amount at stake but according to the difficulty of the legal issue, so that many more would go to county courts. These, in turn, could be relieved of cases hanging purely on facts, by creating a network of lay courts – civil justices of the peace.

Such an approach, though commonplace elsewhere, seems radical in England. Many solicitors criticise Sir John's proposals concerning legal aid. Barristers are likely to be dismayed by any proposal to restrict their speeches.

Absurdly, the slowness, if not absence, of any reform may be due to the accumulation of power in the hands of the Lord Chancellor. The Lord Chancellor presides over the upper chamber of the legislature; as a member of the Cabinet, he is a senior member of the executive; as a member of the judicial committee of the House of Lords, he is a senior judge; and he also appoints judges, from the lowest to the highest courts. Such an accumulation of powers has been made bearable only by a succession of gentle Lord Chancellors who preferred consensus to promoting their own views. Also, one feels sometimes, the Lord Chancellor has too much to do, to do anything.

The difficulty could be solved by a constitutional reform which would divide the office of the Lord Chancellor into three. The appointment of judges, now done on the basis of private soundings, could be put into the hands of a judiciary commission, subject to public control. The Lord Chancellor would be in charge of the legal business of the state, together with the attorney-general and solicitor-general.

Most important of all, there should be one office, the ministry of justice, to co-ordinate the reform of legislative drafting, interpretation of law, and court procedure and administration, none of which can move forward out of step with the other.

Legal reform in Germany

The great machinery of West German justice quivers and creaks under the burden of ever-increasing civil litigation. The nineteenth century concept of a perfectly rational *Rechtstaat* (rule of law) and the more recent experience that obedience to 'properly' established, but essentially wicked, laws and executive decisions may open the gates to hell on earth, in Germany add to the overworking of law which is a feature of industrial society. Far too many disputes are being brought into courts from whose decisions as many as four appeals are sometimes possible.

The federal Minister of Justice, Hans Engelhard, fears that the flood of litigation might clog the courts and prevent their proper functioning. He has initiated a wide-ranging review of civil justice. His objectives are: more easily understood statutes, a greater number of out-of-court settlements and fewer appeals.

By 1980, the number of civil actions reached 1.57m and by 1986 had risen by another by 27 per cent. At the same time, the number of appeals has increased by 32 per cent. The rise in litigation has been accompanied by a corresponding increase in the number of attorneys from 36,000 in 1980 to 50,000 in 1987. However, budgetary restraints have kept the increase in the number of judges to a much slower pace. Between 1980 and 1985, the number of trial judges rose by 7 per cent and appeal judges by only 2.3 per cent.

The West German system of courts can be visualised as several pyramids, ensuring both decentralisation of courts and their far-reaching specialisation. The backbone of the system is the pyramid of ordinary civil courts starting with district court (*Amtsgericht*), dealing with disputes of minor value or importance. The next step is regional court (*Landsgericht*) from which cases can go to an appeal court (*Oberlandsgericht*) in each Land. A further appeal (*Revision*) can go to the Federal Supreme Court (*Bundesgerichtshof*).

There are also specialist benches established in a number of civil courts. The most prominent of these is the Competition Bench of the Berlin

Kammergericht to which go all appeals against the decisions of the Federal Cartel Office, located in the same city.

A single judge sits only in the lowest level of courts – the district courts. In higher regional courts, a bench of three judges is the rule and larger benches decide appeals in the federal courts. A reduction in the number of judges deciding appeals is seen by the Ministry of Justice as a way of alleviating the present difficulties.

A certain over-emphasis of rights to legalistic attitudes and litigiousness, may originate from a belief in the rationality and exhaustiveness of the great nineteenth century codes, the civil code, the criminal code and the two sets of rules of the civil and criminal process. Emanating from the legal and philosophical concepts of pre-industrial society, these codes were out of date by the end of the nineteenth century.

Modern German jurisprudence emphasises that, in an industrial society, law is necessarily a product of compromise between the conflicting interests of major groups. From this, it is only a short step to the recognition that litigation can only rarely, if at all, lead to an absolute justice, and that a settlement by negotiation or conciliation may be the better way. Such legal theory is, of course, also much more convenient to a minister of justice operating under budgetary constraints.

The history of German justice in the Third Reich is the history of an institution which failed to resist and, step by step, sunk to a role of accomplice and executioner of an *Unrechtsstaat*.

The defeat of 1945 and the Nuremberg trial shattered the easy positivism which helped judges to silence their own conscience. In practical terms this led to the adoption of the Fundamental Law, now such an important source of overriding rules which have to be respected by courts, government and Parliament alike.

The application of these rules goes beyond simple, individual human rights, also in effect protecting entire groups of people considered vulnerable. It even goes beyond the limits of a free market economy which, as the German Constitutional Court recognised, is only one of the possible social structures satisfying the requirements of the Fundamental Law.

These are, no doubt, welcome and most admirable principles but one of their less welcome consequences is a further opportunity for litigation and appeals. In an effort to curb this, Mr Engelhard asks attorneys to advise their clients against litigation whenever settlement or another resolution of the dispute appears possible. The way German attorneys are paid already puts a premium on settlement, for which they receive separate remuneration. It is also the duty of German judges to influence parties towards reaching a settlement.

The government will now seek to give further incentives to avoid litigation. At the same time, the review of civil justice will also aim to streamline procedure and assist both judges and court administrators with a wider deployment of electronic information systems.

The great pyramid of German courts, with well over 10,000 career judges, could not be more different than the judicial system of the UK. The causes of its present overload also seem to be different – but the solutions offered do have a familiar sound.

Chinese rituals and mysteries

Doing business with China, the world's most populous market, ought to be a sort of status symbol, if only it did not take so much time to acquire. Negotiating a contract with the Chinese may take years. It is a costly pastime. And often it is only at the signing of the contract that the discovery that this is only the beginning of the real negotiations is made. Why?

Dr. Stefan Messmann, the Volkswagen in-house lawyer and Chairman of a Standing Committee for Standard Contracts of the European Association for Chinese law, provides a plausible answer.[11]

It will no doubt please lawyers that the first reason which Dr Messmann gives for the slowness of negotiations is that the Chinese often prefer to negotiate without lawyers. In his experience, the Chinese team, consisting of technicians, businessmen and officials, tries to make do with non-binding statements and vague formulations, while scribbling down verbatim every pronouncement made by their European partner, in order to bring it out years later when circumstances have changed, and insist that it represented a binding promise. Obviously, the Chinese have not yet discovered the standard incantation of 'without prejudice', which enables lawyers to be precise about mutual obligations under discussion, without giving either party the possibility of referring back to statements preceding the conclusion of the contract.

The tricks employed by the Chinese negotiators do not seem any different from those employed worldwide, but the Chinese have refined them into a ritual, making it easier for those without any great experience to benefit from the wisdom of past generations of astute businessmen. Also, a ritualised negotiating process can be entrusted to middle-ranking officials and watched and directed discreetly by those in real authority who do not wish to show their hand. In this way, those at the top can grant last-minute concessions to save negotiations from failure, or withhold their approval – without losing face.

One of the most important tasks of the Chinese negotiator in the opening phase of the talks seems to be the search for the 'right partner'. This will not necessarily be the most senior of the European negotiators, but the one who seems to be forthcoming to the Chinese side. If they find a member of the foreign delegation who is willing to talk to them and to his colleagues outside the formal negotiations, and appears to be helpful in putting across their point of view, they will shower him with attention and friendliness. The Chinese are great cultivators of friendly feelings, believing that friendship obliges, exposes the 'friend' to manipulation, and makes him dependent. One would expect a wise European delegation to appoint a suitable person to act as such a 'right' partner.

Where should the talks take place? It may be useful to invite the Chinese team to visit, showing them the factory and the application of its products, and acquainting them with the hierarchy of the headquarters. The negotiations, however, can seldom take place in Europe because the Chinese negotiators must constantly refer to their superiors. In addition, those who have real authority may not like the contract resulting from negotiations abroad, which they could not follow and direct on a day-to-day basis.

The Chinese location for the talks is particularly important for the second phase, when the foreign team is asked to present their ideas. These are immediately communicated to the invisible persons in authority. They will then decide the line to be adopted by the Chinese negotiators, reaching their decision on the basis of reports from their negotiators, without discussing it with the foreign party.

After the main line to be taken has been determined by those in authority, the Chinese technique does not seem to be particularly original: there is the usual attempt to play out members of the foreign team against each other, the labelling of its individual members as 'good' or 'bad', attempts to make the foreign partner feel guilty about delays when he opposes unacceptable demands, and finally, attempts to exert pressure through the press and media.

It may happen that the Chinese negotiators will be so good at the delaying tactics designed to tire out the foreigner that they will put themselves under time pressure: suddenly they will forget about all-important principles and essential details in the rush to be able to submit the signed contract to authority. In such a case one should beware: the essential details, left out in the hurry, will come back with a vengeance and the negotiations will be reopened after signature. For this reason, it is of greatest importance to establish who is the ultimately interested Chinese party – an export-import corporation, a production enterprise, a government department, the Bank of China or one of its specialised subsidiaries, or one of the national corporations in the automobile or shipbuilding industry – and try to establish direct contact.

The conclusion of an agreement or contract is still not the beginning of business, as agreements, contracts and articles of association are subject to approval by the appropriate authority. Reporting the Provisions to Encourage Foreign Investment, in force since last October. Jeanne-Marie Claydon of the London School of Oriental and African Studies writes that applications should now be dealt with within three months.[12]

The new Provisions were enacted by the State Council of the PRC to pacify the foreign investors frustrated by the difficulties of obtaining foreign exchange, red tape and high operating costs. However, these guidelines show an ambiguity, resulting probably from the desire to satisfy diverse and often contradictory ideological streams within the government. In response to complaints about interference in the internal organisation of foreign investment enterprises, a 'right of autonomy' is 'guaranteed'. But this does not abrogate any of the existing powers of supervision under the law. The provisions refer to 'support' to be given to foreign enterprises to manage themselves 'in accordance with internationally advanced scientific methods'. This is said to confirm that foreign companies will not be required to copy the management methods of Chinese state enterprises.

Foreign-investment enterprises are given the 'right' to determine by themselves matters such as production and operation plans, the purchase of materials, the sale of products, the raising of funds, and wage and bonus structures, writes Ms Claydon, but she adds, 'questions of the scope of authority under the contract will presumably continue to be dealt with by a process of negotiation between the relevant authorities and the investor'.

The Provisions, like all rules relating to foreign investment in China, are framed in terms of administrative guidelines rather than strictly enforceable rights and obligations. Accordingly, their actual impact will depend upon their interpretation and application by the authorities.

Such interpretation of guidelines will in its turn depend on the relative strength of ideas and political factions transmitted to the businessmen through the bureaucracy. This, by being slow, is a stabilising factor of sorts. Since 1976, western economists ranging from Adam Smith to Milton Friedman and Ota Sik, the Czech theoretician of market socialism, have been translated into Chinese. Even more important may be the influence of growing foreign trade, aid, co-operation and investment activity in China. But the opposition of the 'apparatus' against reform – and the old see-saw of decentralisation and recentralisation – combine with new social tensions.

As Dr Messmann says, the perpetual change from chaos to order and back again is an old established Chinese concept. The western business negotiators will have to adopt either a very short or a very long perspective.

Comecon craves legal integration

Comecon, the Communist parallel of the EEC, seems to be set on creating its own regional and supranational business law. This transpires from the academic argument[13] that the lack of a regional commercial code is now seriously hampering the progress of economic integration of the Soviet bloc.

Lagging some 20 years behind the EEC in its use of law as an instrument of intergration, the Council for Mutual Economic Aid – as Comecon is styled – now feels the need to harmonise certain areas of national laws of member states, and ultimately to create a common commercial code for interstate trade. An intermediate task would be the unification of rules governing conflits of law related to international business.

Legal aspects of Comecon's internal trade could be largely ignored as long as it was completely dominated by dirigism, when centrally planned objectives were pursued by means of administrative, bureaucratic measures. Deliveries of goods and provision of services by state-owned and controlled enterprises took place at the behest of their political masters. Though the degree of dirigism differs from one member state to another – the managements in Czechoslovakia, East Germany and Hungary enjoying a certain degree of operational independence – when it came to any major dispute between enterprises of different countries, until recently these could be settled on the political level. Failing that, an umpire could always be found in Moscow – and *Moscow locuta, causa finita*.

Such political solutions can, of course, hardly be invoked for the settlement of minor problems. They must, in any case, have become a heavy burden on the political strata as economic relations gradually intensified, assuming at the same time more complicated forms of multilateral co-operation, of joint research and development, and of joint ventures. The unwillingness to base joint agencies and companies on the law of one of the member states and the impossibility of having them 'float' in a legal vacuum combined to create a need for a 'Comecon law' to sustain such institutions.

Another pressure towards legal, rather than political and diplomatic, regulation of Comecon business comes from attempts to give managements greater responsibility for economic efficiency. Instead of being held to plan fulfilment and budgetary limits only, managers are now encouraged to gear production to the requirements of their customers. Their bonuses and investment allocations are made dependent on a certain measure of cost-effectiveness. Such considerations always mattered in East Germany, which never stopped comparing its industrial achievements with those of West Germany. They have become gradually more important in Hungary and, with the rejuvenation of its leadership, are now being advanced, at least in speeches and exhortation, in the Soviet Union.

Comecon does not lack quasi-judicial institutions for the settling of commercial disputes. Each of the member states has well-established arbitration courts, replacing the former commercial courts. These should be perfectly able to apply law to commercial disputes, if only they could always say which law is applicable. Section 110 of Comecon's General Conditions of Deliveries states merely that matters for which the parties did not provide by contract should be decided in accordance with the law of the country of the seller. This, however, leaves open the question of the law applicable to multilateral deals, joint research ventures or joint companies.

Moreover, section 110 refers to the general rules of civil law and not to the special business law enacted for relations between national enterprises in Czechoslovakia and in East Germany. There is also nothing similar in Comecon to the 1968 (Brussels) Convention on Jurisdiction and Enforcement of Judgments in Civil and Commercial Matters.

A further difficulty, not unknown in the EEC, is caused by the unforeseeable effects of legal rules once they have been transplanted from one legal system to another. Such difficulties, experienced in the EEC, for example, with the Bankruptcy Convention, are much more pronounced within Comecon, where the legal systems of Czechoslovakia, East Germany and Hungary are closer to the systems of Austria, West Germany and Switzerland than to those of Bulgaria, Romania and the Soviet Union.

Such differences are apparent not only in historically conditioned institutions and in the approach to law, but even in recently developed branches of law, such as motor insurance. In the Soviet Union this is a purely contractual arrangement and Soviet citizens may be indemnified for liability to third parties only in respect of accidents which have taken place outside the Soviet Union. All the other Comecon countries have a regime of statutory insurance where the State Insurance Institute is liable even if the motor car owner fails to pay insurance premiums. The definition of a 'motor vehicle' and of the event triggering liability differs widely from one Comecon country to another.[14]

The differences between the national legal systems give little hope that adoption of rules governing the choice of applicable law would provide more than temporary relief.

Comecon experts had always argued that the organisation could adopt supranational rules only in respect of issues which the civil codes of the member states left to the discretion of the contracting parties – and must not touch any mandatory rules of such national codes. If this view is now rejected by academic lawyers, it indicates that the legal policy of the Soviet Union is undergoing a change. Though the new policy is no doubt dictated by integrationist and federalist aims, against the background of a more complex economic relationship, the legal techniques are likely to be influenced by the Czechoslovak Code of Foreign Trade, 1963 and the East German Law of International Commercial Contracts, 1976.

It is now recognised that better collision rules are not enough: the objective seems to be to prevent collisions by adopting substantive rules governing Comecon internal trade, joint ventures and, possibly, its collective relations to third countries.

Article 15 of the Comecon Complex Programme – its latest policy directive – is now interpreted as establishing the objective of law unification going beyond the former limits of non-mandatory provisions of national civil codes. Instead, unification should be directed positively to those branches of business law where it can best serve the economic integration of the region. It seems that Comecon could do well by asking the European Court of Luxembourg for help.

The General Conditions of Delivery, and similar rules for assembly and construction work, are now seen as a half-way house, not going much further than standard contracts of individual companies in the West. The call is now for Recommendations which, very much like EEC Directives, would oblige member states to harmonise certain areas of their national laws. This legal harmonisation should be based on the duty of member States, embodied in Part 16, b, 7 of the Complex Programme, to create economic, organisational and legal conditions for its accomplishment.

Like the EEC Commission, Comecon interprets such general obligations very broadly: the harmonisation should encompass not only civil and commercial law but also public, administrative, financial and labour law, to name but a few.

Beyond harmonisation looms the objective of rules and codes directly applicable, like the EEC Regulations and some provisions of the EEC Treaty, but this is seen as a distant objective for which the time is not yet ripe.

But even at this early stage it is made clear that a 'socialist internationalised legal regulation' of business should be independent of the proposals for universal unification formulated by the United Nations Commission for International Trade Law (Uncitral). It is said that the Uncitral proposals, sometimes in the form of model laws, do not provide adequately for principles of central planning and of socialist internationalism – another term for *Caesar supra gramaticos*. It is interesting, however, to note that Comecon's member states take a very active part in the work of Uncitral and seem to favour the adoption of its model laws – by others.

Notes

1 In *Deerness v John R. Keeble & Son (Brantham) Ltd* on 15 October 1982, affirmed by the House of Lords 15 May 1983, [1983] TLR 6 May.

2 [1979] 1 WLR 606.

3 (1982) Journal of Business Law 290.

4 Issues of courts and interpretation were discussed by me in *Judges, Law and Businessmen* (1983), Kluwer (Law and Taxation Publishers, Deventer, The Netherlands).

5 Recorded by Sir Harold S. Kent *In on the Act* p 97.

6 May 1975, Cmnd 6053, para 19.1, as quoted by Kent on p 103.

7 Held by Celsus, *Libri Digestorum* 1, 3, 17.

8 FT, 23 February 1984, p 9.

9 H. S. Kent *In on the Act* p 97.

10 'Managing your Lawyers' by Antonia Handler Chayes, Bruce C. Greenwald and Maxine Paisner Winig (1983) Harvard Business Review 84–91.

11 Bulletin of the European Association for Chinese Law (Square de la Quiétude, Brussels) No. 2, vol III.

12 FT Business Law Brief, November 1986, p 7.

13 See Pavel Kalensky 'Methods of Legal Regulation of Civil Law Relations in Socialist Economic Integration and Prospects of their Development' (1985) Pravnik, vol CXXIV, 7th issue, 616–634.

14 According to Immrich Fekete 'Statutory Insurance of Motor Vehicles in CMEA', ibid, 638.

2 New business for lawyers

The legal profession: 'All change'

The English legal profession is in need of radical change brought about by the almost simultaneous maturing of four factors:

- the gradual erosion of the profession's barriers to entry and to internal competition;
- the appearance of external competition, both domestic and foreign;
- the pressure for greater cost effectiveness of the legal services from the government, which became the single most important paymaster of the profession;
- and finally, the rapid development of communication and information technology, which will further intensify both internal and external competition and facilitate the adoption of cost-saving procedures.

Throughout the nineteenth century, the legal profession successfully limited entry to its ranks by premium fees demanded from articled clerks by solicitors and from pupils by barristers, in addition to the cost of maintenance which, in the first years, the young lawyer had to meet out of his private funds.

In the case of the Bar, numbers were kept down further by the rejection of all who were unlikely to become 'gentlemen', and by the weeding out of young barristers who did not make ends meet after a few years of practice.

During the nineteenth century and the beginning of the twentieth, academic legal education was of no great significance for entry into the profession. A dramatic change has taken place in the past two decades as the impact of new universities and polytechnics, and of grants to students, has diminished the importance of on-job training as a barrier to entry. At the same time, legal aid has made possible the survival of many young barristers and some solicitors who otherwise would not have made the mark.

So far, the legal service has maintained its internal market-sharing arrangements. This ensures the barristers a monopoly of appearance in higher courts, and solicitors a monopoly of access to clients.

These changes resulted in a rapid growth of the profession. The number of private practioners at the Bar increased from fewer than 2,000 in 1961 to more than 5,000 in 1984 – over 170 per cent – in spite of the continuing restriction exercised by the shortage of tenancies in chambers. The numbers of solicitors increased in this period by almost 140 per cent.

In the 1970s, women started to make a mark in the profession. They seemed to be less encumbered by traditions and more forward-thinking than their male colleagues. Of even greater importance, the expansion of the last 20 years has increased the proportion of hungry young barristers and solicitors, to whom change could bring benefits.

While the older men may prefer to preserve their privileges and monopolistic practices until they retire, the young men and women of the profession must be concerned about the increasing external competition.

For the solicitors, who have so far derived half of their income from conveyancing. the greatest threat comes from the acquisition of estate agents by banks and building societies, who will then provide a comprehensive property service by employing solicitors or licensed conveyancers in their estate agencies.

One response to this threat has been the formation of a Conveyancing Exchange which, for a negotiated annual fee, offers to market solicitors' conveyancing services, providing them with ancillary services, and attracting clients by a promise to monitor the quality of the services provided by the associated solicitors. This fills a gap sorely neglected by the Law Society.

However, though association, greater cost-effectiveness and improvement of quality may help, it will be an uphill job to defend anything approaching the present share of the conveyancing market once the banks and building societies start to operate in it in earnest. And while solicitors were saturated with conveyancing, probate and family affairs, the more rewarding field of advising businessmen has been occupied by a few specialised firms and increasingly, by accountants.

As a result, 23 leading City law firms look after the business of some 1,500 large companies (an average of some 63 companies per partnership); and 10 leading provincial and Scottish law firms look after 233 large companies (an average of 23.3 per partnership).

Even within the group of 23 leading City firms, there is a heavy concentration of business at the top. Half of the large corporate clients, including the largest of them, are served by the five biggest City law firms. These employ specialists, and are not much concerned with access to the courts – they do most of their commercial litigation in chambers, where they have direct access without the need to employ barristers.

Even more important, perhaps, is the competition from accountants, whom the indolence of solicitors allowed to take over the profitable tax business, and who are now expanding fast into other departments of law – particularly in the field of law compliance, in connection with the growing importance of regulation and self-regulation schemes. They are also acting increasingly as business advisers and as providers of business analysis and economic advice in connection with mergers and acquisitions.

Through legal aid, the government sustains both the Bar and the solicitors and is now a decisive paymaster. It will press for streamlining of the court procedure.

A VISION OF THE FUTURE

A possible scenario runs as follows . . . Though the Lord Chancellor is still believed to protect the Bar, the reforms that he must demand in order to slow down the escalation of legal aid costs will bring about important changes for the profession. The expansion of written procedure will reduce the call on barristers' services, and sooner or later they will be obliged to give up the appearance in pairs – a QC and junior – and the insistence on the attendance of a solicitor.

This, in turn, is likely to lead to the end of the privileged position of silks within the Bar and give a greater chance to juniors. Greater control of the procedure by the judge will deprive solicitors of a steady income from litigations and pre-trial procedures dragging over many years.

The streamlining and speeding up of court procedure is bound to be followed by a similar increase in cost effectiveness of arbitration, further accelerated by the pressure of alternative methods of dispute resolution.

These are expanding, because both litigation and arbitration became too costly in terms of money and managerial time, in addition to damaging business relations, through their adversarial nature.

All of this is likely to lead to a collapse of the present structures. When its own 'big bang' comes, the legal profession will be forced to look across the Atlantic.

In order to survive, solicitors will have to offer a complete service, and to be able to do so will merge or associate with large firms. This will not exclude the continued existence of highly specialised small firms, which will provide services similar to those of barristers at present.

Barristers, who have already tasted the advantages of direct access (and of contingency fees) when acting for or advising foreign clients, are likely to trade willingly their court monopoly for direct access to domestic clients.

As a result, successful solicitors will employ young barristers in their offices, and successful barristers will build up offices employing not only clerical staff but also qualified solicitors. In this way, the fusion of the profession will be brought about – and the client and the state, as the principal paymaster, will jointly determine the pace of the transition.

Ancient customs of law

According to the venerable Gilbert Abbott A'Beckett, 'there are also attorneys, now called solicitors, and barristers, whom we shall now proceed to give a bird's-eye view of. Every man may appear by his attorney, except an idiot, who must appear in person, for the law regards an idiot as one who is naturally qualified to enter personally into a lawsuit' ([1887] CB 3, III, 5).[1]

Though an idiot *must*, everybody else *may* appear as a litigant in person, in all courts of the land. A solicitor will do in tribunals and lower courts and even in the High Court in the judge's chambers. In open court, however, High Court judges, Appeal judges and Law Lords will take notice only of barristers. Barristers, alas, will not come alone but with solicitors, and, possibly a junior, so that the litigant will be impressed, if not by the result, then certainly by the bill.

Barristers tend to believe that the higher courts are their monopoly and have been from time immemorial – one which could be upset only by an Act of Parliament. This illusion was dispelled recently by Sir John Donaldson, the Master of the Rolls, in *Abse and Others v Smith and Radio Trent*.

AUDIENCE

At issue was whether the courts can implement the recommendation of the Royal Commission on Legal Services, that, where proceedings are formal and unopposed, the solicitor should have a right of audience, if indeed the matter cannot be dealt with by letter or telephone.

Sir John said that the collective of High Court judges, or the collective of the Appeal Court judges, could change the present practice and admit solicitors for some or all business of either court if they thought this was in the public interest. The barristers had no monopoly of audience.

The judges, who all started as barristers, are unlikely to think that a radical change would be in the public interest, but unless the Court of Appeal is reversed by the Lords, the solicitors have their foot in the door. Public pressure might ultimately convince the judges that they should let them in.

For a while we will still have to put up with the make-believe that bewigged judges and barristers are very superior eighteenth-century gentlemen and that it takes weeks to explain the simplest thing to the ghosts of an illiterate jury, long removed from civil courts; and that justice would suffer if they allowed new entrants to practise outside the historical chambers, whose inelastic floor space so conveniently keeps their numbers small and their fees high.

REALITY

The reality is vastly different. The big firms of City solicitors increasingly do without barristers. They have lawyers on their staff who can look after their court business which is mostly in chambers. Others will follow their lead.

Many barristers see no reason why they should continue to be approached only through solicitors as the present rules of the Bar want it. They want to have, and many do have, direct contact with big clients, accountants, insurance companies, and banks. There is no reason why they should not employ assistants to look after their paperwork, instead of giving a fat cut of their fees to impresarios – posing as clerks. They want to be allowed to advertise and they will be, to keep step with solicitors.

Whatever the judges may now think, competition will bring about rationalisation, removal of medieval barriers and reduction of legal costs. Even the wigs may go!

Moving the legal profession into the mainstream

The blueprint for the future of the English legal profession presented for discussion by the Law Society last week aims at a unified but not uniform legal service. It should consist of a network of general practitioners and of specialists who could be either solicitors or barristers. Solicitors should be allowed to plead in higher courts now reserved for barristers, and barristers should be allowed to have direct contractural relationships with clients without the intermediary of a solicitor. It follows that High Court judges should be selected not only from barristers but also from solicitors.

The legal profession so re-shaped would be based on common training of solicitors and barristers. Individual lawyers could leave the determination of their career until after they have gained some experience and shape it in accordance with their talents and with the demand for their services.

GRAVE MISTAKE

The purely defensive stance adopted by the Bar in response to the solicitors' pressure does not seem very wise. The public respects tradition and cherishes eccentricity, but only within reason. The Bar's pride in the Inns of Court, quaint mores, wigs and even a certain amount of introspective arrogance could well survive, but not the insistence on continuing the monopolistic practices of mediaeval guilds into the twenty-first century. By mobilising backbench barristers against any change, by opposing in the *Cyril Smith* case the appearance of a solicitor in the High Court even on a purely formal occasion, the Bar brought on itself more than the solicitors dared to hope for: a Court of Appeal declaration that the Bar has no monopoly of the higher courts. The judges are now contemplating whether they should allow solicitors a greater role.

It would be a grave mistake if only the requirements, jealousies and internal pressures of the two branches of the profession were taken into account in any future change. To succeed, the profession must take into account the changing demands for its services. These are at present available only to very large companies or to the impecunious, benefiting from legal aid. The legal profession misses out on the middle strata of entrepreneurs who provide dynamism to the economy. The delays and high costs of patent litigation is only one example of how the present system puts the medium and small entrepreneur and innovator at the mercy of those who can afford the exorbitant costs of litigation.

GREATER MOBILITY

However, the reduction of legal costs, though important, should not be the only aim of change in the legal profession. The removal of the historical and now obsolete division should free the Bar from its dependence on litigation. It should turn the attention away from legal technicalities and towards the need for common sense solutions. It must be repeated that the main task of a lawyer is to prevent disputes, a task which should be made more rewarding than it is at present.

To prepare them for the role of legal advisers to business, the training of lawyers will have to embrace a wider horizon than it does at present. There should be greater mobility between private practice and employment as in-house lawyers. In-house employed solicitors and barristers should have the same access to courts as practitioners and be subject to the same professional discipline. Judges selected from a unified profession embracing practising solicitors and barristers as well as in-house lawyers would be much closer to the reality of disputes brought before them and indulge less in sterile manipulation of formal concepts. The recruitment of academic lawyers as part-time judges could help to put the day-to-day problems of developing areas of law into perspective and to adjust law faster to new demands.

The legal profession is on a side track. It could and should move into the mainstream. The solicitors seem to have grasped this, it is now up to the Bar to follow.

The need for scholarship and specialisation

In the Great Souk of Marakesh – or any other African market – a holidaying English solicitor can watch the beginnings of his profession: squatting on a small carpet in the open, his evolutionary ancestor writes letters and applications – and envelopes – for his illiterate clients who, like clients all over the world, wait patiently for the miracle.

Alas, however nostalgically he may observe this idyllic scene, the contemporary solicitor cannot suppress the deeply disquieting thought that his own clients, or at least most of them, are no longer illiterate and have quite staggering demands on his knowledge and organisational ability. The warnings and exhortations of reformers could be ignored as long as professional barriers and monopolies protected him. These are now crumbling under the impact of market forces. The great souk of London, in particular, is proving to be a stern teacher.

It is no longer possible to ignore the competition of such plain-language presentations of law, which – with Citizens Advice Bureaus and other popular institutions which provide legal advice in all but name – could substantially reduce the cost of legal aid to the Government. Many solicitors now respond to this competition by offering free initial interviews and, in rural areas, by preparing to provide 'motorised law offices' and home calls by solicitors, particularly where clients find it difficult to travel. Another move in the same direction is – or rather will be – arrangements made by employers for free legal advice for their employees. This would be an additional perk which, like the resident doctor and nurse, could reduce both time off and worry.

These developments are a response to the fast expansion of a clientele which is unable or unwilling to support a slow and expensive, elitist legal service. At the other end of the battle front, the profession can be seen reacting to the need to keep up with the avalanche and to interpret much more complex law. One of the possible solutions leads from a narrow-minded attention to 'black letter law' to something which could be called 'legal fundamentalism', where familiarity with the basic principles of the system enables a faster orientation and understanding of the ever-changing legislation and judge-made law. The other path is specialisation. Solicitors are now experimenting with both.

Until recently the legal profession – solicitors, barristers and judges – looked down on the academic lawyer. They felt no need for a rational structure and arrangement of English law. Indeed, some said the more confusing and uncertain it was, the better for the profession. The 'learned journals' used to ignore completely legislative proposals, and only reported judgments with reverence and without any critique. When, in 1950, the Modern Law Review published Professor L. C. B. Gower's complaint that law teachers criticised judicial decisions so humbly that it was no criticism at all, and that their inferiority complex was bad for the whole legal profession, the editor was summoned by the Law Lords and solemnly reproved.

The UK is still unique in excluding academic lawyers from judicial appointments and, indeed, most senior judges still refuse to admit that they could gain anything from studying law as a social science. However, a more enlightened view is gaining ground. Even living authors are nowadays quoted in courts as 'persuasive authority' – a privilege which but a few years ago was reserved to those securely dead.

Both the Law Society and the Bar now encourage entry of candidates with a law degree – entry without it is quite unthinkable outside the UK.

So much for the discreet, but unavoidable, intellectualisation of the profession; but its restructuring is causing much more fuss. The first visible stage, the growth of City law firms and their mergers, may well come to a halt in so far as it was a corollary of the internationalisation of the City, and of the influx of foreign clients accustomed to the sort of comprehensive service offered by US law firms.

The expertise of the large City firms, the fact that they are mostly engaged in uncontentious business and that most of their High Court litigation is in chambers, where they do not need a barrister, reduce their interest in the fusion of the profession and the rights of appearance in higher courts for solicitors. Their partnerships are sufficiently attractive to tempt young talent to leave the Bar.

Is bigness – by merger or internal growth – the right solution?

The time is certainly up for the one-person general practice, and even two or three-member partnerships are vulnerable. The strain which the complexity of law and clients' demands puts on these small firms is reflected in their high proportion of negligence claims and the frequency with which the Law Society has to step in to compensate clients for fraud or malpractice. However, there is room for one-person offices, or small partnerships, narrowly specialised in a certain line, criminal defence, personal injuries, tax or employment law, for example. The existence of such specialised solicitors will be yet another argument for giving clients complete freedom of choice as to who should represent them in court. As the frequent appearances of barristers in tribunals and enquiries of all sorts demonstrate, the exclusive rights of audience in higher courts are not indispensable for a continued existence of the Bar.

This leaves open the question of the small general practice with several partners, still relying mainly on conveyancing, probate, divorce and company work. They could find a new *raison d'être* if they became business solicitors, helping small and medium-sized businesses to cope with the complexities of finance, contracts, product liability, industrial relations and intellectual property.

Some suburban and provincial solicitors will turn to the more demanding new tasks unaided. Others, however, will be able to become business solicitors only by joining hands with accountants, estate agents, insurance brokers and surveyors.

Justice for the not-so-poor

The introduction of class action, assisted by legal aid, proposed in the Legal Aid Bill in March 1988, would solve or at least alleviate the problem of access to the courts in a particular range of cases. In other types of cases, however, the central problem of English justice would remain unsolved – its denial to the vast section of the population not eligible for legal aid and unable to afford the costs.

This, like woodworm, is a problem which ought to be dealt with before it affects the load-bearing members of the social and political structure of the country. The easiest solution, and one which would be in keeping with the preference for giving free play to market forces, would be the introduction of contingent fees. This system, which is used in the US, requires the attorney to finance the litigation for a share in the award, so that the plaintiff pays nothing if he loses.

Contingent fees have been considered at various times by the English legal profession, mostly with revulsion. The Royal Commission on Legal Services, chaired by Lord Benson, rejected a proposal submitted by Justice, the all-party association of lawyers, for a modified system of contingent fees. According to this proposal, a slice of all awards won by successful claimants would be paid into a special fund. Lawyers – whether successful or unsuccessful – would receive their fees for the work done, calculated as at present, from the fund. In other words, successful plaintiffs would subsidise the losers but everything else would remain as it is.

Such a system would help plaintiffs of modest means, though it would not serve other aims of public policy. On the present system of pay, UK lawyers avoid any risk, so that one of the most important advantages of the US contingency fee system, namely the elimination of hopeless actions, is lost. At the same time, the proposed contingency fee fund would open the possibility of going to court to a vast new category of plaintiffs. This would make UK courts busier than ever. Such an escalation of actions would be all the more painful as the system would not provide the lawyers with any incentive to conduct the litigation swiftly.

Others point out that the contingency fee system has not reduced litigation in the US but, on the contrary, may have contributed to its escalation. It would be wrong, however, to conclude that a similar effect can be expected in the UK. The effect of contingent fees in the UK would be much more restrained.

The US legal scene is different in almost every aspect and the escalating effect which contingency fees have had on the volume of litigation there, as well as on the inflation of awards, is the result of many factors:

- The US tendency to resort immediately to litigation and to look to the courts for the solution of many economic and social problems which, in other countries, are a matter for the governments and legislature to decide.

- The important role of juries in US civil cases – from which they were removed in the UK a long time ago.
- The separate and aggressive US trial bar from which most of the highly activist judges are recruited.
- The inability of the successful defendant to recover legal costs from the defeated plaintiff in the US: in the UK he can recover about half of his real costs. This means that the risk to a US plaintiff of starting an action is much smaller.
- The US courts' readiness to support exorbitant demands for the supply of documents in the discovery procedure.

These circumstances expose the defendant to enormous, unrecoverable costs, even if he has no case to answer. In such cases, an aggressive attorney can obtain a substantial settlement from a defendant who, though certain of his case, wants to avoid the enormous costs – in money and managerial time – of the pre-trial procedure.

Fortunately, such conditions do not exist in the UK, and the possibility of introducing contingent fees over here must be considered against the different background of the UK.

The main advantage of a contingent fee system in the UK would be to enable plaintiffs of modest means to invoke the help of the courts. Even without a central contingency fund as proposed by Justice, this system would subsidise unsuccessful plaintiffs from the lawyers' share of awards won elsewhere, as only the gain from successful cases would enable the lawyer to risk loss in others.

English lawyers would be wary of embarking on unjustified litigation because their risks would be so much greater than those of their US colleagues. If defeated in court, they would have to pay the other party's costs, there would be no jury to be influenced by emotional pleading and no 'activist' judiciary with an eye on re-election or reappointment. And except for the rare case of 'aggravated damages', there would be no possibility of obtaining the penal damages which are such a menace in the US.

Another barrier to the escalation of UK litigation on anything approaching the US scale is the UK doctrine of precedent. This would not allow UK judges, however hard-pressed by an aggressive counsel, to stretch the established law of tort or company law to the length now attained in the US.

The damage such legal developments cause not only to individual companies, but also to the competitiveness of US industry abroad has now provoked a reaction. Many states are in the process of limiting damage awards to consumers. But no legislative relief has been achieved so far from the equally huge jury awards for breaches of contract.

Even accepting that contingent fees in the UK would not lead to the excesses in the US, their introduction would probably require much greater judicial control of the pre-trial procedure and of the trial itself. This is badly needed in any case, whether contingent fees are introduced or not.

In fact, the greatest obstacle to the introduction of such a system seems to be the obsolete organisation of the legal profession and its division into two separate branches of barristers and solicitors.

Solicitors could ill afford to bear the risk of a case undertaken for contingent fees alone, while guaranteeing full fees to the counsel. Both solicitor and counsel would have to participate in the venture.

Whatever the arguments for or against, it seems clear that contingent fees could not be introduced without a number of other reforms, of which the strengthening of judicial control and a fusion of the profession, or at least a radical change in the rules of the Bar, are foremost. It is not an easy proposition, but one which can no longer be ignored. If the reform of restrictive practices legislation foreshadowed in the Green Paper encompasses the legal profession, there will, at last, be an instrument for achieving the much overdue change.

The class actions, the contingent fees, the prohibition of lawyers' restrictive practices are all pieces of a jigsaw puzzle falling into place: the emerging picture is of modern times, at last.

Lawyers without frontiers

In a judgment handed down on 25 February 1988,[2] the European Court struck down, as incompatible with European law restrictive conditions imposed by West German legislation on lawyers from other member states.

The decision rules out similar restrictions in all member states and will greatly facilitate the provision of cross-border legal services throughout the European Community. It will be welcomed by companies who wish to employ their own lawyers in transactions or disputes taking place in another Community country; it will be welcomed most by enterprising lawyers wishing to expand their activities beyond national borders; it may not be so welcome to lawyers who fear the competition which this will bring.

The decision will be particularly pleasing to those British lawyers who have already expanded their activities to the Continent, without establishing a permanent office there. There is, of course, the invisible barrier, which no court decision can remove, created by the difference between the substantive and procedural law in civil law countries on the one hand, and in common law countries on the other. However, being much larger, law firms in the City of London are in a better position to employ specialists familiar with civil law and its procedures than the, as a rule, much smaller continental law firms are to employ specialists in common law.

Indeed, the Federal Republic's restrictive interpretation – by a law of 16 August 1980 – of EEC Directive 77/249 on the freedom to provide cross-border services can be seen as a defensive measure designed to protect the smaller and less internationalised German law firms against an invasion of foreign lawyers.

The directive provides, in Article 5, that member states can impose on the foreign lawyer, representing or defending a client within their jurisdiction, the condition that he will provide his services in co-operation and agreement with a local attorney, who is admitted to the court where the action takes place and who is responsible to it.

The German law elaborated this condition in a way which would have made it impossible for a foreign lawyer to make a single move without a German lawyer.

The European Commission thought that this was going too far and the European Court found the Commission's complaints justified, with two unimportant exceptions concerning contact with prisoners and representation before the Federal Supreme Court.

It held that the obligation to act in agreement and in co-operation with a local lawyer must be interpreted with reference to the purpose of the provision, defined in the preamble of the directive as 'the facilitation of the actual provision of cross-border services'. It must also be taken into account, said the court, that the Treaty of Rome prohibits all restrictions of the cross-border services since the end of the transitional period many years ago. It calls for removal of all discrimination based on the nationality or residence of the provider of the service.

Although Article 60 of the Treaty provides that cross-border services can be provided 'under the same conditions as are imposed by that state on its own nationals', the Court held that this must be interpreted restrictively so as to comply with the general principles of the Treaty. As the freedom to provide cross-border services was a fundamental principle of the Treaty, the host country could not impose on the foreign lawyer all the conditions imposed on its own nationals, but only those which were dictated by public interest and were not already met by the conditions imposed on the foreign lawyer in his home country.

The German law provides that, in disputes where representation by an attorney is not required, the party may appear in person or be represented by a layman as long as he does not provide such legal assistance as a business. As the foreign lawyer does provide legal assistance in the course of business, the German Government insisted that he could not appear in such disputes alone, but only in co-operation with a German attorney.

The Court rejected this argument. As the exclusion was not dictated by public interest, it could not be extended to the foreign lawyer, who had to be allowed to represent clients alone, without the co-operation of a German attorney, before courts and authorities whenever representation by an attorney was not obligatory.

The Commission complained that the German law gave much too wide a meaning to the concept of 'co-operation and agreement', particularly when requiring evidence of it at every step and when restricting contacts between a foreign lawyer and a prisoner. The German Government defended these restrictions by pointing to the responsibility which the German attorney bears towards German courts and to the unfamiliarity of the foreign lawyer with German law and procedure.

The court said the German Government failed to explain what it meant by 'responsibility towards the court', adding, somewhat mysteriously, that this responsibility had to be understood with reference to the aim of the directive to facilitate the provision of cross-border services.

As far as unfamiliarity with the foreign legal system was concerned, co-operation with the local lawyer was supposed to compensate for it, said the Court. It should be left to the two attorneys, foreign and local, both subject to the professional rules of the host country, to fashion their co-operation in a way appropriate to the instructions received from their client.

The national legislation could not impose on the foreign lawyer requirements which were disproportionate to the objectives of such co-operation. The Court described as unnecessary the requirements that a German attorney must be constantly present at oral hearings, that he must be the appointed defence counsel or hold the power of attorney for the client, and that the foreign lawyer must, at every step, show evidence of his agreement with a German attorney.

The Court underlined that the possible lack of knowledge of German law was not a matter concerning the responsibility of the attorney to the German court, but of his responsibility towards the client who had the freedom to appoint an attorney of his choice.

German attorneys can appear only before the court to which they are admitted and, under the German interpretation of the directive, only locally admitted attorneys could provide the necessary co-operation with foreign lawyers. The Court said that the territorial restriction was clearly designed for lawyers permanently established in Germany. It was pointless to apply it to foreign lawyers appearing only occasionally. However, it was justified to require that in cases before the Federal Supreme Court the foreign lawyer should co-operate with a German attorney admitted to that court.

Also the restrictions on contact with prisoners were justified by reasons of security, but the court or authority in charge of the prisoner should be able to make exceptions required by circumstance.

Businessmen will find this decision of the European Court reasonable. Lawyers will think it very bold. If foreign lawyers are enteprising enough to make use of it and appear in the High Court, the Court of Appeal and the House of Lords, they will drive a coach and horses through the rules of the Bar and of the Law Society. It could certainly open up the lawyers' world.

Business lawyers east and west

Fascinated as one is by the antics of the English legal profession – judges, barristers, solicitors painfully making up their minds to enter the twentieth century on the eve of the twenty-first – one can easily forget the troubles, other countries have with their lawyers.

JAPAN

Starting with the Far East, one would expect Japan to be a happy place, as it has so few attorneys: only 109 per 1 million population, compared with 803 in the UK. As attorneys are not allowed to advertise, the less well-established remain unknown, while the prominent minority can be expensive and choosy about their clients. Legal costs can rarely be recovered by the successful litigant and legal aid is quite insufficient. Appeals take, on average, five years to reach decision; district court litigation may be over in little more than a year.

There are only 2,200 judges, but in the 500 courts of summary jurisdiction they sit with two lay conciliation commissioners. Scarcity of lawyers, delays and high costs are enough to explain the non-litigiousness of the Japanese. No doubt it also has much to do with the stability of social relations.

COMMUNIST EUROPE

Though Mr Mikhail Gorbachev has a law degree, it would be wrong to conclude that lawyers are of any great importance in the Soviet empire. There are, of course, differences from one country to another. The importance of lawyers is in inverse proportion to the degree of nationalisation, which is complete in the Soviet Union and Czechoslovakia, but enriched by the survival of small businesses or farms in East Germany, Poland and Hungary.

State enterprises have in-house lawyers and take their disputes to the State Arbitration Commission, which replaced the former commercial courts. Private individuals can obtain assistance with divorces, probate, property transfers and petty litigation from public notaries or attorneys, who operate in officially organised and supervised legal advice centres.

GERMANY

Moving west, one encounters in West Germany a very different legal profession, well-trained, self-confident but somewhat over-disciplined. Attached to a pyramid of courts with a base spread evenly over the entire territory of the Federal Republic, the attorneys form dispersed small partnerships. They are not cheap, but their fees are predictable because they are related not to the time spent but to the amount involved in the business at issue. They get paid more if they reach a settlement. This payment, according to the value of a contract, proves very expensive to banks and major companies requiring advice on large contracts or financial schemes. Consequently, they mostly rely on in-house lawyers.

The decentralisation of the courts means that law firms do not reach the size of those in the City of London. One of the biggest, with many foreign clients, is Boden, Oppenhoff & Schneide of Cologne, which has only 25 partners.

So far, the strict prohibition, even horror, of advertising has kept the outsiders outside. But the constitutional court has now broken through the ethical rules of local law societies by outlawing all regulations that are not necessary in the public interest. This may eventually lead to advertising and to abandonment of the rule that each partnership may operate only from a single office. The single-office rule, also observed in France by its very conservative legal profession, has been held to contravene the Treaty of Rome and contemporary requirements by a French appeal court.

US

The law industry of the US surpasses the rest of the world in the number of lawyers, their inventiveness, diligence, enthusiasm and greed. In this lawyers' paradise, the scope for the attorney is enormous, ranging from political lobbying to business guidance and litigation. The judiciary also enjoys enormous power. Judges, elected or appointed on the basis of political orientation, play an important constitutional role and vigorously develop law in response to popular demand.

The US attorneys operate in a labour-intensive way, often forcing the defendant, through a succession of interlocutory hearings, to disclose lorryloads of documents. This, together with the fact that the successful 'defendant is only rarely awarded costs, enables the aggressive and hard-working attorney to obtain for his clients substantial settlements, even from defendants quite certain that they would win if the case came to trial.

This is the unpleasant aspect of the contingency fee system which, on the other hand, opens the court doors to the impecunious claimant. Success – which depends less on legal argument than on the technical skill, perseverance and financial resources of the law firm – leads to large partnerships, a high degree of computerisation and high-powered recruitment. Law schools are being pressed to be less academic and to provide students with practical skills.

However, this industrialisation of the law practice, and the very success it achieves in the form of multimillion dollar awards which can drive even the biggest companies into bankruptcy, has produced a backlash. More than a dozen states have enacted upper limits for punitive damages; joint and several liability, enabling the claimant to go for the deepest pocket, is likely to be modified; and medical practitioners may get some protection against malpractice suits.

By contrast, federal proposals for reform of the law are unlikely to succed in the near future. Ironically, some help may come from judges, who created the present situation. Being political animals, dependent on the electorate, they may sense the apprehension of the public and start to restrain extravagant over-lawyering.

The in-house lawyer needs to have the courage of his convictions

---

It is difficult to speak in one breath of all in-house lawyers. A member of a big legal department, possibly comprising 100 lawyers, will have a different role to that of the only lawyer in a small company or a general counsel of a big corporation whose office is next to that of the chief executive.

In every case, however, he will be more closely linked with the life of the organisation, of which he is a part, than an outside lawyer. He should be able to take into account not only the objectives followed by this organisation in a particular case, but also its general strategy and aims; and, above all, he should have some idea of the intellectual qualities of the managers involved and of their temperament.

If they tend to be reckless and rash, the legal man has to keep a tight rein on them; if they are over-careful they need to be encouraged and told that some degree of uncertainty is unavoidable. When it comes to disputes, it is not enough to know whether the company has a case, but also whether it has the resources, manpower and patience necessary to sustain long litigation.

Every lawyer, but perhaps even more so the head of a big legal department, needs to have the courage of his convictions. Though he will be expected to give reasons, particularly when his recommendations go against what the chief executive would like to hear, he should be able to follow Lord Mansfield's advice 'decide promptly, but never give your reasons. Your decisions may be right, but your reasons are sure to be wrong'. Sometimes, of course, it is difficult to become the head of the legal department with such qualities, but that would clearly be the fault of the chief executive.

But it is not enough if there is courage and independence of mind at the top. One of the great dangers of in-house legal advice is that it is a product of committees which always err on the side of prudence. It is, therefore, of the utmost importance to organise the work of legal departments in such a way that its individual members are as much as possible individually responsible for the advice given to management.

One of the important tasks of a general counsel of a big corporation is to see that the legal specialists, whether employed or contracted by the company, are aware of the changes taking place or expected in their particular field.

Being an in-house lawyer, it seems, is not a profession and not only a job, but rather a state of mind: a schizophrenic state, to be more precise. On the one hand, the in-house counsel must know the law, or at least know about it, must watch out for legal problems before these develop, and must be integrated into the management team to be able to detect any such problems.

On the other hand, he must view law with a healthy scepticism and not let the non-lawyers in the management team rely on it unduly. The best contract will not insure against difficulties when concluded with a man who cannot be trusted, and the fact that an agreement conforms to Sharia, the sacred law of Islam, is no insurance against it being torn up when alliances are swapped or a regime replaced by another one, no matter whether less or more holy than the preceding one.

Though knowing that law will not prevent such disasters, the lawyer must be prepared to use as much law as he can make serviceable and as much common sense as he can master to mount a rescue operation.

The work of an in-house lawyer is often interesting; at times it is also difficult.

Intermezzo: Fairy-tale town where common law and civil law meet

Urbino, one of the many fairy-tale towns of the Marche, is a short drive from the Adriatic coast of Italy. It straddles two hills and, as you approach, its renaissance splendour seems self-enclosed and distant. But once inside its walls, you are instantly engulfed by a very contemporary multitude of university students who clearly outnumber local residents.

The Urbino Law school, though only 100 years younger than my own *alma mater*,[3] seems a much more alive and certainly warmer place. If I were 20 again, I would like to be there as a student. If I were 40, I would like to teach there. And, being what I am, I wish someone had the good sense to convene in Urbino a leisurely symposium at which my presence would be considered indispensable.

The theme of such a symposium would, obviously, be about the bridges between the civil and common law systems, attempted by the drafters of the numerous international conventions and EEC directives; whether these bridges are well placed, broad enough and safe to carry the increasing volume of international legal traffic. And, above all, whether some of these bridges could not be eliminated altogether, if only the civil and common law lawyers knew a bit more about each others' systems.

For such a trans-systematic education of English lawyers Urbino seems to be ideally situated. It is an eminent centre of Roman law studies which, to this day, are the great harmonising factor, providing a common language for all European lawyers, including those of Communist countries – with the single exception of English (though not Scottish) lawyers.

Yet the difference is not so big that the gap cannot be breached. Like the common law today, so the Roman law, as transmitted by Justinian, was a casuistic system, a judge-made law supplemented by statute. Roman law studies, in which continental universities have engaged for the past 500 years, have distilled from the case law of Roman praetors simple principles which were then enshrined in the early nineteenth century codes. The same process of distilling general principles from leading cases is much in evidence at the great law schools in the US, and the tendency to such abstract rules was still much in evidence in the English law reports at the beginning of this century. The present proliferation of law reports about commercial cases – where differences are so minute that they would be lost in any attempt at extracting an abstract ruling – are a fairly recent phenomenon, and the cause of much delay and dissatisfaction in the higher courts.

Is the tide turning? The Law Lords have complained more than once recently about the flood of unnecessarily reported and uselessly cited commercial court judgments. These complaints, together with the 'no frills' approach of Sir John Donaldson, the present Master of the Rolls, seem to have had a beneficial effect. In one of his commercial court judgments[2] Mr Justice Parker, as he then was, refused quite bluntly to discuss a surfeit of precedents on the issue of frustration of a contract. He quoted Lord Roskill, who said that the principle setting out conditions under which a contract may be declared frustrated is now so clearly defined that citation of numerous precedents is unnecessary.

Frustration cases being the bread and butter of arbitrators and commercial lawyers, this move towards a clearly stated principle replacing precedents is very much in agreement with the process which led to the codification of the civil law in Europe and which is at present producing the various 'restatements' of law in the US.

However, a shower of abstract jurisprudence is not the only refreshment that an itinerant lawyer can find in Urbino. A number of practical problems of applied jurisprudence is thrashed out each year at the two-week seminars held in August by the Urbino Centre for European Studies. The subjects range from EEC law applicable to the pharmaceutical industry, to such South European issues as the 'reconstruction of taxable income with the help of external indicators' (the accounts presented to the tax man lacking any credibility). The courses – attendance at three can lead to a diploma in European law – are held in Italian and French only.

The combination of classical, abstract, and modern applied jurisprudence corresponds well to requirements of the students: they all hope for well-paid and safe jobs in banks and industry. The poorly paid and politically unsafe civil service comes next, while the adventure of private practice seems to be last on the list. Only heroic types embark on a judicial career in Italy.

Even a short stay at the Urbino university can teach an English lawyer much about the formative years of his continental colleagues, so different from the life at a UK or US university. It is relatively difficult to enter an English university, but once there you are not expected to kill yourself by hard work. By contrast, it is easy to enrol at the Urbino university – and at most continental universities for that matter. Both university fees and the cost of board and lodgings in heavily subsidised colleges are ridiculously low. Even private 'digs' are cheap. Moreover, in accordance with the continental custom, only about one-tenth of the 15,000 enrolled students are actually in residence at Urbino.

With an almost unrestricted entry it is left to Urbino's examiners to reduce the student population to realistic dimensions. Only about half of those who enrol eventually graduate. Examinations are mostly oral and go on as long as is necessary for the examiner to discover a gap in the candidate's knowledge and to throw him out. Though the law course need not take more than four years plus six months for final examinations, many students take six or even eight years to graduate.

Even so, a university degree is not enough. To be fully qualified students have to sit a state examination after a year of legal practice. No wonder that one finds them immersed in textbooks everywhere: on the little piazzas, in the staircase-like narrow streets, in the surrounding woods. On second thoughts it might be better to avoid an Italian law school in my next life. Instead, I will try to park an ice-cream van on Urbino's Piazza de la Republica and just watch the young people milling around.

Notes

1   *A'Beckett's Comic Blackstone*, a reprint by Southampton Ashford Press.
2   Case No 427/85, Business Law Brief, March 1988, p.19.
3   The Charles University, Prague.

3 The confusing law of finance, insurance and tax

Badly needed: a rational law of credit

The law in England seems to be left to grow like an unkempt forest, and the undergrowth is sometimes impenetrable. The recent wave of insolvencies – the painful aspect of the slimming of British industry – has brought home many unpalatable truths. Among them has been the discovery by many creditors that their security – or collateral, as American readers would say – is not as secure as they had thought. When things come to a crunch, the holder of a registered security may discover that the claim of another creditor has greater priority, even though his security was either not registered at all or registered subsequently with a retroactive effect. If a debt was assigned to him by his debtor, he might find that this assignment was worthless because another assignee to whom the debt was fraudulently assigned for the second time had priority.

Nor is the law without unpleasant surprises for the insolvent debtor. One would assume that he is entitled to receive any surplus realised by the creditor when selling the security, but this is not always the case. The rules established in pawnbrokers' shops live on.

The law still seems to be operating on the crude assumption that the creditor takes possession of the pledge as was the case some hundreds of years ago; modern business cannot operate unless the debtor can continue to have control over the pledged machinery, raw materials, products and accounts receivable. To accommodate this requirement the ancient structure has been changed a great deal in the course of time by piecemeal additions.

As long ago as 1971 the Crowther Commitee on Consumer Credit recommended that the present diversity of rules should be replaced by a legal structure applicable uniformly to all forms of security devices. The model the committee had in mind was Article 9 of the Uniform Commercial Code of the US. Their recommendations were supported by the Finance Houses Association but rejected by the government in 1973.

Since then the urgency of these recommendations has become much greater, not only because of the recession but also because courts have given a wider scope to reservation of title, which has the same effect as a charge but does not require registration.

What should one ask from a rational law? First, that it should regulate uniformly all transactions which have the same substance, irrespective of the form. Second, that there should be a simple filing system from which potential creditors could discover at a glance all the previous charges on the assets which they consider as a possible security. It should be possible to cover a composite inventory by a single entry, and it could be left to searchers to obtain further details from the secured party. Such a registration system would remove the present uncertainty about priorities and protect the bona fide creditor against prior unpublished charges on the assets. Third, the law should ensure that the debtor receives any surplus remaining in the hands of the creditor after the realisation of the security. There should also be no unjust enrichment of one creditor at the expense of others.

No automatic rights to interest

It is unbelievable that a great trading nation should have allowed its law applying to interest on overdue debts to get completely out of step with that of its trading partners and to become more obscure with every half-hearted attempt at reform; it is absurd that at a time when the role of small businesses in the restructuring of industry is recognised, the law of interest does, in the words of Lord Roskill, 'place the small creditor at a great disadvantage vis-à-vis his substantial and influential debtors'; and it is both anachronistic and unfair to treat a supplier's demand for interest as an attempt at usury when his bank can charge him up to 20 per cent for his overdraft merely on the strength of 'banker's usage'. It is unbelievable, absurd, anachronistic and unfair, but it is the law, and the Law Lords said so quite clearly.

Of all the Western countries, with the exception of the Irish Republic, only England and Wales do not give the creditor a statutory right to interest on overdue debts. Various rules of common law, of equity, and a number of provisions, tucked away in statutes where one would not necessarily look for them, now give the courts and the arbitrators the discretion to award interest even if the debt was paid before the judgement or award was made. But there is still no provision to protect the creditor against the debtor who postpones payments for years and then pays in the nick of time before legal action is taken. This situation was called 'the indefensible absurdity' by Mr Justice Parker (as he then was) in his judgment in the *Chandris* case, but he refused to accept Lord Denning's ruling in *Finix* that commercial arbitrators could award interest even if the court could not.

Lord Denning made another brave attempt to alleviate the difficulty in the *Techno-Impex* case. Although he was in a minority with his view that the arbitrators in the City of London were not bound by the strict rule of the common law courts or of the statutes applicable to them, he was supported by Lord Justice Watkins in holding that they have the right to award interest, compound as well as simple, in cases within the Admiralty jurisdiction of the High Court because the Admiralty Court could award it. This decision, helping long-suffering creditors and vindicating the claim that London is a good place for international arbitration, has soon been reversed by the House of Lords in *President of India v La Pintada Compania Navigacion SA*, reported in the *Financial Times* on 5 June 1984.

The common law rule that interest may not be claimed in respect of the non-payment of a contract debt unless the parties have provided for the payment of interest, either expressly or by implication, was laid down by the House of Lords 91 years ago in the *London, Chatham and Dover Railway* case. It brought England and Wales out of step with Scotland, the rest of Europe (except Eire) and the United States, where a creditor has a statutory claim to interest on delayed debts at a rate determined from time to time by statute or by the courts.

The appellants in the case before the Law Lords asked for the 1893 decision to be reversed. Lord Brandon of Oakbrook, ,who delivered the leading speech, said that the need for the reversal of the *London Chatham and Dover Railway* rule had become less necessary because the Court of Appeal limited its scope by saying in *Wadsworth* in 1981 that it applied only to general damages and that the courts had discretion to award interest as 'special damages' if the creditor could prove that the delay of payment caused him a specific loss.

Moreover, a 1934 Law Reform Act gave the courts discretion to award interest where the debt remained unpaid until a judgment was given, and in 1982 the Administration of Justice Act provided that interest may be awarded where a debt was paid late after proceedings had begun but before they had been concluded. At that time the Government and Parliament already had the Law Commission's recommendation that the law should be changed radically by giving the creditor a statutory right to interest on overdue debts. But the Government seems to have been swayed by the argument that in business everyone is both a creditor and a debtor and that the introduction of statutory interest would only bring extra work to the accounts departments. This seems to be a very questionable argument, but whatever the reason was, the Law Lords have now concluded that it would be an unjustifiable usurpation of Parliament's function if they introduced a change which Parliament clearly rejected.

The Law Lords may be 'timid souls', but their hearts were bleeding. Lord Roskill said that he found Lord Brandon's reasoning compelling but freely confessed that he arrived at this conclusion with both regret and reluctance. He expressed the hope that a solution would be found promptly to remove the remaining injustice in this branch of the law. Lord Scarman associated himself with the comment made by Lord Roskill and expressed regret and reluctance at the need to allow the appeal: the sooner there is legislation the better.

Lord Fraser of Tullybelton felt himself driven by Lord Brandon's irresistible reasoning to agree reluctantly that the appeal must be allowed. Only Lord Bridge of Harwich made no reference to his feelings and pointed out that a broad judicial rule could not make adequate provision for the many special cases of which the Law Commission's proposal of legislative change took care.

Having thus placed on record that justice would demand another solution, the Law Lords proceeded to show, like a well-programmed computer, that logic demanded the undoing of the limited improvements brought about by the *Techno-Impex* decision of the Court of Appeal.

Lord Denning was wrong when he thought that arbitrators were not bound by the rules of the court when it came to awarding interest. 'Where parties refer the dispute between them to arbitration in England, they impliedly agree that the arbitration is to be conducted in accordance in all respects with the law of England unless, which seldom occurs, the agreement of reference provides otherwise.' said Lord Brandon. And both Lord Denning and Lord Justice Watkins were fundamentally wrong about the powers of awarding interest in Admiralty jurisdiction.

An Admiralty Court, Lord Brandon said, had neither power to award interest on debts already paid nor to award compound interest in any case. As to the basic common law rule, the Law Lords were prevented from revising their 1893 ruling by what they saw to be the manifest policy of the legislature.

A short survey and suggestions for drafting of interest clauses is contained in *Payment Obligations in Commercial and Financial Transactions* by Professor R M Goode, published by Sweet & Maxwell.

The limping law of insolvency

In the course of the past 100 years the law of insolvency has undergone a great transformation on the continent. It has remained stagnant in the UK where its spirit, and even many details, derive from the Bankruptcy Act 1883 which also determined the approach to subsequent legislation on the winding up of companies. In assessing the spirit of the Act *The Times* reported on 15 June 1883:

> Every interest has been ruthlessly sacrificed that stood in the way of creditors. The floating charge, developed by the courts in the second half of the nineteenth century, had the result that one could now rewrite that sentence to read 'Every interest has been ruthlessly sacrified that stood in the way of the debenture holder.

That such a state of law is against the public interest is now widely recognised. When trade creditors have to bear the entire burden (the assets being absorbed by the tax man and the bank), insolvencies have a knock-on effect. And the interests of creditors are not the only ones to be considered: there are the shareholders who invested their capital, employees who invested their skills, and the community, region or the whole country who may be interested in the survival of the business to maintain a balance of their economy.

By contrast, the continental way of dealing with insolvent, or merely over-geared companies, is to allow them to come to an agreement with their creditors. By proposing such a settlement under the supervision of the court, the debtor can obtain an immediate moratorium applying also to secured creditors, as soon as the court appoints a trustee, and this can be done very quickly.

Parallel with this exists the possibility of a settlement arranged without the court's supervision – continental debt composition may reduce the debts to a certain percentage (not less than 35 per cent in Germany), provide for an extension of credit, assign certain assets to creditors, and even include a scheme under which creditors will become stock-holders in the debtor company. The scheme has to be aproved by a qualified majority of creditors.

The possibility opened to German companies of managing their financial restructuring while leaving the banks in the back seat came as a surprise to most City operators in connection with the collapse of AEG-Telefunken in 1982.

However, that does not mean that German banks are without any unfair advantage over other creditors. Though a bank whose customer applied for the opening of bankruptcy proceedings can be opposed by other creditors if it wanted to use customers' receipts for the reduction of its overdraft, it has been contested in German legal literature whether the bank is subject to the same limitation if the customer applies for a judicially supervised settlement instead.

In Case II ZR 293/1985, the BGH has sided with the banks. It rejected all analogy with the bankruptcy ordinance. To leave no doubt about the desired result, the court also said that the failure of the trustee in insolvency to revoke the authority previously given by the insolvent debtor to his customers, to pay what they owed him into his bank account, was not a prohibited special agreement. This decision clearly infringes the principle of equality of unsecured creditors. It is what they call in Germany *systemwidrig*. German banks, apparently, can get an exemption from the rule of law.

Under the French procedure for provisional suspension of payments, the court grants a three months' delay immediately after the opening of the proceedings. No payment of prior debt or disposal of assets may take place during this period without the consent of the delegated judge.

If the rescue of the enterprise is in the national interest, the plan for its financial reorganisation does not need the approval of the creditors and may also affect secured creditors. The plan prepared by the debtor together with the administrator, or by the administrator alone, should not extend over more than three years. It may include a reduction of debts, extension of credits not exceeding three years, and a change of management.

In the US, the 1979 Bankruptcy Act goes even further. Its chapter 11 greatly facilitates the composition of debts aiming at the survival of the business which takes precedence over the protection of creditors. It enables a company which cannot meet its debts to go to court with a plan for making the business successful and solvent. The court holds a hearing to ensure full disclosure of all relevant facts. The plan has to be approved by the creditors, but the management is not suddenly replaced by a receiver whose main object is to satisfy the creditors. Changes in management may be necessary to convince the court and the creditors that the plan is viable, but the continuity of operations is assured.

The recommendations of the Cork Committee[11] did not go as far as either the French or the US model. It proposed two alternative procedures: one would be under the supervision of a court which would appoint an administrator. Such an appointment would start a moratorium. Business would continue as usual while creditors' meetings would either approve the administrator and give him sufficient time to prepare a scheme of reorganisation, or recommend the termination of his appointment.

The second alternative proposed by the Cork Committee is a voluntary arrangement without the court's supervision, designed for small companies. The board of directors would agree the terms of arrangement with creditors and appoint a provisional trustee. Creditors could substitute a trustee of their own choice and if they approved an arrangement by a specified majority, this would come into effect as soon as it was filed at the Companies Registry.

The Insolvency Act (1985) adopted Cork's proposals for the rescue of failing companies by an administrator. But it did not curb the power of the bank holding a floating charge and it is doubtful whether it will be possible to persuade the banks to approve the administration unless what they are owed is small in comparison with their interest in the debtor's survival. The reform of English insolvency law can hardly be viable without dealing with the floating charge first.

Obsolete insolvency procedures: a European problem

The 1984 Conference of European Ministers of Justice instructed the European Committee on Legal Co-operation to attempt a harmonisation of the principles guiding insolvency proceedings in the 21 member states of the Council of Europe. The conventional bankruptcy and insolvency proceedings aiming at liquidation of the failed enterprise for the benefit of the creditors, as well as the newly emerging concept – variously called rehabilitation, restabilisation or reorganisation – aiming at the survival of the enterprise in the interests of the debtor, of the creditors and of the economy at large, should be taken into account.

The second task which the conference gave the committee was to tackle the numerous problems arising when the debtor has creditors and assets in another state than the one in which proceedings were instituted.

This is a relatively meagre result in view of the fairly ambitious report presented by the Swiss delegation, with its emphasis on the need for new procedures to prevent insolvency and to enable an enterprise to survive it, if viable. That approach was supported by reports presented by France, Germany and Spain.

Curiously, the conference was not reminded of the Cork report which did such pioneering work in this field. The modesty of the British delegation, headed by Mr Leon Brittan, the (then) Home Secretary, was perhaps due to the fact that only a few of the less important Cork proposals survived in the Government's White Paper. The UK was not the only reluctant participant in these discussions. Some delegations doubted that harmonisation was possible at all and, more particularly, were shy of any proposals which would deprive the taxman and public agencies of their privileged position.

Government moves to ease the international problems of insolvencies have been concentrated exclusively on conventional bankruptcies, ie where there has been a liquidation of the failed enterprise. The most ambitious attempt in this field is the EEC draft convention of 1980, but this is still a long way from becoming operative. Within the limited compass of the Community, the convention would remove at least some of the restrictions, which most countries' legislation imposes, following the territorial principle.

The exceptions are Belgium, Luxembourg and Portugal, which adopt the principle of a universal bankruptcy embracing also creditors and assets in other countries. Elements of this are to some degree present also in the Austrian, French and Nordic laws. There is a long history of bilateral agreements trying to overcome the difficulties, the latest being those concluded by Austria with Belgium and France.

However, the improvement of legal techniques, whether by bilateral agreements or a convention, will leave untouched the real problem posed by the wholesale destruction of small and medium-sized enterprises – and some big ones as well – in the course of the recession. The US provides the lead in a new approach which puts reorganisation of the business above the wish to punish the insolvent debtor, and even above the short-term interests of some of the better secured creditors.

But the Cork Report is not the only echo of chapter 11 of the US Bankruptcy Code in Europe. A new Bankruptcy Act which has been in force in Austria since January 1983 is biased in favour of restabilisation rather than liquidation. Belgian legislation introduced at about the same time provided for a commercial investigation department in every commercial court. This would convene creditors and, if necessary, appoint a consultant to assist the debtor in running his business until an agreement with the creditors had been reached.

In Spain new legislation would provide for composition and supervised management as an alternative to liquidation. Similarly, the French reform of insolvency law, consisting of four Acts of which the first reached the statute book in 1984, will enable the court to appoint a conciliator to negotiate deferments and the adoption of a recovery plan. The Swiss draft bill of 1983 provided for a confidential procedure enabling companies to ask for a moratorium earlier than they could previously. There would also be room for an administrator with considerable powers to help the restabilisation of the business.

The German economy has been hit particularly hard by the inadequacy of the conventional insolvency law. In three-quarters of all insolvency cases – and there were 16,119 in 1983 – proceedings could not even be opened because there were no assets to cover the costs. Only about 15 per cent of all banbkruptcies received the full treatment, but practically nothing resulted from these proceedings for the unsecured non-preferred creditors. Composition proceedings, which are usually kinder to this type of creditor, took place in less than 1 per cent of all insolvencies.

The economic and political consequences of this collapse of traditional methods obliged the Boon Government to authorise a major rethink. An independent commission – the opposite number of the Cork Committee – was appointed in 1978. The Ministers of Justice and the Home Secretary, assembled in Madrid, received a preview of its report.

Although German law does not know the institution of the floating charge, German lawyers have so developed the reservation of title and security interests in movables that these achieve almost the same as a floating charge, to the detriment of the unsecured creditors. According to a 1975 study, th creditors benefiting from the German equivalent of the floating charge received 88 per cent of the assets, and of the rest 9 per cent was taken by priority creditors.

The Commission took the view that the secured creditors should no longer be able to dispose of their securities directly without participating in the bankruptcy proceedings. The disposal would be in the hands of the administrator, who should be authorised to make a fixed percentage deduction from the proceeds to contribute to the bankruptcy costs. The Cork Report wanted to achieve something similar when proposing a 10 per cent reduction of the secured debts in favour of the unsecured creditors. The German Commission also thought that statutory preferences, particularly those of the taxman, should be removed, and that back-pay for the period prior to insolvency should be covered completely by insurance financed by a levy.

An important element of the German plan is to remove the veto of the individual creditor. The vote on the reorganisation would be taken in groups, and a reduction of the claims secured by moveables will require the consent of only 80 per cent in that group. In the case of unsecured creditors, the consent of only 60 per cent will be required. Claims secured by mortgage will remain outside this procedure, but both the work council, representing the employees, and the shareholders will be represented on a consultative committee appointed by the court. However, unlike some other European projects, the German proposals centre on the activities of the administrator. The court will decide only on disputed claims and supervise the procedure. It will make no commercial decisions of its own.

Many people think that the German economy has done so well because the relatively large number of small and medium-sized firms gives it greater flexibility and its industrial relations system avoids conflicts as much as possible. The bankruptcy law reform will, if adopted further strengthen, or at least tend to preserve, these advantages. The much too timid Insolvency Act 1985 will allow the destruction of Britain's small enterprises to continue.

Ill-considered rescue makes bank liable to new shareholders

The tale of a bank which postpones the bankruptcy or winding up of a client in debt, in order to get its money home first, is a familiar one, particularly in countries which, unlike the UK, do not put the bank in a privileged position by means of a floating charge. However, it does not often happen that the shareholders of the failing company turn to the courts to compensate them for the loss they suffered as a result of the bank's machinations. Such a case[2] was recently sorted out by the German Federal Supreme Court (BGH).

The BGH has in the past shown great understanding for the dilemma of banks or managements which have to weigh the prospects of a possible rescue operation against the danger that should it fail, the circle of the suffering creditors would be further increased. Sometimes, the court was thought to have treated the would-be rescuers too gently. In the case of the Herstatt Bank – the failure of which caused tremors among German bankers – BGH excused the chief executive from liability to creditors on the ground that he was entitled to exercise his business judgment about the prospects of a rescue which ultimately did not succeed.

No such gentleness of approach was evident when the Westdeutsche Landesbank was sued by twelve shareholders for damages in respect of losses caused by the postponement of bankruptcy of BuM, a building construction enterprise. It was alleged that the bankruptcy was postponed and a new issue made to enable the bank to be repaid its loans and overdraft. The shares became worthless – but not before the bank sold its own shareholding. One of the bank's directors served as deputy chairman of the ailing company's supervisory board.

At the centre of the events was the issue of new shares underwritten by the bank, the object of which was to provide the ailing company with fresh capital and to restore its solvency. The shareholders claimed compensation both in respect of old shares acquired before the new issue, and in respect of newly issued shares. This latter claim can be sub-divided into a claim in respect of shares issued before a prospectus was lodged with the court of registration, and another in respect of shares issued thereafter.[3]

The BGH rejected the claim in respect of old shares but returned the case to the Appeal Court with rulings likely to result in a decision favourable for the holders of the new shares. BGH said that whenever new shares were issued as a means to postpone bankruptcy, those responsible were liable in damages to the new shareholders.

The events took place in the late 1970s. The bank was the main source of credit of BuM AG – a public company – whose overdraft had reached DM 87m in December 1977.

BuM was obliged to reduce its overdraft to DM 20m by the end of 1977 and to achieve this, it intensified the collection of moneys due to it from customers.

On 30 December 1977, the board of the bank resolved to increase the overdraft limit to DM 40m but not to allow it to be overstepped in the future. To keep the company solvent, in January 1978, the bank supported an application by the company for a guarantee of a loan of DM 100m by the regional government of Nordrhein Westfalen – this was granted in March. The bank participated with DM 55m in the loan arranged under this guarantee and at the same time withdrew the earlier increase of the overdraft limit.

However, this loan was not enough to restore the solvency of the company and in July 1978 the company and the bank applied for a federal guarantee of a medium-term loan of DM 50m. This was granted on the condition that the capital of the company would be increased by DM 88m and that the new issue would be pre-financed by the defendant bank in association with another bank and the main shareholder of the company. The defendant bank participated in the new loan with DM 30m.

The prospectus for the Stock Exchange listing of the new shares was issued by the underwriting banks on 7 November 1987, but the new shares had been offered for sale already on 10 October.

Even the money obtained from the new issue was not enough to restore the solvency of the company, which had to apply for the opening of bankruptcy proceedings on 3 April 1979.

The plaintiff shareholders claimed compensation for the loss suffered on buying old shares after the issue of a misleading prospectus for the new shares and for loss suffered on all new shares whether bought before or after the issue of the prospectus. The trial court and the appeal court in Dusseldorf rejected their claims except that concerning the new shares bought after the publication of the misleading prospectus. Against this decision, the shareholders appealed further to the BGH.

BGH confirmed the Appeal Court's decision in respect of old shares. There was no fraud as the bank's alleged deceit was not intended to create an advantage for the sellers of old shares at the expense of buyers. The court did not see why the bank should have been interested in keeping the price of shares up – though this seems obvious since it was planning a new issue.

The court said that though the bank which, to serve its own interests, postponed the bankruptcy of a client in the knowledge that ultimately the failure could not be avoided, was liable to the failed company's creditors, the same did not apply to shareholders who acquired old shares after the bank had taken measures to postpone the failure. The legislature did not want to deter the banks unduly by making them liable towards an undetermined circle of shareholders. These were left to bear their speculative risks alone.

However, the bank was liable to the holders of new shares if the new issue was the means by which it pursued its illicit aim of postponing the bankruptcy of the company at the cost of the new shareholders.

In reversing the Appeal Court's dismissal of the claim for compensation in respect of new shares issued before the publication of the prospectus, the BGH went fairly deeply into the problem facing a rescue operation. It held that a bank carrying out such an operation was obliged to seek an objective assessment of its probable success. It had to investigate the causes of the debtors' difficulties and to consider whether the proposed means of rescue were likely to restore the health and profitability of the company.

If the bank failed to undertake such investigation, or ignored the doubts resulting from it, the court could not dismiss the possibility of intentional damage to third parties. If there was intentional behaviour contrary to public policy, the holders of new shares had a good claim for compensation.

In the present case, the company had been making big losses ever since 1974. It consumed its reserves, and obtained government-backed loans to the tune of DM 150m to improve its liquidity. Its Nigerian subsidiary had no hope of getting DM 127, owed by its customers.

The BGH said that this should have prompted the Appeal Court to doubt that the bank could reasonably expect the success of the rescue. The Appeal Court should not have refused to admit a plaintiff's witness, the bank's former executive and member of the company's supervisory board. The refusal to admit the witness suggested a biased approach to the evaluation of evidence. The Appeal Court was told to get more facts and to think again.

A comfort letter come true and the liabilities of parent companies

---

It must have caused sleepless nights for many group executives when Mr Justice Hirst held to be binding a letter of comfort given by the Malaysian Mining Corporation to Kleinwort Benson, the London merchant bank.[4]

The result is that Malaysian will have to pay the bank some £12m as damages for the failure of their London subsidiary to repay a loan of £10m. The subsidiary, MMC Metals Ltd, is one of the many victims of the International Tin Council's default and is now in liquidation.

Comfort letters, known more aptly in Germany as *Patronatserklaerungen*, are a soft alternative to a guarantee. They are given by a parent company to the creditor of its subsidiary for a variety of reasons: sometimes the parent does not want a guarantee to show on its balance sheet, it may wish to save on tax, or simply to avoid a legal obligation.

Comfort letters are a species of those ambiguous declarations which negotiators often use to save a deal threatened by lack of agreement on an important point. They accept a formulation which allows each of the parties to believe it did not give up any ground. It is a lawyer's cover-up of a disagreement. The lawyer keeps his fingers crossed and prays that there may never be litigation over the meaning of his handiwork.

This, however, is exactly what happened to the comfort letter received by Kleinwort from Malaysian. Kleinwort won, but the problems which Mr Justice Hirst had to solve before he concluded that the letter of comfort created a contractual obligation on the part of its issuer remind us forcefully of the shortcomings of English law concerning groups of companies.

The story of the comfort letter is simple. MMC Metals required additional finance and Kleinwort was willing to grant them a facility of £5m on condition that Malaysian guaranteed the loan. Malaysian said it was not its policy to guarantee the borrowing of its subsidiaries. After much toing and froing their board approved a comfort letter, the crucial sentence of which read: 'It is our policy to ensure that the business of MMC Metals is at all times in a position to meet its liabilities to you under the above arrangements.' The arrangements referred to in the letter were a loan of £5m, later increased to £10m.

Was this the same as a guarantee? Clearly not. A guarantee, which Malaysian refused to give, would have enabled the creditor to sue the guarantor for a well-defined amount of debt using the summary proceedings under Order 14 of the Rules of the Supreme Court. But if it was not a guarantee, was it not at least a contractual obligation to make good any damage suffered by the creditor?

When MMC Metals ceased trading in October 1985, it owed Kleinwort £10m plus interest and the bank asked for immediate payment from Malaysian. Malaysian denied liability. The comfort letter, it said, was not intended by either party to impose any legally binding obligation on them to support MMC Metals. Moreover, circumstances had materially changed since the letter was issued and with them Malaysian's policy regarding the support given to the subsidiary. No assurance had been given, it added, that such policy would not be reviewed in the light of changing circumstances. In due course Kleinwort took Malaysian to the High Court, where the main issue before Mr Justice Hirst was whether the assurance of the comfort letter, quoted above, was of a contractual nature.

English law recognises that some agreements do not give rise to legal rights because the parties had not intended any legal relationship between them. However, when the agreement relates to business – in contrast to social or domestic matters – the burden is on the defendant to prove that no legal effect was intended. It was argued on behalf of Malaysian that any ambiguity in the text should be explained against Kleinwort, which was responsible for providing the original draft of the letter. However, the judge found that the original draft was amended by Malaysian so that this argument did not succeed. Mr Samuel Stamler QC, appearing for Malaysian, then argued that to say 'it is our policy to ensure' was less than 'we confirm'. He did not succeed here either, though the way in which the judge rejected this argument is not entirely convincing.

Mr Stamler's strongest argument was that the prehistory of the comfort letter clearly indicated that Malaysian was not prepared to accept joint and several liability or to enter into a guarantee, and that, in his view, should be enough to remove the presumption that the comfort letter was meant to create a legal obligation.

Mr Justice Hirst rejected this argument. The refusal of a guarantee did not, in his view, exclude the possibility of another contractual obligation. The bankers clearly relied on the comfort letter when agreeing to the loan. In addition, Malaysian treated the letter as a document of great consequence, as was evident from the fact that it was backed by a formal resolution of their board.

The judge concluded that the letter formed an important and integral part of a commercial agreement; and as Malaysian was unable to prove that both parties intended that it should not be legally binding, it must be taken as creating a contract under which Malaysian was bound to make good any losses suffered by the failure of its subsidiary.

The decision was clearly not an easy one, and was preceded by many others solving similar difficulties. Not only does English law not make parents liable to their subsidiaries' creditors, it even allows subsidiaries to be made liable for the debts of parent companies to the detriment of their own creditors – see *Newperor Holdings v Lloyds Bank*[5]

The statutory position is not very different in France but the courts go a long way to satisfy the creditors of a failed subsidiary. They often use mixed arguments, such as that the subsidiary was not really independent and was in fact controlled by the parent, or, that it appeared so to the creditor because the subsidiary had the same or similar name, the same corporate location and engaged in the same kind of activities as the parent company.[6] The French courts will consider whether the subsidiary did not perhaps act for the whole group, or was put forward as a front for another company in the group or the parent itself.

The obligation of the parent to the creditors of its subsidiary is more clearly defined in German company law. The 1965 law on companies limited by shares (AG) provides for two situations. If the group is formed by contract, the parent company is obliged to stand in and make good any loss resulting from the company's trading at the end of the business year. If the group is not contractual but only results from the ownership of equity by the parent, the parent is obliged to indemnify creditors for losses caused by any disadvantageous actions which the subsidiary took at the behest of the parent in the interest of the group. This, of course, poses a number of questions concerning the relative advantages and the influence which may have to be sorted out in the courts, but it still gives the creditors a better position than they have in English law.

I am seldom enthusiastic about the EC Commission's proposals, but one has to recognise that its regulation on groups of companies, proposed in 1970, has it just about right. It provides in Article 239 that a parent company located in or outside the Community should be jointly liable for its EC subsidiary's obligations to creditors within the Community. This would be an improvement on present English law but one should go further: a Community aspiring to world trade should not cut out foreign creditors from the benefit.

Eurodollars in English courts

The case of the Libyan dollars deposited with the London branch of Bankers Trust (BT) was one of the many generated by a clash between US laws, aspiring to extraterritorial application, and national laws of other countries. Similar litigation was only narrowly avoided during the blocking of Iranian assets by President Carter.

On 9 January 1987, the Court of Appeal held that the issues were far too complicated for a summary judgment earlier handed down by Mr Justice Evans in favour of the Libyan Bank. A full trial was indicated and Lord Justice Kerr listed the main issues involved.

After a most thorough consideration of these issues, Mr Justice Staughton reached the same conclusion as Mr Justice Evans: the deposits were in London, subject to English law. The presidential freeze of Libyan assets could affect the usual transfer via New York clearing, but this was not the only possible way to repay the money to the Libyans. The American bank was obliged to use all methods open to it to discharge its obligation: it could pay cash in dollars or in sterling, and it was obliged to pay not only the $131m (£80m) on the London Deposit Account but also an additional $161m, which should have been but was not transferred from a New York current account of the Libyan bank to the London deposit account. It was further liable in damages, to be assessed, for flagrant bad faith in changing the calculation of interest to the Libyan bank's detriment.

Whatever the ultimate fate of this judgment, it is bound to remain on record as an excellent source of information about English law applying to eurodollars.

The charm of eurodollars is in their exemption from the obligation imposed on American Banks by Federal Reserve Board regulation D, to keep 12 per cent of their deposits either in the form of vault cash or as an interest-free deposit with a Federal Reserve bank. This requirement, according to section 204(c)(5) does not apply to any deposit which is payable only at an office located outside the United States. For this reason American banks can pay higher interest on their eurodollar deposits.

BT treated the Libyan Bank's London account as such an exempted deposit and at first glance it seems that this settled the problem. However, things are rarely what they seem. According to a memorandum submitted by the Federal Reserve Bank of New York as *amicus curiae* in the case of *Wells Fargo Asia Ltd v Citibank SA*, the fact that settlement of US dollar deposit liabilities takes place in that country between US domiciliaries does not determine where the deposit is legally payable. Virtually all US large-dollar transactions between parties located outside the country must be settled in the US.

Clearly, the exemption is not limited to deposits denominated in a foreign currency and is available to foreign branches of US banks that book deposits denominated in US dollars.

'If there were not some such interpretation', commented the judge, 'the whole eurodollar market might well be thrown into disarray, or even disappear altogether.'

The original arrangement between the Bankers Trust and the Libyan Bank was for a managed account which provided the Libyan Bank with the speed and efficiency of current account payments in New York and the advantage of an interest-bearing account at eurodollar rates in London. If this arrangement still existed, the London account could be used only for transfers to New York, caught by the presidential freeze.

However, the judge held that the Libyan Bank has in fact brought to an end the managed account arrangement, either implicitly by asking for payment in London, or later expressly by their solicitor's letter. The London account remained an interest-bearing account from which BT was obliged to make transfers on the instructions of the Libyan Bank, as long as these avoided an infringement of the US law in the US. The termination of the managed account arrangement also resolved all doubts about the law applicable to the relationship; the London account was then clearly governed by English law.

As the next line of defence, BT submitted that even then only transfers through the New York clearing were permitted by implication from the usage of the international market in eurodollars, or from the course of dealing between the parties since 1980. After hearing expert evidence, the judge concluded that there was no such implied term.

The judge rejected the opinion of two authorities, Dr Franciss Mann in his book, *The Legal Aspects of Money*, and a concurrent opinion expressed by Professor Roy Goode in *Payment Obligations in Commercial and Financial Transactions*, that eurodollar deposits cannot be withdrawn in cash. He concluded that there was no possibility in this case to effect payment by in-house or correspondent bank transfer, and that bankers draft on London would not have been eligible for London dollar clearing.

The only possibility open to BT – and one which it was obliged to make use of – was to pay in cash. It was the customer's fundamental right, he said, to demand payment in cash. Such demand was in fact made. It has not been argued that the delivery of such a great sum in cash in London would involve any illegal action in New York. Accordingly, BT was liable to deliver. The judge also held that the customer is entitled to demand payment in sterling if payment cannot be made in dollars. 'If I had not held that payment should have been made in cash in US dollars I would have held that it should have been made in sterling'. Sterling notes would have been available from the Bank of England in London.

In the view of the judge no arguments diminished the importance of the general rule that the proper law of a bank's contract is the law of the place where the account is kept. 'Political risk must commonly be an important factor to those who deposit large sums of money with banks.'

The security of the deposits is, no doubt, a very important consideration.

However, there is also an international interest in containing and combating terrorism and preventing it from destroying the very foundation on which the banking business exists. Dr Mann wrote in 1979, on the occasion of the blocking of Iranian accounts, that international public policy required courts of all countries to assist in the elimination of international illegality in the interest of the world community at large. In his view it is necessary to support an allied nation's policy of retaliation. He also thinks this is not a point of politics but a matter of judicial conscience.

Few judges will agree that it is their business to take the hot potatoes out of the fire to save the politicians' skin, and the politicians do not like to fight a fire in other people's houses – they prefer to wait until it spreads to their own.

Financial Services – a prophecy not heeded

It was ordained that I should not be left out of the song and dance preparing for the Big Bang. Still hopeful, I went round the office looking for annotated copies of the Financial Services Bill which would save me from thinking. All I found was a library copy in pristine condition, its 174 pages craving for human sympathy and attention.

I read it all before leaving the office but it did not help much. I took it home and read it again. To no avail. Next morning, I woke up with a high fever. The doctor was called and strictly prohibited the reading of any legislative material.

When I recovered, I still could not say what was in the Financial Services Bill. In desperation, I keyed it into my desk computer and asked what the main idea was. The computer took inordinately long to answer and then said: 'Never mind the idea, implementation is unlikely before mid-1987, probably much later.' 'But Big Bang is scheduled for 27 October 1986. 'I pointed out. 'You will just have to make do with common law, the Prevention of Fraud Investment Act 1958 and the Licenced Dealers' Rules.'

I asked what was likely to happen in 1987 when the Secretary of State, the Securities Investment Board and all the self-regulating organisations should have brought out their various rules. 'CAN'T SAY' appeared in glaring green letters on the screen.

'Don't be silly,' I said to my computer, 'there are 166 clauses and 13 schedules. Do your work properly and tell me what will happen.'

'NOTHING,' in big green letters. 'Explain,' I ordered, losing patience. 'There are too many "ifs" and "buts"', chirped the computer, evidently trying to appease me. 'Only one thing is certain. The breach of the as-yet-unknown rules will entitle those concerned to mount a civil suit under section 57. All documents will be capable of discovery. Litigation will proliferate to figures beyond my capacity. Authorised persons threatened with suspension, injunctions and restriction orders will fight back in courts, making complaints against the self-regulatory organisation, the SIB, the

Secretary of State and his inspectors. They will be busy convincing the DPP that no evidence is available.'

There was a silence, and then my computer added: 'Can't say how anyone will have time left for the investment business.'

At this point, concluding that I would not get any sense out of the machine and flouting the doctor's orders, I decided to make another attempt to digest the Financial Services Bill by human methods. I am sorry to confess that I did not get much further than my computer and can offer no more than these meagre gleanings about the Bill.

There will be two broad categories of persons to whom the legislation should be of concern. One consists of those engaged in, or attempting, investment business. The other are the investors. The first difficulty is that these are only imaginary categories. Some investors will themselves be engaged in the investment business. In relation to the dealers, brokers and advisers, the investors can be classified either as customers or as clients. They are customers when they only buy or sell, but clients when they receive advice.

Those engaged in the investment business will fall into three broad categories. Thos who are exempt from the impact of the legislation, like the Bank of England, the Stock Exchange and Lloyd's of London, will apparently be able to do whatever they want. Those who are authorised persons will be subject to rules made by the Secretary of State, except that these rules will not apply to them if they are members of a recognised self-regulating organisation. Finally, there is a third category, those who attempt doing invstment business without being authorised: they will find that their deals cannot be enforced.

The crucial prohibition of the Bill is contained in section 44 which says that any person who makes a misleading statement or dishonestly conceals any material facts is guilty of an offence for which he can be sent to prison for up to seven years. This sound pretty tough, but the reality is different. First, it does not apply to statements made outside the UK, or made in the UK but affecting persons who are outside the UK, or affecting agreements entered into or exercised outside the UK. One can see the prices of Zurich office accommodation rocketing.

Second, if anyone is so careless as to mislead UK investors from a UK office and commits an offence against section 44, the matter will have to be referred to the Director of Public Prosecutions, who will give the culprit complete protection from publicity and plenty of time to find refuge for himself and his money in one of the many warm islands specialising in such hospitality.

The Bill would, of course, give the Secretary of State many other theoretical possibilities of how to move against those who do not play the game, for example, by withdrawing or threatening to withdraw or limiting their authorisation.

Given the existence of the one big family linking politicians with City institutions, as demonstrated by the past treatment of insurance frauds and the exemption of Lloyd's of London from the impact of the proposed legislation, one would have to be foolishly optimistic to expect that the political powers will be used effectively.

There is, of course, also the remedy of common law private action for those who have been swindled and who should be able to recover any profits fraudulently obtained by those who pretended to act as agents but preferred their own interests. Those who need the protection of the law most will not have money to risk on such private litigation, and some of those who have the money will use litigation just to annoy their competitors, or to bring them into disrepute. And what about the duty of an agent representing two principals whose interests clash? The Bill does not provide an answer.

Finally, there is the underlying idea that conflicts of interests – between the agent and his principal, and between several clients of one agent – can be somehow prevented by the erection of Chinese walls separating the dealing, advising and investment organising departments in a multi-purpose financial institution. My computer tells me that as many as 50 Chinese walls might be necessary within a conglomerate to provide for all possible situations. As it may be difficult to erect so many, it suggested that partners might sit in spacesuits and lunch apart.

There is indeed very little to recommend in the Bill. The City stands and falls on the confidence it enjoys. The Bill will do nothing to strengthen that confidence and a lot to frighten dealers away from London.

Is there a better way?

There is no perfect solution, but it could be done better. First, whatever legislation is made, it should be simple and understandable to non-lawyers and even to those coming from other jurisdictions and are used to more direct legal thinking. It could rest on two basic rules, one saying that anyone who misleads another person, or lets him fall into error for his own or other people's gain, commits a fraud – and forget about dishonesty on which you need a jury to pronounce. The second rule should be that no one can serve two masters.

From these two rules everything else can be derived according to the circumstances of the particular case. The forms which dealers and brokers use with customers and clients should clearly state how they deal with what profit or other interest they have in the transaction.

Second, enforcement should be simple, cheap and predictable. There should be no reliance on remedial actions depending on political decision of ministers and no references to the Director of Public Prosecutions. Private actions should be only a last resort and so circumscribed as to prevent abuse.

The main burden of enforcement should be concentrated in the hands of a Securities Investment Board with statutory power to impose restrictions on dealers and severe fines capable of putting culprits out of business. There should be the right of appeal to courts in the same way as there is judicial review for other administrative decisions. It would rarely have to come to that. The possibility of sending a mob of investigators on a dawn raid, the ignominy of a well-published investigation, the risk of initiating class actions on behalf of the small investors harmed by illicit operations: such threats would probably be enough to put the fear of law into City dealers in the same way as raised eyebrows used to do in the good old days.

And one more thing. It could have a most salutary effect if the threat of libel law was lifted from the financial press and if it had at least the same freedom of reporting as the Wall Street Journal has in the US.

Sovereign debtors: New York judges bending as straws in the wind

Bankers need not fear any punishment for throwing good money after bad: if they do so individually they will be rescued by a kindly central bank; and if they act collectively for sovereign borrowers, no-one dares to mention it for fear of shaking the house of cards known as the 'international credit system'.

All this comes very much to mind as one reads the two entirely contradictory judgments passed by the same three appeal judges of the US Court of Appeals for the Second Circuit in one and the same case, namely the *Allied Bank International v Vanco Credit Agicola de Cartago*.

In 1984, the first of these judgments[7], Allied I, made New York law and New York courts unsafe for international lenders. The court bent over backwards to prevent a 'rogue' bank from spoiling a settlement, designed to paper over Costa Rica's default on promissory notes issued by its three state-owned banks. It achieved the desired result by concluding that what the Costa Rican Government did was not much different from a moratorium accorded to a US insolvent company under chapter 11 of the US Bankruptcy Code. Moreover, the court said, this moratorium was in line with the policy of the International Monetary Fund, enjoying the support of the US Government. Hence, comity – the mutual respect of courts – demanded that Allied should not be allowed to enforce the payment of the bills in New York.

It seemed to me then that such extraterritorial application of US insolvency laws at the cost of American and non-American creditors was outrageous. It would deter potential lenders from making their loans payable in New York and from choosing New York law and New York courts for the settlement of disputes. My feelings were echoed on the other side of the Atlantic. As a result the Appeal Court decided to think again and ordered a rehearing.

To please the banks, which were now afraid that Allied I might drive international loan business away from New York, the court bent the following year again, this time in the opposite direction, and held, in Allied II[8] that the payment of the promissory notes should be enforced. To reach this conclusion, the judges performed some remarkable self criticism, worthy of Communist deviationists seeking re-admittance to the Party.

Leaving aside the doctrine of comity, the court this time concentrated on the applicability of the Act of State doctrine. In the light of past jurisprudence US courts will not sit in judgment on acts of a foreign government that are effective only within that government's own territory. And they will respect such acts even if these have effect within the US, so long as the effects are compatible with the law and policy of the United States.

The first question which the newly assembled court had to answer, therefore, was whether the loans were situated in the US or in Costa Rica.

The court chose to be guided by an earlier ruling of the Fifth Circuit in *Tabacalerott,*[9] according to which, for the purposes of an Act of State, the location of a debt depends largely on whether the Act of State – a confiscation as a rule – can 'come to complete fruition within the dominion of the (foreign) government'.

The court reasoned that not only were the loans negotiated and the bills payable in New York and the Costa Rican banks submitted to the jurisdiction of New York courts but that the US also had 'an interest in maintaining New York's status as one of the foremost commercial centres in the world'. But the lucidity of this statement was rather spoilt when the court added that Costa Rica's interest in the contract was 'essentially limited to the extent to which it can unilaterally alter the payment terms'.

Having thus reached the conclusion that the *situs* of the debt was in the US and not in Costa Rica, the court had to consider whether the act of the Costa Rican Government might, even so, command respect because it was consistent with US law and policy.

This time the court had the benefit of *amicus curiae* brief from the Department of Justice, stating that the US supported the debt resolution procedure of the IMF only on the understanding that the underlying obligations to pay remained valid and enforceable. *Ergo*, the Costa Rican Act of State was inconsistent with US policy as it aimed at making the promissory notes unenforceable. *Ergo*, the Act of State doctrine was not applicable. The payment of the bills would be enforced.

However, the banks still seem to be unhappy. The first judgment did make New York a rather undesirable place for such business, but they also dislike the second judgment because it gives individual banks too much scope for spoiling a tidy renegotiation exercise. They want to have their cake and eat it.

But this seems to be one of the few desires which New York cannot help to achieve.[10]

Banks in need of international rules

A succession of upheavals – Iran, Afghanistan, Poland and the Falkland Islands – should have brought home to bankers that international law is a very uncertain concept and provides little guidance on how they should behave when caught between conflicting interests of governments, depositors and performance bond holders – not to speak of their own stake in the survival of international loan arrangements which sometimes can be achieved only by firmly closing one's eyes to the fact of a debtor country's default.

Realisation of the inadequacy of both international and national rules when confronted with such exceptional situations came at a time when national banking laws were under review, necessitated by the recession. The trend towards greater disclosure and stricter surveillance, as well as efforts to reform insolvency laws, will have to be harmonised internationally.

The freezing of Iranian assets brought to the forefront of attention the

US doctrine of 'nationality jurisdiction', according to which foreign subsidiaries of American companies should obey American laws and regulations. The 1980 Special Powers of the President Act purported to extend to embrace foreign subsidiaries of US banks which, however, were subject to the banking laws of the countries in which they were established. The measure put the City of London in an extremely difficult position and could well have damaged it as the major financial centre of the world.

Similar problems, though on a smaller scale, were created for banks in Frankfurt, Paris and Zurich. Legal suits brought in English, French and German courts and aimed at establishing that the Iranian deposits in Europe were subject to the local law of banking contracts had every chance of success but the subsidiaries of US banks, were under pressure from the US to resist such actions. In the end the issue was resolved without the assistance of courts by the release of the hostages and the Algerian agreements.

In their guidelines on the blocking of Argentinian assets by the British Government, the Bank of England and Treasury avoided making a similar mistake. Following legal advice they decided that the blocking could not be enforced on the overseas branches of UK banks; they expressed only the hope that the overseas branches would abide by the spirit of the guidelines.

One cannot assume, however, that other governments in a similar situation would follow the British example; there is urgent need for an international convention which would establish the rule, binding on national courts of law, that no parent company has the power to compel its foreign subsidiary to disregard local laws and should not attempt to do so. Such a convention could also go into some detail about the treatment of international syndicated loans and other forms of credits caught in governmental freezing of banking transactions.

The unresolved problems of application of national laws to business activies in other countries create difficulties also on a more mundane plane. The US securities regulations provide for criminal penalties and are, therefore a combination of consumer protection legislation and criminal legislation. This combination leads to the punishment of infringements which took place in the US even if no US citizens or residents suffered any damage. If they had suffered damage the US courts would punish such acts even if they took place outside of US territory. Although the US courts have somewhat curbed this tendency towards the universal application of the Securities Exchange Commission rules, current legislative proposals point towards its expansion which is likely to lead to more friction and litigation.

A Federal Securities Code, proposed by the American Law Institute is said to aim at a broad substantive coverage within the limits of international law but in fact enlarges on the requirements developed by the courts. Its section 1905 would provide that the Code is to apply to non-residents of the US who have registered, or should have registered, under the Code as issuers, brokers, dealers, investment advisers or persons who submit tenders, as well as to insiders of such companies. Non-resident operators falling within these categories would be exempt from registration if they do business with persons outside the US or with a person who is not a US citizen and is in the US on a visit and was previously a customer or client of the broker.

The calls for greater disclosure and stricter surveillance – reappearing periodically since the Herstatt Bank failure in Germany – were greatly reinforced by the international events affecting the credit system. When the US Federal Reserve proposed new reporting rules for foreign banks operating in the US in November 1979 it was severely criticised but submissions made to the Fed revealed that bank accounts and the supervision of banks could be much improved in several countries and that the whole international credit system could benefit from greater cooperation in this field.

The US proposals led to a protest from central banks in Belgium, West Germany, Italy, Japan, The Netherlands, Sweden and Switzerland as well as from the Bank Control Commission in France. There were fears, possibly justified, that the US operators wanted to extend their regulatory jurisdiction to non-American banks. The Swiss Bankers' Association argued that there was no need to disclose secret reserves: 'A regulator can have no legitimate interest in determining the degree of understatement [of bank's capital] if the stated capital is sufficient.'

This discussion, however, stimulated new proposals. The European Community is moving towards greater disclosure and towards international co-operation between the supervisory authorities.

The best illustration of the changing opinion is the fact that the Swiss Banking Commission has revoked the famous Circular 4 which approved the holding of secret reserves. The Swiss Federal Court held that the parties interested in bank accounts were not only shareholders, creditors and debtors but also the public at large. And in another decision, it indicated that the requirement of truth and clarity in accounts had greater weight than a bank's desire to cover up losses. A qualified disclosure, perhaps under the heading of 'diverse income', may be required in the future when secret reserves are mobilised and that would of course have the consequence that losses too would have to appear in the balance sheet.

The public's suspicion that in a political turmoil banks are exposed to very great losses may in the end do greater harm if imagination is given a free rein. Disclosure may act as a stablising factor.

Insurance: the Lloyd's way

The confidence of the customer is a rather important asset. Once overcharged, he is likely to go to another market, and electronic communications make that easy.

Unfortunately, many ways are still open to those who want to rip off the customer seeking insurance.

Also, those who finance insurance and put their entire assets at risk, the 'names' at Lloyd's of London, can be cheated in a variety of ways which, curiously, receive much more publicity than shabby treatment of the insurance seekers, though these are more numerous and more important for the economy: excessive insurance premiums tend to reduce the efficiency and competitiveness of production directly or indirectly.

Let us take them first. Though its terms of reference were focused on protection of names, the committee chaired by Sir Patrick Neill recognised[11] in its report published in January 1987, that this implied also the safeguarding of the interests of the policy holders who otherwise may run away.

Unfortunately, this is about all the committee has to say on this subject in its report. It notes with approval that the brokers were ordered by the 1982 Lloyd's Act to divest themselves of managing agencies, which dominate Lloyd's syndicates. But it turns a blind eye to the fact that they are still allowed to own underwriting agencies representing (mainly foreign) insurance companies, that they hold 'binding authorities' – which make them into agents and representatives of insurance companies – and they may be, and often are members of insurance syndicates at Lloyd's.

These links lead necessarily to a conflict between the client's and the broker's interests. It is argued, in defence of this system, that to retain the client's account, the broker must serve him well.

This may work in favour of large clients able to shop around and check. A medium to small enterprise, however, does not employ an insurance specialist on its staff and is easily fobbed off with usual sales talk explaining a higher premium by 'better terms' or even 'better quality insurer' – factors which are difficult to prove and impossible to quantify. A consumer seeking motor, household or life insurance is, of course, even more at sea than a small business firm.

There is a strong case, therefore, for severance of brokers' remaining links with insurers.

Turning to the protection of names: these successors of the insurers, who used to sit in Mr Lloyd's coffeehouse, sipping coffee and underwriting policies brought to them by waiters acting as brokers, became somewhat distant from the actual operation of the world's most famous insurance market. First, they gave authority to one of those sitting at their table and these became the 'underwriters'. In the second phase, the underwriter and his deputy, keeping the list of names of the members of the syndicate, became bosses. They established parallel syndicates – baby syndicates – of themselves and their friends, to whom they would steer the more profitable business.

The Neill report says that such parallel syndicates should be discarded within two years – as well as special links with reinsurers, which sometimes were owned by the underwriter and through which profits could be syphoned to tax havens.

In the third phase, an additional layer was imposed between the names and the underwriters: the 'names agent' whose function it was to recruit investors willing to become 'names' and to place their business with managing agents. The names are captives of the agent who recruited them, and who may not have the right contacts or be too closely linked with the managing agency. They must not seek busines of a certain class – marine, for example – with more than one agent. The Neill report recommends that they should be given the freedom to go to any agent they wish.

However, there is yet another, almost unavoidable pitfall in store for the name. The 'managing agents' have become limited companies and the 'underwriters' are no longer insurers acting for themselves and other members of the syndicates, but employees and often directors of the managing agency, owing their allegiance and fiduciary duty directly to the shareholders of the agency and only very indirectly to the names. By a similar development, the names' agencies became limited companies with shareholders to look after.

This results, of course, in a fundamental conflict of interest between the shareholders of these agencies and the actual insurers, the names. A complicated and mostly opaque structure of commissions on premium income, expenses and participation in the profits, but rarely in the losses of the insurance business has been designed mainly for the benefit of the agencies.

Even more serious may be the tendency to build up premium and undervalue the outstanding liabilities, so that the agency can be sold at great profit. The money to be made by selling a profitable, or apparently profitable, agency seems to have become a widespread obsession at all levels of the Lloyd's hierarchy.

The Neill committee sought to improve the position of the names by increasing the number of non-professional members of the Lloyd's Council, by redrafting agency agreements, by greater transparency of the commissions and charges, and by offsetting losses of one year against the profits of another before calculating the agency's share of profit.

These are, no doubt, welcome paliatives which, however, do not touch the cause of the disease. This can be cured only by removing the conflict of interest between names and the shareholders of the agencies – by making the names into the only shareholders.

There is no reason why syndicates have to be reconstituted each year. They can form mutual societies running the agencies. Only such a shift in the economic power – which could be achieved gradually by ruling that agency shares may be sold only to names which they represent – can achieve a radical improvement. Avoiding this essential problem, the Neill committee instead leaves it to the Council to find solutions for problems, or calls for more reports, policy statements, declarations of faith – all paperwork which, going by past experience, is only increasing administrative costs with little other effect.

Insurance: the West German way

There are two ways to protect the insured's or the insurance seeker's interests: one is by vigorous competition among the insurers and the other by state regulation of the insurance industry.

Historically, the UK took the first road, the only one open to a world trading nation. Germany, like most Continental countries, took the path of regulation.

It resulted in government supervision not only of the solvency and managerial efficiency of insurers but also of screening and approving the terms of standard insurance policies for the benefit of the insured. In the field of fire insurance, the only mass insurance before the advent of the motorcar, this paternalistic attitude led to the establishment of state-owned insurance organisations controlled by the Laender and operating in each of them as a monopoly.

These differences in historical approach are so great that English and West German experts often find it difficult to understand each other, even if they both speak either English or German. While institutions and their supervision still differ greatly in their form and concepts, the actual differences in operation and in the market are being gradually eroded.

In the UK a number of institutional insurers are in no way different from their West German counterparts and Lloyd's itself is no longer a place of vigorous competition between syndicates of insurers.

In West Germany the original aim of protecting the insured has been eroded as private households, small farmers and small businesses have been joined as insurance takers by large enterprises, whose interests often span the world.

These large enterprises have their own insurance departments dealing directly with the insurers. They are perfectly able to look after their interests and need no nanny to look after them. These big enterprises are also allowed to contact foreign insurers without any great difficulty. One-off insurance contracts which result from the initiative of the West German insurance taker are considered by West German law to be outside the regulatory framework.

The majority of insurance seekers, however, have to go through brokers. It is a criminal offence for these brokers to place insurance abroad, that is with a foreign insurer who is not established in West Germany.

Looking at the same problem from the other side, a foreign insurer intending to do business in West Germany on a continuous basis will need to equip his local broker with binding authority to write policies on his behalf. Such a broker will be viewed by the German authorities as his agent.

According to the insurance supervision law as amended on 29 March 1983, all Community insurers – with the important exception of transport and marine insurance – wishing to do business in West Germany through salesmen, representatives, agents or other intermediaries, must be established and authorised in West Germany. This, together with the prohibition on brokers to contract insurance for risks located in West Germany with outside insurers, has now become not so much a measure for the protection of the insured against the powerful insurer as a measure for the protection of the West German insurance market against the penetration of insurers from other member states. This is felt most in the UK, the country with the most developed insurance industry.

Though the European Court in its recent judgment on co-insurance (in Case 205/84) distinguished between the requirement of establishment which it finds incompatible with the EEC treaty, and the requirement of authorisation which it finds more acceptable. The second can be hardly met without the first, if all commercial documents relating to policies, separate accounts and technical reserves have to be located in West Germany.

Moreover, a foreign insurer after going to the expense of such an establishment may be at a certain disadvantage when seeking the approval of the terms of his policies. These are now negotiated between associations of West German insurers and the supervisory office so that the policies of individual insurers can be certain of approval if they conform to the model agreed with their association.

A certain concession to foreign insurers wishing to participate in large-scale insurance contracts has been obtained by the EEC coinsurance directive 78/473. However, in implementing this directive, the supervisory office fixed very high thresholds for contracts benefiting from this directive. Thus, to benefit under the coinsurance directive, the policy insuring against fire, other damage to property and miscellaneous financial loss must not be for less than DM 125m (£42.4m). Aircraft liability has a threshold of DM 75m and general liability policies benefit from the coinsurance directive only if the insured enterprise has a turnover of at least DM 500m.

These thresholds are too high to allow a normal flow of business. In its complaint to the European Court, the EEC Commission said this, but later in the proceedings attacked the very existence of the thresholds. This change in pleadings was used as an excuse by the court for avoiding the issue altogether.

When adopting the coinsurance directive, the Council of Ministers left open the question whether insurers from other member states wishing to participate as coinsurers in a business in another member state might be required to establish local branches or to obtain local authorisation to do business. The council left this hot potato to the European Court.

In its coinsurance decision, the court held that West Germany was wrong in requiring the establishment and authorisation of the leading coinsurer. This, said the court, was not necessary in view of the co-operation between the supervisory authorities of member states established by the directive. Not only the requirement of local establishment but also that of authorisation was, said the court, contrary to Articles 59 and 60 of the EEC treaty and, consequently, also contrary to the coinsurance directive.

The court took the view that in other situations the requirement of authorisation might be justified by the need to protect policyholders.

The West German authorities are now conducting an inquiry with their trade associations to find out what practical interpretations this ruling could be given. The court's judgment is a certain retreat from the proposal of the second insurance directive which would exclude all commercial insurance from the scope of mandatory rules of all the states in which the service is provided. The court found it impossible to make a general distinction between situations where protection is required and where it is not.

A second decision of the European Court[12] (in Case 45/85, of 27 January 1987), finding against a West German fire insurance cartel, will be of greater impact because it clearly brings insurance under the EEC competition law. Though the insurance industry in West Germany is not entirely immune from West German competition rules, their impact is softened because their enforcement has to be agreed between the Cartel Office and the Supervisory Office for Insurance which, understandably, defends the interests of the insurance industry. In dealing with the specific case of the fire insurance cartel, the court did not adopt a radical line, saying merely that the recommended increase of premiums was more than was necessary to ensure the solvency of insurers, and did not leave room for cost competition.

The German authorities seem to be very pleased with the outcome of the Luxembourg litigation, saying that it requires very little change in their system. They expect that Lloyd's of London will establish an office in West Germany. The representative of the Association of Lloyd's Insurers would be able to sue and be sued on behalf of its members. The Lloyd's office in Germany would have to keep a complete documentation of the policies issued but there would be no need to make the contracts in West Germany. These could continue to be made at Lloyd's in London.

Both parties think they have won in Luxembourg. The time may have come when a more aggressive commercial policy would bring better results than lawyering in Brussels, Berlin and Luxembourg.

A US judge succeeds in slaying the hydra of insurance litigation

Judge John R. Brown of the US Court of Appeals for the Fifth Circuit is justly proud that the American courts have succeeded in slaying a veritable hydra of insurance litigation, where each dispute disposed of threatened to give rise to two new ones.[13]

Most of these disputes have now been settled or are likely to be abandoned but the question remains why was this Herculean effort on the part of the American courts necessary? First, is there not something wrong with Lloyd's procedures allowing a broker to create – whether by error, misunderstanding or fraud – the conviction on the part of the insurer that he obtained 100 per cent coverage from the reinsurer while leading the reinsurer to believe that he covered only an excess, only a part of the insurance risk, and, second, should not Lloyd's policies include a clause providing for joining of all disputes in the hands of one judge, preferably in the Commercial Court in London?

The disputes spawned by the Early American Insurance and its various associates – compared by the judge with the mythical hydra – indicate that some improvement of Lloyd's policies may be overdue now that the insurance business has achieved global dimensions.

The story, which involves at least 45 separate insurers, started to unfold when Edinburgh Insurance underwent voluntary liquidation and withdrew in 1982 from the marine insurance business. Edinburgh Insurance acted as reinsurer for Early American, an Alabama corporation that insured vessels plying the inland and coastal waters of Louisiana. On learning of Edinburgh's withdrawal of reinsurance cover, Early American decided to give up its entire marine portfolio. This involved obtaining a 100 per cent reinsurance of the entire portfolio.

Early American turned to its agent, World American Under-Writers, a Delaware corporation. World, in its turn, used the services of A. W. Knott Becker Scott (KBS), a Lloyd's insurance broker.

KBS approached Syndicate 420 at Lloyd's and placed with it a reinsurance contract authorising KBS to issue a cover note to Early American which would allow World to reinsure certain risks with Syndicate 420. In fact

KBS issued the cover note to an intermediary, Channel Underwriters, and Channel in turn issued the cover note to World in Louisiana.

Early American is now undergoing liquidation and bankruptcy proceedings and the question of whether it succeeded in obtaining a complete takeover of its marine insurance portoflio by the Lloyd's syndicate is of considerable importance to the parties whose vessels it insured and other creditors.

However, Syndicate 420 disputes that such a contract was validly agreed, alleging that the brokers, KBS, totally misrepresented the nature of the risk. The syndicate contends that the brokers failed to disclose an adverse loss ratio suffered by Early American, did not tell the syndicate that Early American sought 100 per cent reinsurance of its entire portfolio without retaining any part of the risk itself, and misled the syndicate by stating that its cover note would be issued only for a specific layer of reinsurance – business concluded after July 1982.

To extricate itself from its obligations imposed, as it alleged, by the deceit of the brokers, the syndicate started a number of legal suits in the eastern district of Louisiana. It sought a declaration that the syndicate was not liable to Early American under the KBS cover note and indemnification from World and Channel, should such a declaration be denied.

More suits followed. Having been named as defendant, World claimed indemnity for all losses and damages from KBS. A similar claim against KBS was filed by Early American which, in addition, filed a cross-claim against World and a counter-claim against Syndicate 420.

However, this is not the sum of the multiple suits and claims. Like most insurance brokers, the KBS had a negligence or malpractice policy under which it was promised indemnity for errors and omissions committed by it in the course of brokerage. In fact it had two Errors and Omission policies, one for 1982–83 and the other for 1983–84. Some 29 syndicates subscribed to the 1982–83 policy and more than 40 to the 1983–1984 policy.

One would expect that the two E and O syndicates would be drawn into the dispute only in case the brokers were found liable for negligence or malpractice. However, Louisiana has a Direct Action Statute which permits injured parties to sue directly the insurer of whoever caused the injury. This statute obviated the need to sue the brokers either before or after obtaining a declaration as to the liability of the insurers. It enabled Syndicate 420, Early American and World, as parties injured by the allegedly wrongful conduct of KBS, to claim directly against the two syndicates of the Errors and Omission underwriters.

The main problem facing the US courts now was whether they should deal with these direct action claims or refer the claimants to London where the E and O underwriters initiated declaratory proceedings against KBS in the Commercial Court.

The claimants wanted to have the benefits of the Louisiana statute, enabling them to go straight to where the money was ultimately to come from. The E and O underwriters, on the other hand, were trying to get these Louisiana actions dismissed. Fifteen of the underwriters contended that they lacked minimum contacts with Louisiana which would justify the American courts in exercising what is called *in personam* jurisdiction. All the E and O underwriters argued that the American courts were not a suitable place for resolving a dispute originating at Lloyd's, subject to English law and, moreover, already submitted to English courts.

Like Hercules, who cut off the hydra's heads with a sword and cauterised the wounds with a torch to prevent two heads sprouting in place of each cut off, the American courts used a two-pronged approach, dismissing the direct-action claims on condition that UK courts would deal with all associated disputes.

Turning a blind eye to the 15 underwriters objecting to *in personam* jurisdiction, they dealt immediately with the second and more important objection that London was a more convenient forum for dealing with these disputes. They concluded that a dismissal would satisfy both the private interests of the litigants and the public interests of Louisiana.

The critical issue in the direct actions against E and O underwriters stemmed from the policies solicited, negotiated, issued and delivered in Britain. The coverage was extended by British underwriters to British insurance brokers at the underwriting floor of Lloyd's of London. Most of the documents were in London, as were the witnesses who might be required to enlighten the court on the unique practices at Lloyd's. The disputes would have to be decided on the basis of English law and business practice. The cost of doing so in Louisiana might well be prohibitive.

It was also in the public interest to avoid unnecessary problems and conflicts of law or the application of foreign law, said the court. These were not local controversies which Louisiana would have preferred to have decided at home. On the contrary, the disputes would cause tremendous administrative difficulties to US courts. Both private and public interests, therefore, spoke for confirming the decision of the district court which held that London would provide a more convenient forum.

However, to preserve the rights of other parties, the American courts made the dismissal of the direct action conditional on an undertaking of E and O underwriters that they would not contest intervention by World, Early American or Channel in the London litigation; that they would waive any jurisdictional defences or defences based on the statute of limitation and that they would accept as binding any Louisiana decision regarding liability of KBS.

Finally, the dismissal of the Louisiana suits was made conditional not only on the consent of the E and O underwriters to litigation in London but also on the willingness of English courts to deal with such litigation. These conditions, in the view of Judge Brown, cauterised the wounds left after the heads of the litigation were cut off and prevented new heads from rising in their place.

What Lloyd's should now do is to prevent the proliferation of more hydras.

Punishing the insured for the sins of the insurer

It has become fashionable to remind managements that they should be aware of the legal environment in which their businesses operate.

However, the time has come to remind the courts and government departments that the law they make will be applied to business and that utter confusion and frustration will result if they ignore that environment. It was so ignored by the Commercial Court in *The Bedford Insurance Company* case[14] (that insurance contracts are null and void if made in the UK by an unauthorised insurer), which was only partly removed by a subsequent judgment in the *B. A. Stewart* case.[15]

In the first judgment, Mr Justice Parker (as he then was) held that as the 1974 Insurance Companies Act prohibits in Great Britain the effecting and carrying out of contracts of certain classes of insurance without prior authorisation by the Department of Trade and Industry, any contracts concluded by an unauthorised insurer were not valid and the insured could not claim under them.

The ruling was expressed so broadly that it applied to a great proportion of business transacted in London with foreign companies. It might have nullified not only the policies held by the insured but also contracts between insurers and their reinsurers. It threatened to penalise the consumer by declaring void his policy and to benefit the unauthorised insurer whose illegal operations would be made more profitable because claims against him would be unenforceable in English courts.

The judgment caused great consternation, not only on the London insurance market where it upset the peaceful indulgence in many weird and remarkable practices that were considered perfectly legal in the past, but also in the EEC where it was seen as threatening the freedom of insurance services from which the UK can only benefit. An opportunity to rectify this situation appeared when a similar case, *B. A. Stewart v Oriental Fire and Marine Insurance Company*, came before another Commercial Court judge, Mr Justice Leggatt.

There was, however, a difficulty: both parties urged the reversal of the *Bedford* judgment, but there was a danger that its overruling would be of little precedental value if the merits of the *Bedford* judgment were not argued before the Judge. For this reason Mr Justice Leggatt asked the Attorney-General to appoint an *amicus curiae* whose sole task was to defend Mr Parker's judgment, although one assumes that under the circumstances he did not do so with any great personal conviction.

Mr Justice Leggatt held that the words of the 1974 Act did not say that contracts by an unauthorised person were prohibited and void. He cited a great wealth of English, Australian and US dicta in support of the view that in looking for the implied meaning of the statutes one must have regard to the language used and to the scope and purpose of the statute; that, as Lord Justice Devlin said on an other occasion, the purpose of the statute was sufficiently served by the penalties prescribed for the offender and that avoidance of the contract would cause grave inconvenience and injury to innocent members of the public without furthering the object of the statute. As a matter of commercial practicality contracts of insurance such as these should not, except of necessity, be rendered unenforceable by an innocent insured,' he declared.

Nevertheless, Mr Justice Leggatt refused to make any ruling or *obiter dictum* on how contracts between insurers and reinsurers would be affected. He ended his judgment by saying 'Cetera quis nescit?' which I take to mean 'who does not know the rest?'

However, talking to insurance lawyers and practitioners in London left me in no doubt that none of them knows the rest.

There are several lessons to be learned from this upheaval. First it can lead to damaging absurdities if statutes are interpreted without regard to their purpose, and it would greatly assist the courts if the purpose of every statute was clearly stated in a preamble.

Second, one should avoid creating unjustified suspicion that there is a judicial policy aimed at keeping foreign insurers out of the London market – should there be one, the weapon allegedly employed in the *Bedford* judgment would be like trying to hit a sparrow with a cannon ball.

Third, in commercial matters, every judgment must be related to the contemporary practice and usage of merchants; and finally it would be a great help if the drafting of crucial provisions of statutes was not left to be settled by two opposed and exhausted MPs assisted by an equally tired official at 11 pm in the committee room of the House of Commons.

This much I wrote in 1984 when there was still hope that the Court of Appeal would put things right. It did not: it confirmed the Parker judgment. Promoted in the meantime, Lord Justice Parker was sitting on the bench.

Tax avoidance in fog and darkness

There is little doubt that the House of Lords decision in Furniss (H. M. Inspector of Taxes) against various members of the Dawson family will go down as a milestone in the history of English tax law, although it is not certain whether it will be remembered more for reinforcing the principle of honesty in tax matters or for creating confusion in their administration.

Those who live in ignorance of the intricacies of English tax law may be surprised that the principle of good faith, and the rule that only transactions which have a real business purpose will impress the taxman are not of general application in the UK as they are in most other advanced countries. The UK started on its separate path in 1936, by the House of Lords' decision in the *Duke of Westminster*, with the ruling that everyone is entitled to order his affairs so as to pay the least tax under the appropriate legislation. At about the same time the Federal Supreme Court of the US confirmed the same principe in *Helvering v Gregory*, but with the condition that such arrangement of affairs must have a real business purpose and must not be 'a mere device'.

UNCERTAINTY

The omission of this condition, defining the manner in which the taxpayer may legitimately arrange his affairs, led to the growth of a tax avoidance industry. By 1979 it became uncomfortably big. Starting with the *Rossminster* case, the House of Lords began a process of cutting it down to size. The decision in Dawson can be seen as a culmination of this process; it has now reinstated in English tax law the condition of real business purpose, omitted from the *Duke of Westminster* ruling. Lord Roskill expressed the hope that the *Dawson* decision would be sufficient to exorcise the ghost of the *Duke of Westminster*. In so far as this means more honesty and realism in tax affairs, the decision must be welcome: the tax burden which those using artificial schemes can avoid must necessarily be borne by the rest of us.

There is, however, another side to the coin. The tax bar is up in arms because of the uncertainty which this decision has increased by its vagueness. Purposive interpretation of law, stressing the intention of Parliament rather than the letter of the statute, is still a foreigner in English courts, and the Law Lords provided no guidance on the determination of the frontier between a fictitious device and real business. Lord Scarman said that the limits within which the new principle was to operate remained to be probed and to be determined by the courts. This will be of little help to managements who cannot wait for years to learn about the effects of their decisions. By contrast, Lord Brightman said that it was for the Commissioners to determine whether a composite transaction contained steps inserted without any business purpose.

So it is not clear who will determine the impact of the judgment: will it hit international loans arranged through the intermediary of a country with which there is a double taxation treaty to avoid withholding tax on interest? Will it prevent, as some fear, offsetting capital gains and losses within a group of companies, a procedure which has so far not been objected to by the Inland Revenue? The sale and repurchase of shares on the 'bed and breakfast' basis has become vulnerable, but how does one prove that a repurchase of shares has been dictated by business reasons?

This vagueness, combined with the delay and cost connected with going to court, is bound to increase enormously the discretion of the Inland Revenue. Practice notes and prior clearances will replace Acts of Parliament. None of the Law Lords is a tax specialist. The only hope is that both Mrs Thatcher, the Prime Minister, and Mr Peter Rees, the Chief Secretary to the Treasury, as former tax lawyers, will have some understanding for the need to establish some certainty, possibly by short legislation requiring Inland Revenue guidelines to be laid before Parliament.

Tax lawyers ask for Glasnost

Four years after the Law Lords put a seal of disapproval on artificial tax avoidance schemes in their 1984 decision in *Furniss v Dawson*[18] and the tax lawyers are still refusing to concede defeat. Erratic decisions in the chancery, where some judges disapproved of the new approach, encourage them. The cry has been 'Only Parliament can impose taxes and if the words of the legislation can be read so as to bring an unintended benefit to the taxpayer, so be it.'

True, the tortuous drafting also produced unintended disadvantages for taxpayers – but these could and often were removed by amending legislation or by special concessions granted by the Inland Revenue.

Sensing a certain softness and confusion in the 1988 composition of the Judicial Committee of the House of Lords the tax lawyers renewed their attack under the flag of the Special Committee of Tax Law Consultative Bodies. The first two parts of their report[17] on Tax Law after *Furniss v Dawson*[18] is a lament on the blow inflicted to the tax avoidance industry, which will hardly bring me to tears. The three remaining parts, however, contain a number of valuable suggestions for the improvement of tax legislation and its interpretation which deserve every support.

The two issues are inextricably connected. The tax avoidance industry could never have reached the proportions it reached in the 1970s – no doubt in response to the confiscatory rates of income tax on higher incomes – but for the peculiar way in which English statutes were drafted and interpreted.

The report analyses the effects, real or possible, of the new approach, finding the Law Lords' speeches lacking in precision and consistency. It concludes that these judgments achieved some flexibility at the cost of certainty and that it is inappropriate for courts to take such a far-reaching reform upon themselves. The determination of taxation policy should be left to Parliament.

The report blames the courts for having gone well beyond their traditional role in formulating public policy. It has a point when it says:

> Under the uncertain regime of the new approach, the results of taxpayer transactions may be judged not in accordance with the law as they understood it to be at the time the transactions were undertaken, but in accordance with principles of interpretation developed subsequently.

The committee which produced the report would obviously like to see the new approach outlawed, though it does not go so far as to ask for it. But they do say that it should be allowed to fall into desuetude. (So much for their craving for legal certainty!) Failing that, the courts should restrict the retroactive effect of their judgments, as US courts and the European Court do sometimes, or, at the very least, the Inland Revenue should exercise a self-restraint in applying anti-avoidance judgments to transactions which were completed earlier. Another solution would be to replace the judicial 'new approach' by statutory anti-avoidance measures which, the committee hopes, could be better defined (and which, one fears, could be also better avoided).

So much for the first two parts of the report with which I am out of sympathy. However, in its three remaining parts, the report contains recommendations which ought not to be ignored.

The committee recommends the establishment of an expert advisory committee which would sift representations, comments and evidence and report its findings directly to Parliament. Parliament should scrutinise draft legislation in a special standing committee. To make consultations really effective, budget secrecy would have to be reduced to the bare minimum.

The report further recommends that to clarify the intention of Parliament and to facilitate the interpretation, notes explaining their purpose should be placed against the individual sections and subsections of financial legislation. This would certainly be a substantial improvement. Better still, of course, would be to draft the legislations in such a way that it is self-explanatory – but that seems an Utopian proposition as long as the monopoly of the Parliamentary Counsel is not dislodged.

The explanatory process, according to the report, should be continued by allowing courts to refer to reports of parliamentary debates and, further, by publication of the internal guidance notes of the Inland Revenue. Advance rulings and decisions in individual cases should also be published. The committee saw the danger that Inland Revenue could in this way become the judge in its own case, but this is already so, as only very few people can afford the costs of litigation, said to amount to at least £100,000 in a simple dispute. Publication of rulings which could be criticised in Parliament would probably have a restraining effect on the tax authorities.

To sum up what is needed, and not only for taxation:

- Statutes properly prepared and clearly stating their purpose; this would also bring UK legislation in methodical conformity with Community legislation.
- A general rule that laws must not be abused by pitting their technical provision against their general purpose.
- A Freedom of Information Act.

Mafia, US taxmen and the courts

Transnational criminal organisations – whether engaged in the conventional rackets of protection, extortion and prostitution, or in the more advanced forms of securities fraud and drug trades, or in providing mercenaries and terrorists for political causes – use multinational banks for laundering dirty money and for keeping it tucked away in tax havens.

Because all these organisations operate on the Mafia principle, it is extremely difficult to obtain evidence about them except by establishing who are the real beneficiaries of the proceeds of crime.

In this respect, the US authorities appear even more hamstrung than others by their criminal investigation procedures and rules of evidence. It seems that they are resigned to the use of a tax fraud investigation whenever they scent organised crime.

The US investigators, therefore, deserve great sympathy. However, in the pursuit of their prey, they often adopt a parochial and insensitive approach to other countries' laws, particularly those concerning bank secrecy. The idea that US citizens carry their law in their saddle-bags and that US law rules over bank accounts funded with US dollars, wherever located, seems natural in a union of states reaching from one ocean to another where state frontiers, never very visible, have been gradually deprived of most of their legal importance by federalist bias of the Supreme Court. This, together with the superpower complex, may explain why American lawyers, as the ancient Roman lawyers did before them, tend to view their law as universally applicable wherever US interests are concerned. Such attitudes are often viewed by other countries as insolent even if adopted for a good cause, and generate the now familiar extraterriality conflicts of which that with Hong Kong is the most recent illustration.

The flow of cash between Hong Kong and US banks has multiplied tenfold in recent years and US investigators suspect that this reflects the movements of illicit funds into Hong Kong banks. They would like to crack the secrets of these bank accounts and they believe that a recent decision by Judge Arthur L. Nims in the US tax court may help them to do it. Some US enthusiasts even believe that his decision in the *Hong Kong and Shanghai Banking Corporation* tax case will not only open the door to foreign bank secrets but also provide access to records of multinational corporations in general.

Without access to accounts and documents located outside the US, the investigators must make do with financial statements and tax data provided by the company or its auditors. The *Hong Kong and Shanghai Banking Corporation* decision would give them authority to examine records in the head-quarters of a foreign bank which has a US branch office. This, however, is not the view of the Hong Kong court. Its Court of Appeal made it clear in a recent decision that it would not allow bank secrets to be transferred from its jurisdiction at the request of US courts.

In *FDC Co Ltd v Chase Manhattan Bank*[19] information wanted by the American authorities was located in the Hong Kong branch of Chase Manhattan and the American revenue authorities used the familiar shortcut: instead of sending a letter rogatory to the Hong Kong courts asking them for assistance in obtaining evidence (which would probably be denied anyhow), they asked the New York head office of the bank to obtain information from its Hong Kong branch.

A plaintiff, suspected of tax avoidance, turned to the Hong Kong courts for protection, asking for an order prohibiting the Hong Kong branch of Chase Manhattan from transferring the information to its US headquarters. He obtained an injunction from the trial judge and this was confirmed in the Court of Appeal. The bank, said the court, was not entitled to disclose information about the taxpayer's account with the Hong Kong office.

The Hong Kong Court of Appeal held:[20]

All persons opening accounts with banks in Hong Kong, whether foreign or local banks, are entitled to look to the Hong Kong courts to enforce any obligation of secrecy which, by the law of Hong Kong, is implied by virtue of the relationship of banker and customer.

The court recognised that Chase Manhattan might be exposed to contempt proceedings in New York for refusing to transfer the information from its Hong Kong branch. It took the view that it could not assess whether this was likely to happen or not, and that, anyhow, this hazard was irrelevant.

In a similar case[21] an English judge prohibited the transfer of information to the US, but his reasoning left open the possibility that the transfer would be allowed if great harm would otherwise be caused to the bank. A group of oil companies maintained accounts with the London branch of an American bank. Only one of these had any dealings in the US, but the American Department of Justice asked for information concerning all members of the group. A *subpoena* was served on the bank's head office ordering the production of London records. At the request of the oil companies, the transfer of information was prohibited in London by the High Court.

Mr Justice Leggatt said that giving effect in the UK to the order of a US District Court was a matter of public interest. The order required a breach of secrecy but he did not reject it absolutely because of its extraterritorial nature. Instead, he reasoned that the US District Court was unlikely to go ahead with contempt proceedings if the bank was prohibited from disclosing the information by an English court within whose jurisdiction the records were kept.

The judge decided the isue on the balance of convenience: to grant the injunction prohibiting the transfer would not cause any real damage to the US bank, but to refuse it could cause very great harm to the group of oil companies. Therefore, it was not proper to allow the bank to breach the duty of confidentiality.

It seems that the judge could have found a firmer ground for disallowing the transfer in the House of Lords decision in the Westinghouse uranium litigation. His soft approach is in line with that adopted by the House of Lords more recently in the *Laker* case.

In the opinion of Professor E. P. Ellinger[22] such conflicts between courts can be avoided only by an international convention. Positive rules of co-operation are desirable not only to prevent the extraterritorial excursions of US investigators, but also to facilitate the detection and elimination of organised crime.

The possible heads of such a convention are outlined in the bilateral convention concluded between the US and Switzerland in 1973[23] – the first treaty of this kind, concluded by the US after arduous negotiations which lasted four years and seen in Washington as a possible model for similar pacts with other countries. In that treaty, the Swiss made an important concession by promising assistance in the investigation of tax fraud or other offences unknown to the Swiss criminal code if these could be shown to be part of organised crime.

However, some time after the treaty was signed, the *Marc Rich* case revealed that by itself it would not eliminate conflicts. That case arose because US taxmen suspected that the US subsidiary of Rich had avoided declaring profits of $20m by means of inflated transfer prices charged by its Swiss parent. The US investigators probably doubted that their case was strong enough to obtain Swiss legal assistance and, ignoring the treaty, tried to achieve their objective by means of direct orders from US courts. The Swiss would have nothing of the sort and the ensuing jurisdictional conflict resulted in a major diplomatic row.

The lesson from this is obvious: an international convention is necessary but not in itself enough. US lawyers must also be prepared to abide by it.

Notes

1 Insolvency Law and Practice, Cmnd 8558, SO £13.35.
2 BGH II ZR 109/84. Judgment of 11 November 1985.
3 BGH dealt with this issue of the misleading prospectus on 12 July 1982 (11 ZR 172, 175/81).
4 FT Law Report, 12 January 1988.
5 Discussed in A. H. Hermann's *Judges, Law and Businessmen* (Kluwer) pp 176–178.
6 See Court de Cassation in Immobiliere Lambert (D 1968 J 337 PL).
7 733 F 2d 23 (2d Cir 1984).
8 757 F 2d 516 (2d Cir 1985).
9 *Tabacalero Severiano Jorge v Standard Cigar Co* 392 F 2d 706 (5th Cir 1968).
10 See International Financial Law Review, August 1985, pp 26–31.
11 Regulatory Arrangements at Lloyd's. Report of the Committee of Inquiry, Cm 59, 117 pp, SO £8.10.
12 Case 45/85, judgment 27 January 1987 (FT Business Law Brief, February 1987).
13 US Court of Appeals for the Fifth Circuit, No. 85-3353, corrected opinion by Judge John R. Brown in *Syndicate 420 v Early American Insurance Co . . .* Transcript received by courtesy of Fishbourn Boxer & Co, solicitors, London.
14 *The Bedford Insurance Co Ltd v Instituto de Ressaguros do Brasil and Others*, FT Comm LR, 16 November 1983.
15 *B. A. Stewart v Oriental Fire and Marine Insurance Co*, FT Comm LR, 2 May 1984.
16 'Unauthorised Insurers and Reinsurers', briefing seminar, organised by Insurance and Reinsurance Law International.
17 Published by the Law Society, £6.50.
18 *Furniss v Dawson* [1984] STC 174.
19 Judgment of 17 October 1984, Nos. 65 and 131 (civil).
20 As reported by Professor E. P. Ellinger (1985) Journal of Business Law 445.
21 *XAG v A Bank* [1983] 2 All ER 464.
22 (1985) Journal of Business Law 446.
23 Treaty between the US and Swiss Federation on Mutual Assistance in Criminal Matters signed on 25 May 1973.

4 The obscure law of intellectual property

How to make the patent system serve innovation

Mrs Margaret Thatcher, the Prime Minister, never misses an opportunity to stress the importance of intellectual property for the prosperity of Britain. She is right. Unfortunately, it remains at exhortations. Little is done to make the system responsive to new needs and what is done is confused, confusing and heavily biased towards the interests of the patent bar.

The defenders of the intellectual property system focus in the first line on its external enemies: the protection of intellectual property is eroded by the EEC, which gives higher priority to competition rules and free movement of goods; and by the developing countries' policy of 'technological decolonisation under duress' – that is, by sequestration of patents and trademarks.

Innovation is threatened also by product liability programmes and, increasingly, by the free exploitation by imitators of technical and health safety tests carried out by the innovator. This diminishes the rewards for pioneering work in a wide range of products, from building materials to medicines.

However, the greatest threat to innovation is not from outside of the system designed to protect it, but from its inner, unresolved contradictions.

Once upon a time patents were mainly required to protect and stimulate clear-cut and generally understandable innovations, mainly in the field of mechanical engineering; they prove ill-designed to protect innovation in the communication industry and chemical or genetic engineering where no judge can be sure whether the extra circuit or molecule are an innovation or merely a disguise employed by an imitator. Trade marks introduced to tell the consumer who made the product, are now means of consumer indoctrination; copyright once designed to protect authors of original artistic and literary work is now used to give monopoly of production and exploitation to the makers of spare parts and to computer programmes designed by a multitude of anonymous authors and which are neither original, artistic or literary.

The originally intended balance between the disclosure of the innovation required to stimulate further technological advance and the temporary monopoly granted to the inventor making it can no longer be upheld. If the disclosure is complete, the patent can be made worthless by small additions. If it is incomplete, the monopoly is not justified. The cost in time and money of obtaining a patent and of defending it puts off any inventor with limited financial means – and this includes also quite substantial enterprise.

PATENTS FOR LITIGATION
The concept of the petty patent and postponement of examination until such time as the invention has proved to be commercially viable, or until there is need to defend it, have been put into practice in many countries. Some experts go as far as to maintain that the best protection is publication of the invention in a little known language, in a periodical of small

circulation, which would suffice to disprove the novelty of any future patent applications by competitors.

The next logical step would be to replace the patent system by a form of copyright protection, but this excellent idea is quite unacceptable to the powerful interests vested in the present patent system and, therefore, hardly worth considering.

The proportion of patent applications lodged by small or medium-sized firms has steadily diminished over the past decade in most countries. But the UK's experience has shown that, although more research establishments are associated with big companies, small firms more often produce radically new ideas.

All this was well known, considered and rejected. The 1977 Patent Act, by putting forward the publication of the patent application, and by introducing stricter standards of examination, shifted the balance of the British patent system to the advantage of big companies. These are more interested in information that can be gleaned from the patent libraries than in a quick grant of the patent, indispensable to an individual inventor or small firm in need of finance and backing for the commercialisation of their invention.

If the examination procedure adopted for the granting of a patent makes it more difficult for a small enterprise to succeed, the court procedure makes it quite impossible for an individual inventor or small firm to defend a patent.

PROHIBITIVE COST OF LITIGATION

The enormous costs of patent litigation between giant companies such as Polaroid and Kodak are well-known. Such litigations often stretch over a decade and the costs run into many million of pounds. Even a relatively simple patent dispute can easily cost each side well over £100,000 and despite the award of costs, the winner may still be out of pocket by more than £50,000. In addition, managerial time and energy are wasted not only on the business side but also on the technical side.

These factors make patent litigation quite impractical for small companies which have to concentrate their human resources on the development and marketing of new products. If a financially strong competitor covets their patents, or wishes to stop their exploitation, they must consider themselves lucky to be asked for a licence and given some hope of future royalties. Not for them dreams of business expansion.

The preparation of an infringement action takes from 18 months to five years and can involve extensive discovery of documents as well as practical experiments. Eight to 10 lawyers will sometimes attend these tests, which may last for weeks, rather than days, though only a few lawyers really know what to look for.

When all the experiments are completed and thousands of pages of paper assembled, the case is ready for trial. However, due to the peculiar notion that surprising the other party is an essential feature of the adversary procedure, the parties may still be in the dark about the case of their opponent. This will be revealed only during a trial which, typically, lasts between five and 30 days.

The judge or judges like to find the perfect solution according to the law, if not justice, but the piles of documents and reports of tests obscure the issue. In most cases, therefore, the decision is based on facts little different from those known at the beginning of the action. And the legal view taken of these facts seems to be highly subjective as a large proportion of decisions are reversed on appeal.

WHAT IS TO BE DONE?

First, taking into account that commercial viability will determine the money which should be spent on obtaining a patent, it should be left to the applicants whether they wish to have their application examined right away or only later on.

Second, as the patent is worth having only if it can be defended, the defence costs should be drastically reduced, taking a lesson from the way the Patent Office handles patent disputes. Proceedings concerning validity or applications for declaration that a certain action does not infringe a patent can be argued in the Patent Office at one-tenth of the cost involved in High Court proceedings. Evidence is mainly written, there is little or no discovery and the hearing usually lasts for not more than two days.

All parties should have the right to insist that any Patent actions should be heard and decided by the Patent Office and this right should not be restricted by the need to obtain agreement of the other party to the dispute. Appeals should go to an appeals board within the Patent Office – an arrangement adopted by the European Patent Office – and be subject to leave. The Patent Office or its Appeal Board should be able to refer important and novel issues of law to the High Court or directly to the Court of Appeal.

The Copyright and Patent Act 1988 leaving the possibility of appeal to court unrestricted, can achieve some improvement only when the dispute is between parties of equal financial muscle. The small firm or individual inventor will remain at the mercy of the giant competitor.

Genetic engineering: no protection for cost-reducing innovation

---

The failure of UK patent law to take into account reduction of production costs achieved by an innovation was again demonstrated when Mr Justice Witford, on a petition by the Wellcome Foundation, revoked patent number 2119804 for Human Tissue Plasminogen Activator (t-PA) granted to Genentech Inc on 26 February 1986.

With his usual elegant lucidity, the judge analysed and explained a subject of enormous complexity, far beyond the imagination of most of us: how elemental chemical codes and messengers, determining the recreation and perpetuation of living matter, visible (often with utmost difficulty) only by means of electron microscopy, can be separated and recombined to achieve a useful purpose: in the present case, an economically viable production of t-PA in exactly the form it exists in human tissue.

This achievement by Genentech, an independent Californian research company specialising in genetic engineering, makes it possible to produce t-PA in sufficient quantities to treat diseases caused by partial or complete occlusion of arteries or veins. These include heart attacks, strokes, pulmonary embolism, deep vein thrombosis, peripheral arterial occlusion and venous thrombosis – all major health hazards.

Other products used for the same purpose have undesirable side-effects and disadvantages. A patent monopoly for the production of pure t-PA by recombination of elements of living matter could bring its owner enormous financial benefits. Genentech is now moving from research into production and t-PA should be its main line. Its European licensee is Boehringer Ingelheim Limited which also took part in the patent litigation.

To define the framework of reference for this litigation one can do no better than to use the judge's own words:

> A long time elapsed between the publication in the last century of the Mendelian theory of the control of heritable characteristics by genes, and the discovery and acceptance of the fact that dioxyribonucleic acid, DNA, is the essential genetic material . . . It was only in the later 1960s and early 1970s that significant developments in the field of genetic engineering took place. Recombinant DNA was an infant – albeit a lusty and rapidly growing infant – in the 1970s. I have had the great advantage of hearing evidence from a number of witnesses of international repute, including Dr Berg, who in 1980 received a Nobel award for work including the first report on the synthesis of a recombinant DNA.

Dr Berg started to work on protein synthesis in 1957. Soon he moved into the area of transcription and translation of genetic messengers into sequences of proteins. He has shown that it was feasible to join DNA molecules in the living body and to isolate the resulting structure. By 1979 cloning was practised by scientists and, according to the evidence of Professor Brammar, the expert called by Wellcome, at the date of the patent all of the techniques described therein were known.

The invention claimed by Genentech arises from the alleged discovery of a particular DNA sequence and the amino-acid sequence of human plasminogen activator deduced from it. However, a discovery by itself cannot be patented unless the inventor tells people how it can be usefully employed. The Judge found that this was not described in sufficient detail.

Also, Genentech were not the only people who looked for a way of obtaining t-PA by recombination of DNA molecules. The Cold Spring Harbor laboratory in the US is presently working on the same problem in association with the Wellcome Foundation. However, the whole of the evidence highlighted the difficulties which faced the researchers working in this particular field. Genentech researchers seemed to have cracked the problem by July 1980. The announcement of the discovery of the full sequence by Dr Pennica, one of their researchers, at a conference in Lausanne in July 1983 received a standing ovation.

The Judge accepted that the information was novel and had practical application, but he took the view that it did not justify the broad claims of the patent. When a patent is taken out, he said, for a new result not known before, the patentee is entitled to protection against all other processes for the same result. However, if the patent is taken out for a process for arriving at a result known earlier, any other person may take out a patent for another process or use another process without a patent to arrive at the same result. Genentech, in the view of the Judge, was asking for too much. It wanted not only protection for the process, but also for the result which was known before they started their research.

> As a claim to a product, t-PA produced by any known or hereafter discovered route in the field of recombinant DNA technology is too wide and is bad . . . It is a claim to an obviously desirable and potentially possible end, reached by routes on which only limited guidance is given.

The Judge did not seem too happy with the conclusion which he thought unavoidable:

> What Genentech did was achieved by what, in my judgment, was rather more than the exercise of proficiency; it involved laborious and costly effort and to deny any monopoly protection to those who are prepared to put as much time, skill and money into research as Genentech did, is only too likely to discourage workers in this field from making advances which may be of the greatest public benefit.

But was it really unavoidable? Lord Diplock said in *American Cyanamid Company (Dann's) Patent (1971 Patent Cases 425)* about a new antibiotic:

> The task of finding such a strain of micro-organism calls for the exercise of technical proficiency and is laborious and very costly, for the odds against success are large. It is not easy to see what inventive step, as distinct from the mere exercise of proficiency and practice, is involved in this kind of research, but the result of success in it is a new product useful to humanity which does not exist in nature.

However, even the same kind of antibiotic or biological agent can be a different product commercially if it becomes available in massive quantities instead of the minute quantities used for laboratory purposes or for exceptional clinical use at exorbitant cost. The question of production costs was taken into account in a Chancery judgment some 100 years ago, when a new method was discovered for the production of aspirin at a fraction of the previous cost.[1]

Confirming the decision of Mr Justice Witford on 31 October 1988, the Court of Appeal disappointed those who hoped that it might take the production and commercial aspects into consideration and moving from simple logic to dialectic reasoning, will conclude that quantity transforms into quality. It seems now that it would require legislation bringing the Patent Act into the age of genetic engineering.

Why the European patent is useful and the Community patent will be too costly to defend

Can there be a real common market as long as patents, trademarks and copyright are based on national laws and lead to individual monopoly rights separate for each national territory?

The European Commission has battled for years for the unificiation of these intellectual property rights, arguing that their use compartmentalises the common market and contributes to higher price levels in some member states. The Commission also argues that it is not enough just to remove this negative effect but that it is necessary to establish truly common patents and trade-marks extending over the entire territory of the Community. The Commission succeeded in substantially eliminating the restrictive effect of patents and trademarks by 1982. Some progress has been made towards a Community patent and a Community trademark.

The Commission's efforts to remove intellectual property barriers to trade has been highlighted by a series of defeats suffered in the European Court by most of the big names in the pharmaceutical industry. Winthrop, Sterling Drug, Hoffman La Roche, American Home Products, Pfizer and Hoechst, one after the other, were told with increasing emphasis that once they put their product on the market in one member state they must not stop 'parallel' importers; that is importers not authorised by them, buying such products wherever they were cheaper and importing them irrespective of whether separate patent or trademark rights were held by the manufacturer or his distributor in the country of importation.

The European Court developed a doctrine according to which intellectual property rights may not be used in a way infringing the principle of free movement of goods or the competition rules of the Community. Under certain conditions the parallel importers may not only import from a cheaper market but also re-package the branded product and, in the case of multi-brand products change the brand to that used by the manufacturer in the country of importation.

But on the other front, aiming at the unification of intellectual property rights throughout the common market, progress has been slower.

The first achievement was the 1973 European Patent Convention and the establishment of the European Patent Office in Munich. The 'European patent' administered by the Office is a misnomer. All the Munich office can do is process a single application which results in a batch of national patents, each subject to the appropriate national law.

However, even this modest achievement provides a useful service to industry.

In the first place it enables inventors to obtain several patents without the need of multilingual translations. The Munich procedure, thought to be expensive at the start, offers now better value because the European Patent Office fees have risen only by 20–25 per cent – substantially slower than the fees of national patent offices. As a result, the number of applications examined by the UK Patent Office diminished from 35,000–40,000 a year to some 18,000–20,000, while the number of applications processed in Munich has reached 35,000 a year.

The real ambition of the Commission, however, is a Community patent which would have validity throughout the EC. For this purpose it proposed that a single Community patent be made available on the basis of a Convention, the text of which was adopted at a diplomatic conference almost ten years ago. The diplomats reached agreement relatively quickly, but when it came to ratification, the Convention had such a rough sailing that it seemed it would never come to port.

One of the greatest difficulties was the provision which would leave it to national courts to deal with infringement actions while the European Patent Office would decide whenever validity of the patent was contested. All familiar with patent litigation know that these two issues are always linked: when the patent-holder brings an infringement action the defendant attacks the validity of the patent. The UK, together with some other countries, opposed the artificial division of these two issues. Some had a protocol on litigation appended to the Convention to enable national courts to decide both on infringement and on validity.

In order to assure uniformity of judge-made law throughout the Community a special Community Patent Court will be established to which it would be possible to appeal from national courts on issues of validity, though on the assessment of damages and royalties the national courts would have the last word.

The second, unsolved problem is the complication and high cost of the proposed Community patent litigation system. In most litigations, the Common Patent Court would have exclusive jurisdiction on all matters brought before the national appeal court in so far as these did not involve questions of national law. The appeal would, therefore, generally, be subject only to formal proceedings in the national appeal court which would refer it to the Common Patent Court.

Surprisingly, the Common Patent Court would deal not only with issues of law arising from the Community Patent Convention but would also undertake a complete retrial of the dispute, even dealing with questions of fact. In some cases there could be a further reference to the European Court of Justice in Luxembourg. The mind boggles when one tries to imagine the time and costs involved!

EEC patent licensing exemption – a bad solution of an unnecessary problem

---

Of all the countries forming the European Community, the UK probably has most to lose by a legal regime hostile to the commercialisation of innovation and industrial developments by means of patent licensing. The export of British know-how makes an important contribution to the country's invisible earnings.

It was therefore particularly irksome when British industry discovered, soon after UK's accession, that exclusive patent licenses are viewed by the Commission as prohibited restrictive agreements.

Such view is not justified by the competition rules of the Community. The monopoly created by every patent is exempt from the impact of these rules, and whether the patent owner exercises his patent rights directly or through others makes no difference. Of course, patent licensing agreements provide an opportunity for negotiating restrictions which go beyond the monopoly created by the patent and if these are important enough and affect trade between member states, the Commission may prosecute them. However, aiming at all exclusive licences, it cast its net so widely that it was never able to haul the fish out of the water.

Ever since the UK joined the Community, patent licensing applications have formed the bulk of the competition department's unfinished and unmanageable business. At the end of 1983, out of a stockpile of 3,654 notifications 62 per cent concerned patent licensing agreements.

The Commission makes between 10 and 15 decisions each year. At this pace there was little hope that companies would obtain any decision about the validity of their licensing agreements within the life of the patent.

A regulation which would exempt all licensing agreements satisfying certain specified conditions was the obvious solution from the beginning. The Commission drafted one in 1976, but it did not meet the needs of industry and was widely regarded as inadequate. The British Government declared that the regulation would make things even worse, and blocked the project.

After 10 years of unrelenting struggle, worthy of a better project, the Commission succeeded in obtaining member governments' approval of an improved draft.

The regulation published on 16 August 1984, in the Official Journal, has been in force since 1 January 1985.

The block exemption applies to licences to manufacture and sell (not to sell only) agreed between two parties concerning national, Community or European patents and, further, to utility models and inventions for which an application will be made within one year. Know-how relevant to the working of the patent may be included. Joint venture licences, however, are expressly excluded.

There is a 'white list' of clauses that are permissible and a 'black list' of clauses that are prohibited.

YOU MAY
- exclude the licensee and licensor from each others' territory for the life of the patent;
- prohibit the licensees from manufacturing or actively seeking sales in the protected territory of others for the life of the local patent;
- prohibit licensees from accepting unsolicited orders from other protected territories for five years after the marketing of the product anywhere in the EEC;
- impose your trademark as long as the licensee can put his name on the product;

– if necessary for a technically satisfactory exploitation of the invention, you may impose quality control and a sourcing obligation; include a non-exclusive reciprocal improvements clause.

YOU MUST NOT
– prohibit the licensee from challenging the validity of the patent, though you may provide for termination of the licence if he does;
– impose any other restrictions on competition with the licensor or other licensees than those specifically allowed;
– restrict the licensees' freedom of action in respect of customers prices or products;
– ask for royalties on unpatented products;
– prohibit sales to exporters or to oblige the licensee to sue parallel importers;
– extend the licence beyond the life of patents existing when the licence was granted, unless there is a mutual right to terminate annually;
– oblige the licensee to assign to the licensor patents for improvements or for new applications of the licensed patents.

It is a great pity that the Commission is unable to see the advantage of legal certainty and always prefers a solution which enables it to have the last word. Article 9 of the Regulation provides that the Commission may withdraw the benefit of the block exemption where it finds that an agreement, though falling within the Regulation, has certain effects incompatible with Article 85/3; for example, when the product is not exposed to effective competition or the parties try to prevent parallel imports. As these and other conditions can be construed broadly the parties will, in fact, always be at the mercy of the Commission.

Some licensing experts think that in these circumstances the best policy is to grant a non-exclusive licence and never go near Brussels. In the case of a joint venture it may be possible to use management control instead of a restrictive agreement.

If legal security is very important, it may be necessary to notify, even if the agreement can be cleared only under the 'opposition procedure'. If it cannot, or if this is doubtful, it may be better to consider a different arrangement. For example, there is the possibility of assigning the patent and taking a reverse non-exclusive licence.

Though experts are pessimistic, there is some consolation in the attitude of the European Court which in recent years has twice refused to go the whole way with the Commission's exorbitant doctrine.

Know-how licensing regulation tastes bitter under the icing

At long last, in 1987, the European Commission has taken out of its oven the draft block exemption for know-how licensing agreements. The Commission maintains it is still edible, though only the future will tell.

It will certainly not give 'absolute legal protection to know-how licences' as an official of the Commission said, but it will exempt from the prohibition of restrictive agreements certain know-how licences under specified conditions and for a limited period of time.

The draft regulation defines know-how as a body of non-patented technical information ranging from descriptions of manufacturing processes, through recipes to designs and drawings. Licensing of such know-how will be exempt only if it is secret and substantial. The licence can be either exclusive or non-exclusive.

'Secret' does not mean that each individual component of the know-how must be unknown outside the licensor business; rather it applies to the entire package of information. 'Substantial' means that know-how must be of decisive importance at least for a major part of the manufacturing process, for the product or its development.

To be able to verify that the licensing agreement meets these conditions, the Commission will require that know-how is identified in the agreement in as much detail as possible and that the parties keep detailed records of any subsequent improvements. As agreements concluded before this exemption comes into force will benefit from it only if notified to the Commission, the block exemption opens access to valuable and secret business information—all notifications are passed on to member governments.

Officials will be bound by secrecy but knowing the leaky state of 'apparatus' some firms may conclude that under the icing the cake has a bitter taste.

An important omission, by no means unintentional, concerns franchising agreements which always include the communication of some know-how. The Commission dealt with these separately. The exemption applies only to production technology. Agreements concluded for the purpose of sale of products are excluded, except for supply during a preliminary period, before the licensee starts production of his own.

The *Maize Seed* decision of the European Court obliged the Commission to recognise that territorial exclusivity granted by the licensor may be justified if it is necessary for the introduction of a new technology which required lengthy and costly research. Article 1 of the regulation will therefore approve of an undertaking given by the licensor that he will not himself exploit or allow others to exploit the know-how in the licensee's territory which may embrace part of the Common Market or all of it. The agreement may also provide that the licensee will not use the know-how in territory reserved for the licensor or for other licensees:

The exemption from the impact of Article 85 of the treaty will be granted for a maximum period of seven years from the date of the first licensing agreement concluded in respect of the same technology in the Community.

Further periods of territorial protection may be allowed only where new substantial and secret improvements will be added and only by conclusion of new agreements in which the improvements are described in detail. The agreements can also oblige the licensee to use the licensor's trade mark or packaging or 'get-up' determined by the licensor so as to distinguish the product from others, provided the licensee is allowed to identify himself as the manufacturer.

To enjoy the benefit of the block exemption the licensing agreement will have to satisfy the general requirements of Article 85/3: consumers should have a fair share of the benefits by improved supply; the agreement must not contain restrictions which are not indispensable; and competition at the distribution stage must be safe-guarded by the possibility of parallel imports.

The exemption will not apply to agreements which prohibit the use of the know-how after the expiry of the agreement or when the know-how became publicly known otherwise than by the action of the licensee. Excluded from the benefit of the exemption will also be know-how resulting from practical experience gained in working an expired patent previously licensed to the licensee.

The licensee must not be obliged to assign to the licensor rights to improvements or new applications of the licensed technology, or to grant him an exclusive licence for such improvements or new applications.

The exemption will also be frustrated if the licensing agreement imposes on the licensee quality specifications or other unwelcome conditions which are not necessary for a satisfactory exploitation of the technology. He must not be prohibited from contesting the secrecy of the licensed know-how or the validity of any connected patents. He must not be charged royalties on goods or services which are not at least partially produced by means of the licensed know-how.

Neither party must be restricted to a category of customers or to a certain maximum quantity of the licensed products within the technological field. And, of course, there must not be any price-fixing or non-competition clauses.

However, certain restrictions of this type can be introduced if notified to the Commission and not opposed by it within six months. Such tacit clearance could be used, for example, for an obligation to continue the payment of turnover-related royalties for more than three years after the licensed know-how has become publicly known; or for an obligation of the licensee to supply only a fixed quantity of the licensed products to a particular customer, where the know-how licence is granted to provide a territory with a second source of supply.

Some of the clauses explicitly allowed by the regulation are evident from the reversal of the prohibitions, for example, that the licensee may be required to pay royalties for three years after the know-how became public, though if he discloses the secret he may be obliged to pay royalties till the expiry of the full term of the agreement. Other approved clauses concern confidentiality, prohibition of sub-licensing by the licensee, obligation of mutual communication of experience and specifications of quality as far as technically necessary. The licensee may also be obliged to buy certain goods or services from the licensor or from a supplier designated by him, as long as such tie is necessary for a satisfactory exploitation of the technology.

The agreement may oblige the licensee to use the know-how only for a certain technical application or for one or more products and may oblige him to pay a minimum royalty or to produce a minimum quantity. It may also include a 'most favoured licensee' clause – that is that no one else may be granted a licence on better terms.

These are the main points of the 29-page draft. It is a mouthful and the regulation will take some time to digest. The first impression is that it will bring some good but not as much as it could if the Commission accepted that know-how agreements are concluded between consenting adults who can look after their interests.

The perils of the EEC trademark

Coca-Cola is a trademark which secures a world market for a fizzy brown liquid. It is probably the best known example of the advantages that can be gained from promotion concentrated on a single name, but it is not a method suitable for everybody. Distillers, for example, successfully market another brown liquid under a variety of trademarks, and their usefulness goes beyond the identification of differences in the taste for Black and White, Johnnie Walker, White Horse and 47 other brands. They also enable a better exploitation of different price levels, both within one country and in several countries.

The protection of national markets where high prices can be obtained is particularly important for the pharmaceutical industry which, because of direct or indirect price control, or absence of patent protection, is obliged to sell in some countries at low prices. Trademarks licensed to the local sole distributors of pharmaceuticals and protected under national trademark laws in a high-price country were in the past often used as a barrier against imports of identically branded goods sold by the manufacturer on another national market at a lower price.

The EEC Commission has been waging a long and successful war against such trademark-assisted compartmentalisation of the Common Market. It has received powerful support from the European Court.

But the Commission is not satisfied. It wants to consolidate and extend its achievements by harmonising European trademark law and by creating a Community trademark. The Commission has some good arguments for this, but the project has many weaknesses.

The EEC plan for trademark law harmonisation, the creation of a Community trademark, and the establishment of a Community Trademark Office, was believed to be in the final furlong in 1982.

It took another six years before the member governments finally agreed to adopt it and it may take some more years before the plan becomes a reality. The delay was due not only to the squabble about the location of the European Trademark Office but also to inherent weaknesses of the plan, all of which were evident in 1982.

The establishment of a Community trademark office in London is the most easily visualised part of the project. The London patent agents want it; the London municipality wants it; the British Government wants it. It would be the first EEC institution located in the UK.

Munich – with its European Patent Office and contingent of patent agents – had always a rational claim while other cities have a strong political argument.

The examination system proposed for the Community trademark by the Commission could probably be better handled in London than anywhere else because it is similar to the UK system. A more subtle argument for

London is the need to increase the British sense of belonging to the Community.

In short, it would be nice to have the Community Trademark Office in London provided that such an office would be a useful institution. This, however, is by no means certain.

It is difficult enough in a single country to find a suitable name which is not already in use. It would be many times more difficult to find trademarks which are acceptable, free, and commercially effective, in all the countries and language areas of the Community. Even the most enthusiastic proponents of the Community Trademark concede that the number of registrations at the Community Trademark Office would be relatively small and that they could be achieved only by a lengthy and costly process.

The price exacted for the relatively few Community trademarks is a dangerous surgical operation aiming at an automatic removal of all multiple brands of one and the same product. The European Court ruled, in the American Home Products case, that two different trademarks must not be used for the same, or similar, product with the sole purpose of separating the national markets, or at least they must not be used to stop the parallel importer. The Commission's project would go much further. It would lead to an automatic invalidation of trademarks if the protected goods were marketed in another member state under another trademark.

Such surgery would have painful side effects. First, neither of two trademarks may be suitable in any two countries, and the manufacturer might be obliged to give up both and to undertake the expensive promotion of a new trademark. Second, the trademarks which manufacturers may have to abandon under this rule, could be picked up and registered by their competitors.

There exist basically three types of trademark protection: one protects rights acquired by using a trademark or name over a period of time. This is achieved by the common law 'passing-off' action – which is aimed at people who try to 'pass-off' one produce as another – and to a lesser degree also by the 'unfair competition' legislation of the continental countries. The second registers trademarks without preceding examination – such is the French system of *marque déposée*. Other continental systems are close to the French. The third system, used in the UK and Eire, makes registration dependent on examination by the trademark office – and registration is, therefore, much harder to get.

The Community trademark would be based on the examination system, like the UK trademark. But some British companies believe that not only should the French system be adopted for the Community trademark, but that Britain should have used this opportunity to give up examinations in its national system. The critics of the present UK system argue that the examination is arbitrary, costly, time-consuming, and, in view of the protection given to unregistered trademarks under common law, provides no certainty.

If Britain gave up the examination system, it is argued this would open up the possibility of joining the Madrid agreement which all the other member countries of the EEC have been successfully using for over 100 years. Under this agreement one application lodged with the national registry may be extended to a further 23 countries.

A number of technical objections raised in 1982 pointed out that the

EEC trademark plan would put at a disadvantage owners of common law trademark rights, protected in the UK by the passing-off action; this has been removed in a more recent draft. The plan had also its usual dose of drafting ambiguities and contradictions, some of which, one would hope, have been ironed out in the meantime.

However, even without such contradictions, an EEC regulation establishing the European Trademark and a directive for harmonisation of trademark laws will give the Commission and the European Court vast opportunities to escalate its impact by case law. It is high time to study not only the immediate impact of the scheme but also its likely transformation by European case law.

Cable TV and the German Fundamental Law

Unlike local radio stations, whose impact can be balanced by tuning to distant stations, local television, and cable television in particular, contain the seed of a monopoly over a particularly addictive form of publicity. In its judgment of 4 November 1986, the West German Federal Constitutional Court stated the requirements which must be satisfied by German legislation to prevent any restriction, distortion or abuse of the freedom of broadcasting, guaranteed by Article 5 of the Fundamental Law.

The Constitutional Court takes the view that this pithy rule means that the freedom of broadcasting must be protected not only against the intervention of the state – that is, of the government in power – but also against private monopoly and abuse by sectional and economic interest.

In reviewing legislation adopted in Lower Saxony on 23 May 1984, the court held that broadcasting programmes of radio and television must try for a 'balanced diversity' in order to support the democratic order. Broadcasts should provide an opportunity for all schools of thought except those opposed to the democratic system of government.

But the representation of minorities cannot be achieved arithmetically. Rather, it is important to prevent the assumption by one group or another of a superior, dominant influence on the formation of public opinion. In a way, this concept owes much to the competition law, where free competition is protected not by allocating market shares but by measures restraining the abuse of dominant market power and monopolies.

The law adopted in Lower Saxony (GVBR p 147) is one in a series of legislative attempts by German Länder to regulate broadcasting in the transitional period while private stations and cable transmissions of foreign television broadcasts appear side by side with state broadcasting stations, but before private enterprise has completely taken over and integrated the European and possibly worldwide audience, as some observers expect it will do.

While in radio, the required balanced diversity is therefore an automatic result of the technical ease with which distant broadcasts can be heard, the problem is quite different in the field of television. Reception from television satellites requires costly equipment. And the cable systems capable of bringing foreign television broadcasts, whether from foreign stations or from satellites, to the doorsteps of the local audience have only a limited reach.

The West German post administration aspires to a cable network covering 80 per cent of the territory but at the beginning of 1986 it was accessible to only about 18 per cent of all households, of which only a third – 6 per cent of the total – made use of it.

The Constitutional Court had to start, therefore, with the premise that television broadcasting is, and for some considerable time will remain, a localised issue of a terrestrial nature, meaning that the influence of satellite broadcasting has not yet opened the air to worldwide competition and that law is still needed to protect the balanced diversity and to prevent the emergence of private monopoly in the formation of public opinion. The legislation adopted by Lower Saxony tries to achieve this by introducing a licensing procedure for private radio and television stations. Political parties or their enterprises are not eligible, and no programme maker can obtain a licence for more than one complete radio channel and one complete television channel. This limitation also embraces all associated enterprises.

It is laid down that, preferably, there should be two radio and two television channels produced by operators satisfying professional requirements. Broadcasting times should be mutually agreed but, if not agreed, can be regulated by the authority – a regional broadcasting commitee operating as a public agency independent of the government.

It is the task of this authority to watch over the balanced diversity of programmes, which can be achieved either by balancing each programme or by collective balancing of several programmes. The ultimate sanction available to the authority is to revoke the licence.

The key requirements of supervision are contained in section 15, applying to programmes produced in Lower Saxony or imported there from other parts of West Germany. The individual channels, or all channels combined, must provide for the expression of views of all important political, ideological and social groups. Section 11 prohibits programmes opposed to free democratic order and to the country's constitution. Section 13 requires factual and comprehensive information. And section 14 provides for the protection of juvenile listeners and viewers.

The broadcasting programmes should be aimed at the entire Lower Saxony audience, though they may exceptionally also provide programmes for a smaller area. In such a case, no more than half of the channel programmes may be supplied by a publisher of periodicals which has a dominant position in the locality.

Advertising matter may be inserted only in blocks and only in programmes lasting more than 100 minutes. Advertisements must not amount to more than 20 per cent of weekly broadcasts.

Programmes imported from abroad do not require a licence; only notification to the authority is needed. Their contents must not infringe human dignity or contravene the prohibition on pornographic, violent or racist sequences.

Programmes imported from the West German territory must also satisfy the requirement of balanced diversity laid down in section 15. Imported programmes are not subject to the duty to publish replies by those who feel that their interests were harmed by misleading information.

The Socialist party (SPD) met this legislation with intense hostility. A constitutional complaint was signed by 201 SPD members of the German Parliament. They complained that the balanced diversity of the programmes is not properly specified in the legislation, which also does not ensure proper control and prevention of undue influence over the formation of public opinion. In private, market-orientated broadcasting, the balance of information and opinion will not be produced automatically, they asserted, it must be regulated. They further complained that the legislation did not provide sufficient control of sponsorship and private subsidies as well as control of combined press and broadcast enterprises.

Because of these alleged shortcomings, the plaintiffs asked the Court to declare the entire statute null and void.

The Court rejected this main claim and held that the legislation was in principle compatible with the requirements of the Fundamental Law. But it called for it to be amended.

The Court rejected the demand for a detailed regulation of the 'balanced diversity of programmes'. This, said the judges, was a target for which broadcasters must strive but it was impossible to say exactly how they should do it.

However, the complaint was justified when it pointed out that the statute provided no guidance for the transition from internal balancing within one programme to external balancing between several programmes. This shortcoming could be removed by providing that the existence of four mutually independent channels of the same sort creates the presumption of external balance. This presumption however could be disproved by the broadcasting authority. Such an arrangement, adopted in Schleswig-Holstein, also provided for clarity and certainty of the law.

The Court also said that imported programmes should not be exempted from the requirement to contain factual, comprehensive and true information, and they should not be absolved from the obligation to publish replies from those harmed by misleading information.

The Court called also for removal of a provision which leaves the government free to decide a licensing application if the independent authority did not decide within three months or additional time allowed to it. The Court said this would leave too much discretionary power in the hands of the prime minister of Lower Saxony.

The decision demonstrates how a Bill of Rights can serve not only for protecting individuals but also as a powerful weapon in the hands of opposition.

Cable TV and EEC rules of competition

The expected expansion of cable television will increase the importance of copyright protection of films. In the UK, films picked up from domestic broadcasts may be freely transmitted by cable and the re-transmission of films picked up from foreign broadcasts may be exempt from copyright fees by the Performing Rights Tribunal. Very much the same effect is achieved in Germany, where courts view cable television as a sort of extended aerial of the receiving set.

By contrast, Belgium and Luxembourg follow the Berne Copyright Convention under which the holder of exclusive distribution rights can obtain a court order prohibiting cable transmission of a film picked up from a foreign broadcast. The problem is unsolved in Italy and Denmark and a matter of controversy in France.

On top of these uncertainties come problems of EEC law. The European Court held in 1980[2] that it was not against the EEC freedom of cross-border services if an exclusive film distributor prevented a cable television company from transmitting a film to which he had exclusive rights, even if the company picked up the film from broadcasts authorised by the film-maker in a neighbouring country. That was clear enough and most people assumed that film distributors who had been granted exclusive licences had nothing to fear from EEC law.

Unfortunately, the Belgian Court of Cassation gave the European Court a second chance to look at the case which prompted its 1980 decision. This time the question was whether the exclusive distribution rights clashed with EEC rules of competition. In its 1982 Coditel judgment[3] it deftly kicked the ball back into national courts without giving them any real guidance.

Coditel is the name of three Belgian companies transmitting by cable TV broadcasts of German stations which have poor reception in the regions served by the companies. As part of this service they relayed from Germany a French film, Le Boucher, to which exclusive distribution rights in Belgium were held by Cine Vog. Cine Vog sued the Coditel companies for infringement of copyright.

When the case reached the Belgian appeal court, questions were sent to Luxembourg concerning the compatibility of Belgian law, which protects the distributor, with the freedom of cross-border services, and Article 85 of the EEC Treaty which prohibits and declares null and void agreements which restrict or distort competition and adversely affect trade between member states.

The Coditel companies received strong support from the EEC Commission. According to the Commission, exclusive licensing of films was a restriction of ecnomic freedom to which Article 85 applied. The aim of exclusivity was to prevent potential competition by other distributors. The Commission denied that the ability to grant exclusive licences was an essential function of the right to exploitation of a cinematographic work. On the contrary, a contractual renunciation of free exploitation of film rights was tantamount to the abandonment of copyright.

But it was not enough if the exclusive licence distorted competition. It was also necessary, concluded the Commission, to show that it had a perceptible adverse effect on trade between member-states. The question whether an exclusive licence was or was not contrary to Article 85 was, therefore, economic rather than legal. It could best be decided by national courts.

The EEC Commission which, in essence, asked the court to apply to film copyright the same restrictions which it had already applied to patents, trademarks and industrial design was opposed by Britain, Holland and France. Both the British and French governments agreed with the film distributor that prohibition of exclusive licences would make film distribution quite impracticable. Moreover, said the British Government, prohibition of exclusive licences would favour big film companies which distribute through their own fully owned subsidiaries. It would operate to the detriment of small, independent film-makers who have no organisation of their own and depend on distributors.

The Court's judgment is a compromise, but it comes much closer to the Commission's view than the 1980 judgment which, for all practical purposes, can now be forgotten. The granting of an exclusive licence to a film distributor was not in itself a prohibited restrictive agreement, the court said. One had to take into account that such a licence might be necessary to ensure the dubbing of films and the financing of their production.

However, the Court said the exercise of such exclusive licences could, in certain economic and legal contexts, lead to consequences prohibited by Article 85, in particular, if it created barriers to trade unjustified by the needs of the cinematographic industry or if it provided for exorbitant royalties or for an excessively long duration of exclusivity. It would be up to the national judge to keep these dangers in mind when deciding whether an exclusive film licence had been put to a use which infringed Article 85 and was, therefore, prohibited.

EEC limits to industrial design rights

In spite of the work done by consumer organisations, products are often sold by their looks protected by industrial design rights or *Geschmackgmusterrecht* as it is called in Germany.

In a judgment handed down on 14 September 1982, in Case 144/81, the European Court refused an invitation to venture into the almost impenetrable jungle of disharmonious national laws applicable to this type of industrial property.

It ruled that whatever rights are created by national legislation or national courts in respect of industrial design protection, their exercise within the EEC is subject to the same limitations which the court earlier imposed on the exercise of patent and trademark rights.

The case which provided the Luxembourg judges with an opportunity to extend the doctrine of exhaustion of rights to industrial designs, originated from an infringement action brought into a Dutch court by a Dutch importer of ladies' handbags made in Taiwan.

The Dutch appeal court addressed two questions to the European Court:

whether it was not contrary to EEC law if the Benelux legislation deprived all other persons (except the author of the design or his employer or assignee) from the possibility of opposing the grant of rights to the first depositor of the model;

whether EEC law would allow the grant of an injunction preventing the importation of the product from another EEC country where it was lawfully distributed without any infringement of the applicant's rights.

The Court said that EEC law presented no obstacle to the application of the Belgian legislation as interpreted by the Dutch court.

Turning to the substance of the matter, the Court ruled that the exercise of industrial design rights established by whatever method must be subject to the same limitations as the exercise of patent and trademark rights: such rights must not be used to oppose the importation from another member state of products which have been placed on the market by the owner of these rights or with his consent, or by someone who is legally or economically dependent on him.

Further the rights to an industrial design must not be used to enforce restrictive agreements between those involved. Finally, these rights may not be used with the intention of partitioning the Common Market to prevent imports of such goods to which the design protection rights have been established by different persons in the different member states concerned.

Ladies' handbags may not be a product exciting the minds of big business, but motor car spares are. The Luxembourg decision is likely to have an impact here.

The gradual erosion of spare parts copyright

Starting with the Design Copyright Act 1949, Parliament made it abundantly clear that it does not intend copyright protection for purely functional designs. However, by a grammatical analysis of a 1968 amendment adopted to meet a special difficulty of Birmingham jewellers, the courts concluded that three-dimensional functional products derived from drawings retained the benefit of copyright if they did not qualify for registration. As a result, while inventions are protected by patents for 20 years and registered artistic designs for 15 years, functional designs which have neither of these merits enjoy a protection of over 50 years. Moreover, infringement of design copyright can result in the award of higher damages than infringements of more inventive forms of intellectual property.

In the spring of 1986, the House of Lords considered the copyright protection of BL exhausts. It upheld in principle the absurd copyright protection of functional products which survive the designer by 50 years.

The Law Lords said only that it must not be used so as to interfere with the right of a car owner to have his car repaired. By a logical jump of considerable audacity, the majority of Law Lords concluded that this freed from copyright restriction anyone who wished to produce and supply spare parts to a car owner.

As far as it goes, this is a welcome decision, but it does not go far enough. It upholds a rule which was created by courts against the clear intention of parliament – as Lord Griffith pointed out in his dissenting opinion – and tries to temper its effect by an exception based on a principle of law of which no one was aware so far. This is likely to create no end of confusion and much unnecessary litigation. Lord Griffith's clear rejection of copyright protection for functional designs would be much preferable.

In May 1988, the Law Lords took another step to diminish the three-dimensional absurdity. Their dismissal of a Hong Kong appeal concerning the Lego and Duplo children's model-building systems is likely to have considerable business impact. There must be many more products like Lego bricks, where the penetration of the market by a competitor is made almost impossible by the design copyright of a well-established and dominant product.

A similar problem in the patent field has been recently considered in the case of IBM, which dominates the computer market to such a degree that new hardware producers have little hope of success unless they make their products IBM compatible. Both US and EC antitrust agencies pressed IBM, with some success, to announce their specifications ahead of new models so that competitors could keep their products compatible.

In the case of Lego the competitors consider that they have no hope of penetrating the model building market unless they produce a system that is compatible with Lego. After the expiry of Lego's patent and design protection in the US, the Tyco group did exactly that: it copied elements which formed the core of the Lego system, adding to them elements of its own design. Some, or all, of the modular units were to be manufactured in Hong Kong.

As was to be expected – Tyco made no secret of what it was doing – Lego brought a copyright infringement action in Hong Kong. When it failed in the Hong Kong Appeal Court, Lego pursued the appeal further in the Privy Council. The Hong Kong laws under which the action was brought are replicas of the UK's Registered Designs Act 1949 and Copyright Act 1956. The problem with which the Law Lords were invited to deal is essentially the problem of copyright for 'three-dimensional reproduction of original drawings'.

The judgment of the Privy Council reveals a welcome realism. The original Lego bricks were a copy of designs made by Mr Hilary Page, whose UK patents for the system expired in 1954 and 1959. The Lego Group then obtained further protection by new patents and designs which expired in 1975, and these enabled them successfully to resist all competitors producing model systems compatible with Lego.

The Lego's improved designs were registered in 1958, Lego argued that these designs ought not be have been registered because they were incapable of registration and consequently that they qualified for copyright protection. The reasons why the designs were incapable of registration, Lego claimed, was first that they were functional and not artistic, and second that they were not novel.

On the first point, Lord Oliver said that there was substantial evidence that Lego's draughtsmen aimed not only at functional efficiency, but also at the eye appeal of the product. Lego was wrong to argue that the designs were not capable of registration and thus available for copyright protection because they were purely functional.

On the point of novelty, Lord Oliver said that the words 'capable of registration' had to be traced back to the Copyright Act 1911. It seemed in the highest degree improbable that the framers of this Act, which denied copyright to works intended to be used as models for industrial production wanted to give copyright protection to such excluded works only because they also lacked novelty. The words 'constituted a design capable of registration' aimed at works which had the essential characteristics of designs at the time they were made, one of which was originality and novelty. It was absurd, said Lord Oliver, to maintain that a design sufficiently novel to qualify for registration would be excluded from copyright protection, while a 'design' lacking novelty – and therefore unable to obtain 15-year protection by registration – would qualify for copyright protection for the entire life of the author and a further 50 years.

It is this aspect of the Law Lords belated conversion to ordinary common sense which opens to lower courts the possibility of removing the 'three-dimensional reproduction of original drawings' argument.

Lego's second claim, which concerned post-1973 designs, failed because the Law Lords concluded that these contained no visually significant changes or improvements from the earlier designs. In this connection Lord Oliver discussed 'originality', for which no statutory definition exists. It had been said, in the context of literary copyright, that it depends on the degree of skill, labour and judgment involved in preparing a compilation. It was a gross error to apply this as a universal test, said Lord Oliver. A reproduction of a drawing, though requiring skill and labour, would become an original work only by some material alteration or embellishment.

To sum up, copyright protection of spare parts and other products made on the basis of engineering drawings, models or other documents has received a blow but it will depend on lower courts whether this will prove fatal. Their Lordships can get some credit, but not full marks.

Notes

1 *Von Heyden v Neustadt* (1880) 14 ChD 230.

2 European Court, Luxembourg, Case 62/79, *Coditel v Cine Vog Films*; judgment 18 March 1980. FT, 10 April 1980. FT European Law Letter, April 1980.

3 *Coditel v Cine Vog Films*, Case 252/81, judgment 6 October 1982, unreported.

4 Privy Council Appeal No. 43/1987, *Interlego AG v Tyco Industries Inc and others*, FT Law Report, 11 May 1987.

5 Consumers and other victims of civil wrongs

Consumers' law: slow progress from the corner shop era

The broad field of consumer protection, the impact of UK's civil, criminal and administrative law and the likely impact of the measures proposed by the EC Commission was reviewed comprehensively by Sir Gordon Borrie, the Director General of Fair Trading, in his 1984 Hamlyn Lectures.[1]

Miss Emma Warburton Hamlyn of Torquay, a patriotic lady who died in 1941, wished the lecturers to praise the advantages of English law. Sir Gordon had some difficulty in trying to comply with her wish.[2] True, he could record considerable achievements over the past 15 years, but if one takes account of the 'bold' and of the 'timorous' judges and legislators whose deeds he discussed, it seems that the timorous are in the majority: Sir Gordon, who as a public servant has the good fortune of being able to combine the authority of his office with academic freedom of criticism, does not suffer a dearth of ideas on how things could be further improved, and how the consumers' society could be made safer for the consumer.

The integration of the British retail trade was almost completed in the first two decades after the war, and was accompanied by the domination of the market by pre-packaged branded products. This has radically altered the relationship between the manufacturer, the distributor and the consumer. A local grocer who knew his customers' tastes, the corner shop where the buyers went not only for the goods but also for advice, was replaced by impersonal multiple stores in which the consumer is left to his own devices and has to rely on information, if any, contained in manufacturers' advertisements or printed on the package. Law always lags behind life, but in the consumer field the lag is particularly great: the fundamental element of the British consumer's protection was, until 1 March 1988, when the Consumer Protection Act 1987 came into force, his contract with the shopkeeper and this was made even more absurd by excluding those who use the product from the benefit of the seller's liability if the product was not bought by themselves but, for example, by a member of their family.

The principle that only the immediate seller is responsible to the buyer, was already breached in 1932 when the House of Lords held that a manufacturer could be made liable for negligence to anyone who had been killed or injured or whose property had been damaged by a defective product if there had been insufficient care on his part or on the part of his employees. Courts are now inclined to also allow damages for distress and for disappointment. In 1982 the House of Lords went still further and held, in *Junior Books Ltd v The Veitchi Company Ltd*,[2] that where the proximity between the producer of a faulty product and the user was sufficiently close, the producer had not only a duty to prevent harm being done by the product but also to avoid faults being present in the work or article itself.

Sir Gordon feared that the courts are likely to interpret this new rule fairly narrowly, maintaining the fiction that the consumer, in general, relies on the immediate vendor and not on the manufacturer. However, it will be increasingly difficult to uphold this fiction where the manufacturer's advertising, and brand advertising in particular, are the key factors in consumer choice. This was recognised by Lord Wilberforce when he said that the proximity between the consumer and the manufacturer was sufficient when the manufacturer could envisage that carelessness on his part may cause damage to the consumer. Sir Gordon would like this view to find more general application.

The hesitant progress of common law from the 'freedom of contract' to the protection of the weaker party to the contract, pioneered by Lord Denning, was supplemented by legislation: the Supply of Goods (Implied Terms) Act 1973, the Unfair Contract Terms Act 1977, and the Supply of Goods and Services Act 1982. Sir Gordon regretted, however, that some of the basic notions of this legislation remained unclarified because few consumers have the courage and financial means to go to court with their complaints, and such decisions as there are, were made mainly by county courts and do not constitute a precedent.

The Director General of Fair Trading can attack in the Restrictive Practices Court standard forms of contract recommended by trade association, but no other, and it seems that Sir Gordon would very much wish for legislation enabling him to obtain in courts a prohitory injunction in respect of contract clauses that are 'unreasonable towards the consumer', as his Australian and Swedish counterparts can. He also lacks powers to attack terms at which public corporation do business with the consumers, although these may have a greater and much more general impact than those recommended by trade associations.

Sir Gordon takes a critical view of the various sectorial schemes designed to indemnify the consumer if he suffered by bankruptcy or fraud of the supplier. Such schemes range from the statutory policyholders' protection to schemes organised by the federations of builders, glaziers, and of newspaper associations in respect of mail orders. He points out that honest traders often complain that such indemnity schemes oblige them to compensate customers of their more reckless competitors who often collapse for the very reason that they offer their goods and services at unrealistically low prices. Sir Gordon welcomed the Cork proposals which would provide automatic and immediate safeguards by disqualifying from directorships a person who has been responsible for the failure of a company, and make personaly liable for company debts directors guilty of reckless and unreasonable behaviour.

The provisions of criminal law enacted in aid of the consumer seems to be even less effective. Statutory regulation of bargain offers and similar promotional devices appears to be too complicated and poorly defined. Sir Gordon would prefer a single, general rule prohibiting false or misleading statements about the price of goods or services – this type of legislation provides an excellent starting point for achieving fairer trade practices in Australia. Another weakness of the criminal law provisions concerning trade descriptions, food, drugs, weights and measures, is the very low level of fines compared with the profit which can be unfairly achieved. Although the courts can now award compensation in criminal proceedings, this is still a novelty which judges and magistrates are slow to take up.

There seems to be no great enthusiasm to inform the courts of the facts of trading life, and to achieve a long-term effect on the trading climate by consistent prosecution. Sir Gordon quoted Edmund Burke's 'For the triumph of evil, it is necessary only that good men do nothing'. However, with the courts overtaxed as they are, only administrative penalties imposed by a 'ticket' on the spot – and leaving it to the trader to appeal to the court if he wishes – could compensate for the effect of Burke's rule.

Compensation for injury could be facilitated by a revolving fund

The iniquities of the UK and US laws of liability for personal injuries have again been brought to the forefront of attention by the *Opren* case in the UK and the *Dalkon Shield* case in the US. In the first a staggering disparity appeared between the damages awarded to claimants in the US and those offered in the UK.

The second case demonstrates how US juries can drive manufacturers into bankruptcy. Neither the UK nor the US system seems to produce reasonable results and both produce them only after a delay of many years – a whole decade sometimes – so that they are of little value to those in need at the time their need is greatest.

The Opren litigation was five years old when settled by the majority of claimants – and would take many more years if pursued to the end. To win under the old law, the claimants would have had to prove that the manufacturer and the UK authority which licenses medicines were negligent – a most difficult task, to say the least – and there was some doubt whether the legal aid fund would continue to support them in it. But even when there is no longer a need to prove negligence in respect of faulty products supplied after 1 March 1988, when the product liability provisions of the Consumer Protection Act 1987 came into force, the claimants will not be much better off.

The 1987 Act opened to the manufacturers the defence that the product was made and supplied in accordance with the scientific and technological knowledge available at the time. It would again take many years and exorbitant legal costs to prove them right or wrong on this point. No doubt the position of the claimants could be improved by revamping the litigation process but the welcome changes suggested by the Civil Justice Review with the support of Lord Hailsham, then Lord Chancellor would not be enough.

Modern disasters produce hundreds of victims – many thousands in the case of an unsafe drug; hence the need for the disposal of a large number of related claims in single proceedings. Under the latest legal aid legislation the class action procedure, supported both by the judiciary and the Law Society, is going to be available also to legally aided claimants.

The need for a modified contingency fee system, which would free claimants from the unbearable risk of legal costs or dependence on the uncertain support of the legal aid fund, is also now being considered by both the Law Society and the Bar. It would remove the absurd situation in which only the very rich, whose dependence on compensation for injury is least, can afford to sustain a prolonged litigation, while those who are neither rich nor poor cannot even think of starting it.

More reform would be required to remove the other fundamental injustice; that if two people suffer similar crippling injuries in two accidents, only the one who can prove that it was due to somebody's negligence has a chance, while the other is bound to remain empty-handed.

All these matters were considered in the (Pearson) Report of the Royal Commission on Civil Liability and Compensation for Personal Injury. Its unanimous recommendations, made in 1977 warmly supported by Lord Denning and Lord Scarman later, have been mostly ignored by the government.

Compensation for personal injuries should not depend on proving negligence and the ability to litigate. It should be proportional to need and paid quickly or by periodic payments according to need, supplementing what is available through the National Health Service and social security. The time has come to bring these Pearson recommendations one stage further.

Present day needs might be best met by a revolving fund from which compensation would be paid to victims of major disasters, unsafe drugs and other accidents whose nature and scope would have to be carefully specified. The fund would be replenished by contributions collected from those responsible for accidents or disasters. The fund would be in a much better position than individual victims to obtain a reasonable settlement or to litigate with a large company. Claimants dissatisfied with the decisions of the board or ombudsman in charge of the fund could appeal in much the same way they can now appeal against decisions on social security benefit. Such an approach would be both kinder to the victims and still oblige industry to remain safety conscious.

Product liability – US moves towards curbing its excesses

Asked recently whether the EEC product liability proposal is 'a good thing', Mr Richard K. Willard, the US Deputy Attorney-General,[3] suggested that it might be a good thing for the US which already suffered a loss of competitiveness as a result of its own stringent product liability laws. Mr Willard, who is in charge of product liability legislation and chaired the US Tort Policy Working Group (TPWG), thinks there is growing awareness of the enormous social cost of product liability laws. The total tort litigation costs were estimated for 1985 between $29bn (£17.8bn) and $36bn (£22bn) – of these claimants received at most $14 to £16bn.

In addition to the legal costs there is a proliferation of costly defensive measures. For example, the cost of unnecessary medical tests, Caesarian deliveries and other surgery, is estimated at some $20–30bn per annum.

While the European trend is clearly towards greater product liability, the US seems to be retreating in horror from its consequences. Last year, the TPWG recommended a return to a fault-based standard for liability and a number of other reforms. The past year saw an unprecedented bout of legislation and, so far, two thirds of the states have adopted some reform of the tort law.

The pioneers of reform argue with considerable success that the social security system now provides a safety net allowing the limitation of awards and that the present system operates in favour of wealthier plaintiffs who can claim greater loss of income than poorer victims.

They point out that the system is inefficient because the victim gets less than half the money paid by the manufacturer, the rest being absorbed by legal costs and that it is unfair in that it favours victims of manmade accidents against victims of natural disasters.

There are also the old arguments that product liability law discourages innovation, which would not apply to European legislation, if, as in the UK, it provides an exemption for development risks.

The US insurance crisis, which meant that manufacturers could not obtain insurance cover or could not afford the insurance premiums asked for it, has ameliorated somewhat, mainly as a result of higher excess thresholds and lower limits of cover. Moreover, there is an increasing reliance on self-insurance and captive insurance programmes.

But the impact of the no-fault liability laws is still felt. In 1986 commercial general liability and medical malpractice insurance produced 13 per cent of the premium income but accounted for 33 per cent of the insurers' total underwriting losses.

The defenders of the present system argue that the insurance crisis is caused by collusion among insurers, imprudent business practices, a decline in investment income and trade regulation. However, the US Justice Department concluded that these are unlikely causes of the crisis. It attributes the crisis to unforeseen changes in the court's determination of liability and assessment of damages, together with the uncertainty generated by these changes.

The rise of average jury awards is accelerating. Most of the increase which has taken place since 1960 occurred in the 1980-84 period. In this period, product liability awards increased by 212 per cent in Cook County, Illinois, and by 1016 per cent in San Francisco, California, the two judicial districts in large conurbations for which good reports are available. Medical malpractice awards rose in the same time by 2,167 per cent in Cook County and by 830 per cent in San Francisco. Of particular interest is that the proportion of £1m-plus awards rose steeply in the last 20 years, reaching by 1984 over 85 per cent of the total damages awarded in Cook County and 58 per cent in San Francisco.

Punitive damages, originally introduced for intentional wrongs only, and now applied to no-fault situations, increase awards, are an obstacle to settlement, and lead to abuse of litigation. Another cause of the escalation of liability litigation is traced back to legal theories seeing the role of courts in distribution of risks by means of insurance rather than in resolution of disputes.

The adoption of popular social engineering theories by US judges can be partly explained by the fact that state judges are elected and try to please the voters.

There are, of course, also more specific reasons. For example, motor insurance is often inadequate, limiting the compensation of victims of accidents to $50,000, and this must have been an important incentive for the development of product liability laws.

Another notorious incentive is, of course, the contingency fee system in which the attorney finances the litigation for a share of the award. It must be said, however, that the contingency fee system also eliminates hopeless claims and thus prevents a good deal of unnecessary litigation.

In its updating report on the liability crisis, of 11 March 1986, the TPWG urges more reform legislation. It should be drafted simply and clearly to survive the attempts of judges to limit its effect. Such legislation should remove the joint and several liability which enables the plaintiff to seek compensation from whoever has the deeper pocket, even if his share of responsibility is only minimal. Instead, liability should be proportionate to the share of fault or responsibility for the injury.

The most controversial reform proposal concerns the non-economic damages awarded by courts for pain, mental anguish and emotional distress. The TPWG originally recommended a limit of $100,000 on such non-economic damages, but has now increased its recommendation to $200,000. It recommends that punitive damages should be included within the overall limit on non-economic damages.

Another way of curbing punitive damages would be to restrict attorney's contingency fees to no more than 5 per cent of punitive awards. But the TPWG makes a wider attack on the contingency fee system when it proposes a sliding scale descending from 25 per cent of the first $100,000 of an award to 10 per cent of any amount in excess of $300,000.

The US experience contains many lessons for Europe, not least of which is that state laws get entrenched and are not an easy object of a uniform, Union-wide reform. By 1992 this could well be a European problem. It might have been better to introduce European product liability not by a directive, but by a directly applicable EEC regulation: this could then be revoked or changed throughout Europe at a stroke, by another regulation.

US product liability law and world trade

Unfashionable as it is, I must confess a certain sympathy for the eagerness of the US state courts to protect US consumers, irrespective of where the acts which had adverse consequences took place. After all, it has always been accepted that if a bullet is fired across the frontier and hits some one, that is a sufficient ground for criminal prosecution in the courts of the country where the injury occurred. By similar logic, the European Court ruled some years ago that pollution of the Rhine by waste released upstream could be viewed downstream as an act done in another country where the pollution took effect.

As the world grows smaller and the world market integrates, with the result that manufacturers cannot foresee where their mass-produced goods will end, it would be good to have international harmonisation of product liability laws and an international convention on jurisdiction over product liability claims. Unfortunately, we have neither and no prospect of getting them within the foreseeable future.

Manufacturers exporting their products worldwide have to live, therefore, with the fact that the US courts award compensation for the effects of faulty products, and sometimes for misuse of perfectly sound products, on terms incomparably more generous than the courts of any other country. As a result, everyone, if he can, tries to sue in the US for his product liability claims – and also anti-trust claims – even if the manufacturer's connection with the US markets is of the flimsiest type.

Such a case came before the Supreme Appeal Court of California when a Taiwanese tyre manufacturer, who was held responsible for a motorcycle accident in California, thought to involve as a third party a Japanese tyre valve manufacturer, whose valve was used in the blown tyre which caused the accident.

The valve manufacturer, Asahi Metal Industry Co Ltd, supplied less than 1.25 per cent of its products to the Taiwanese tyre manufacturer. Only 22 per cent of the Taiwanese manufacturer's tyres used Asahi valves. Asahi had no control over the distribution of tyres fitted with its valves, did not ask that they be marketed in California and was not asked to design any valve assemblies to comply with specific Californian standards.

When the dispute reached the California Court of Appeal, this said that it had no personal jurisdiction over Asahi as 'It would not be reasonable to require Asahi to respond to California solely on the basis of ultimately realised foreseeability that the product into which its component was embodied would be sold all over the world including California.'

However, the Californian Supreme Court thought otherwise. It held that as California had a substantial interest in protecting its consumers, and both California and the Taiwanese tyre manufacturer had an interest in avoiding inconsistent results and a multiplicity of litigation, the dispute should be governed by the substantive law of California and fell under the jurisdiction of Californian courts.

Asahi appealed to the Supreme Court of the US and this agreed to review the Californian decision. The Washington law firm Sutherland, Asbill & Brennan submitted an *amicus curiae* brief on behalf of the Confederation of British Industry, and the American Chamber of Commerce in the UK.

These decisions encouraged hope that the Supreme Court would take the opportunity offered by *Asahi* to clarify the law by limiting the liability of the unwilling foreign supplier of parts which, incorporated in the final product, find their way to the US market without his prompting.

The Supreme Court disappointed such expectations.[4] It reversed the Californian decision on the grounds that it was unfair and unduly burdensome for Asahi to have to go to California and submit to a foreign judicial system. The Court split 4:4 with one abstention on the crucial question of degree of a foreign company's involvement in the US 'stream of commerce', required to justify the US courts' jurisdiction.

Four justices, including Chief Justice Rehnquist, said that the mere awareness that the components would reach the US 'in the stream of commerce' was not enough – only an act of the company 'purposefully directed' towards the US would justify US courts jurisdiction.

The other four justices took an opposite view:

As long as a participant [in the flow of products from manufacturer to consumer] is aware that the product is being marketed in the [US] state, the possibility of a law suit there cannot come as a surprise.

The courts could assume jurisdiction even if there was no 'purposeful act' directed towards the US market.

Justice Stevens abstained, saying that the appeal could be allowed without getting into this issue. He may yet sway the court one way or the other in the future.

Zeebrugge disaster: how verdict of unlawful killing affects claims for compensation

The verdict of 'unlawful killing' returned by the jury on the Zeebrugge ferry disaster will have no direct legal consequences on the prosecution of those responsible but may substantially improve the position of those claiming compensation.

It was not the task of the inquest to apportion responsibility and guilt when finding that there was an unlawful killing. It is a matter for the prosecution service to decide whether to prosecute or not and whom.

The prosecution service already had the report of the inquiry into the disaster conducted by Mr Justice Sheen.

The fact that disciplinary proceedings conducted by the shipping company against the master and officers of the Herald of Free Enterprise were not postponed to await the result of criminal prosecution suggests that criminal prosecution was not contemplated at the time, though the inquest jury verdict introduced a new element of psychological and political pressure towards prosecution.

The verdict will however influence the civil claims for compensation. The limit on compensation imposed by the 1974 Athens Convention and the Merchant Shipping Act, which since the disaster has been increased to £80,000 per passenger, does not apply in a case of intentional or reckless misconduct on the part of the shipowner.

The coroner told the jury that they should give a verdict of unlawful killing only if they find that there was gross negligence. The difference between that and recklessness is very small or none.

Would a UK court impose punitive or exemplary damages as US courts do in similar situations?

The leading dictum on this is by Lord Devlin in *Rookes v Barnard* (1964) when he said that exemplary damages may be awarded if the defendant's conduct has been calculated by him to make a profit for himself – a profit that may well exceed the compensation payable to the plaintiff. This principle was later approved by the House of Lords in *Broom v Cassel* (1971).

If the Zeebrugge victims succeeded in convincing a High Court judge that the ship owners' negligence was due to the pursuit of profit, to achieve quick turnround of ferries, they may well claim not only compensation outside the Convention limit but also exemplary damages.

The coroner rejected moves to consider a verdict of 'corporate manslaughter' and this underlines the principle that a limited company cannot be guilty of unlawful killing.

This ruling was upheld by the High Court, which rejected an application for judicial review of it on the grounds that he had been right to find that there was no evidence against the company.

No such case has ever succeeded in English law. An attempt to indict Ford in the US in connection with the death of occupants of some of its Pinto cars also failed.

Finally, the disaster is a reminder of the urgent need to rationalise UK law governing liability for accidents taking place abroad which, as the English and Scottish Law Commissions reminded us,[5] is in a mess.

The lesson of Bhopal

The disaster at Union Carbide plant at Bhopal, India, one of the greatest industrial tragedies of all time, is further compounded by the uncertainty of law and slowness of procedures which should bring relief and compensation to survivors while it still can help them. It calls for an international treaty providing greater certainty of law and division of liability between the multinational company and the host government.

As long as that is not achieved, parent companies investing in less developed countries should abandon the now fashionable permissive attitude to subsidiaries and control their safety arrangements and environmental impact strictly by their own inspectors on the spot. They should abandon the project rather than succumb to the host government's pressure to give up technical control of potentially dangerous plants.

WHOSE RESPONSIBILITY?

What are the legal issues of Bhopal from which lessons can be derived? First there is the issue of responsibility. How is it divided between Union Carbide, its Indian subsidiary and the Indian authorities? The burden on Union Carbide is very heavy, not only because it owns 51 per cent of the Indian subsidiary's equity but because it admits responsibility for the training of the Indian personnel. It might be found liable for designing and supplying unsafe plant, for failing to use its controlling power to enforce observance by the local management of safety instructions and, finally, for not having adequately trained local personnel.

As to the responsibility of the Indian authorities, this may extend not only to unsatisfactory inspection but also to any pressure which the authorities may have exercised on Union Carbide to employ staff qualified rather by their politics than by their managerial ability. Above all, the

Indian authorities seem to bear responsibility for one of the major causes of the tragedy, which was the proximity of the shanty town to the plant.

According to Indian environmental rules, the factory should have been sited 15 miles from urban settlements. This distance may have been respected in the planning stage, but thereafter the authorities did not prevent workers and their families from settling in shanty dwellings close to the plant. Indeed, when the danger was pointed out to them, the answer was that the plant could not be moved. The possibility of moving the people does not seem to have been seriously considered.

WHICH LAW?

The second issue is the question of which law should be applied. The answer to this could make a tremendous difference to the victims as US law of liability for wrongful acts is much stricter than Indian law, which is said to reflect the state of UK law at the time of the declaration of Indian independence.

The basic jurisdictional rule would guide judges towards the law of the place where the claim arose, but this need not necessarily be India as much of the design and manufacture of plant and equipment, training of personnel and managerial decisions or omissions, probably took place in the headquarters' establishment of Union Carbide in the US. Moreover, many US judges are inclined to temper the basic rule, that one should apply the law of the place where the claim arose, by other considerations. These include predictability of results, simplifications of the judicial task and preference for a system of law which sets a higher standard of conduct and protection against injury. It is evident that US law would win, at least on the second and third considerations.

WHICH COURTS: US OR INDIAN?

The third issue is: which courts have jurisdiction for litigation. US lawyers preparing class actions on behalf of the victims – some of whom are said to have received Rs 100 (about £7) for signing a power of attorney – are naturally interested in having the dispute decided by US courts. A panel of US judges has already decided that the proper place for bringing any suit in the US is the Federal District Court for the Southern District of New York.

To decide jurisdiction, the US courts will have to consider whether US or Indian courts are more convenient for the resolution of this dispute. The availability of witnesses may favour Indian courts though Union Carbide will, no doubt, call some witnesses from its US headquarters. Ease of enforcement of any awards would speak in favour of US courts.

The main argument canvassed so far in favour of US courts is that Indian courts require the plaintiff to deposit 5 per cent of the amount of damages claimed, but none of the Bhopal victims could manage anything approaching this sum and so would be deprived of the possibility of taking their claim to court. The other argument is that the backlog of cases in the Indian courts, with Supreme Court lists running into the 1990s, would deprive most claimants of any hope of getting compensation within their lifetime.

However, precedent would lead the US judges to ask whether there is a court available for the claimant to go to in his country, not how good that court is or how favourable or unfavourable is its procedure. Moreover, the Indian Government could remove the 5 per cent deposit requirement by legislation and the courts could give priority listing to any consolidated action for compensation.

SETTLEMENT

A settlement would be in the interests of all parties concerned except the lawyers – in the recent asbestos litigation 63 per cent of the compensation paid was consumed by expenses and legal fees. An out-of-court settlement would enable survivors of the tragedy to get some compensation when they need it instead of waiting for the outcome of litigation which could easily drag on for ten years. Union Carbide would also be better off if it could pay reasonable compensation now instead of having the threat of claims running into billions of dollars hanging over its head, to the detriment of its goodwill and creditworthiness.

Finally, the Indian Government would be spared the embarrassment of having the dirty linen of its local and central administration laundered in US courts where the Union Carbide lawyers would be bound to bring it to establish that the Government had at least partial responsibility for the tragedy. This concern must have played a role in the swift legislative action by which the Indian Government assumed powers to sue Union Carbide for compensation on behalf of the victims, and in this way to establish for itself a position in the negotiations for a settlement.

Sandoz pollution of the Rhine: no great legal problems

If taken to court, claims for compensation for damage caused by the Sandoz accident and subsequent pollution of the Rhine should prove a rich source of business for international lawyers without requiring them to solve any particularly difficult legal problems.

The main principle according to which claims for damages can be decided by international or national courts as well as the determination of jurisdiction, were surveyed and re-affirmed in two European Court judgments in 1976 and 1979.

By contrast the Convention on the Protection of the Rhine against Chemical Pollution concluded in 1976 between West Germany, France, Luxembourg, the Netherlands, Switzerland and the European Community, has nothing to say on the settlement of such claims.

In the Rhine Water case No. 21/76, the European Court held on 30 November 1976 that according to the 1968 Brussels Convention on Jurisdiction, of which Switzerland is not a signatory, a plaintiff has an option to sue either in the country where the damage occurred or in the place where the event leading to the pollution took place.

In its second Rhine Water judgment (Case 3789/77) of 8 January 1979, the court went much deeper into the matter. It established first that claims can be brought only by those who suffered damage and not by bodies whose function is to promote environmental purity.

With reference to the 1976 Convention, the Court ruled that the existence of international treaties regulating pollution and consequently allowing a certain degree of it, does not affect private rights of action under the ordinary rules of international law.

Dealing with the question of applicable law, the Court said that in the absence of special treaty provisions, or of special rules of international customary law, a national court should go by rules of international law derived from treaties, international custom and practice, general principles of law recognised by civilised nations, and teaching of outstanding international lawyers.

It followed from these sources that the basic principle of international law applicable to this case was that everyone should behave so as not to cause damage to others, and was liable in damages if violating this legal duty.

Discharge of toxic waste into an international river, said the court, constituted a violation of this general principle and created an obligation on the polluter to compensate for the damage caused. Private persons, no less than states, were bound by this rule of international law, and the national courts before which the claims were brought were bound to apply it.

Liability for Chernobyl: need of firmer international rules

On 19 July 1986, the Soviet Politburo accepted the conclusions of the Chernobyl commission of inquiry that the disaster was due to negligence and, in some instances to criminal negligence, of local as well as central government officials. Criminal proceedings were initiated against some, others were sacked and the Politburo went as far as to say that Mr Anatoly Mayorets, the Power Industry Minister, deserved to be dismissed, though he escaped with only a reprimand.

The Politburo report put on entirely new and firmer ground what were previously academic speculations about Soviet liability for the injury and damage caused outside its frontiers by the disaster. Like anybody else, the Soviet Government is responsible for its servants' acts and omissions in the course of carrying out their duties.

According to the report, the accident was due to the irresponsible handling of experiments. What appears as gross negligence to the commission would no doubt be viewed as outrageous recklessness if it is true that the containment vessels and structures of the reactors did not meet the minimum standards of other countries.

In addition to liability for negligence, there appears to be liability for failure to take steps which could reduce the adverse consequences or help the afflicted states to take timely preventive measures. There was no forewarning of the experiments and no immediate information after the accident.

The applicable rules of international law have been much discussed particularly in France and West Germany.[6] Neither the Paris Convention on the liability towards third persons in the field of nuclear energy concluded in 1960, nor the Vienna Convention on the liability for nuclear damage of 1963 were signed by the Soviet Union, so one has to consider international rules of more general application.

The Soviet Union, and the Ukraine separately, adhered to the 1979 Geneva Convention on Long Range Transboundary Air Pollution. Though this Convention, in force since 1983, has no provision about liability of member states, and does not deal specifically with radiation, it refers to air pollution in general and establishes certain principles applicable to any pollution of the atmosphere which has international effects, even to such types of pollution which we cannot envisage at present. The OECD 1974 recommendation on principles concerning transfrontier pollution (document C), which preceded the conclusion of the Convention, defines pollution as the introduction into the environment of deleterious substances or *energy*, and this would cover radiation.

The Convention provides for an exchange of information and consultations on application by countries which are or might be substantially affected. After the Chernobyl disaster, information was provided only long after the radioactive clouds had reached other countries. This was a breach of Article 5 of the Convention for which the Soviet Union can be held liable even if the Convention has no specific provisions about liability.

Soviet liability follows also from the fundamental rule that a state which causes damage to another by an act or omission contrary to international law is liable to restitution, damages or satisfaction – 'one of the principles most deeply rooted in the doctrine of international law and most strongly upheld by state practice'.[7]

No country may engage in activities on its territory which cause another state substantial and unusual damage. This principle has become part of the customary international law through numerous international agreements and decisions. Liability for negligence or internationally illegal acts is explicitly laid down in the UN 1982 Convention on the Law of the Sea, and more generally by the UN International Law Commission in its codification drafts on state responsibilities.

International law seems also to impose stricter requirements on information than those which can be derived from the Geneva Convention. This follows from a number of declarations and recommendations concerning the planning of activities capable of leading to environmental pollution. The OECD recommendation C (77)28 in particular, requires the country which is the source of environmental pollution to provide appropriate information on pollution affecting or threatening the territory of another state 'on its own initiative or at the request of the state concerned'.

Going still further, agreements between the Nordic countries as well as the German-French Convention of 1981 concerning nuclear accidents impose on the signatories the duty to issue warnings over events or accidents which might lead to radio-active pollution on the territory of another state, and so do the guidelines in Resolution 2 of the 1982 Montreal Conference of the International Law Association.

These issues are viewed as particularly urgent in West Germany, not only because it is nearer to the accident than other members of the European Community, but also because under Article 38 of the Atomgesetz, the

German Government has to pay out immediate assistance to farmers and traders who suffer adverse consequences. The payments made and likely to be made in Germany are substantial in themselves, but if one tries to add up the damage in other countries, particularly also in Comecon countries, they are likely to amount to billions of pounds, while the long-term damage is almost impossible to assess.

There seems little doubt that the states affected by the consequences of the Chernobyl disaster have claims in damages against the Soviet Union. Enforcement is another matter. Even the strongest claims in international law cannot be satisfied without the co-operation and consent of the Soviet Union. Even if these claims were taken to the International Court of Justice in The Hague, this could help only if the Soviet Union recognised the competence of the court to decide the issue. The Soviet Government is unlikely to do that.

However, a friendly solution by some sort of arbitration or more probably through diplomatic negotiations seems not altogether impossible. In the case of the Soviet Kosmos satellite which crashed in Canada, the Soviet Union agreed to meet half of the Canadian claim for $3m. The claims from the Chernobyl disaster are likely to be so enormous that no more than a goodwill payment can be reasonably expected. But even this may help the worst affected and contribute to the development of a branch of international law in which the Soviet Union should be as much interested as other countries.

There is need to clarify governments' responsibilities for damage caused in other countries by accidents resulting from peaceful use of nuclear energy and to provide ground for new agreements which would make the enforcement of damages easier. Such measures should not be seen as a means of retribution against countries where nuclear catastrophes of the Chernobyl type occur, but rather as an incentive to prudence.

While many governments find it easy to ignore damage caused to their own citizens, an efficient international machinery for adjudication and enforcement of damages caused in another state would be a powerful incentive to take the best possible precautions and to abstain from dangerous experiments.

Notes

1 Published by Stevens & Sons under the title *The Development of Consumer Law and Policy – Bold Spirits and Timorous Souls* p 138.
2 [1983] AC 520, [1982] 3 WLR 477.
3 Speaking in London at a meeting arranged by Barlow, Lyde and Gilbert, solicitors, on 9 April 1987.
4 *Asahi Metal Industry v Superior Court of California, Solano County (real party Cheny Shin Rubber Industrial Co Ltd)* No. 85-693, decided 24 February 1987.
5 Working Paper No. 87 and Consultative Memorandum No. 62, Choice of Law in Tort and Delict (HMSO, £6.25) pp 293.
6 So particularly by Dr Alfred Rest in [1986] Versicherungsrecht 609-620, Heft 25(A), to whom the author feels much indebted.
7 PIC Series A No. 17, p 29 – Factory at Chorzow.

6 The pitfalls of commercial law

The Walrus and the Carpenter – the bad cabbage seed

'If seven maids with seven mops
Swept it for half a year,
Do you suppose,' the Walrus said
'That they could get it clear?'

In the last judgment he delivered on 29 September 1982,[1] Lord Denning gave an optimistic answer to this question. He said: 'The time has come, as the Walrus said, to talk of many things.'

In short staccato sentences he proceeded to deal with the appeal of seed merchants against a High Court judgment awarding damages of £100,000 to farmers whom they supplied with 'cabbage seed' for £192. The merchants did not deny that the seed did not produce any cabbage but claimed that the small print on their contract form limited their liability to £192.

Lord Denning used the opportunity to recount the long struggle of judges to protect the weaker party to a bargain against the hard letter of the contract. He told of the devices to which judges had to resort during the 38 years he had sat on the Bench, striving for clarity and supremacy of justice over the law. Not all, but some battled for these aims throughout the past two centuries, at least since Lord Mansfield, the eighteenth century Lord Chief Justice.

Law is backward looking and the progress of the enlightened judges was uncertain and slow. As recently as in 1980, before the two Securicor decisions,[2] Lord Denning would have felt obliged to get round the small print by saying that the seed supplied was different in kind from that which was ordered, so that the seed merchants were not protected by the limitation clause. However, in the second Securicor case, Lord Wilberforce said: 'Clauses of limitation . . . must be related to other contractual terms, in particular to the risk to which the defending party may be exposed, the remuneration which he receives and, possibly, also the opportunity of the party to insure.' This opened the door to a more direct attack on the unfair limitation clause.

The words of Lord Wilberforce completed the reversal of the 'freedom of contract' doctrine which constrained judges at the time when Lord Denning was called to the bar. Exemption clauses printed in small print on the back of tickets and order forms, catalogues and timetables, were then held to be binding on those who took them without objection. No one ever did object, no matter how unreasonable the exemptions were.

The 'freedom of contract' was freedom for the big man with the printing press. Unable to attack the 'freedom of contract' as an abuse of the weaker party, judges developed a secret weapon called 'the true construction of the contract'. If a ship deviated from the agreed voyage, if goods were stored in the wrong warehouse, if the seller supplied goods different in kind from those ordered, the words of the exemption clause were found by the judges to be not strong enough to exempt from liability.

In 1956 the Court of Appeal took another small step forward, formulating the doctrine of the 'fundmanetal breach': if the big concern was guilty of a breach which went to the very root of the contract, it could not rely on the printed clause to exempt itself from liability. But such open disdain of the 'freedom of contract' displeased the House of Lords. The Law Commission came to the rescue with its report on exemption clauses in 1969. In 1973 the Supply of Goods (Implied Terms) Act provided that a term in a contract of sale is not enforceable if it would not be fair and reasonable to allow it.

So it is no longer necessary to do violence to language and say that the seed supplied was not really cabbage seed. It is now possible to concentrate on the real issue: would it be fair and reasonable to allow the seed merchants to rely on the limitation clause? Lord Denning said that the clause was not negotiated; the farmers could not check the quality of the seed. The seed merchants could insure against the risk. The mistake could not have happened without serious negligence on the part of the seed merchants or their Dutch suppliers. It would not be fair to enable them to escape responsibility for it.

When is plant not plant?

The moral of this piece is that before investing heavily in electrical light fittings, one should make sure that one is within the jurisdiction of right-minded Special Commissioners who recognise such fittings as plant and allow the expenditure against the first year's trading income. There is little point in appealing if they do not.

On 4 March 1982, the House of Lords ruled[3] that electrical light fittings do enjoy such tax advantage. A week later, on 11 March 1982, the Law Lords confirmed[4] that they do not.

It all depends on the meaning of the word 'plant' – perfectly clear to a manager but full of mysteries to lawyers.

The two contradictory judgments were both unanimous. The leading opinion was delivered in the first case by Lord Wilberforce, and in the second by the Lord Chancellor, followed by Lord Wilberforce.

The House of Lords has recently created great uncertainty about the approach to tax avoidance schemes. After a long period of grammatical interpretation favouring the tax avoider, if turned against the tax avoidance industry by shifting the emphasis from forms of transactions to their reality, only to return again to the grammatical method in its recent decisions. The two judgments concerning electrical light fittings illustrate perhaps even better, how the lack of a consistent method adds to the unpredictability of law.

*　　*　　*

The first case concerned the installation of new electrical light fittings and of various pieces of decor and murals, such as plaques, tapestries and pictures in hotels belonging to the Scottish and Newcastle Breweries. In one hotel these included a set of two elaborate metal sculptures representing seagulls in flight.

The Special Commissioners disallowed electrical wiring but held that the fittings, decor and murals, including the seagulls, were plant, in that they created the 'atmosphere' or 'ambience' which could attract customers. The Law Lords agreed with them that all these fittings and artefacts should be regarded as apparatus of the trade, and so, as plant, attracting 100 per cent tax allowance in the first year of its installation.

The word plant, frequently used in fiscal and other legislation, is one of those which have no statutory definition. Lord Justice Buckley said about it not so long ago, in 1979, that it was an ordinary English word which should be interpreted as having the meaning which it would be given under the circumstances of the particular case by a man who speaks and understands English accurately but not pendantically.

In 1981, Lord Justice Oliver added that 'The English speaker must, I think, be assumed to have studied, though, authorities.' Once he had, he forgets about plain English! 'No ordinary man, literate or semi-literate,' said Lord Wilberforce,

> would think that a horse, a swimming pool, moveable partitions, or even a dry dock was plant – yet each of these has been held to be so: so why not such equally improbable items as murals, or tapestries, or chandeliers? . . . In the end each case must be resolved, in my opinion, by considering carefully the nature of the particular trade being carried on, and the relation of the expenditure to the promotion of the trade.

One can hardly quarrel with this, but is it a question of fact or of law?

Lord Lowry said that, though the meaning to be given to the word plant was a question of law for the courts to interpret, there were cases which, on the facts, were capable of decision either way. Evidently, as soon as it became as difficult as that, it was no longer a question of law but a question of fact and degree, and in such a case the decision cannot be upset as being erroneous in point of law, except when the Commissioners misunderstood or misapplied the law.

But how could they err in law if it was all a question of fact? At this point the plain English speaker is lost for the second time. How can you say that the Commissioners drew the wrong conclusions in law when you started with the premise that law does not provide an answer and that the case should be decided on facts, he argues. Whatever the logical weakness of such reasoning, it leaves the courts free to do as they please.

*   *   *

In spite of all this the next appeal was dismissed by their Lordships because they found that the interpretation of the word 'plant' was a question of facts which were better left to the Commissioners. In this case the plant, or non-plant, at issue were electrical light fittings in the Brent Cross Shopping Centre. Having approved, in the case of the hotels, that the fittings were plant in law, the Lords proceeded to uphold that they were not plant in the case of the shopping centre as it was a question of fact.

One would say that in a retail business, good lighting may be as necessary to attract the customers and to create a cheerful ambience as in a hotel, and even more necessary to enable the customers to see the goods they want to buy. Indeed, one could say that special care is necessary to select such lighting in which the materials can be seen in their true colours. Yet, in this case, the Commissioners thought that lighting was not plant. So be it, said their Lordships, but not with any great conviction.

*   *   *

In this second judgment the leading speech was made by Lord Hailsham, the Lord Chancellor. He reminded the House of the words of Mrs Piozzi in 1789 when the word 'plant', applied to a large portion of ground in Southwark destined to the purpose of extensive commerce, caused her some difficulty or, as she said, 'gave me much disturbance from my inability to fathom the meaning of it'.

Lord Hailsham then proceeded to analyse the meaning of 'plant' in the botanical and in the industrial context and in the UK and Australian usage. He wondered whether the whole form in which special cases have recently come to be stated does not add force to the doubts as to the value of the present four-tier system of appeal.

In this sea of uncertainty, Lord Hailsham finally found a tiny island of firm ground on which he could rest his foot and push away the mountain of legal argument which, by now, seemed somewhat overwhelming. He took refuge in the Commissioners' statement that the multiplicity of elements of which the electrical installation consisted prevented them from treating it as a single entity. Lord Hailsham wondered why – in the hotel case the Commissioners did not suffer by any such hang-ups – but thought that the Commissioners entered clearly the realm of fact and degree. There was no question of law. Their Lordships would wash their hands of it. The contemporary ordinary man will be caused no smaller disturbance than Mrs Piozzi suffered in 1789.

Beware of judicial definitions of standard contract clauses

What is the price of nostalgia? To Shell International it was some £35m which the oil company did not recover from its insurers for the loss of crude oil loaded on the *Salem*.[5] The master and crew of the ship, in conspiracy with its owners, loaded the oil in Kuwait, manifestly for a European destination, unloaded almost all of it surreptitiously in a South African port (having previously obtained South African money) and then to cover up the theft scuttled the ship with the remaining oil on the high seas.

Shell relied on an insurance policy, the wording of which can only be explained by nostalgic hankering after things long past. The list of perils insured against read as follows:

> Touching the adventures and perils which we the assurers are contented to bear and do take upon us in this voyage: they are of the seas, men of war, fire, enemies, pirates, rovers, thieves, jettisons, letters of mart and countermart, surprisals, takings at sea . . . and of all other perils, losses and misfortunes,

that have or shall come to the hurt, detriment or damage of the said goods and merchandises, and ship, etc., or any part thereof . . .

Not only does the language sound strange, but even those words which still sound familiar have been qualified by legislation and judicial decisions so that they became 'terms of art' and no longer have their ordinary meaning. Thus, one might come to the conclusion that Shell was covered because the policy insures against thieves, but Rule 9 of the construction of a marine policy in the First Schedule to the Marine Insurance Act 1906 excludes 'clandestine theft or theft committed by crew or passengers'.

One would have thought that Shell could have fallen back on the Institute Cargo Clauses (FPA) which were appended to the policy and of which Clause 8 reads:

> In the event of loss the Assured's right of recovery hereunder shall not be prejudiced by the fact that the loss may have been attributable to the wrongful act or misconduct of the shipowners or their servants . . . .

But marine insurance lawyers agree that this could not apply because it was first added to rectify a 1924 decision of the Lords, excluding scuttling of a vessel from the perils of the sea.

The only peril on which Shell could fall back was the 'taking at sea'. For some 300-400 years this was taken to mean capture or seizure and not embezzlement (in the Scottish, wider meaning) of the cargo by the owners of the ship, its master or its crew. However, in 1969, a Denning Court of Appeal held in *The Mandarin Star* that 'taking at sea' included also conversion of the goods by the master of the ship to the use of the shipowners. When the *Salem* case first came to trial in the High Court, Mr Justice Mustill was bound by *The Mandarin Star* to find in favour of Shell. On appeal, however, Lord Denning recanted and said that his much-criticised judgment in *The Mandarin Star* was based on a misunderstanding. The judgment was made *per incuriam* and should not be binding. Mustill was reversed, and Shell appealed further to the House of Lords.

There, Mr Gordon Pollock QC argued on behalf of Shell that as the insurance cover was taken in the period between 1969 and 1982, when *The Mandarin Star* decision was law, it must be assumed that it was the intention of the parties to insure also against 'taking' by shipowners and their servants. There was no sign of the London and other insurance markets having taken any steps to alter the standard form of policy or any of the institute clauses to circumvent that decision.

The Law Lords unanimously rejected this plea, agreeing with Lord Roskill who said that a decision only a few years old, and now conceded to be wrong, should not be deemed to be right because of the principle of *stare decisis*, especially when it was but a single deviation from several centuries of orthodox doctrine. Moreover, adherence to the heresy would in his view, cause great practical difficulty as endless disputes would be likely to arise whether and when any such 'taking' was a 'taking at sea'.

As a result of this unanimous decision of the Law Lords, it will no longer be possible to rely immediately on the rulings of the Court of Appeal, binding as they are on lower courts and on the Court of Appeal itself. One will have to wait and see whether they are not later declared a heresy.

How long? Twelve years is obviously not enough, particularly if the judgment is criticised by commentators. Would 50 years be more acceptable, or should one extend to judgments the ancient rule that only dead authors are a recognised authority in court?

How much more simple it would have been had the Law Lords said that the insurers could have excluded the consequences of *The Mandarin Star* by adding to the policy after the 'taking at sea' the words 'but not by the owners, master or crew of the ship'.

One can take different views of the doctrine of precedent. Some believe in its virtue – to others its shortcomings are more evident, but few will settle for a compromise under which one has to go to the House of Lords to establish whether a precedent was binding or not at the time a contract was made.

US lawyers accept that

> it must be presumed that if the terms in use in such [insurance] contracts have been judicially construed, that the parties contemplated that construction,[7]

and also that

> the judicial construction . . . made prior to the insurance of a policy will be presumed to have been the construction intended to be adopted by the parties; otherwise the language of the policy should have been modified to make the contrary intent clear.'[8]

The archaic formulation of the Lloyds marine policy will soon be replaced by a modern form and one hopes that the confusion about 'taking at sea', 'barratry' and 'mart' and 'countermart', whatever they may mean, will disappear. But the confusion created by the Lords' decision in the *Salem* is more fundamental and will persist. While we should still believe that the intention of the parties is decisive for the meaning of the contract, we are no longer allowed to believe that when choosing the words to express their intention the parties followed the latest meaning given to the words by judges.

The confusion springs from the Lords' adherence to two contradictory and unreconcilable doctrines: the one says that judicial rulings are binding until reversed by a superior court, and the other that judges do not create law but only uncover it – which means that some of the binding precedents can be non-law and not binding.

Hidden defects – insurance may help where legislation failed

Hidden defects, whether in buildings, other works or legal documents may be caused by breach of contract, lack of professional skill, negligence or other wrongful acts. They are probably bothering more people in England than anywhere else because house ownership is there more widespread. Latent damage cases due to building defects outnumber all others by nearly

5 to 2 in England. And they cause extraordinary legal problems. Until 1986 it was good law that the victim may sue for compensation only within six years from the time when physical damage occurs to the building, although it may not be discovered or reasonably discoverable until later. The defect which ultimately caused the hidden damage may have occurred even earlier.

The law is full of uncertainty because it is difficult to prove when the damage occurred: the plaintiff will argue that the defect in foundations led to structural damage during the last drought, even if this was 25 years or more after the completion of the building, while the architects or builders will maintain that the damage is of an earlier date and remained unnoticed, and certainly unclaimed in court, for more than six years.

The Scots approach is different, counting the period of limitation during which it is possible to sue from the time the plaintiff has, or with reasonable diligence could have, discovered the damage. This agrees with the continental approach, stated with classical lucidity in section 1489 of the Austrian (Maria-Theresian) Civil Code:

> No action for damages can be brought later than three years from the time when the victim learned of the damage and who caused it, whether by breach of contract or otherwise. If the victim did not learn of the damage or who caused it, or if it was the result of felony, the right to sue is extinguished only after 30 years.

Because of the obvious unfairness of a law depriving those who suffer damage which remained hidden for more than six years of all remedies, judge-made law has moved towards starting the period of limitation at the point of discoverability. The Court of Appeal favoured this approach in *Sparham-Souter* ([1976] 1 QB 858) but this was a deviation from the general principle that the period of limitation runs from the accrual of the cause of action. Also, there was no 'long stop', like the 30-year limit in the second sentence of section 1489, and the liability for undiscovered damage could run into perpetuity. The law was felt to be uncertain, unfair, and in some cases unenforceable. The Law Reform Committee was therefore asked in 1980 to recommend what should be the limitation period in negligence cases involving latent defects, other than latent disease or injury to the person.

Before the Committee could make up its mind, the trend towards discoverability was completely reversed by the House of Lords in *Pirelli* ([1983] 2 AC 1). This made it clear that the six-year limitation period runs from the date of the damage, and not from the date of its discoverability, and that if the time runs against one owner, it also runs against all his successors in title.

In its report, presented to Parliament by the Lord Chancellor last November, the Committee tried to soften the harshness of the law in respect of negligence cases generally, not only in the building industry.

Its recommendations led to the enactment of the Latent Damage Act 1986.

The 1986 Act gave house owners another three years from the date when they discovered the damage in which to claim and provided an overriding time limit of 15 years from the date of the wrongdoer's breach of duty, beyond which he could not be sued. This sounds simple, but in fact the statute is unintelligible in the best tradition of English statutory drafting.

Professor Phillip Capper of Keble College Oxford, author of the Latent Damage Act 1986, the first book published on this subject, says that the Act is 'a dense web of barely intelligible inter-related rules (introducing) a range of overlapping and inter-related time periods . . . the Act cannot be understood without extensive knowledge of other relevant pieces of legislation and case law'.

British architects are unhappy: 'In practice the proposal will result in cases coming to trial more than 25 years after the events in dispute,' they say. 'Whatever small benefit may accrue to a few potential claimants and defendants is far outweighed by the added complexity and confusion of rules.'

A better solution might be a three-year period of limitation from the date of discoverability with a long stop running from the completion for a period of 12 years during which the liability of the defendant would start to diminish gradually, say, after six years. During the second half of the period it would fall from 100 per cent to zero.

The whole tangle could be untangled, if viewed as an insurance problem. Architects should be covered by an obligatory indemnity insurance with premium related to the architects past record. If house-owners insured as well, any recovery from architects would be a matter for the insurers. Any disputes should be resolved by arbitration.

Commodity brokers' ill-fated German gamble

It is dangerous when doing business in a foreign country to rely on legal and moral concepts acquired at home – even if the country is so close as West Germany. London commodity brokers seem to ignore, to their own peril, the German disapproval of differential deals, options or futures where no commodities change hands, and only profits and losses calculated on the movement of the price are credited or debited to the customer's account.

German law treats such deals much the same as gambling, so that any claims arising from them are unenforceable. There are, however, certain exceptions. Enforceable debts are incurred by German residents who have 'market capacity', for example, because they are registered merchants.

Rayner-Harwill, acting as agent for J. H. Rayner (Mincing Lane), seems to have opened an account for a Bonn man, MN, without checking whether he was a registered merchant. It seems to have relied on his word. It was agreed, in October 1980, that Rayner (Mincing Lane) would carry out for MN differential deals on the London and US raw material markets, receiving an initial deposit of 1,000 Krugerrands as security. The agreement was in German but provided for the application of English law and the jurisdiction of English courts.

The Bonn client deposited the Krugerrands with the Bank fuer

Gemeinwirtschaft, instructing it as follows: 'The deposit should be delivered to me against a receipt, but only with the agreement of Rayner-Harwill Ltd, London.' Of course this was not a deposit in favour of Rayner-Harwill but merely a deposit by the client which could be blocked by Rayner-Harwill.

Nevertheless, the bank sent to Rayner-Harwill a telex which went beyond the instructions received from its client. It said: 'We confirm that we are holding the 1,000 Krugerrands to the order of Rayner-Harwill Ltd, London, as security against transactions effected by Rayner-Harwill Ltd, on behalf of MN.'

The deals carried out by Rayner on behalf of MN soon resulted in losses, and Rayner asked for a further security. Acting through his limited company, the German client (who had previously dealt in a personal capacity) instructed the bank to provide two guarantees for a total of DM 2.5m.

This the bank did in the following form:

> (With reference to the current business connection between you and the company), we undertake irrevocably to pay on your first demand amounts due to you by (the company) up to a total of (DM 1m and DM 1.5m) against your declaration in writing that (the company) did not pay the required amount when due.

No one seems to have made any fuss, neither then nor later in the courts, that the company had no contractual relationship with Rayner and was unlikely to incur any debts.

However, the parties which were so easy-going as long as they were making agreements fell out completely when the debit balance on MN's account reached DM 2.38m. Rayner asked for a settlement within 14 days and, as no payment was forthcoming, called on the German bank to pay under the two guarantees. The bank did not pay, and Rayner brought an action against it in the High Court in London. The bank's objection, that the dispute was not subject to the jurisdiction of English courts, was rejected by Mr Justice Staughton.

In the meantime, the true dimensions of the case had been unfolding in the German courts where the two Rayner companies predictably lost a legal battle which they fought all the way to the Federal Supreme Court (BGH). They were sued by MN and his company, who asked the courts to order Rayner-Harwill to release to them the 1,000 Krugerrands held by the Bank fuer Gemeinwirtschaft and to order Rayner (Mincing Lane) not to make any demands under the two bank guarantees. They argued that as MN was not a registered merchant, the debts arising from differential deals made on his behalf on foreign markets were unenforceable.

The Federal Supreme Court ruled in 1980,[9] in Case BGH II ZR 269/79, that claims from differential deals were unenforceable in Germany even if the deals were subject to foreign law and binding under its provisions. The Landgericht of Bonn and the Appeal Court of Cologne had no difficulty in concluding that the claim of the two Rayner companies against the German speculator must not be enforced. The two UK companies were ordered to release the gold coin deposit and to refrain from making use of the bank guarantees.

The only straw which the two UK companies were still clutching when they reached the Federal Supreme Court was reliance on section 55 of the Boersengesetz, according to which one cannot reclaim the payment of an unenforceable debt once it has been made. They viewed the security of the Krugerrands and the guarantees as payment of the unenforceable obligation and were fortified in this belief by a BGH judgment of 1971.[10]

However, that judgment was reversed[11] in 1982: a security can now be binding only if it covers stock exchange futures and only if strict formal requirements have been satisfied. Commodity futures are not covered; Rayner-Harwill was rightly ordered, said the BGH, to relinquish the possibility of blocking the return of the Krugerrands to the depositor.

Much the same applied to the bank guarantees. These could not be recognised as payment but only as security for a future payment. The BGH found nothing wrong with the injunction preventing Rayner (Mincing Lane) from claiming payment under the bank guarantees.

One of the defendant's arguments was that the injunction granted by the German courts represented an inadmissable intervention in the jurisdictional sphere of UK courts. The BGH did not agree: the plaintiff did not ask for any penal sanctions to be attached to the injunction, nor were such sanctions threatened by the courts below.

Speculating without risk in Germany

If you have a reluctant but solvent debtor in West Germany – or anywhere else as long as the debt is governed by German law – you stand a good chance of making some extra money, courtesy of the Federal Supreme Court (BGH) in Karlsruhe. All that is needed, is to think of a good speculative share and to tell the debtor how many shares you would buy had you received his money. Should the price drop, you had better forget the whole thing, but should it rise you can tell him that you would now sell the shares you never bought, and ask him to pay you the profit you could have made.

The ruling[12] which makes such profits on imaginary transactions possible is very untypical of the BGH, which has a deserved reputation for common sense and sound legal craftsmanship; but even a master carpenter sometimes cuts himself and this seems to have happened here. The Bonn legislators have been landed with a problem.

A partner expelled from the company by a resolution of the other partners, contested the validity of this resolution, but then agreed to sell his stake in the company for DM 400,000. Subsequently, he sued the company, claiming more money under different headings, and in 1975 obtained a judgment for DM 600,000 plus interest. The plaintiff's claim leading up to this judgment was quantified in the course of a hearing which took place on 21 February 1975 but the sum awarded by the court was received by him only at the end of August 1979.

The former partner, whom we shall call EB (in deference to the wish of the court which does not like names to be disclosed), then brought a second action against the company – this time claiming damages for a loss of profit due to the delay in receiving his money. He submitted evidence that he had informed the company by two letters of 21 June and 14 October 1976 that he would like to buy with the money owned to him a specified number of particular shares for a total amount of DM 368,350.71. He urged the company to let him have the money, but without success.

About a year later, on 16 May 1977 (while the debt was still unpaid) EB informed the company that, had he bought the shares as originally intended, he would have sold them on 11 May 1977, for a profit of DM 31,675.56. He claimed damages for that amount, plus interest. The action was first brought in Dusseldorf, where it was dismissed both in the regional court and in the Appeal Court.

The Appeal Court did not see a sufficient causal link between the delay and the loss of profit on an imaginary speculative deal. Such a link, the court said, could be assumed in speculative deals of that type only when the creditor took steps to proceed with the transaction in the expectation that he would receive the money on the due date, that is before the debtor delayed matters.

It was, however, quite a different matter when the decision to make a speculative deal was taken only when the debtor was already in delay. In such a case, it was impossible to establish how the creditor would have disposed of the money had he received it in time and had the investment been connected with a risk. To allow damages for the loss of a fictitious profit when no risk had been taken would open the door to an arbitrary and uncontrollable increase in the obligation of the debtor, said the court.

This perfectly reasonable conclusion did not, however, satisfy the BGH. Interpreting section 252/2 of the German Civil Code the court said that 'lost profit' was a gain which would probably have been achieved in the usual course of business or, in special circumstances, where measures had already been taken to achieve it. The Appeal was wrong when it thought that the purpose of the provision was to limit the compensation for lost profit to such profit as could be expected at the time of the loss-producing event – here when the debtor began to delay matters.

On the contrary, said the BGH, the purpose of section 252 was to make it easier for the damaged party to prove loss. Consequently, section 252 also provided for gains on transactions which the creditor decided to make while the debtor was already holding up payment. The party claiming damages needed to prove only that there was a probability of profit, had the debtor paid without delay.

The BGH resolutely rejected the Appeal Court's view that to award damages in this case would be to allow creditors to engage in speculation at the expense of the debtor and free of risk to themselves. This would be the case, said the BGH (revealing a great innocence in these matters), only if the probability of profit depended solely on the timing of the purchase and sale of the shares, without taking into account the development of the share price in the intervening period.

If the price of the shares had fallen in the intervening period, said the BGH, a subsequent rise would no longer count. It was necessary to establish how the plaintiff would have behaved in the face of the actual share price development, had he speculated on his own risk.

These were, however, not issues of law but issues of fact, and the BGH decided to return the case to the Appeal Court for retrial in accordance with the new interpretation of section 252. Almost as an after-thought, the BGH pointed out that the Appeal Court should also consider a possible co-responsibility of the creditor for the lost profit, according to section 254. Such a co-responsibility would have existed, had he been in the position to obtain bank credit for the purchase of the shares. If that had been the case, the loss would have been reduced to the cost of the credit.

This seems to be a case which cannot be resolved without some unfairness to one of the parties. However, the restrictive interpretation of section 252 adopted by the appeal court in Dusseldorf seems to be the only practical one. It might be just possible to prove what would have been achieved in the ordinary course of business, and on transactions already initiated, had the money come home when it was due. For the rest, a proper rate of interest ought to be enough.

Good faith and bills of lading

The queue of ships waiting for unloading during the dock strike is likely, sooner or later, to lead to a long line of disputes about who should pay for the cost of waiting known in the trade as demurrage. In this connection a number of old and some new, questions may crop up about the nature of the bill of lading (B/L).

Is the B/L, as a rule signed only by the carrier or on his behalf, an agreement or is it simply a negotiable receipt for the goods? And, even if it is an agreement or confirmation of one, does it bind third parties, such as the consignee?

This problem seemed to worry civil lawyers, including those of the EEC Commission so much that a claim of a mere $334 in damages for a short delivery of a shipment of timber was allowed to take the time of three Belgian courts only to be referred by the Court of Cassation to the European Court of Justice[13] which is responsible for authoritative interpretation of the 1968 Brussels Convention.

CHOICE OF FORUM

The plaintiffs received the shipment of timber under a B/L issued by the defendant carrier. It contained the following clause: 'All disputes relating to the present Bill of Lading should be resolved by the court of Hamburg.' Nevertheless, the plaintiffs sued in Antwerp, where the consignment was unloaded. They insisted that the choice of Hamburg jurisdiction was invalid because it did not satisfy the requirements of Article 17 of the 1968 Brussels Convention.

The Antwerp court accepted jurisdiction and this was confirmed by the Court of Appeal. It was only on further appeal to the Court of Cassation that the two questions concerning the binding nature of the jurisdictional clause were formulated and referred to Luxembourg.

Before the European Court the plaintiffs and the Commission argued that the Hamburg clause could be valid only if expressly accepted both by the shipper and the carrier. The Commission maintained that in interpreting Article 17 of the Convention no account should be taken of general practice and usage. An agreement presumed merely on the strength of usage was not an agreement in the meaning of Article 17. The Commission admitted that the jurisdictional clause might be valid if a continuous commercial relationship had existed between the parties and a denial of the clause by the shipper could not be made in good faith.

The British Government, in its observations to the court, insisted that the issue was of fundamental importance, and not merely a matter of judicial policy. It suggested that the real question was: 'Was the jurisdictional clause included in the Bill of Lading in a manner which shows that a real agreement exists between the two parties, taking into account the principle of good faith?' In the British view an answer to this question could be given only by the national judge on the basis of all the facts of the case.

The court concluded that a B/L clause might satisfy the requirements of Article 17 as confirmation of a previous verbal agreement concerning jurisdiction. Even in the absence of such a previous agreement, it might be sufficient if there existed a current commercial relationship between the parties as all Bills of Lading had the jurisdictional clause pre-printed. It would be contrary to the principle of good faith to claim that the choice of forum expressed in this way was not part of the rules governing a continuing commercial relationship. The clause was also binding on the consignee or other bearers of the Bill of Lading if they succeeded in the shipper's rights and obligations on the strength of the applicable national law.

CONSIGNEE AND DEMURRAGE

Somewhat nearer to home appeared the question whether the consignee or any other holder of the B/L could be made liable for demurrage on the strength of a clause saying that the B/L incorporated the terms of the charterparty. The charterer is, of course, normally responsible for any loss caused to the shipowners by keeping the ship in port longer than agreed, and an arrangement which would shift this responsibility to the consignee who has no control and mostly no knowledge about the movement of the ship would make little sense. Curiously, the Miramar Maritime Corporation,[14] the shipowners, pushed its claim against Holborn Oil Trading, the consignee, all the way to the House of Lords. After having suffered defeat in Mr Justice Mustill's court and in the Court of Appeal, they were told by Lord Diplock that no businessman who had not taken leave of his senses would intentionally enter into a contract which exposed him to a potential liability of that kind, and that this in itself was an overwhelming reason for not indulging in verbal manipulation.

ARBITRATION CLAUSE

But what about the incorporation of an arbitration clause of the charterparty into the B/L? This question was raised before the Italian Supreme Court[15] which held that the incorporation could be effected only by a reference which had a 'perfect relation' with the arbitration clause.

The case before the Italian court concerned a shipment of soya seed which arrived seriously damaged in Venice. The consignee asked the Tribunale of Venice to determine whether the seller, the shipowner or the insurer was liable for damages. Not only the charterparty but also the contract of sale and the insurance policy provided for London arbitration and all three defendants objected to the jurisdiction of Italian courts. Both the Tribunale and the Court of Appeal accepted the objection but, on further appeal, their decision was reversed by the Supreme Court.

Having decided that the claim based on the B/L was not subject to arbitration and should be decided in Italian courts, the Supreme Court held that all three claims should be decided together by an Italian court. That meant a virtual invalidation of the two other arbitration clauses. The court reasoned that both logic and justice demanded that connected suits should be dealt with by the same judge, and that this principle was supported by Article 22 of the 1968 European Judgments Convention. As it was within the power of the court to derogate from the jurisdiction of state courts, it was 'logical' that it could also derogate from the jurisdiction of an arbitration tribunal.

The logic may not be immediately apparent, although the solution might have been sensible in view of the delay the plaintiff would suffer if he had to litigate first in Italy and, if not successful, arbitrate later in London.

When management takeover is a fraud

Sybron's managers who established a mirror-image company for themselves while still in Sybron's employment – taking over at least part of their employer's business without its liabilities – seemed to have persuaded themselves that it is possible to do such a thing and still remain within the law.

They were disenchanted by Mr Justice Walton, whose judgment[16] surveyed the law applicable to this type of commercial conspiracy. It stakes out a demarcation line between the healthy competitiveness of employees who exploit knowledge gained in past employment in a business of their own, and an illegal breach of confidential and fiduciary duties.

The law can hardly be understood without the background against which it was developed by the court. Sybron is an American corporation: in the UK it operated through its subsidiary, Gamlen, with further subsidiaries in the Netherlands, Germany and Italy. In the early 1970s, within the space of about 10 months, all the top managers of the European zone of Gamlen resigned. What on earth had been going on?

The answer provided by the judge was that it was a conspiracy by the managers to take away the chemical cleaning operation of Sybron previously conducted through the European wholly-owned subsidiaries. The conspirators took away customers and employees, adopted the formulation of Sybron's chemical products and the style and content of their leaflets. They took details of pricing policies and knowledge of the precise discounts granted to particular customers, and in this way obtained a 'jet-propelled start' in competition with the 'remnant business' of Gamlen.

On top of all this, Mr W. S. Roques, chief executive of Sybron's European subsidiaries, who, as the judge said, served as the conspirators' look-out man to the last, left the company in September 1973 with a golden handshake and a handsome pension for himself and his wife.

The first question of law which the judge had to answer was whether the conspirators who set up a mirror image business to that of Sybron owed their duties to Sybron or to the subsidiaries by which they were employed. He concluded that, looking at the commercial realities, it was primarily Sybron which was injured, and that Sybron was able directly to claim damages in respect of the organisation as a whole – there was no need to assess separate damages to the individual subsidiaries.

The next important question to be answered was whether the combination followed an unlawful purpose or a lawful purpose by unlawful means. The establishment of a competing business is clearly a lawful purpose, but breach of contract is an unlawful means to achieve it. The breach of contract in the Sybron case was plainly fraudulent. Was it necessary for all conspirators to have full knowledge about all that was intended and/or done by the others?

Using a parallel from criminal law, the judge said that, as the driver of a getaway car waiting patiently in the side street is a conspirator – once the conspiracy has been established – even if he does not know what is actually going on in the bank vaults, then acts done and admissions made by any of the conspirators are acts and admissions which are evidence against the others. But the conspirator must know the facts which make the combination unlawful though there is no need for him to appreciate their significance. Deliberate failure to open his eyes, for fear of what he suspected he would see, was no excuse.

In short, as Mr Justice Goulding said in his judgment of 12 November 1979:

> For servants during their employment and in breach of their contractual duty of fidelity to their master to engage in a scheme, secretly using the master's time and money, to take the master's customers and employees and make profit from them in a competing business built up to receive them on leaving the master's service, I would have thought that commercial men and lawyers alike would say that is fraud.

Mr Justice Walton said that the whole essence of the operation was that the conspirators would compete with Sybron and Gamlen while they, or some, or one of them were still employed. The conspiracy came to an end when there was no conspirator left working for the plaintiffs. As to the individuals, the crucial question was: what was the state of knowledge of those who joined the 'new business' at the time they joined it?

In the end, there was a claim for damages in respect of the conspiracy and another for breach of the contracts of service by the individual conspirators. There was also a claim in relation to the pensions of Mr and Mrs Roques, which they were given in ignorance of the facts. The damages awarded were believed to be the highest so far in an English court.

Notes

1 *George Mitchell (Chesterhall) Ltd v Finney Lock Seeds Ltd*, 29 September 1982.

2 *Photo Production Ltd v Securicor Transport Ltd* [1980] AC 827 and *Ailsa Craig Fishing Co Ltd v Malvern Fishing Co and Securicor*, 26 November 1981.

3 House of Lords, *Commissioners of Inland Revenue v Scottish and Newcastle Breweries Ltd*, judgment 4 March 1982.

4 House of Lords, *Cole Brothers Ltd v Phillips* (Inspector of Taxes), judgment 11 March 1982.

5 See FT Comm LR, 22 February 1983.

6 [1969] 2 QB 449.

7 *Appleman's Insurance Law and Practice* (1976) p 7,404.

8 *Couch on Insurance*, 2d, 15:20.

9 11 ZR 10/83.

10 BGH Z 58, 1.

11 BGH Z 86.

12 Case II ZR 80/82, judgment 29 November 1982.

13 Case 71/73, *Partenreederei ms. Tilly Russ v Haven & Vervoerbedrijf Nova*, FT Business Law Brief, August 1984, p 12.

14 FT Comm LR, 6 June 1984.

15 *SIAT v Société de Navigation Transocéanique and others*, Case No. 6035, Yearbook Commercial Arbitration, vol IX, 1984, p 416.

16 *Sybron Corporation and Gamien v Tocham Ltd and others.*

17 *Sybron Corporation and Another v Barclays Bank plc*, judgment 24 February 1984, (1984) TLR 9 March.

7 The inequality of state and private traders

States and multinational companies

International arbitration of disputes between states and companies is a relatively recent phenomenon. The need for it springs from the increasing role played in the world economy by the multinational corporations on the one hand, and by state traders, the new merchant princes, on the other. To this development, prominent since 1945, has been more recently added an unprecedented expansion of loans granted by banks to foreign states, and the inevitable defaulting on these loans.

The magnitude of these investments, developments and credit operations, makes political involvement of governments unavoidable; indeed, many of these transactions were preceded, stimulated and helped by governmental and intergovernmental actions, pursuing strategic and foreign policy objectives often in combination with an effort to secure export contracts by means of credits, guarantees or aid grants.

We have the unenviable privilege of watching the forces at work which made it true that, as Dr F. A. Mann wrote (*Studies in International Law*, p 239): 'Public international law and private law . . . are branches of the same tree. They apply in conformity with the demands of reasonable justice and practical convenience.'

Unfortunately, these forces seem to be so violent and contradictory at present that it is most difficult to say what is the shape of the tree and of its branches and that at times one fears it might be uprooted altogether.

The combination of commercial and political interests is more evident on the side of the state trader or the government granting or nationalising an oil concession; but it is no less real on the other side where the commercial and political subjects retain separate identities. This would by itself lead to an internationalisation of the contracts in which the relations between countries are materialised. Moreover, though multinational corporations may have more business muscle than the state with which they contract, they are at a disadvantage when it comes to law. These companies need, therefore, to take the settlement of any disputes out of the territorial jurisdiction of the other party to the contract.

Even when it escapes the jurisdictional territory of the contracting state, the company is still at a great legal disadvantage: courts of most countries are slow to accept that the international contract, on the security of which the attainment of a better economic balance between East and West, and between North and South, depends, supersedes the traditional notions of 'sovereign immunity' and of 'act of state'. Hence the need to avoid as much as possible interference of courts in arbitration of disputes arising from such international contracts and the need for their assistance in the enforcement of awards.

But a few years ago such *desiderata* could be brushed aside as pious but unrealistic. Starting with the *Lena Golfields* dispute in 1930, and increasingly with the proliferation of disputes between states and the oil companies after 1950, arbitrators tried to solve these problems with great ingenuity and inventiveness but without much hope of success. A turning point came in 1981 when the conflict between the US and Iran led to the establishment of a truly international arbitration tribunal, and the placing at its disposal of substantial funds for the settlement of claims by the nationals of the US and Iran against the government of the other country.

The experience with this tribunal is likely to encourage similar arrangements in the future. One expects that there will be a great need for them as the financial squeeze is likely to oblige debtor countries to abandon many of their ambitions and unprofitable projects.

However, such better institutional arrangements modelled on the Iran/US Arbitration Tribunal can hardly be attempted unless some measure of agreement is reached on the fundamental issues. Of these the question whether an act of state can be a *force majeure* for a state controlled corporation seems to me to be the most important.

The blurred divide between governing and trading

Two issues concerning the mode of the state in dispute with a company are of crucial importance for the decision to arbitrate and for the possibility of enforcing any award. The first is the question whether the behaviour by which the company is aggrieved can be classified as the state's governmental activity or its commercial activity. The second issue concerns the standing of governmental agencies, often incorporated in the form of trading companies: are they identical with the state, or do they operate at arm's length, so that either the government cannot be held responsible for them or they have a defence of *force majeure* if the government orders them to abandon or otherwise breach their contracts?

By coincidence, the three recent English decisions trying, not quite successfully, to illuminate these problems were all made in the course of reviewing arbitration awards concerning sugar contracts.

The House of Lords decision of 6 July 1978 in *C. Czarnikow v Rolimpex*[1] rests on the finding of the arbitral tribunal that Rolimpex, one of the Polish foreign trade organisations, was an entity with a separate will, following its own commercial strategies and, indeed, that at the critical time it pleaded that it should be allowed to fulfil its contracts.

The House of Lords decision in favour of Rolimpex had been at the time explained by this finding of facts from which the judges could not depart. Subsequently, however, this 'finding of facts' has been given a general validity. Thus, in *I Congreso del Partido*, Lord Wilberforce said, on 16 July 1981:

> State-controlled enterprises, with legal personality, ability to trade and to enter into contracts of private law, though wholly subject to the control of their state, are a well-known feature of the modern commercial scene. The distinction between them, and their governing state, may appear artificial: but it is an accepted distinction in the law of England and other states.

The dangerous consequences of this attitude are evident. In the Rolimpex case several western sugar merchants, of which Czarnikow was one, suffered losses amounting to some £40m, when the Polish government decided not to honour its 1974 sugar contracts after a disappointing sugarbeet harvest and a substantial rise in the world price of sugar. The artificial distinction between the state and its trading agency, which I will call the Wilberforce doctrine I, enabled Rolimpex to claim *force majeure*, and that it fulfilled its obligation to obtain necessary export licences though these were later nullified by an export ban. It is a threat to all contracts with state controlled corporations, but it stands on feet of clay.

The arbitrators and all the judges involved were impressed by the fact that Rolimpex executives manifested a desire to honour the contracts and secured the backing of their immediate boss, the Minister for Trade. They were overruled by the government. Both arbitrators and judges concluded that the distance between the trading organisation and government was sufficiently demonstrated to justify the defence of 'government intervention'.

This conclusion revealed a misunderstanding of the theory and practice of state monopoly of foreign trade in Communist countries. The concepts of 'state monopoly' and 'government intervention' are mutually exclusive – the government cannot 'intervene' in its own business. Not only was the doctrine of the state monopoly of foreign trade entrenched in the constitution of all Comecon countries, but it was one of the few fundamental rules which were meticulously followed in everyday practice. Every state trading agency is linked to the state budget and subject to directions, general or specific, formal or given over the telephone, by the ministry of foreign trade. Only very recently, as part of economic reforms now in progress, have enterprises also outside the sphere of the Ministry of Foreign Trade been allowed direct participation in exports and imports. Moreover, it is quite unthinkable that a foreign trade organisation anywhere in Comecon could conclude contracts concerning the entire exportable surplus of a future harvest without being expressly authorised by its government to do so. Such speculative contracts are always a gamble. The Rolimpex decision of the House of Lords opened to Communist governments the possibility to gamble without any risk – as long as this possibility will not frighten away potential trading partners in the West.

The 'Wilberforce doctrine I' was applied in aid of Cuba in its dispute with IANSA, the Chilean importer of sugar, after it lost the first leg of its defence based on the common law doctrine of sovereign immunity (the State Immunity Act 1978 did not yet apply) which continues to form part of the international law.

The dispute came before English courts twice. The first time in the form of a case stated by the arbitral tribunal which awarded damages to IANSA for breach of contract and wrongful coversion of a cargo of sugar while it was being unloaded in Valparaiso from *Playa Larga*. When about a quarter was discharged, the Communist government of Chile was toppled and the Cuban Government ordered the master to sail out of the port immediately.

The arbitrators also held that IANSA was entitled to damages for breach of contract and the restitution of money paid in respect of cargo on *Marble Islands* diverted from its course to Valparaiso at about the same time. They declined to award damages in respect of the unshipped balance of the contract, holding that it was frustrated by the events in Chile.

Mr Justice Mustill affirmed this award with the exception of damages for the diverted cargo of *Marble Islands*. He held that a commercial contract, which would not be concluded if friendly relations did not exist between the exporting and the importing country, is frustrated if the regime of one of these countries is replaced by another of which the other country disapproves.

His judgment was appealed, but before the appeal could be heard, another case arising from the same events reached the House of Lords – it concerned the arrest of *I Congreso del Partido*, a sister ship of *Playa Larga* and *Marble Islands*, all owned by the Republic of Cuba. IANSA, as owner of the converted and diverted cargo on the two last named vessels had the *I Congreso del Partido* arrested in an English port as security for damages claimed from Cuba. Cuba answered the arrest with a defence of state immunity.

When this case reached the House of Lords, Lord Wilberforce said that, though a state remains capable at any time of acts of sovereignty, the instructions passed on to the master of *Playa Larga* were in the nature of operational instructions issued by the owner of a ship through his agents. They were not an act done *jure imperii*. It followed from numerous decisions of English, US and German courts, that an act done *jure gestionis*, as the instructions to the master were, could not be granted immunity only because it was politically motivated.

> If immunity were to be granted the moment that any decision taken by the trading state were shown to be not commercial, but politically inspired, the 'restrictive' theory (of sovereign immunity) would almost cease to have any content and trading relations as to state-owned ships would become impossible. It is precisely to protect private traders against politically inspired breaches, or wrongs, that the restrictive theory allows states to be brought before a municipal court.

I will call this the Wilberforce doctrine II. It disposed of the view adopted by Mustill J that contracts concluded in view of friendship may be abandoned when the friends fall out. But his judgment was upheld by the Court of Appeal[2] on 2 December 1982 on different grounds. Lord Justice Ackner said that the contract in respect of the cargo on *Marble Islands*, and of the unshipped balance, was frustrated by the antagonism between Cuba and Chile and was made illegal by the Cuban Law No. 1256, passed subsequently. There was no crucial difference between *Rolimpex* and *Cubazucar*, he said. Though it was subject to direction and control by the Cuban government, *Cubazucar* had a separate legal existence. Thus, a judgment undone by the Wilberforce doctrine II was rescued by the Wilberforce doctrine I.

Surprisingly *Rolimpex v Czarnikow* was not even mentioned by Mr Justice Parker when giving judgment in *Atisa v Aztec* in 1983, although this case was eminently suitable for its application. There was even no need in this case to apply the Wilberforce doctrine I as the independence of the exporter of the state was not in doubt. Atisa, the exporter, was a commercial company based outside Kenya, and if Rolimpex could benefit from the *force majeure* clause, Atisa had an even better claim to it. As in the Polish case, also here the government was the monopoly supplier of sugar and decided to repudiate a contract concluded with Atisa because of a bad harvest. However, in contrast with the Polish case, the arbitrators found that the Kenyan government was at all times acting as a private trader. If they failed to deliver to Atisa, this was a private matter and did not entitle Atisa to a defence of *force majeure* against Aztec's claim of damages for breach of contract.

Note. The *Rolimpex*, *Cubazucar* and *Atisa* cases are discussed in greater detail on pp 153–155.

The state and its agents

The willingness of courts to ignore the legislation establishing a state monopoly of foreign trade and to treat trading agencies of Communist countries as separate entities, encourages states occasionally to disclaim responsibility even for the acts of its government departments. Thus, in the Topca/Calasiatic case, the Libyan government objected that arbitral proceedings were instituted against the Libyan Arab Republic while the deeds of concession were concluded by 'The Minister of Petroleum'.

A similar object was made later by the Government of Iran when opposing a claim before the Iran/US Claim Tribunal: the contract in question, it asserted, was not with the Iran government but with its Ministry of Defence.

No need to say that the arbitrator, R. J. Dupuy, did not appreciate the Libyan objections. He held that it clashes with the principle called 'the unity of the State', by virtue of which 'conduct of any State organ having that status under the internal law of that State shall be considered as an act of the State concerned under international law, provided that organ was acting in that capacity in the case in question'.

The question which legal entities operating in France can be considered to be 'emanations' of the Libyan state was studied by 'three wise men' appointed by the Paris Tribunal de Grande Instance presided by Mme Simone Rozes, when lifting attachments of the funds of Libyan companies obtained by LIAMCO under its award which received exequatur from a lower court. The study by the 'three wise men', however, was not concluded at the time the two parties reached a settlement and was, of course, discontinued then.

The most recent positive contribution to this issue can be found in the Algerian (Iran/US) Claims Settlement Declaration of 19 January 1981, which states in Article VII/3: 'Iran' means the Government of Iran, any political subdivision of Iran, and any agency, instrumentality, or entity controlled by the Government of Iran or any political subdivision thereof.

The separateness of a state trader from the state owning and controlling it cannot be justified even on the formal criteria of municipal company law.

The 'lifting of the corporate veil' or 'disregard of legal entity', well established in common law countries, are used particularly when a sole shareholder, or a small group of shareholders, use the corporate veil to enrich themselves on account of the company creditors or contracting parties. The doctrine of 'Durchgriff' serves the same purpose in Germany and Switzerland.

Does this doctrine apply equally to where the sole shareholder hiding behind the corporate veil is a state? The English Rolimpex case would suggest a reluctance to apply it. The US courts, by contrast, see in the fact that the shareholder is a state, an additional reason for disregarding the corporate entity as demonstrated in a series of cases cited by Professor K. H. Bockstiegel.[3]

The international variety of corporations and of rules applying to their 'unveiling' is much greater than that encountered within a single municipal system. The parties to international contracts, and arbitrators, may not be always familiar with the particular domestic law.

The issue is, of course, of particular importance when dealing with the state trading, mainly Communist, countries which operate a monopoly of foreign trade, but whose foreign trading agencies are in the form of separate corporations, sometimes even in the form of companies limited by shares. In the view of Professor Bockstiegel one should start with a presumption that these state trading agencies have a separate and independent existence. This presumption should be maintained in the face of general measures, legislative or executive, adopted by the state as long as these measures are motivated by general considerations – that is not by considerations relating primarily and mainly to a contract which the government wishes to avoid. Such general measures should justify a defence of *force majeure* on the part of the state trading agency. However, the presumption of separate identity of this agency should be abandoned as soon as the measures taken by the state are addressed to the particular contract or, at least, are clearly motivated by a desire to avoid its consequences. Such specific measures should, therefore, not be allowed to trigger a *force majeure* clause.

This view may sound well in theory, but is useless in practice, as even measures specifically designed for the evasion of contractual obligations will always be disguised and presented as being of a general nature. Moreover, even a general measure promoted by a bad harvest, and appropriate for the needs of the internal market, may be quite unnecessary in the international context when the commodity to be delivered under contract in question is available on the world market and can be bought there either by the state trading agency or by the other party which then has a claim for any difference in price in comparison with the contract.

One can, therefore, conclude that it would greatly simplify matters if it was accepted that the rules of public international law prevent states from excusing, by legislation or executive measures their own breaches of contracts concluded by themselves or their agencies.

State traders and the rules of the game

There is a general consensus that the state trading corporations should benefit from the same rules as corporations owned privately, and in particular from the recognition of their separate legal entity – as long as they observe the rules of the game. In the vast majority of their dealings the state traders do observe the rules – they could hardly expect to be accepted as business partners if they did not.

The same practical necessity dictates that courts should not hesitate to accept evidence disproving the assumption of separateness from the state and pull down the corporate mask if the state disowns its trading agency in order to avoid contractual obligations.

The principle that a state may not abuse legal technicalities to avoid its obligations was recognised by the Permanent Court of International Justice (PCIJ 1926 A 7, 30, and 1930 A 46, 167), and by courts in the US and West Germany. But even specific legislation designed to avoid contractual obligations is from time-to-time respected by national courts – for example Swiss.[4]

In a dispute concerning an abandoned project of hotel and tourist development agreed between *South Pacific Properties and Egoth*, the Egyptian state agency for tourism,[5] the arbitral tribunal held that Egyptian legislative and administrative acts which made the project impossible did not relieve Egypt from its liability for breach of contract which its government endorsed.

Many of the great arbitrations between state and private traders concerned concessions for the exploitation of mineral resources granted by the host state to a foreign company. Such disputes are invariably about a unilateral abrogation or modification of the concession by the government. The crucial issue before the arbitral tribunal can in most cases be boiled down to the question: which substantive law applies? If it is the domestic law of the host country, the foreign company has lost its case. It can only win if the concession contract can be brought, either under the public international law, or, unlikely, under the law of another state which does not recognise nationalisation or sequestration without compensation, and where the execution of any favourable award is not barred by sovereign immunity.

Public international law would, for all practical purposes, apply when the parties have agreed at least that the domestic law of the host country should apply insofar as it is not contrary to generally accepted principles of law, in which case it should be superseded by these principles or, better still, by the rules of public international law. The minimum safeguard is probably that which was used in the *Lena Goldfields* concession which was made subject to 'any present or future Soviet legislation' with the exception that the Soviet government may not modify the contract unilaterally.

No such exception was included in the concession contract between Saudi Arabia and the Arab American Oil Company (Aramco). When it came to the dispute, the arbitral tribunal, chaired by Professor Georges Sauser-Halle, held that as the Saudi Arabian law did not previously contain any specific rules for the exploitation of oil deposits, the 1933 Concession

Agreement 'had the nature of a constitution'. The state, said the tribunal in its 1958 award, had the legal power to forbid itself to withdraw certain rights which it had granted.[6]

This reasoning seems to be somewhat thin on the ground, but the tribunal was even more daring when it concluded:

> Lastly, the tribunal holds that public international law should be applied to the effects of the Concession, when objective reasons lead it to conclude that certain matters cannot be governed by any rule of the municipal law of any state, as is the case in all matters relating to transport by sea, to the sovereignty of the state on its territorial waters and to the responsibility of states for the violation of their international obligations.

The 'legal' acrobatics which the Aramco tribunal was obliged to perform to arrive at a fair award taught the next generation of lawyers to draft concession agreements more carefully. The Libyan concessions, for example, were at first drafted with a clause that the contract was governed by Libyan law insofar as this agreed with the 'principles of international law'. In more recent concessions the clause contains the further provision that in the absence of such conformity reference should be made to 'general principles of law'.

Such a clause enabled Professor Rene-Jean Dupuy to hold in the *Topco/ Calasiatic*[7] case that the legal order from which the binding nature of the contract derived was international law, and that the law which governed the contract was the two-tier system provided by the parties – the first tier being Libyan law as long as it was not contrary to international law, and the second tier, the general principles of law.

The well-established principle of public international law that a state cannot avoid its international obligations by reference to its municipal law is likely to remove the many problems damaging to trade, which originate from the contradiction between the commercial and the sovereign activities of a state whenever its contractual obligations are subject to a municipal law, even if this is not its own.

The question may be asked whether a private party can choose public international law to govern its contract, whether it can in this way promote itself to a level normally reserved for sovereigns. Dr Francis Mann gives the following answer:

> Nothing prevents a contract between the German state and a Dutch firm to be submitted to French law. Similarly, the fact that one party is not a state should not prevent the contract from being submitted to public international law.[8]

This view is also supported by most arbitration awards concerning oil concessions, but there are more objections to be dealt with. The 1969 Vienna Convention on the Law of Treaties, by its Article 46, gives to a state the possibility to escape its contractual obligations if their fulfilment would be a manifest violation of an internal law of fundamental importance. Nationalisation of industry may, of course, be taken for such an internal law of fundamental importance, but in that case also the other rule of public international law would apply which requires fair compensation to be paid for the nationalised property.

Enforcement of awards and sovereign immunity

When it comes to enforcement of awards made against a state or its trading company, courts will hesitate to act; they fear – though they rarely admit it – that it may have unpleasant consequences for their own government or banks if they treated a foreign sovereign too harshly. Common law countries were particularly slow to abandon the doctrine of absolute sovereign immunity and relapsed into it gladly – but civil law courts, in Switzerland for example – were no less ingenious in achieving the same end. No one, however, displayed greater judicial inventiveness to protect foreign sovereign debtors when it suited domestic banks than the US Appeal Court for the Second Circuit, in the Portorican debt case. For a short time it made New York forum and law highly suspect for the creditors in international loan agreements, but soon recanted, reversing its own judgment.

The restrictive interpretation of sovereign immunity – that in civil and commercial matters a sovereign is a private person in another's territory – was adopted in civil law countries in the course of the 80 years preceding 1960, when it was also embraced by Japan.

The US courts had been moving towards excluding immunity in commercial issues since 1952, but the exclusion was completed only in 1977 by the Federal Sovereign Immunity Act. In the UK the restrictive theory of sovereign immunity was first recognised by the Privy Council in the *Philippine Admiral* in 1975, but its definitive absorption by the common law was achieved only by Lord Denning's judgment in *Trendtex*, approved by the House of Lords in *I Congreso* in 1982. In the meantime Parliament adopted the State Immunity Act of 1978, which the courts have now interpreted for the first time in *Alcom v Republic of Colombia and others.*[9] At issue was whether a foreign government's bank account in the UK may be frozen by the courts, to secure the payment of the foreign government's commercial debts. Mr Justice Hobhouse said 'no'. Sir John Donaldson's Court of Appeal said unanimously 'yes', and the Law Lords, again unanimously 'no'.

The result is that foreign states' bank accounts will be open to enforcement of judgments only if the foreign governments' lawyers are particularly dim or negligent.

The Swiss courts recognise in principle that sovereign immunity may not be claimed for a state's acts of a commercial nature or by its public or state-controlled corporations but the Federal Supreme Court developed two other obstacles to enforcement of awards or judgments.

One is the rule that assets of one state corporation must not be seized to satisfy a claim against another.

The other, more serious, obstacle is known as the requirement of 'Binnenbeziehung'. This means that Swiss courts will approve the enforcement in Switzerland of a judgment or award against a foreign state or its corporation only if the obligation was contracted or was to be performed in Switzerland. The assignment of a foreign private party's claim to a Swiss resident and even less the mere location of the debtor's assets in Switzerland, is not enough. The location of the arbitral tribunal in Switzerland is no help in this matter.

Thus, in the *Liamco* case the Swiss Federal Supreme Court lifted nine attachment orders against Swiss banks holding Libyan assets because the award 'lacked sufficient domestic relationship'.

In the *Bangladesh* case,[10] this court refused to recognise an award against the Bangladesh state though this state dissolved the debtor corporation by administrative measures which had the sole purpose of preventing the exposure of the corporation to arbitration. The court said that it would have decided differently if the claimant was a Swiss creditor: in such a case the court would have found it necessary to rectify those consequences of foreign law which were incompatible with the fundamental principles of justice respected in Switzerland – in the usual shorthand it would have admitted the objection of public policy.

In this connection it should be noted that in *Arab Republic of Libya v Wetco Ltd*,[11] the court said it could not correct the effect of foreign laws by means of the public policy exception when the foreign state did not act with a discriminatory purpose as it did in the Bangladesh case. *Wetco* contended that LINOCO was an *alter ego* of the Libyan state and that it was consequently bound by the arbitration agreement concluded with LINOCO – a problem which appeared again in the already mentioned *South Pacific Properties*.

This attitude favourable to the state whose trading agency defaulted was further reinforced by the passage of the 1981 Swiss Federal Enforcement and Bankruptcy Bill restricting pre-trial attachment to the assets directly owned by the foreign state trader. The measure would exclude any recourse to the assets of the foreign state or of its other corporations. On the other hand, the proposed code of Swiss private international law could preclude a successful pleading by a foreign state or its corporation of immunity or non-arbitrability on the basis of its domestic law.

Rolimpex and Cubazucar – call for legislation

The sugar cases – *Rolimpex* and *Cubazucar* – have already been discussed but there seems to be need to point out the confusion which ought to be removed by legislation.

In a monumental judgment written as a text-book Mr Justice Mustill held, in February 1980, that commercial contracts which could not have been concluded had friendly relations not existed between the exporting and importing country, were frustrated if the regime of one of these countries had been replaced by another of which the other government disapproved. This ruling transposes into the realm of politics the doctrine that the intention of the parties, at the time a contract is concluded, is of overriding importance for its interpretation. Such extension of this perfectly sound doctrine offers to state traders the possibility of avoiding commercial obligations under the pretext of political necessity.

The doctrine that commercial contracts can be cancelled for foreign policy reasons with retroactive, and extraterritorial effect, is contrary to the legal policy of the UK and of other major countries of Western Europe. It was successfully opposed when the US prohibited the Siberian pipeline contracts and tried to prevent European companies from fulfilling them.

Dealing earlier[12] with the arrest of a Cuban ship connected with the now decided dispute, Lord Wilberforce said that sovereign immunity is now not granted in respect of commercial activities of a foreign state. He said 'it was precisely to protect private traders against politically inspired breaches or wrongs that the restrictive theory of sovereign immunity allowed states to be brought before a municipal court.' Three Law Lords (though not Lord Wilberforce) held on that occasion that Cuba could be responsible for the conversion of sugar loaded for Chile and diverted on the high seas to Vietnam.

However, Mr Justice Mustill's judgment was now confirmed by the Court of Appeal. In view of what the Lords said on the same day in *Hannah Blumenthal* about frustration – that it could not be brought about by the fault or default of the parties, the reasoning in the Cuban case had to be changed, so as to emphasise an artificial distinction between the government and the state trader. 'It is accepted,' said Lord Justice Ackner, 'that they [Cubazucar] are not an emanation or a department of the Cuban state and that they have an independent legal existence.' He relied on the House of Lords decision in *Czarnikow v Rolimpex*[13] – a case in which Poland failed to deliver sugar to British and other western importers. The Czarnikow doctrine enables the government, which makes a contract in the hope of making profits, to get out of the contract if the market turns against it, claiming political motives or economic necessity. It puts it in the fortunate position of being able to pose as *force majeure* when reneging on its obligation.

The doctrines laid down in *Cubazucar* and *Rolimpex* are masochistic, bad for business and contrary to the public interest. They should be removed by Parliament.

Atisa v Aztec – a sane decision

Perhaps it was just a product of the hot summer, but should the conclusions reached by Mr Justice Parker in *Atisa v Aztec*[14] survive in the appellate courts, something good may come out of them.

The remarkable thing which should not be overlooked by commodity dealers and their legal advisers is that one of the precedents on which Mr Justice Parker turned his back was the infamous case[15] of *Czarnikow v Rolimpex* which enabled state traders to gamble on the commodity markets without running any real risk.

In that case Rolimpex, a foreign trade organisation, fully owned and controlled by the Polish state, successfully claimed that the *force majeure* clause in the Refined Sugar Association's contract relieved it of all contractual obligations when the Polish Government decided not to export sugar which it said was needed on the domestic market. The arbitrators, the commercial court judge, three appeal judges, and five Law Lords all agreed that, although Rolimpex was an organisation of the state, it was not so closely connected with the Government as to be unable to rely on 'Government intervention' under the *force majeure* clause.

They also held that it fulfilled its obligation to obtain the necessary export licences even if these were later nullified. On this point, however, Lord Justice Lane, as he then was, and Lord Salmon dissented. They thought that the obligation to obtain an export licence was met only if the export licence remained valid until required to pass the goods through customs.

The case before Mr Justice Parker was similar in almost every respect, and the point on which it differed made it even more suitable for the application of the *Rolimpex* doctrine than that case itself. The dispute was between Atisa which sold to Aztec 13,000 to 14,000 tons of Kenyan white sugar. Unlike Rolimpex, Atisa was an independent commercial company. It was based outside Kenya, and its dealings with the Kenyan Government were at arm's length. Its contract with Aztec was dated 24 January 1980 and, before signing it, Atisa agreed a corresponding contract with the Kenyan government, which was the monopoly supplier of Kenyan sugar to the market. This verbal contract was subsequently replaced by a formal contract, signed on or after 25 January. Delivery was agreed for April 1980.

On 20 March, however, Kenyan newspapers reported that the national assembly had passed a resolution recommending that no surplus food should be exported without presidential or cabinet authority. In spite of this, the Ministry of Commerce wrote to Atisa on 11 April, assuring it that the ministry had every intention of fulfilling the contract and proposing a postponement of the shipment to the second half of June 1980 because one of the sugar refineries had been shut by a fire and heavy rains had reduced production.

Within a week this was contradicted by a decision of the Kenyan Cabinet which approved an export order for 14,000 tons, and directed that all other contracts, including that with Atisa, should be cancelled.

The Kenyan authorities declared that the contract was not made with the authority of the Government, and had not been signed by an authorised person. Atisa informed Aztec, the buyers, who initiated arbitration in December 1980.

Though the case was a replica of *Rolimpex*, the arbitrators dealt with it differently. The sellers' defences of *force majeure*, frustration, premature termination of contract and waiver by the buyers all failed. Atisa asked for leave to appeal on all four points, but was granted leave only on the frustration point. On this, the arbitrators had little to say: 'The sellers have not shown that the contract became impossible of performance.' When the case came before Mr Justice Parker it was argued on behalf of the sellers that, when concluding the contract, the two parties had in mind a monopolist supplier, the Kenyan Government, and that its failure to supply the sugar constituted frustration because it was due to an entirely unforeseeable change in government policy for reasons of state.

There was no question that Atisa was not an 'emanation' of the Kenyan Government. The arbitrators decided that the Kenyan Government was acting as a private trader which found it necessary for internal reasons to withhold performance. In their view that did not amount to *force majeure*, still less to 'government interventions'. If the sellers' supply contract was unauthorised and invalid, that was a private matter between them and the Government. The fact that the Government was the sole supplier of Kenyan sugar did not excuse the sellers from delivery to Aztec.

The judge said there was no finding in the award that, when making the contract, the parties had in mind that the Government was the sole source of supply. He refused to infer that it was in their minds. Though the arbitrators were not asked the right questions, he would have reached the same decision. There was, in his view, no change in the law, and nothing in the nature of a failure or destruction of the subject of the contract. At all times an export licence was required, and the risk of it being refused was upon the sellers.

There is, of course, a formal difference between the two judicial decisions: *Rolimpex* deals with *force majeure*, and *Atisa* with frustration. But these words change nothing of commercial substance. In both cases the background was the rising price of sugar on the world market. In such a situation sellers look for an opportunity to get out of old contracts. In both, the Government claimed a shortage of domestic supplies, probably rightly. In both, the Government could have bought on the world market, as any other trader who sells short. The approach adopted by Mr Justice Parker will be seen as a great improvement by the trade.

The Colombian Embassy Account – State immunity in civil and common law

The question whether a foreign government's bank account in the UK may be frozen by the courts, to secure the payment of the foreign government's commercial debts, was described by Lord Diplock as of outstanding international importance. He said so on 12 April 1984 when the House of Lords unanimously reversed[16] an equally unanimous judgment of the Court of Appeal,[17] delivered by Sir John Donaldson, Master of the Rolls, that the answer to this important question should be affirmative.

Sir John Donaldson's judgment brought a step forward the gradual restriction, over the past 100 years, of the immunity of sovereigns engaged in business in a foreign country. What was an exceptional occurrence in the nineteenth century has now become of very great practical importance.

The decision of the House of Lords was a step back, depriving the 1978 State Immunity Act of much of its bite and likely to make the enforcement of commercial judgments and arbitral awards more difficult.

Alcom, a company supplying security equipment to the Colombian embassy, obtained a default judgment against the Republic of Colombia, and a *garnishee* order on the embassy's account with a London bank. The default judgment had in the meantime been set aside, but the appeal on the question whether a sequestration of a foreign embassy account was possible continued because of the importance of the issue.

International law was cited in aid of the reversal of the *garnishee* order, first by Mr Justice Hobhouse, and again when he was confirmed to have been right by the House of Lords when Lord Diplock said that a judgment of the German Federal Constitutional Court in the *Philippine Republic* case of 13 December 1977 was wholly convincing and particularly helpful because it decided a similar dispute by reference to public international law. It may, therefore, be useful to attempt a brief timetable of developments in this field as an indication of the general direction in which the law of nations moves.

As far as easily accessible reports go, the principle of international law, according to which in civil and property matters 'a sovereign is a private person in another's territory', was applied in Belgium by the Appeal Court of Ghent in 1879, and in Italy by the Florentine Court of Cassation in 1886. Between 1893 and 1909 the Civil Cassation Court of St Petersbourg made a series of decisions to the effect that foreign governments do not enjoy sovereign immunity in commercial matters. In 1907 this principle was adopted in Austria and in 1920 the Austrian Supreme Court, dealing with a builder's claim against the Turkish embassy in Vienna, ruled out the granting of sovereign immunity in commercial matters.

The Swiss Federal Court rejected a claim to absolute immunity in 1918, and in 1927 the Swedish Government proposed that in a codification of international law immunity should not be granted in commercial matters. In 1960 the Japanese Government made a declaration in favour of excluding immunity in commercial cases, and in the same year this view was adopted by the Consultative Committee of the Asian and African States. The Austrian decision of 1920 had an echo in a 1963 judgment of the German Constitutional Court in an action brought by a central heating contractor against the Iranian embassy.

Sovereign immunity has proved much more resistant to change in common law countries. The US courts had been moving towards excluding immunity in commercial issues since 1952, but the exclusion was completed only in 1977 by the Federal Sovereign Immunity Act. In the UK the restrictive theory of sovereign immunity was first recognised by the Privy Council in the *Philippine Admiral* in 1975, but its definitive absorption by the common law was achieved only by Lord Denning's judgment in *Trendtex*, approved by the House of Lords in *I Congreso* in 1982. In the meantime Parliament adopted the State Immunity Act of 1978, which the courts have now interpreted for the first time in the Colombian Embassy case.

This is not the place to analyse in detail the reasoning by which Lord Diplock and Sir John Donaldson reached such different results. When the convoluted text of the Act is unwound, it appears that a foreign state's property is immune against enforcement of a judgment if it is not used for commercial purposes, and that a declaration by the ambassador that it is not so used shall be accepted as sufficient evidence unless the contrary is proved. Such a declaration was delivered by the Colombian ambassador, but the Court of Appeal held that it was disproved by the fact that the bank account was used to pay for air tickets and loans to stranded citizens which, in itself, was not an exercise of sovereign authority.

In taking the immediate application of the money rather than its ultimate aim, the Court of Appeal judgment was firmly based on the House of Lords decision in *I Congreso*. It could have also referred to the 1975 Frankfurt Landgericht judgment in the Nigerian cement case, when it was held that a letter of credit was commercial by its very nature, and its purpose irrelevant. The same can be said of a bank account.

Lord Diplock, by contrast, considered the ultimate purpose of the account and, in interpreting the 1978 Act, considerably reduced the possibility of disproving the ambassador's certificate. He held that the bank account was safe from execution 'unless it can be shown by the judgment creditor . . . that [it] was earmarked by the foreign state solely (save for *de minimis* exceptions) . . . for commercial transactions [such as] documentary credits for goods sold to the state . . .'

The result is that foreign states' bank accounts will be open to enforcement of judgements only if the foreign governments' lawyers are particularly dim or negligent.

Settebello – when a friendly government is accused UK courts look firmly the other way

---

The tanker ordered by Settebello, the Liberian outpost of the Thyssen group, from Setenave, the Portugese state shipyards, was to be delivered originally by 31 January 1978. Article 6 of the contract provided that in case of delay exceeding 12 months, the purchaser would have the option to rescind the contract. However, the delivery date was extended several times, finally until 30 April 1982, and it was provided that if the vessel was not completed in all respects on that date, Settebello should be entitled to terminate all its obligations by a written notice and that the shipyard would repay previous instalments amounting to some $11m.

During the period of the delay, the market was becoming glutted with tonnage so that Settebello probably could not have made any use of the tanker if delivered. Its market value fell from the agreed contract price by about one third. There was no doubt, therefore, that Settebello would make use of the cancellation clause if the tanker was not delivered by 30 April.

At this point, the Portuguese Government stepped in like a *deus ex machina* and a mere 10 days before the cancellation date enacted the decree-law No. 119/82. Though it was drafted in general terms, it was in fact tailor-made to solve the predicament of the state shipyards. It applied only to contracts concluded by companies later declared by the government to be 'in critical economic situation' and only to contracts governed by Portuguese law. The decree gave a Portuguese company the right to avoid cancellation for delay in delivery but not cancellation for any other reason.

The cancellation clause could be avoided under the decree by a declaration made by the company that it would deliver within a further two years. As a fine detail, the decree provided that such a declaration by the Portuguese company would be effective from the day it was posted – in contrast with the general rule of Portuguese law which makes communications effective only from their receipt – a provision included, no doubt, because of the short time available to the shipyard.

After it had served its purpose, the decree was never again invoked. It has been publicly referred to in Portugal as the Setenave decree.

Settebello never recognised the pseudo-legislative intervention into its contractual rights. It insisted on the legality and effectiveness of its cancellation notice and claimed repayment of the $11m already paid. Setenave on its part claimed that the cancellation notice was illegal and asked for $31m plus interest. After about two years it sold the tanker to another party for $20m.

The dispute between the two parties came before Dutch arbitrators. Another dispute between Settebello and the Banco Totta and Acores which guaranteed the performance of the contract by the Portuguese party came before the English courts. Their attitudes to the preliminary legal issue concerning the intervention by the Portuguese Government could not be more different.

The Dutch arbitrators concluded that

> to give effect to the decree-law would be to deprive Settebello, without compensation, of a contractual right to cancel for the default of Setenave, a shipbuilder whose delays had already placed it in breach of contract well before the decree-law was passed. It would equally deprive Settebello of its right under Article 11(b) of the contract to recover some US $11m with interest in respect of instalments already paid by it. No compensation is granted by the decree-law for such losses.

The arbitrators pointed out that the decree-law was no enactment of general effect postponing the rights of all creditors like a moratorium. It was designed to destroy the right of Settebello to cancel the contract for failure by Setenave to deliver and to recover the $11m it had paid. Though worded in general terms, it struck at no-one else. The award in favour of Settebello, said the arbitrators, was the only one compatible with elementary canons of equity.

*   *   *

In the meantime the action against the guaranteeing bank[18] had its run in England.

English courts have been traditionally reluctant to sit in judgment over the actions of foreign governments. They have retained longer than judges in any other country an exaggerated respect for foreign sovereigns entering the market place. One reason for this might have been that the principle of sovereign immunity helped the UK when it faced a number of actions as a result of wartime sequestrations made under the 'trading with the enemy' legislation. Another reason might have been the Foreign Office's distaste for vulgar business interests souring relations with friendly countries.

However that was, a turn came with the passage of the Sovereign Immunity Act. In 1979, in the dispute between Czarnikow and the Polish state trading organisation Rolimpex, although the House of Lords decided in favour of the state trader, Lord Wilberforce said that if a foreign government were taking action purely in order to extricate a state enterprise from contractual liability, such action might be denied the character of government intervention. This, he added, would require clear evidence and definite findings.

Such evidence and definite findings about the nature of the decree by which the Portuguese Government interfered with the contract between Setenave, its shipyards, and Settebello were required when Settebello sued Banco Totta and Acores in the High Court over a guarantee to pay £25m in connection with the Portuguese 'shipyards' failure to deliver. However, Mr Justice Hurst, before whom this case was brought, did not feel the same way as Lord Wilberforce. He said that to grant requests to obtain evidence in Portugal that the decree was made at the initiative of the shipyard would be meddling in the legislative business of a friendly power. The plaintiff's interests, he said, had to yield to a higher legal principle.

Mr Justice Hurst was confirmed by the Court of Appeal and the House of Lords refused to grant to Settebello leave to appeal, thus indirectly confirming the Court of Appeal decision.

Such legal policy is bound to cause more difficulties for British firms in the future and to render British practice out of tune with that of other countries. Another unwelcome consequence will be that international arbitrations, which are very often about disputes between a private company and a government-owned enterprise, will continue to avoid London.

ITC – a divided Court of Appeal finds member government immoral but not obliged to pay

The Court of Appeal's principal judgment in the series of actions brought against the International Tin Council (ITC) left London traders and banks with some £900m of unsatisfied claims against the insolvent international body. Half of the burden may well fall on the Inland Revenue, assuming that the unlucky creditors will be able to deduct the loss from their profits.

However, the blow to the business community's confidence in the ability of UK courts to uphold commercia claims against defaulting governments cannot be expressed in figures. Its consequences are certainly greater than the financial loss – and will not be undone by a possible future out-of-court settlement.

The judgment in *J. H. Rayner (Mincing Lane) and others v DTI and others* (FT Law Report, 3 May 1988) which cleared the 22 governments of liability for the debts of the insolvent ITC, revealed a fundamental fault in the London system combining the trading and banking practice as well as the law applicable to it. If only the judgment was perverse, the House of Lords will be able to provide a remedy on appeal. If, however, it finds the judgment right, the perversity is entrenched in the entire system where confidence extended to trading governments has no justification in the law.

As Sir Geoffrey Howe, Foreign Secretary, once said, 'If the system is perverse, the law on which it is based comes into disrepute.' In the case of the ITC, the British government by siding with the unwilling debtors, has much contributed to the perversity of the system, and one suspects that Foreign Office considerations for the interests of some of the governments reluctant to pay – the British Government was willing to pay its share – were at the back of this decision.

Unfortunately, the case is in no way isolated. It is only the last in a series of UK courts' decisions which favoured state traders not only unfairly but also in contradiction to what is generally assumed to be the law. The UK courts' tendency to overlook that princes entering the market must be treated on an equal footing with private traders, became evident in the Polish and Cuban sugar disputes, and later in the case of Uganda Holdings, Portuguese Shipyards, the Colombian Embassy London account and Spanish Rumasa trade marks. The rejection by the Court of Appeal of claims against member states of the insolvent International Tin Council, however, has even wider consequences going beyond the privileged treatment of state traders. It can be seen as a reversal of the general assumption underlying not only UK law, but also commercial laws of all industrialised countries, that companies and partnerships can limit their liability towards creditors only by entering such limitation into a public register, showing it on their letterhead and complying with whatever legislation has been made for the protection of creditors of such limited companies.

Should the Law Lords confirm the Court of Appeal, there will be urgent need for introducing legislation which would make it clear that governments wishing to trade in the UK with limited liability can do so only by incorporating their agencies as prescribed by UK company law. At the same time and by the same legislative act, the State Immunity Act should be re-stated in a way which would remove the restrictive interpretation given to it by the Court of Appeal judgment.

There is, however, some hope that such legislative action will not be necessary. The Court of Appeal was disunited on the main issues and only one of the three judges, Lord Justice Kerr, rejected all liability on the part of the member states. The other two accepted liability in international law but one of them, Lord Justice Ralph Gibson, held that the claim against the member governments could be pursued only by the British Government in the International Court of Justice in the Hague. In other words, that it cannot be enforced by English courts. In this way the two Appeal judges, each for a different reason, prevailed over Lord Justice Nourse who alone held both that the member states are liable and that the claims are enforceable against them in English courts.

The Appeal judges felt that the ITC case represents a novel problem on which no specific authority exists. They found the behaviour of the ITC and of the member states abhorrent, verging on fraud, particularly in view of the fact that the member states instructed the buffer stock manager to continue trading when it must have been known to them that the ITC was insolvent. They did not mince or spare words to express their moral indignation, yet when it came to law they fell collectively as short of the task as the debtors. Though the judgment quotes Lord Simonds' dictum (in *National Bank of Greece and Athens v Metliss* [1957] AC 509 at 525) that in the absence of authority binding the court the question is simply, what does justice demand, the Appeal judges, with the exception of Lord Justice Nourse, paid no attention to their own appreciation of justice, not to speak of what the international business community considers to be just.

The principle of unlimited liability is firmly anchored both in English and in international law. It springs from the fundamental axiom that obligations should be kept, without which contractual law of any legal system would simply disappear into thin air. From this it follows that the fundamental duty of living up to one's obligations can be restricted only by specific and explicit measures, which may be either mandatory provisions of a statute or reservation made by parties in a contract. This underlying principle of law comes to the surface in section 5 of the Limited Partnerships Act 1907, which states:

> Every limited partnership must be registered as such in accordance with the provisions of this Act, or in the default thereof it shall be deemed to be a general partnership and every limited partner shall be deemed to be a general partner.

And section 4(2) of the Act goes on defining a 'general partner' as one who is liable for all debts and obligations of the firm.

The law could not be clearer, yet Lord Justice Kerr reasoned that the Headquarters Agreement between the UK and ITC interposed between the members of the group and third parties a legal entity and that this meant that member states had no liability for the contracts made by the ITC, adding that English law does not know the institution of Scottish partnership. This reasoning contradicts the 1907 Act which enables a partnership to have rights and obligations of its own and makes it therefore into a legal entity of the same sort as the partnership in Scottish law and in the civil law systems.

The parallel in German law is the 'open commercial partnership' which like the English partnership and any English body corporate can acquire property, rights and undertake obligations, sue and be sued, but for whose obligations the partners are jointly liable to creditors personally. Section 128 of the German Commercial Code goes even further: the personal and joint liability of the partners is mandatory on all open commercial partnerships and any agreement to the contrary is ineffective against the creditors. This is not only an academic question of comparative law. The German Government has been most reluctant to live up to its obligations from ITC membership and its stand is likely to have greatly influenced the British Government. It should take a leaf out of its own book.

There is no force either in the conclusion of Lord Justice Ralph Gibson which combined with the partnership argument of Lord Justice Kerr to defeat the correct view reached by Lord Justice Nourse.

Lord Justice Gibson accepted that the ITC had a claim against the member states but was obviously unwilling to enforce it. He thought this claim resulted from transactions between foreign states which in the absence of statutory provision, were not subject to municipal law unless parties have shown the intention that it should. He concluded that enforcement of rights arising under the ITC Treaty, not incorporated into UK law, could not be pursued in English courts.

This, of course, is an escape from the reality of the case into an irrelevant legal theory. The relevant fact is that the member states were trading on the London market as a partnership with unlimited liability, and both under English and international law they were liable jointly and severally. The State Immunity Act of 1907 is a clear expression of Parliament's intention that sovereign states should be treated no differently than private traders in respect of their trading operations. The House of Lords clarified further (in the Cuban Sugar case *I Congresso*) that the political motive behind transactions which are essentially commercial is of no consequence. There is also no reason why UK courts could not apply international law in the same way as they apply foreign laws.

The arguments for reversal of the Court of Appeal seem irresistible; unfortunately, the Law Lords proved to be able to resist the irresistible more than once.

ITC – the root of the trouble

The real problem, however, which must be faced is the state of the law which made such a debacle possible and may yet drive much other business from London.

To look for the real cause is, of course, something which the government is even more reluctant to do than to pay out money. Poor government! Poor legislators! How can one suggest that they are at fault when for years they just looked on and did nothing?

If it is right to accumulate mountains of butter, grain, meat and lakes of wine and olive oil by keeping prices artificially high, why not the same for tin?

The simple explanation is that tin producers do not have the same political clout as the agrarian lobby in the EEC. The London metal brokers' cardinal sin was that at their own peril they overlooked this simple fact. Indeed, refusing to look more than three months ahead – or the length of their forward contract – they made things worse by lending money to ITC to enable it to buy from them at unrealistic prices.

As everyone can now see, it was rather naive to rely on the member states to pay up; or to hope that the 'authorities' would not allow a default to shatter the entire system. The ITC creditors were clearly over-confident:

in cavalier fashion a few did not even insist on those precautions which the ITC was obliged by law to accept, such as arbitration clauses. If sheer incompetence deserves punishment, one could hardly think of a better example.

Unfortunately, the punishment will hit the innocent with the guilty unless the government takes speedy and energetic action to restore confidence in the London market. This cannot be done by pumping money into a leaky vessel, but only be redesiging it. There is need for emergency legislation: first, to assure the functioning of the LME as a proper market – its tin sector was a one-way betting shop in which the ITC was taking all the losses; second, to ensure that obligations undertaken by sovereign traders on the London market are clearly enforceable by English courts, so clearly that it would not even pay to let it come to legal action. Both issues have a significance reaching far beyond the problems of LME and ITC. They should have been solved long ago.

The LME demonstrates the fallacy of self-regulation. It has done wrong all that could be done wrong (and nothing to avert the disaster). It is accepted wisdom that to ensure the functioning of a market, its brokers should not be exposed to price fluctuations and the dealers' exposure should not exceed a certain proportion of their capital reserves.

It should in every case be clear whether someone is acting as a broker or as a dealer and in neither capacity should he be allowed to provide credit to other dealers or international stock managers. To ensure these basic rules, the operations should be made transparent by means of a clearing. This wisdom is no novelty to the gentlemen at the LME, but they think it applies only to other people.

Nothing short of a statutory authority supervising the market can restore confidence at this late stage. To make the authority do its job properly, it would have to be liable in damages to dealers for any dereliction of its supervisory duties. This is the only way to make supervision effective. The body of law developed by the European Court in respect of non-contractual liability of the EEC Commission provides a starting point for the development of a suitable model for English needs. It could be extended to all self-regulatory and statutory supervision in the City of London.

Notes

1 [1979] AC 351, [1979] All ER 1043.
2 FT Comm LR, 17 December 1982.
3 The Legal Rules Applicable in International Commercial Arbitration, note 32 – a paper presented at the Symposium held in Paris in October 1983 to mark the 60th Anniversary of the ICC Court of Arbitration.
4 'Arbitrage International et Ordre Public Suisse' Revue de Droit Suisse 97 (1978) 529.
5 ICC Arbitration 3493, ELL, August 1983.
6 Wetter *The International Arbitral Process I* p 427.
7 Wetter, p 411 and following.
8 Mann 'Contrats entre Etats et Personnes Privees Etrangères', Rev. Belge D.1. 562 (1975) 564-556.
9 Court of Appeal judgment 24 October 1983, FT Comm LR, 26 October 1983, House of Lords judgment 12 April 1984, FT Comm LR, 17 April 1984.
10 *Soc. des Grands Traveaux de Marseille v Bangladesh*, 6 May 1976 (1978) Swiss Yearbook of International Law 34, p 387.
11 (1981) Swiss Yearbook of International Law 37, p 446.

12 *I Congreso* [1981] 3 WLR 328.
13 *Czarnikow v Rolimpex* [1979] AC 351.
14 FT European Law Letter, August 1983.
15 [1978] 3 WLR 274, [1979] AC 351.
16 FT Comm LR, 26 October 1983.
17 FT Comm LR, 17 April 1984.
18 *Settebello Ltd v Banco Total and Acores* FT Comm LR, 21 June 1985.

8 National laws and international business

Trade wars and law

The governments opposing each other in the trade war between the EEC and the US are torn by conflicting desires. They oscillate between long-term strategy and short-term expediency, between contracts now and unpaid debts later, between the wish to preserve alliances and the necessity to satisfy business interests and the electorate.

In such a situation, politicians could be helped out of their quandary by a set of rules which would balance out the advantages and disadvantages over a longer period, to the ultimate benefit of both parties to the dispute.

Both sides to the dispute resort occasionally to legalistic arguments which are quite inconsistent with their past behaviour. The US which insists on its right to impose embargo rules on foreign companies opposed, by legislation, the Arab boycott of Israel. France and the UK, which opposed the US embargo on supplies for the Siberian pipeline, were quite willing to tolerate the Arab boycott and opposed the US attempts to penalise European companies complying with its rules.

Indeed, the legislative experience gained by the US in opposing the Arab embargo of Israel could be useful to European governments should they decide to fortify their blocking legislation. The US introduced a range of severe civil sanctions for violation of the anti-boycott provision of the Export Administration Act.

The sanctions include revocation or denial of export licenses and export privileges and loss of foreign tax credits and tax deferrals on foreign profits reinvested abroad. The civil and administrative penalties are reinforced by the possibility of imposing fines. Attorneys, accountants, consultants, forwarding agents or any other organisation acting in a representative capacity for the company taking part in the boycott or secondary boycott may be excluded from handling export licence applications.

In 1976, the Department of Justice charged the Bechtel Corporation (of which Mr George Shultz was a leading executive until he became Secretary of State), with a conspiracy to boycott US sub-contractors and suppliers blacklisted by Arab League countries.

The action brought by the department was directed also against Bechtel's subsidiaries in Canada. Although such actions were most unwelcome in Canada, no blocking legislation was enacted.

On the contrary, to show its solidarity with the US, the Canadian Department of Industry, Trade and Commerce passed a regulation designed to withhold government financial assistance from those Canadian companies which failed to give assurances, when requested, that they did not comply with certain aspects of the boycott.

The Canadian Government did not, however, go as far as to make compliance with the Arab boycott laws illegal: Canadian exports to Saudi Arabia rose by 343 per cent between July 1975 and July 1976.

The history of the Arab boycott and of US anti-boycott laws provides an illustration, if one was needed, of the point that the acceptance or rejection of another country's laws to a domestic situation depends on their economic and business effect rather than on some abstract notions of sovereignty.

The Canadian business community, as well as the British and French, preferred compliance with the extraterritorial Arab boycott laws to compliance with the US extraterritorial anti-boycott laws. The latter meant a loss of additional business while the former meant the chance of more.

The placid stance of the Canadian Government in 1976 was not due to any lack of statutory defences. Suitable blocking legislation had been adopted in 1975 to oppose the US enforcement of the embargo on trade with China and Cuba. The US Department of Commerce, acting under the Trading with the Enemy Act 1917, had classified as a 'US affiliate', subject to the embargo, any foreign company in which a US company owned at least 10 per cent of equity.

The prohibition caught not only direct supplies to a country on the US list of enemies, but also any sub-contracting to suppliers of such a country. The US tried to stop exports from Canada of locomotives, of which certain parts were produced by subsidiaries of US corporations.

Canada took legislative countermeasures by adopting amendments to the Combines Investigation Act. These gave powers to the Canadian Restrictive Trade Practices Commission to review and to prohibit the implementation in Canada of foreign judgments, laws and directives 'which would adversely affect competition, efficiency or trade'. Failure to observe an order of the commission is punishable by fines and imprisonment.

As in 1964, when the French took resolute judicial steps to ensure the delivery of Berliet trailers to China, the US retreated also in 1976. The Department of State announced that 'trade in non-strategic items by US subsidiaries in Canada would recieve virtually automatic approval except in cases where a significant percentage of US componentry is involved'). However, US parent corporations were kept waiting for approvals and, therefore, tended to veto any deals with Cuba proposed by their Canadian subsidiaries.

Should one conclude that conflicts of this type cannot be prevented by the adoption of international rules or resolved judicially because their nature is economic, commercial and political? Such a conclusion would ignore the fact that economic interests, human passions, and the struggle for power are at the root of most disputes subject to the rule of law. But in the absence of a superior authority, such disputes can be subject to the rule of law only if the parties recognise that it is by far the most economic method of resolving them.

Whose law is it anyway?

When individuals or companies are subject to conflicting regulations, it is a sure sign that 'muddling through' is undermining the rule of law – or that a powerful state is trying to clip the sovereignty and independence of another. Law is an exclusive system of enforceable rules, identified with the state, and conflicts of legislative jurisdiction, therefore, always disturb international relations.

The opposition of the US to its allies' participation in the Soviet gas pipeline project was understandable. That, however, is not the issue here.

The question was whether the US could prevent existing contracts from being fulfilled. Indeed, one could add that any attempt to make US domestic law effective in the countries of its allies, and to impose US policies on them in this way, was bound to weaken the alliance at a time when it was already under strain. Lord Cockfield, the Trade Secretary, ruled under the Protection of Trading Interests Act 1980 that the US controls were damaging to the trading interests of the UK, thus preventing British companies from complying with US requirements or prohibitions.

Statutes blocking extraterritorial application of US laws have been adopted also by Belgium, Denmark, Finland, France, Germany and the Netherlands and, in addition, by Australia, Canada and India. The question is whether blocking legislation is an effective and suitable remedy.

It can be very effective. The US so-called 'nationality jurisdiction' over foreign subsidiaries, did not come out too well from a test to which it was exposed in France in connection with the US embargo on trade with China.

Fruehauf-France was, in 1964, one of the 10 foreign manufacturing subsidiaries of the Fruehauf Corporation of Detroit, a major producer of heavy trucks. The French subsidiary was organised as a company under French law. The US parent owned 70 per cent of its shares, French shareholders the rest. Of the eight directors, five were nominated by Detroit headquarters, and the others by the French shareholders.

When the US Treasury learned that Fruehauf-France had received a sub-contract in connection with the delivery of semi-trailers to China, it instructed Fruehauf-Detroit to cause the French subsidiary to cancel the contract on pain of criminal penalties to the parent company and its directors. The French Government protested that, by obeying the US orders, the directors of the French subsidiary would become liable to criminal prosecution in France for violation of French company law. In the end, the conflict was solved in the civil courts. At the request of the French directors, a French commercial court appointed a temporary administrator to secure the implementation of the Chinese contract.

Of even greater interest was the US reaction. The Treasury announced that as the subsidiary ceased to be under the control of Detroit, no sanctions would be taken against the parent company or the American directors of the French subsidiary. The Treasury lawyers closed both eyes to the US Foreign Assets Control Regulations which spoke of subsidiaries 'owned or controlled' by US interests – the French subsidiary remained in US ownership. The lesson was learned, and the Rhodesian Transactions Regulations, enacted three years later, were not made applicable to foreign subsidiaries in which US corporations had only shares without effective control.

Unilateral legal measures to curb the extraterritorial application of US laws and policies can evidently have some effect, but are they a suitable and safe remedy? The side effects of such remedies are always unpleasant and may be dangerous. They aggravate the underlying political conflict, and in any case lead to legal uncertainty, to the detriment of trade. One is driven to the conclusion that this is a problem which should be solved by international agreements overruling national laws and providing national courts with a firm basis for decisions.

An international highway code of legislative jurisdiction should ensure that foreign subsidiaries are subject only to local law, should decriminalise foreign enforcement of anti-trust and should secure the same treatment for domestic and foreign export cartels. Such a code would also provide that offences against market regulations should be punishable only by the exclusion of the foreign dealer from the national market.

The refinement of such an international convention and its uniform interpretation should be entrusted to an international tribunal acting on references from national courts or governments. It could share the personnel and facilities of the International Court of Justice in the Hague.

Large companies on both sides of the Atlantic feel that something better than angry confrontation over individual instances is necessary, and proposals[1] for an international solution, have been commended for consideration by the governments of Canada, the US and the UK, by the British-North American Committee – a group of top executives drawn from the private sectors of the three countries. One of their members is Mr George Shultz, the US Secretary of State designate. Let's hope that he will not forget.

Arbitration in the aftermath of trade embargoes

In 1973 the Mississippi floods caused the US Government to declare a prohibition of soya beans exports which lasted only four days. This was followed by a steep rise in prices of soya beans. Nine years later, disputes between sellers who claimed frustration of the contract by *force majeure* and buyers who did not want to give up contracts concluded at the old price, still reverberated in the Royal Courts of Justice in the Strand.

Even greater complications resulted from the suspension of trade and freezing of Iranian assets after the toppling of the Shah's régime and the imprisonment of the US diplomatic mission in their embassy in Tehran. In accordance with the Algerian agreements, all court decisions obtained by US firms against Iran were then annulled and all claims were referred to a special arbitration tribunal established in The Hague.

The agreement establishing the tribunal was concluded in January 1981 and $1bn of the Iranian assets were placed with the Central Bank of The Netherlands to be used for the satisfaction of the tribunal's awards. It was agreed that Iran should replenish the fund whenever it fell below $500m. The inadequacy of this part of the agreement became evident within a year. Not only was there a big question mark over Iran's ability and willingness to replenish the fund, if necessary, but a dispute is now raging between the parties about who should pay the cost of keeping the account and whether the interest accruing on it should be handed over to Iran or kept on the account.

The Supreme Court of the US firmly shut the door through which the American parties could back out of the claims agreement by ruling that it was within the President's power to settle the international crisis by suspending private suits against Iran and transferring Iranian assets out of the US. The Iranian side, however, was left with the possibility of frustrating the operation in several ways. One of these was to flood the tribunal with counter-claims. Thus a major US company claiming about $2m from the Iranian air force for maintenance work, was faced with demands for 'necessary compensation' for its alleged failure to comply with contractual obligations amounting to $10m.

By the middle of March 1982 the Iranian side made 11 counter-claims in a total of 19 statements of defence filed so far. Some of the counter-claims can be seen as such only in the wider context, as they are addressed to other companies than those which made the original claim. In addition, the State Department received 43 Iranian claims against US banks which rejected Iranian calls on performance bonds, in compliance with orders received from US courts. Iran has also filed some 1,500 claims against the US Government, various companies and individuals but more than two-thirds of these may be inadmissible because the tribunal ruled that it had no jurisdiction over claims against American citizens.

The already mentioned Supreme Court ruling left open the question whether the Presidential order did or did not constitute a confiscation of property contrary to the Fifth Amendment. In a dissenting judgment, one of the justices said he would leave this issue open for the US Court of Claims to decide on a case-to-case basis. In his view, the Government should pay compensation to those whose claims it annihilates in order to achieve its foreign policy objectives.

One such suit, for compensation amounting to $6m, was filed in the US Court of Claims by E-Systems Inc.[2] This company did some work in 1978 and 1979 on two Boeing 707s belonging to the Iranian Government. After Iran defaulted on payment for this work, the company obtained liens on the aircraft before President Carter blocked Iran's assets. However, later on, the Government refused to allow the company to foreclose on its liens, and this was claimed to be the same as confiscation on the grounds that the value of the aircraft would rapidly diminish through deterioration and obsolescence. The Justice Department argued that E-Systems Inc must first exhaust the possibilities offered to it by the International Claims Tribunal in The Hague. That might take a very long time indeed.

The tribunal consists of three Americans, three Iranians, two Swedes and one Frenchman. Iran objected to one of its own nominees and then to the Swedish judge, Nils Mangard, who was accused of 'lacking neutrality'. It was alleged that he criticised the execution of judges in Iran. Mr Mangard's version was that he spoke of problems with the execution of judgments in Iran.

The objections were submitted for a decision to the president of the Dutch Supreme Court, Mr M. J. A. Moons. Mr Moons found that Iran had not submitted a sufficiently clear statement of facts and no relevant dates and rejected the objections.

The tribunal operates within the framework of UNICITRAL rules. However, in its day-to-day business, it uses a draft of more detailed rules which it has so far failed to adopt formally. American lawyers voiced a number of objections to these draft rules. They claimed the right to cross-examine witnesses unless denied by the tribunal instead of requiring its permission as at present. They wanted it to be made clear that unrelated set-offs and counterclaims were outside the tribunal's jurisdiction.

The American Bar Association Committee on Foreign Claims also argued that the secrecy of the arbitration proceedings operated to the disadvantage of the US claimants. They cannot attend hearings in cases with similar issues, while the Iranian parties are, in fact, offshoots of the Iranian Government and know all. But dire need creates its remedy: an excellent Iranian Assets Litigation Reporter[3] twice monthly provided a wealth of information on legal and administrative issues in short articles and reprints of court submissions and decisions. So there is a source on how to do better in future calamities.

The Laker dispute: a case for international arbitration

'At the root of the conflict are the fundamentally opposed policies of the United States and Great Britain regarding the desirability, scope and implementation of legislation controlling anticompetitive and restrictive business practices.'[4] This is how Judge Wilkey summarised the conflict between UK and US courts concerning the attempt of Laker's liquidator to obtain substantial damages from a number of Iata air companies alleged to have brought about the downfall of Laker Airways by predatory pricing and by preventing the realisation of a refinance scheme when the company was in difficulties.

The conflict produced the rare and unedifying spectacle of court injunctions shooting across the Atlantic in both directions, first forbidding Laker to prosecute British Airways and British Caledonian in US courts, and then in the opposite direction prohibiting KLM and Sabena from obtaining similar protection from British courts. It was this last injunction made by Judge Harold Greene in the US District Court (Civil Action No. 83-0416) with which the US Court of Appeals for the District of Columbia dealt on 6 March 1984.[5]

The appeal by KLM and Sabena was dismissed by a majority opinion which contains a very impressive discussion of the issues of concurrent jurisdiction and extraterritoriality and reaches conclusions with which it is difficult to quarrel.

The UK Court of Appeal made the affirmation of Judge Greene's injunction easy by basing its own prohibition addressed to Laker in respect of the two British airlines on the activation by the British Government of its powers under the Protection of Trading Interests Act. These, as the Court of Appeal said, made the case untriable because the two airlines were prevented from co-operating in any way with US courts. The US Court of Appeals based its decision, among other things, on the argument that the Belgian and Dutch companies could not obtain the same protection from the British Government.

Dissenting from the majority, Judge Starr took a much softer line. He said:

> A tempest has been brewing for some time among the nations as to the reach of this country's antitrust laws, and today's decision strikes a strong blow in favour of what will be viewed by many of our friends and allies as a rather parochial American outlook.

This was, in his view, incompatible with the orderly operation of the two nations' respective judicial systems. He would return the case to the District Court for narrowing of the injunction in a way consistent with the principles of comity to facilitate 'the seemly accommodation of sharply divergent and competing national interest'.

The narrowing of the injunction which Judge Starr had in mind would prevent KLM and Sabena from seeking in London an order banning Laker's liquidator from prosecuting them in the US, but would not prevent them from asking for a declaratory injunction in the UK courts to establish that they were not liable with a view to the regulations and treaties applying to transatlantic air transport. Reading between the lines, one can see that the main objective of Judge Starr was to provide time for an out-of-court or political settlement of the whole dispute.

Although the majority opinion strikes a much firmer note in defence of the US courts' jurisdiction over alleged anticompetitive behaviour affecting the American travellers on transatlantic airlines and the overwhelmingly American creditors of Laker Airways, it discloses the same awareness of the need to resolve the issue extra-judicially, possibly by international arbitration. It states: '. . . this court has neither the authority nor the institutional resources to weigh the policy and political factors that must be evaluated when resolving competing claims of jurisdiction.' In contrast, diplomatic and executive channels could negotiate and reconcile such conflicts.

The opinion focuses attention on the provisions of the Bermuda II Treaty[6] for the arbitration of disputes regarding its terms. It points out that neither the US nor the UK Government has yet invoked its right to call for an arbitral decision on the scope of the immunity from US anti-trust laws which this treaty provides in Article 17.

By affirming the injunction, granted by Judge Greene and depriving KLM and Sabena of a hypothetical and not-too-probable protection by the UK courts, the US Court of Appeals has done all it could do judicially. Even those who disagree with some of its reasoning regarding the effects doctrine will have to admit that there is much in the opinion's emphasis on the wider problem and on the need to seek a political solution. It says in a footnote:

> It may be that further efforts by the governments of both countries would help resolve the deadlock which appears to be developing to the detriment of the litigants' interests and the ultimate frustration of the national policies of the US and Great Britain.

The majority opinion of the US Court of Appeals also strikes a much more realistic note than many US proposals which see the solution of the conflicts created by US long-arm legislation in the judicial balancing of competing national interests by the spirit of comity – that is, mutual respect for the law and courts of another country.

I have missed no opportunity to argue that the vague concept of comity, developed by well-meaning judges, is being offered by politicians as a sop and can have the effect only of delaying the solution of the real issue. The view that comity is irrelevant to the solution of extraterritoriality conflicts was recently endorsed by the Berlin Appeal Court in the Rothman/Morris merger case.[7]

It is, therefore, very gratifying to see this realistic view adopted by a US court. While the dissenting opinion invokes comity, the majority opinion states that the balancing-of-interests approach has not gained more than a temporary foothold in US law. 'Courts are increasingly refusing to adopt the approach. Scholarly criticism has intensified. Additionally, there is no evidence that interest-balancing represents a rule of international law.'

It is futile to expect courts to find a solution by balancing national interests. Most judges will refuse to take this role, and most of those that will accept it will only find that the interests of their own country carry the greater weight. The majority opinion of the US Court of Appeals rightly suggests that international arbitration of such disputes would be a better solution. The opinion is an outstanding contribution to the discussion of the wider problem underlying the present Laker dispute. One would wish the governments concerned to take note of what Judge Wilkey said, instead of just waiting for something to turn up. If they do nothing, the extraterritoriality tangle will go from bad to worse.

Lords' judgment in Laker and British public policy

Laker's attempt to introduce competition into transatlantic air transport has stirred a hornet's nest. Its failure and the subsequent attempt of the liquidator to blame the established air companies forming Iata (and to recover over $1bn in damages), caused even greater agitation among the hornets. What seemed justice to Laker's US creditors, was perceived as injustice by the Iata air companies.

Some hoped that the Law Lords would find a just solution – other, less ambitious, would have been content with a pragmatic solution making easier the settlement of the US/UK controversy. Still others would have been satisfied with an elucidation of the legal problems, in particular of the impact which the 1980 Act for the Protection of Trading Interests can have in such situations.

They were all disappointed.[6] Admittedly the Law Lords were faced with an impossible task: to resolve judicially, as between private parties, a dispute which, in fact, was one in international law and between two governments. This difficulty was recognised quite clearly, not only by Lord Scarman but also on the other side of the Atlantic by Judge Wilkey[7] of the US Court of Appeals for the District of Columbia. Both suggested that international arbitration could provide a better solution.

To sort out the legal problems which made the two eminent judges prefer a non-judicial solution, it may be useful first to rehearse the basic facts.

After winning against a reluctant British Government in English courts,[8] Laker Airways obtained a licence for its Trans-Atlantic 'no frills' Skytrain first from the UK and then from the US authorities. It attracted about one-seventh of the North Atlantic passengers. The established Iata airlines then reduced their air fares to the level of Laker's, but their service included the usual frills and advantages following from their membership of Iata, which Laker did not join. Laker soon met with financial difficulties, and a rescue attempt failed. In this attempt McDonnell Douglas, the aircraft manufacturer, was to play a part by participating in Laker Airways.

These events became the subject of judicial scrutiny in the US, both on the civil and on the criminal track. Laker's liquidator brought a civil anti-trust suit against a number of US and foreign airlines, including British Airways and British Caledonian. He alleged that they agreed to lower prices to put Laker out of business and, when, as a result, he met with financial difficulties, that they put pressure on McDonnell Douglas and frustrated the rescue operation. In parallel with these proceedings the Department of Justice initiated a grand jury investigation concerned with the criminal aspect of the same events.

The British air companies applied in the High Court for Laker to be prohibited to continue its US action as it could result only in great injustice. If Laker won, they argued, it would be only because the US Government ignored the air services agreement between the two countries, the so-called 'Bermuda 2', under which fares were regulated and when approved by the authorities should enjoy anti-trust immunity in the US. But even if they should win in the US courts they would still suffer injustice, because they would be unable to recover the enormous legal costs which such proceedings involved.

Mr Justice Parker (as he then was) rejected their application in a judgment which the Law Lords greatly praised and which will long serve as a source of information on this obscure corner of the law. He said that by operating in the US the two companies became subject to US domestic law. If the alleged scheming really took place, he could see no injustice in allowing them to be answerable. 'Indeed, it would seem a manifest injustice to allow them to escape . . .' As to the undesirable features, such as the high and irrecoverable legal costs, these were common to all US actions.

By the time the case reached the Court of Appeal the Government had activated the provisions of the 1980 Protection of Trading Interests Act, prohibiting BA and BCal from co-operating in any way in the US proceedings. The Court of Appeal held that in view of this the case became untriable in the US and prohibited Laker from pursuing the action. This conclusion was rejected by the House of Lords.

Agreeing with Lord Diplock, the Law Lords embraced the reasoning and conclusions of Mr Justice Parker. They differed from him only where he tried to interpret the 'Bermuda 2' agreement (and reached a conclusion favourable to the US stand). Their Lordships said this agreement was not part of UK law. It was up to the US courts to interpret it, as it was part of US law.

The Law Lords also took a very detached view of the protection orders made by the British Government under the 1980 Act and of the public policy underlying it. This is all the more surprising as Lord Diplock said (on page 10 of the judgment) that 'in the relatively narrow field of international relations between sovereign states which is still reserved to the prerogative', the view of the Government was a source of public policy to which courts of justice gave effect.

On the strength of this, one can hardly avoid asking, what is the view of the British Government in this matter. It has been revealed by the *amicus curiae* in the US litigation. The observations transmitted by the British Government to the US on 6 February 1984 state that airlines do not operate in a free market. Indeed, the US licences require British airlines to observe Bermuda 2, which provides that tariffs are subject to approval of the two contracting states. The UK authorities encourage airlines to discuss prospective tariffs before they are submitted for approval – it is the allegation that such an inter-carrier agreement took place before the tariffs were submitted for approval on which the US anti-trust proceedings rest.

Laker's complaint that the new air fares of its competitors were predatory was first made before the tariffs were approved, and was considered and rejected by the UK authorities. At that time US authorities also pressed for British approval of the new fares. The essence of Laker's complaint is therefore that the British Government, in exercising its rights under an international agreement, failed to protect it from competition.

If the US courts accepted that tariffs charged by Laker's competitors were predatory, this would be a direct challenge to the decisions and requirements of the British authorities. Britain contends that it would be incompatible with Bermuda 2 if the US applied its domestic law so as to judge whether past decisions of the British Government adequately protected Laker, and indirectly its creditors, from the effects of the tariffs charged by Laker's competitors.

The same applies to the second count of Laker's anti-trust action. Although it is alleged that BA and BCal discouraged McDonnell Douglas from participating in the financial rescue, the offer of such participation remained open but, together with other offers of support, was judged to be inadequate by the Civil Aviation Authority.

To cut a long story short, the British Government takes the view that it is contrary to international law if the US attempts to enforce or permits the enforcement of its anti-trust laws in such circumstances. This view is evidently a matter of British public policy: to ignore it is likely to weaken the effectiveness of judicial decisions.

Taking a broader view, one can see that the adoption of statutes blocking the extraterritorial application of other countries' laws – the only remedy seriously tried so far – has had little effect. It aggravates the political aspect of the conflict. While US courts respect the foreign policy of their government the Lords' latest decision speaks with a voice different from that of the UK's executive.

Unavoidably, one is driven to the conclusion that extraterritorial application and effects of national laws are an international problem which can be solved only by international agreements providing national courts with a firm basis for decisions. And there should be an international tribunal available for their interpretation.

US voices of reason

The intransigence of Judge Harold Greene of the Federal District Court in Washington has certainly inconvenienced the British Government by making it necessary to postpone the privatisation of British Airways; it may have even embarrassed President Reagan's Administration – or those of its departments which do not wish to have their foreign relations spoiled by exorbitant anti-trust litigation. However, Judge Greene's radicalism may yet prove to be a blessing in disguise. It has provoked some US judges and legislators to have second thoughts on the merits of an unbridled extraterritorialism in the application of US law.

The first and immediate reaction came from the Federal Court of Appeals[9] on 4 March 1984 in the course of reviewing one of the interlocutory decisions made by Judge Greene. In the appeal judgment, already discussed on pp 172–174 Circuit Judge Wilkey (as he then was), though a staunch extraterritorialist, said that international arbitration appeared more suitable than litigation in disputes of this kind; and Judge Starr, in a dissenting opinion, strongly attacked the long-arm tactics of the District Court.

This sweet voice of reason was followed in November 1984 by a denial of the US court's jurisdiction in the anti-trust suit of *McGlinchy v Shell*.[10] On 27 December 1984, another Federal Appeals court refused to apply US anti-trust law in *Timberlane II*[11] because foreign interest appeared to the court stronger than US interest, and this was followed by an introduction of a Bill[12] by Senator DeConcini on 6 February 1985, seeking statutory confirmation of such respect for comity.

Circuit Judge Scalia now Justice of the Supreme Court strongly underlined the importance which the presumption of only territorial reach of US laws has for sparing the Executive Branch embarrassment in handling foreign relations. His was a dissenting judgment in a case[13] where the majority extended accident liability of the US Government for acts or omissions of its servants to the legal no-man's land of Antarctica.

Of the decisions referred to above, that in *McGlinchy v Shell* is of particular interest because it is one of the first to interpret the 1982 amendments to the Sherman Act. These exempt from US anti-trust law conduct that lacks the requisite domestic effect, even where such conduct originates in the US or involves American-owned companies operating abroad.

The court held that this exemption applied to the allegedly anticompetitive activities of Shell International Chemical Company (Sicco). Moreover, while in the past US courts have often assumed personal jurisdiction over foreign companies on the slightest pretext, in this case the court concluded that Sicco's activities were not sufficiently pervasive to subject it to general personal jurisdiction in the US.

There is a school of thought which would avoid legislative restrictions of the extraterritorial application of US laws by relying on the courts' respect of comity, that is by their balancing the interest of the US and of foreign countries involved in a particular case. Such a balancing test was outlined for the first time in the US Court of Appeals for the Ninth Circuit when dealing, in 1977, with the complaint of Timberlane Lumber Company that the Bank of America conspired with others to prevent Timberlane from milling timber in Honduras and exporting it to the US. Dealing with the *Timberlane* case for a second time, the court applied this test and concluded that US interests did not predominate over foreign interests so as to justify an extraterritorial application of US anti-trust laws.

The court refused to exercise jurisdiction because it found that the potential for a conflict with Honduran economic policy and commercial law was great, while the effect of the attacked behaviour on US commerce was minimal. Only the US citizenship of both parties and easier enforceability of any decision in the US spoke in favour of exercising jurisdiction – but the court thought that was not enough.

The idea that the harmful consequences of the long-arm practices of US courts could be avoided by judicial self-restraint and respect for important interests of other states was also adopted by Judge Weis Jr. in the US Court of Appeals for the Third Circuit, but is by no means generally accepted in the US or in Europe. The Berlin Court of Appeal, for example, to which all appeals from decisions of the Federal Cartel Office go in the first instance, denies that comity is part of international law. The attempt by Senator DeConcini to have it entered in the US statute book is therefore of considerable interest.

Yet even if the US courts should be guided, as proposed in the Bill, by the balance of US and foreign interests when deciding whether to assume jurisdiction in anti-trust matters, it would still remain a great gamble for foreign parties to rely on such a highly subjective test. US interests, seen from greater proximity, are likely to loom larger than less familiar interests and legal policies of distant countries.

According to the Bill, jurisdictional issues should be decided early on as a preliminary issue and would extent the doctrine of the 'most convenient court' to anti-trust cases. Most important of all, the Bill would give the courts the freedom to decide that a case against foreign defendants should not be for treble but only for single damages – treble damages with their punitive effect being probably the most frequent cause of foreign protests against the long-arm operations of US laws.

Finally, a few more words about the 1985 dissenting opinion of Circuit Judge Scalia based on 'the canon of construction which teaches that legislation of Congress, unless a contrary intent appears, is meant to apply only within the territorial jurisdiction of the US . . .' This presumption against the extraterritorial application of US law was employed by the judge in *Martin John Beattie v US*[13] as an argument against extending the waiver of sovereign immunity (contained in the Federal Tort Claims Act) to claims arising in Antarctica.

The litigation arose out of the crash of an Air New Zealand aircraft in which all persons on board were killed. It was alleged that the crash was due to the negligence of the US navy air traffic controllers at a naval air station situated in the Antarctic region.

Judge Scalia's argument was further strengthened by a provision of the Act which excludes any claims 'arising in a foreign country.' However the majority opinion, the last written by Malcolm R. Wilkey in his capacity of Senior Circuit Judge of the Federal Court of Appeals in Washington, held that Antarctica was not a foreign country even if it was not part of US territory. US law could be extended to it in the same way as it could be extended to events on the high seas or in outer space.

Though I like Scalia's principles better, I prefer Wilkey's conclusions. Law, like nature, abhors a vacuum. it seems wise to extend the protection of the law to those who are left out in the cold of a legal no-man's land.

A trial by ordeal

Anything connected with Laker's cheap air travel has always been an emotional issue. First he was the air travellers' hero, fighting the established and expensive airlines. This hero worship was only partly washed out by the disappointment of those who booked trips and could not travel after the collapse of Laker Airways. Later he became an anti-hero of those who wished the privatisation of British Airways to go ahead, and were cross that the huge claims for damages brought in the US courts were holding up the operation.

Like in every good tragedy, there are only victims in the Laker saga. In a system where one half of the air transport is regulated while the other half should obey market forces and thrive through competition, the result must be the same as if all white cars had to keep to the right side of the road, all red cars to the left, and the other colours as they choose. Such arrangements can be profitable only for the repair shops and lawyers.

To make things worse the House of Lords held[14] that this essentially British mixture of competition and regulation should be sorted out by US courts, which were thus left with private actions for the settlement of a dispute which was really between the two governments. This difficulty was recognised in England by Lord Scarman, and in the US by Judge Wilkey of the US Court of Appeal, DC. Both suggested that international arbitration could provide a better solution, a proposition which has been duly welcomed in this column but hardly anywhere else.

Guided unavoidably by their Lordships wisdom, Mr Justice Leggatt lifted an earlier injunction preventing Laker's liquidator from pursuing his claim against the Midland Bank and others in US courts.

He held that an English plaintiff could not be stopped from proceeding in the US under the US anti-trust laws in respect of alleged acts committed in the UK if, (1) those acts were part of an alleged world-wide conspiracy, (2) the allegations, if proved, would disclose a good cause of action, and (3) such action could not be brought in England because the behaviour complained of was not unlawful there.

The judge also held that it was much too early to decide whether the claim was frivolous and vexatious as the Midland Bank alleged. He relied on Lord Diplock's dictum that the truth or otherwise of such an allegation could become evident only after pre-trial discovery in the US.

Let us take the last point first, because in fact it is the pivotal point. To be exposed to the oppressive and costly US pre-trial procedures, often with a number of interlocutory judgments thrown in for good measure, with no chance of recovering the costs of defence even in the case of total victory, may compel even a very stubborn and rich company, totally convinced that the law is on its side, to settle rather than to risk the enormous legal costs.

The growing complexity of transatlantic business relations brings with it the danger that a party to a dispute will try to combine the procedural devices available on both sides of the Atlantic to its greatest advantage. The invoking of US discovery of evidence may cause the other party great expense and put off the resolution of the dispute by raising preliminary issues before the trial judge as well as in superior courts.

This is so even if the main trial has to take place in an English court. Such a situation was considered by the Court of Appeal.[15] It was reassuring to hear Lord Justice Griffiths say, with the agreement of the other two appeal judges, that in the future a party would be justified in asking foreign courts for help in discovery and evidence without referring the matter first to an English court only in entirely exceptional circumstances – for example, if there was the danger that the evidence would otherwise be destroyed. The US courts could and did order discovery before the disputed issues were defined with any precision – a procedure which was not permissible in English courts as it could easily be abused for harassing the other party.

This seems to be a wise judgment. Unfortunately, the rule which it establishes can be easily avoided by starting the action in the United States, which can be done on the flimsiest of assertions.

In the Midland Bank case the alleged behaviour of the bank and of its Receiver is at least described in concrete terms, according to an affidavit sworn by Mr Beckman, Laker's US attorney, presented in the High Court.

As far as the Laker/Lonrho claim is concerned, the 'evidence' I was shown by Sir Freddie and Mr Paul Spicer, a Lonrho director, is hardly evidence of conspiracy. It merely shows that British Caledonian's directors thought that the re-entry of Laker into the long haul transatlantic business would have a highly desabilitating influence on British air transport. To prevent it they were considering the possibility of paying a much higher figure for the facilities in the hands of the receiver than they ultimately paid. They also thought that in this matter British Caledonian and British Airways had a common cause.

That such an interest existed is common knowledge, but its existence is no evidence of conspiracy. This would require further evidence of an agreement to act jointly, at the very least.

After the House of Lords ruling in the BA/BCal case, the deficiency of evidence was not enough to prevent proceedings in the US. However, there were the three conditions articulated by Mr Justice Leggatt in the Midland Bank case.

The first two, that the alleged behaviour in the UK was part of a world-wide conspiracy and that, if proved, would disclose a good cause of action under US anti-trust laws, are easy to satisfy.

However, the third, that the action could not be brought in England (and, therefore, the US courts are the only courts which could deal with the claim), did not seem to be satisfied either in the Midland Bank case or in the Laker/Lonrho case: the EEC rules of competition defined in Articles 85 and 86 of the Treaty reflect very closely the Sherman and the Clayton Acts of the United States and are part of English law.

Claims under the EEC competition rules can be pursued by private actions in English courts. There is no need to go for this to the US unless one aims for a trial by the ordeal of discovery and other preliminary torture.

Conflicts courts cannot resolve

At a seminar of the Public Finance Foundation on the painful encounters of British enterprises with US anti-trust laws the mood was one of bitter helplessness. Sir Alan Neale, deputy chairman of the Monopolies and Mergers Commission, discussed at some length the idea put forward originally by Professor Kingman Brewster, a former US ambassador in London, that conflicts of legislative jurisdiction could be solved by comity – the mutual respect of courts of different countries – and that US judges should be able to weigh the relative national interests involved and refuse the application of anti-trust laws if foreign interests prevail.

Sir Alan did not seem convinced that this offered a solution. The comity proposal had been shown repeatedly to be nothing but a sop to pacify foreign governments whose companies were exposed to a trial with immensely costly discoveries of evidence and interminable litigation of preliminary issues.

It is quite natural that American judges will consider the economic policies of their own government more important. Universal application of its laws has come naturally to every great empire since Roman times. The relative unimportance of state frontiers within the US makes it tempting to transfer rules governing the relationship of American states to relations with foreign countries. As the world shrinks and interdependence of trade intensifies, the universal application of a single system of law appears necessary and often seems unavoidable.

However, there seems to be no end to the difficulties which result from the misguided belief that such a single system of law can be applied unilaterally. The freezing of Iranian accounts in foreign subsidiaries of US banks posed a threat to the City which was removed only by the release of the US hostages. In the Siberian pipeline embargo, the attempt to impose US rules on foreign firms provoked a rare example of co-ordinated defensive action by European countries, Australia and Canada.

The conflict of policies in the field of shipping generated anti-trust suits against some 15 leading companies which form line conferences but was removed in 1984 when Congress exempted shipping from the impact of US anti-trust laws. US shipping is rather weak and needs to be protected against competition. No such exemption is available to civil aviation where the US is in a strong position and desires competition.

The Westinghouse uranium litigation has been settled but it will take some time for the trading partners of the US to recover from the realisation that US courts were prepared to award crippling damages and to punish non-US uranium producers for nothing worse than adopting defensive restraints on competition after the US had threatened their survival and development by an embargo on imports and by releasing its stockpiles – two measures which have at the time taken the bottom out of the market.

The Sherman Act was brought in after the Civil War, when the US Government feared the emergence of trusts in a predominantly agricultural country with a sprinkling of small industries. These circumstances no longer exist.

The real motive for the application of anti-trust laws was better stated by Mr Joel Davidow of the US Department of Justice, when he said[16] that the US applied its anti-trust laws '. . . to punish, remedy and deter international offences which cause direct substantial injury to important economic and legal interests [of the US]'.

It is abundantly evident – and not least to judges called upon to try such disputes – that conflicts of important economic interests cannot be resolved by courts. As Judge Wilkey, of Laker fame and later US Ambassador in Uruguay, asked in a public lecture recently:

> If there is conflict of political/economic policy between nations when those policies spill over borders, does this not call for negotiation and adjustment of the perceived political/economic needs of the nations in conflict? First to define and then to adjust those political/economic needs is whose primary task, the courts or the political organs of our Government?

Litigation is a very clumsy and very costly method of resolving conflicts on economic policy. It is also unfair if governments leave it to individual firms, however big they may be, to fight out in court what are essentially national issues. These can be properly solved only by bargaining but unfortunately, neither the US nor the UK seem to be well equipped institutionally for such bargaining.

Though there is the office of the President's Trade Representative, the US still speaks with many voices when it comes to conflicts of this kind, and in the UK the division of responsibility between the Department of Trade, Foreign Office and the Lord Chancellor's Office is not very helpful either. A Department of Foreign Trade which could integrate foreign and domestic interests of the UK and assemble an expert and effective negotiating team might be of use.

UK bows to US pre-trial discoveries

Whitehall is good at scoring an own goal. In doing so, it follows the example of the House of Lords. To demonstrate how well they can do it, the government has presented the Supreme Court of the US with an *amicus curiae* brief which, by implication, abandons the principle of territorial judicial sovereignty. Instead, it appeals to the US courts to consider 'comity' and the balancing of US and foreign interests before allowing discovery of evidence to proceed abroad by means which are not recognised by the local government.

Comity, or mutual respect of courts, is all things to all people, and the balancing of interests has, in spite of all the noble language wasted on this subject, worked out in favour of American interests which, quite naturally, appear more weighty from the perspective of a US judge.

The case,[17] in which a team of counsel, led by Mr Douglas Rosenthal of Sunderland Asbill & Brennan, presented the brief on behalf of the UK Government was about a product liability claim against two French companies, Société Nationale Industrielle Aerospatiale and Société de Construction d'Avions de Tourism. An aircraft made by these companies was involved in an accident and the two French companies were sued in the US District Court of Iowa by three accident victims.

The French companies appealed further to the Supreme Court.

The US courts' habit of making direct orders for the disclosure of documents within the jurisdiction of foreign courts is an old problem. The US Supreme Court – after washing its hands of the issue on several earlier occasions – agreed at last to say what, if any, are the limits to such extraterritorial orders defying the Hague Evidence Convention, on the application of Messerschmitt Bolkow Blohm,[18] the German aircraft manufacturers. However, the parties have settled their dispute, and hopes turned to a similar case of Anschuetz[19] and Co, another German company. In the meantime the present French case appeared on the scene.

The Hague Convention was designed to avoid conflict between countries with differing rules on evidence in civil litigation. The difference is particularly great between common law countries, where discovery is managed by attorneys, and civil law countries, where judges decide what evidence may or should be produced.

A substantial difference between the US and most other countries is that the US courts are willing to compel pre-trial discovery of documents which are only vaguely defined, held by third parties or of uncertain relevance to the dispute. Often such documents are requested by US plaintiffs to find some cause of action that is still undefined at the time of the request.

Most other countries, including the UK and Germany, are strongly opposed to such 'fishing expeditions'. The Hague Convention provides that requests for documentary evidence from abroad may be addressed to the court within whose jurisdiction they lie and a non-US court is likely to reject fishing expeditions.

Though the US ratified the Hague Convention in 1972, it was not until 1981 that a defendant insisted on the use of its procedure in the US courts. Since then, the number of cases has rapidly increased. About 1,500 cases are pending and at least 27 have already been decided.

The decisions of the courts are not uniform, though most seem to insist that there is no obligation to use only the procedure provided by the Convention and that a US court can compel a defendant over whom it has personal jurisdiction – as in the case of Messerschmitt, which has a US subsidiary – to bring documents to the US and make them available to the other party.

Messerschmitt's plea for judicial review was supported by the German Government which argued that the vast majority of requests for the production of documents located in Germany was made by parties subject to an American court's *in personam* jurisdiction. To limit the application of the Convention to such cases where the US courts did not have such jurisdiction would render it meaningless.

Germany also argued that it was a violation of its sovereignty when a foreign court used the threat of sanctions to force a person under the jurisdiction of German courts to remove documents from Germany to the US for the purpose of pre-trial discovery.

The US Government, in its *amicus curiae* brief, insisted that the history of the Convention revealed no intention of prohibiting the accepted practice of conducting extraterritorial discovery according to US federal and state rules.

American courts might exercise jurisdiction over a foreign party if its US contacts were sufficient to make it reasonable and just and, though they might use the procedure prescribed by the Convention, they could also make direct orders. The US courts were virtually unanimous that the Convention was not exclusive, the US Government said.

It admitted that international comity obliged US courts to give 'respectful consideration to claims of foreign judicial sovereignty'. But, for this, there could be no fixed rules; in each case, the interests of the US and of the foreign state had to be carefully balanced.

The US argued that, as the Convention allowed foreign countries to refuse pre-trial discovery of documents, it could not be accepted as the exclusive means of obtaining evidence abroad, if it were, foreign authorities could become final arbiters of discovery disputes in American proceedings, so displacing the authority of US courts to employ traditional devices provided by federal and state court rules. As General de Gaulle used to say, 'I am for the law as long as it does not run against our interests.'

Like the two German companies before them, the French appellants argue that the official procedure of the Hague Convention is exclusive and that US courts should not be allowed to issue direct orders concerning evidence located abroad.

The French companies are prohibited by France's penal code from providing documents or information on economic, commercial, industrial, financial or technical matters for use in foreign judicial or administrative procedures. The British Government suggests that if US courts order the production of evidence prohibited by such foreign blocking laws without considerations of comity and balancing of interests, this would in the end undermine not only the authority of foreign nations over their subjects but also the authority of the US Government over the conduct of persons in the US. This is whipping a dead horse: US courts have repeatedly said that they will not compel a foreign subject to transgress his country's laws.

Turning to the wider issue of the Hague Convention, the British Government accepts the US view that the official channel provided by the Convention for obtaining evidence abroad is not exclusive as the Convention states that this method *may* be used, not that it must be. From this observation, the brief moves immediately to the argument that the US should moderate its freedom of making direct discovery orders to foreign subjects aboard by considerations of comity and the balancing of interests.

The brief appears to ignore entirely the basic rule of international law that the jurisdiction of a state over its own nationals and all property within its own frontiers is complete and exclusive. American attorneys *may ask* for evidence located abroad and foreign parties may provide it as long as they are not prohibited from doing so by their own countries' laws.

But US courts *cannot compel*, by sanctions applied in the US, foreign companies to comply with such requests.

The Hague Convention merely enabled US or other courts to gain access to foreign nationals and property with the help of local courts – provided these courts found the US request justified and in keeping with their own rules for obtaining evidence.

This is the substance of the problem, and the British argument should have rested there, on the firm basis of international law, instead of begging for comity, which, if not used as a synonym for public international law is, as Dr Francis Mann says in his latest book[20], 'so elusive and imprecise a term as to render its use unhelpful and confusing'.

Supreme Court's universal application of US rules of discovery

The vexing practice of US courts to see the world as their playground was, in June 1987, confirmed by the US Supreme Court in *Aerospatiale*. Not without some hesitation: the court was divided 5:4 and even the majority admonished lower courts to give proper consideration to foreign interests when deciding whether evidence situated abroad should be obtained by internationally agreed methods or by direct pressure and sanctions which might require litigants to violate the law of their home country. But it clearly said that such pressure may be applied, although it did not provide lower courts with any useful guidance as to how such weighing of domestic and foreign interests should be conducted.

The Rehnquist Supreme Court appears to be deeply divided in its approach to international conflicts of jurisdiction. This became evident in February 1987 when in *Asahi*[21] it split 4:4 (with one abstention) on the question of the applicability of US product liability laws to a foreign manufacturer of components which reach the US market as an integral part of products made in a third country. Four Justices thought that it was enough if the manufacturer knew that the products containing his components would eventually reach the US market, while the other four decided that he would become liable only if he took positive action to bring the products into the US market.

The Supreme Court's decision in *Aerospatiale*[22] was swung towards the doctrine of universal application of US laws by the vote of Chief Justice Rehnquist and is bound to provoke more friction between the US and its allies. As the FT commented on 10 September 1986, this would make a tightening of the legislation protecting British trading interests inescapable.

The decision may ultimately boomerang, impeding US efforts to restrict the transfer of technological information for economic and military reasons. As Justice Blackman said in a footnote to his dissenting opinion: 'It may not serve the country's long-term interests to establish precedents that would allow foreign courts to compel production of the records of American corporations.'

To put it more bluntly: if a Soviet court followed the *Aerospatiale* decision and, relying on its rules of civil procedure, ordered a major US corporation to submit unlimited documentation and evidence on the research, development, production and testing of a type of helicopter, one of which had crashed in the Soviet Union causing injury or loss of life, and if this court threatened and proceeded to penalise the US corporation by sequestrating its assets or receivables in the Soviet Union as long as the documents and witnesses did not arrive there, we would have another of those now familiar incidents leading, if not to an intercontinental war, then certainly to the postponement of a meeting between President Reagan and President Gorbachev.

However, if US courts do the same to the UK, Germany and France, US lawyers representing foreign companies and governments do not dare go further than to ask humbly that the US courts try to balance the foreign interests against those of the plaintiffs – an act as impossible as striking a balance between a ton of metal and a quantity of electrical energy.

The *amicus curiae* brief presented to the Supreme Court on behalf of the UK contributed to the unfortunate decision. In contrast with the German government in a similar case,[23] the UK accepted the US view that the official channel provided by the Hague convention for obtaining evidence abroad is not exclusive. It merely asked that US courts should moderate their freedom to make discovery orders direct to foreign subjects abroad, with considerations of comity and the 'balancing of interest'.

The faint-hearted British government lawyers should read carefully the opinion of the four dissenting justices:

The Court ignored the importance of The Hague Convention by relegating it to an 'optional' status, without acknowledging the significant achievement in accommodating divergent interests that the Convention represents. Experience to date indicates that there is a large risk that the case-by-case comity analysis now to be permitted by the Court, will be performed inadequately and that the somewhat unfamiliar procedures of the Convention will be invoked infrequently. The Court's decision means that courts will resort unnecessarily to issuing discovery orders under the Federal Rules of Civil Procedure in a raw exercise of their jurisdictional power to the detriment of the United States' national and international interests.

And further:

The majority ignores the policies established by the political branches when they negotiated and ratified the treaty. The result will be a duplicative analysis for which courts are not well designed. Not only is the question of foreign discovery more appropriately considered by the Executive and Congress, but in addition, courts are generally ill equipped to assume the role of balancing the interests of foreign nations with that of our own. Although transnational litigation is increasing, relatively few judges are experienced in the area, and the procedures of foreign legal systems are often poorly understood.

The US government told the Supreme Court recently[24] that the Convention 'must be interpreted to preclude an evidence taking proceeding in the territory of a foreign state party if the Convention does not authorise it and the host country does not otherwise permit it'.

The dissenting opinion concludes:

> In most cases in which a discovery request concerns a nation that has ratified the Convention there is no need to resort to comity principles; the conflicts they are designed to resolve already have been eliminated by the agreements expressed in the treaty. Many of the considerations that lead to the conclusion that there should be a general presumption favouring use of the Convention should also carry force when courts analyse particular cases. The majority fails to offer guidance in this endeavour, and thus it has missed its opportunity to provide predictable and effective procedures for international litigants in United States courts. It now falls to the lower courts to recognise the needs of the international commercial system and the accommodation of those needs already endorsed by the political branches and embodied in the Convention.

It would be wishful thinking to believe that the lower courts of the US will take this plea of the dissenting opinion to heart.

The only way to achieve its highly desirable objective is if other countries insist that whenever US courts do not make use of The Hague convention procedure when seeking evidence abroad, they are not then entitled to commit breaches of international law and that the enforcement of evidence or of the appearance of foreign witnesses outside the US jurisdiction by sanctions and penalties on property within the US jurisdiction is an infringement of judicial sovereignty and a breach of international law.

Notes

1 A. H. Hermann *Conflict of National Laws with International Business Activity – Issues of Extraterritoriality* (British–North American Committee, London and Washington).
2 *E-Systems Inc v US*, No. 987-81 C, Iranian Assets Litigation Reporter (March 1982) p 4,363.
3 Published by Andrews Publications Inc, PO Box 200, Edgemont, Pennsylvania 19028.
4 Judgment of 6 March 1984, see note 5.
5 US Court of Apeals, DC, Nos. 83-1280 and 83-1281.
6 US/UK agreement concerning air services, 23 July 1977.
7 See FT Business Law column 29 March 1984.
8 *Laker Airways v Department of Trade* [1977] QB 643, [1977] 2 All ER 182.
9 US Court of Appeals, DC, Nos. 83-1280 and 83-1281.
10 *Wm. J. McGlinchy et al v Shell Chemical Co et al,* US District Court, North District of California, No. C-84-0474-SC.
11 *Timberlane Lumber Co v Bank of America . . .* US Court of Appeals, Ninth Circuit, No. 832008 1985-1 TC 64,565.
12 S. 397. A bill to amend the Sherman Act and the Clayton Act to modify the application of such Acts to international commerce.
13 *Martin J. Beattie et al v US*, No. 84-5413, US Court of Appeals, DC.
14 *BA v Laker Airways and others; British Caledonian v Laker; Laker Airways v Secretary of State* FT Comm LR, 24 July 1984.
15 *South Carolina Insurance Co v Assurantie Maatshappij 'De Zevan Provinvien' and others* FT Comm LR, 19 June 1985.
16 International Chamber of Commerce Conference, Paris, 12 March 1981.
17 *Soc. Nat. Industrielle Aerospatiale and another v US District Court for Iowa,* Supreme Court No. 85-1695.
18 *Messerschmitt-Bolkow-Blohm GmbH v Walker,* Supreme Court No. 85-89.
19 *Anschuetz & GmbH* 754 F 2d (5th Circ. 1985).
20 F. A. Mann *Foreign Affairs in English Courts* (Clarendon Press, Oxford) p 136.
21 *Asahi Metal Industry v Superior Court of California,* Supreme Court No. 85-693, 24 February 1987. FT Business Law Brief, March 1987, p 21.

22 *Soc. Nat. Industrielle Aerospatiale and another v US District Court for the S. District of Iowa,* No. 85-1695, 15 June 1987.
23 *Anschuetz & Co and Messerschmitt-Bolkow-Blohm,* FT Business Law Brief, September 1986, pp 3-4.
24 In *Volkswagen v Falton.*

9 The pains of European integrating

Limping towards European Union

The 'Single European Act' is a treaty expanding the scope of the European Economic Community, changing the distribution of its powers in favour of the Commission and providing a legal basis for transforming the EEC into a political union.

It is a pity that the true meaning of this momentous step has not been revealed more frankly. Even Lord Denning was lured to the front gate, to defend long-lost sovereignty, while the thieves were stealing washing in the back yard; how can one expect lesser mortals to glean the truth from the extraordinary obscurity of the documents placed before Parliament?

The process of disinformation started by calling this new European treaty a 'Single European Act'. The ratification instrument, entitled European Communities (Amendment) Bill, makes matters even worse. The explanatory memorandum attached to it was misleading on the main point of European Union when it said that the Bill did not provide for those parts of the Single European Act which relate to co-operation in the sphere of foreign policy.

Though the Bill excludes Title III of the Single Act providing for the mechanics of European co-operation in the sphere of foreign policy, it lets it in by the back door. It provides ratification for the preamble and the common provisions of Title I which obliges the institutions of the European Communities and the bodies responsible for European Political Co-operation to exercise their powers and jurisdiction under the conditions and for the purposes laid down in Title III of the Act and in the 1983 Solemn Declaration on European Union.

Title III provides that the external policies of the Community and of European Political Co-operation – the name given to the embryo European Union – must be consistent. The Commission will have responsibility for ensuring this in its sphere. There will be many institutional links.

However, these provisions may not be of immediate practical impact. It is the expansion of the economic tasks of the Community, foreseen in the Single Act, which is likely to have an impact within the near future. This concerns mainly, though not exclusively, a number of measures usually lumped under the heading 'internal market'. The new Article 8A inserted into the EEC Treaty provides:

> The Community shall adopt measures with the aim of progressively establishing the internal market over a period expiring on December 31 1992, in accordance with the provisions of this Article and of Articles 8B, 8C, 28, 57(2), 59, 70(1), 84, 99, 100A and 100B and without prejudice to the other provisions of this treaty.
> The internal market shall comprise an area without internal frontiers in which the free movement of goods, persons, services and capital is ensured in accordance with the provisions of the treaty.

With its aim of an area 'without internal frontiers', this provision appears to go much further than the EEC Treaty which enumerated only specific tasks, like free movement of goods and of workers, freedom of services and of establishment, and ruled out only anti-competitive practices likely to have an adverse effect on internal trade. The Commission now appears to be given a free hand in proposing no end of new guidelines and conditions, directives and regulations towards achieving the new, more ambitious aim by the end of 1992.

However, a cautious, protectionist attitude remains hidden behind this bold face. A declaration on Article 8A appended to the Single Act states: 'Setting of the date of December 31 1992 does not create an automatic legal effect.' This means that the European Court will be unable to enact after 1992 measures which the Commission and Council in its view should have introduced but did not.

Another escape clause for protectionist policies is provided by Article 8C obliging the Commission to take into account the weaknesses of certain member states and to provide for these in the form of temporary derogations from the uniform rules it proposes. Moreover, a new Article, 100A, will provide a further escape from harmonisation measures adopted by the Council only by a qualified majority and not unanimously.

The protection of 'environment and working environment' are added to the exemptions of Article 36 for public policy, health and patents, trade marks and copyright.

We have heard repeatedly that the Single Act will increase the role of the only elected institution of the Community, the Assembly, now renamed the European Parliament. It creates an elaborate co-operation procedure between the Council, the Commission and the Parliament, too complicated to describe here in detail. The resulting change is that the Parliament now will be better able to delay a decision of the Council – as if the Council was not slow enough – and that the Council will have to act unanimously when adopting a measure opposed by the Parliament. In between the two, the Commission has a role of proposing and re-examining proposals.

The exercise of authority delegated by the Council to itself or to the Commission was for a long time a bone of contention between these two institutions and the European Parliament. In its Article 10, the Single Act decides this in favour of the Council and the Commission and against the Parliament, by a supplement to Article 145. In exercising such delegated authority the Council and Commission need not consult the Parliament or secure its co-operation.

Much attention was also focused on the new rules concerning voting in the Council. The Single Act replaces the requirement of unanimity by qualified majority when voting on measures concerning customs duties, recognition of diplomas, provision of services and transfers of capital, and the implementation of sea and air transport policies, though the establishment of such policies will still require unanimity.

The Luxembourg compromise requiring unanimity where vital interests of a member state are at stake remains important because on many occasions the UK would now find it difficult to get together a majority vote, or even a blocking minority.

One can say, therefore, that the Single Act does nothing to give any real power to the Parliament. It gives much greater scope to the Commission without removing any of its shortcomings; the haphazard choice of subjects for legislation, the secrecy and lack of consultation with interested parties in good time. It does nothing to make the Commission and the Council pay attention to the Court of Auditors and nothing to oblige either of them to propose solutions or to deal responsibly with such major failures as the common agricultural policy.

Unfortunately, new rules do not make new people and even a better Single Act would not make much difference until the member states take the manning of the Community institutions more seriously.

Single market requires regional policy

The basic economic contradiction of the Community which no amount of solemn declarations will charm away is between the need, on the one hand, to have a big European home market if European industry is to compete successfully with the American and Japanese, and, on the other hand, the understandable desire of the industrially weaker regions not to be completely de-industrialised after the protective barriers are removed.

In the absence of an effective regional policy which would subsidise the infrastructure in the less developed regions so as to make them equally attractive for new industries as the old established industry centres, it is hardly surprising that this fundamental contradiction results in a schizophrenic approach to the problems of the Community's internal market.

Let us take the case of motor car standards. Countries which, like France, have a quota for Japanese imports, fear that after completed harmonisation, Japanese vehicles could be imported into France from other member states in addition to the direct imports under the quota.

If the type approval is based on the EEC directives, it offers easier market access to other member states. The US-based companies, General Motors and Ford, make the greatest use of the optional EEC standards but the European companies are still very shy of them.

The reason for this shyness may well have been the detailed nature of the EEC directives. Instead of providing in directives a rigid production specification, it is intended to specify in the future only the minimum standards of safety or of environmental protection to be achieved, leaving it to the manufacturers to achieve them in their own way.

There are two other reasons why motor-car makers prefer national standards to the optional EEC directives. First, it is more expensive to produce to the more demanding EEC standard, and second, the national type approval takes two to three times as long if the vehicle is manufactured according to the EEC standard.

To achieve a common market in vehicles, there would also be need for harmonisation of taxation and removal of price controls. Will the Single European Act help to achieve this need?

Mr Pierre Pescatore who, until his retirement, was considered the intellectual leader of the European Court in Luxembourg, takes the view that the Single European Act opens new possibilities for protectionist policies of member states. This, he thinks, will not only choke the development of a real common market but will also cause external difficulties to the Community with respect to its Gatt obligations.

As Mr Pescatore points out, the amendment of the Treaty achieved by the Single European Act will enable member states to introduce unilateral prohibitions and restriction of imports on the basis of Article 36 and, in addition, also for reasons of protection of environment whenever the EEC harmonisation was adopted only by a majority vote. The Commission will be able to oppose such unilateral measures only if it can prove that they are a means of arbitrary discrimination and disguised restriction of trade.

It will be obliged to take into account special difficulties of individual member states and to keep the harmonisation moving simultaneously in all sectors of industry, which will legalise the present horse trading.

Dr Martin Seidel of the German Federal Ministry of Economics hopes that the Single European Act will speed up harmonisation but at the same time fears its protectionist elements. 'The future development is burdened by some risks and uncertainties,' he said, 'so that the interpretation will depend to a considerable extent on cases to be decided by the European Court.'

In other words, no one knows what will happen, except that the Brussels lawyers will surely have a lot of fun.

Only a really effective regional policy, helping the less developed regions to keep in step with the more industrialised, could convince member states that they can do without hidden barriers to trade.

Ideological limits to unification of company laws

The European Commission believes it to be essential to have a uniform company law in the common market. The real need for this is open to dispute. The US manages to survive as a common market of 50 states with different company laws, and a Federal Securities and Exchange Commission into the bargain.

Nevertheless, the harmonisation of company law might play a useful part in bringing the European market place together and seeing that European companies compete on an equitable basis and can be better compared one with another.

The EEC has made important progress towards bringing the national company laws closer together in the field of accounting and disclosure. But it has stumbled over the Commission's attempt to impose the West German model of two-tier management and worker participation throughout the EEC. And it has not so far tackled some rather important varieties, such as the distinction between issued and paid up capital which is known only in Britain and the Netherlands.

Harmonisation started to bite with the Fourth directive, adopted in 1978. Its purpose is the harmonisation of accounting and disclosure by private and public companies, with the exception of banks and insurance companies. It deals with the layout and content of the annual accounts.

The next important directive was the Seventh requiring the consolidation of group accounts and prescribing their format, audit and publication in the group's annual report. Complementary to these two is the Eighth directive on the qualifications and independence of auditors. These directives have been adopted and must now be honoured in national laws.

A draft of the Ninth directive is designed to protect minority shareholders and creditors.

The Commission has on the table three further projects concerning accounts and disclosure: two of these would extend the accounting rules to banks and insurance companies, while the third would deal with the accounts of EEC-based subsidiaries of banks with headquarters outside the EEC.

The Fifth directive, and the so-called Vredeling proposal, have been the two most controversial projects of the Commission because of their proposed involvement of workers in management. Two two-tier management structure with workers represented on the supervisory board, proposed in the draft Fifth directive, is a norm in West Germany but is viewed with suspicion elsewhere.

The second objective of the draft Fifth directive is the representation of workers in the management structure. The idea is taken from West German company law where the ground for it was prepared gradually, starting in the 1870s when Bismarck realised that consensual industrial relations were indispensable to a country relying on a large conscript army.

But despite the apparent advantage of consensus, of a single trade union for each separate industry, and of mutual trust achieved by giving workers access to information about their company's affairs, Brussels will find it hard to impose the system on the essentially adversarial system of settling industrial disputes in the UK.

Even greater alarm, not only in Europe but also in the US, was caused by the Vredeling project which proposed mandatory information and consultation of employees about the worldwide activities and plans of multinational companies.

In parallel with this slice-by-slice approach to harmonisation, the Commission has also attempted to introduce a uniform EEC company law by the back door, in the form of a European Company Statute. A Draft Statute produced in 1970 envisaged the facilitation of co-operation between national companies incorporated in different member states. European companies at home in the entire Community could, according to this proposal, result from a merger or could serve as a joint subsidiary or holding company of national companies situated in different member states.

This project was keenly supported by the European integrationists. It failed because it was again burdened with a controversial provision for two-tier management and for worker participation. Moreover, the project provided no solution to the problem of multinational taxation.

A more modest approach to building cross-border bridges between companies is the recently revived project of the European Economic Interest Grouping (EEIG). This would avoid the taxation problems and has a fair chance of success. An EEIG is proposed as a partnership without legal personality, whose profits would accrue directly to the individual companies forming it.

It is modelled on the *groupement d'intérêt économique* introduced in France in 1967. The Commission's intention is to make cross-border co-operation between smaller firms easier. The EEIG would be precluded from independent manufacturing activities, but it could co-ordinate purchases, sales and research for its members. It could tender for contracts on their behalf, provide transport services or manufacture component parts for them, and should have no more than 500 employees.

The EEIG may be a tempting proposition in countries such as France where it takes six months to establish a private limited company. However, it has the disadvantage of making each member of the group liable for the unpaid debts of the grouping directly and without any limit.

Another danger is that the grouping could attract suspicion that it operates as a cartel. If it placed on the activities of its members any restrictions prohibited under EEC rules of competition, it could be voided right from the beginning by the effect of Article 85/2 of the EEC Treaty.

Brussels has so far achieved quite a lot of good work on company law harmonisation, particularly in areas free from ideological conflicts. More could perhaps be done, and faster, if the Brussels apparatus was less introvert. Some years ago I talked to one of the Commission's officials, who had spent the best 15 years of his life drafting and re-drafting a company law directive which the member states would not accept. I suggested a few visits to member states to discover the basis of the resistance.

'I have no time for travel,' was his surprising answer. 'It is completely taken up by meetings and correspondence with other departments of the Commission.'

European default judgments

Contrary to most businessmen's assumption, the European Convention on Jurisdiction and Enforcement of Judgments in Civil and Commercial matters (the EEC Judgments Convention) is by no means some sort of innocent 'lawyers' law'. It will bring about a very profound change by ensuring 'free movement' of judgments throughout the Community. It is likely to prove as important for the integration of the European Community as the 'full faith and credit' rule was for the integration of the United States. Embedded in the Constitution, it obliged US courts to respect and enforce the judgments handed down by any other court throughout the Union.

The Convention, concluded in 1968, has been in force between the six original members of the EEC many years. It is now part of UK law.

To avoid undesirable jurisdictions, contracts should include now not only choice of applicable law but also choice of the court before which dispute should be brought. Specific provisions should be agreed for addressing and delivery of notices and warnings of any legal action contemplated by one of the parties.

The European Court has been trying for years to translate the somewhat academic exercise of the EEC Judgments Convention into a language understandable to judges and taking greater account of the realities of business. Two recent judgments illustrate that it can do much but not enough to bring the convention down to earth.

In *Debaecker and Bouwmen*, (Case 49/84) the Court held, on 11 June 1985, that when enforcing a foreign default judgment, the national judge should look beyond the purely formal satisfaction of the requirements of service in the country where the judgment was given. He should consider also any exceptional circumstances which might have prevented the defendant from learning that a legal action had been initiated. The judge should also take into account any responsibility which the defendant might have for not receiving this information.

Some continental courts, particularly in the Benelux countries, are satisfied with a fictitious service of documents – for example, at an address where the defendant is not present or by delivering the document to an authority appointed for this purpose by the statute. It does not matter to them that no actual delivery of the document has taken place. It is *deemed* to have taken place.

In the Netherlands, for example, the documents are deemed to be delivered if they have been transmitted to a court official or to the Dutch Ministry of Foreign Affairs. From that moment on the time given to the defendant for arranging his defence runs – though he may not know about it. Indeed, the first thing he may learn is when a court in his country, or in another EEC country where he has assets, is asked to enforce the default judgment.

The wording of Article 27/2 of the EEC Judgements Convention is ambiguous: it provides that the court asked to enforce a foreign judgment need not do it 'if the defendant was not *duly served* with the document which instituted the proceedings in sufficient time to enable him to arrange for his defence'. What is 'duly served'? Only three years ago the European Court still held that it 'does not require proof that the document . . . was actually brought to the knowledge of the defendant'. But the Court softened this ruling by saying that the enforcing court 'may, exceptionally, consider whether a formal service was fair if it did not require actual communication to the defendant'.

This approach to the default judgments is particularly dangerous in the case of actions initiated in the Netherlands because that country made use of the possibility to modify Article 20 of the Convention so that Dutch trial courts may give judgment in absence of a certificate of service.

The Court seems to have come on the side of the angels. While previously it would only allow the enforcing judge exceptionally to consider a possible unfairness on the formal service, it now requires the judge to consider exceptional circumstances which arise after the 'regular service' has been effected – In the case, the plaintiff learned but made no use of the new address of the defendant after a formal but ineffective service.

A failure to defend an action in a foreign court may also eliminate the possibility of offsetting any counterclaim which the defendant may have and which the trial court may be competent to decide, either under the general rule of the Convention or under one of the exceptional provisions. Though the Convention provides for such exceptional jurisdiction over a claim which should normally be tried elsewhere, in connection with the enforcement of a judgment, the European Court has now sadly restricted and possibly altogether ruled out this provision in its judgment in *AS-Autoteile v Pierre Mahle* Case 220/84 of 4 July 1985.

The German Federal Supreme Court (BGH) referred the issue to the European Court asking whether, under the Judgments Convention, national courts are competent to decide an action, opposing execution of a domestic judgment, based on a counterclaim which, if it was the object of a separate action, they would not be competent to decide. The counterclaim was for an earlier award of costs.

The general rule of the EEC Judgments Convention is that actions should be brought in the Court of the signatory state where the defendant is resident. Article 16, however, provides a number of exceptions to this general rule, one of which is for the court of the place where a judgment is being enforced, if the claim has a special relation to another signatory state than that in which the defendant resides.

The European Court would not have it. It said, rightly, that the opposition proceedings against the enforcement of an order for costs had been used for an ulterior purpose, namely, to make German courts decide an issue for which they did not have jurisdiction according to Article 2 of the Convention; it was an abuse of the process.[1]

However, from this correct finding the European Court regrettably drew a broad ruling which excludes the application of the exceptional jurisdiction in proceedings by which a judgment debtor opposes the enforcement.

As a result, though judgments can cross the frontiers, counterclaims cannot, certainly not at the enforcement stage, which may be the first in which the defendant learns of the existence of a foreign default judgment.

Lords alarmed by EEC's 'external competence'

The principle of the Community's exclusive competence in the field of foreign trade relations, obliging member states not to do anything running contrary to agreements concluded by the Community with third countries, has proved to be very elastic.

A report by the House of Lords select committee on the European Communities made it plain that the UK, as well as other member states, is rather irritated by the Commission's very broad interpretation of this legal doctrine.

Though Article 113 of the EEC Treaty provides merely that '. . . common commercial policy shall be based on the uniformly established principles . . .' the European Court held in a series of rulings that this gives the Community an exclusive competence to conclude commercial agreements with which member states must comply.

The EEC doctrine of the 'external competence' of the Community goes even further; member states must no longer enter into international agreements in any area which is subject to internal EEC Community rules, whether these are laid down in the EEC Treaty or in secondary EEC legislation. As the House of Lords Select Committee states: 'In law, the external competence of the Community is wide and there are few limits to its possible exercise.'[2]

Still, things are never so bad that they could not be still worse and their lordships found numerous occasions to raise their eyebrows and wag their fingers. They seemed to be somewhat alarmed by the Commission's assertion that member states must refrain from adopting national measures not only when these might affect the Community's external obligations, but also whenever such measures could in any way hamper the *future* evolution of Treaty obligations. In the view of the Select Committee, it would be 'rarely appropriate' to exercise external competence under the infinitely elastic Article 235, authorising anything which, though not provided for in the Treaty, is thought to be necessary for the attainment of its aims.

The Committee made clear that the impact of the Community powers should be clearly understood by the British Government and borne in mind when authorisation of further negotiations is sought by the Commission from the Council. It is at this stage that the British Parliament should be informed – and not only after the conclusion of the negotiations, too late for the exercise of any influence, as is the practice at present. By contrast, the Committee sees no reason why the European Parliament should be given any additional powers or influence, and is opposed to its attempt to achieve a veto power by refusing to deliver the Opinions required by the Treaty unless the Commission undertakes to abide by them.

DIVIDING LINE

The Select Committee noted that it was not always easy to say where was the dividing line between the competence of the Community and that of member states. It was equally difficult to say which of the treaties concluded by the Community were directly applicable to the member states in the same way as their national law. They saw dangers in any further development of direct applicability, particularly if it were to extend to provisions which create rights and obligations between one citizen and another, possibly disregarding conflicting national laws.

Such direct applicability and the supremacy of EEC law derive from the notion that all the Community treaties, legislative instruments and other formal Acts constitute a new legal order for the benefit of all citizens of the Community.

There is no doubt that it is a new legal order. If one were also convinced that it benefited all the citizens of the Community, that it was a system providing a minimum of legal certainty and that its purposeful interpretation served the purposes of the Treaty rather than those of its servants, one would find it much easier to subscribe wholeheartedly to its supremacy.

Community law: a tide slow to come in

'The Treaty is like an incoming tide. It flows into the estuaries and up the rivers. It cannot be held back.'

Lord Denning said so years ago and many have repeated the metaphor since, hoping that it would be possible to build a Federation of Europe based on a comprehensive Community Law.

Repetition did not make Denning's prophecy come true. 'I don't think we have seen any such tide on a big scale yet.' Lord Hailsham, then Lord Chancellor, told me in 1987.

Why is it then, that such a big elephant gave birth to such a little mouse?

Let us take the issue of equal pay and sex discrimination in social security cases. Article 119 of the EEC Treaty says: 'Each member state shall . . . ensure . . . the application of the principle that men and women should receive equal pay for equal work.' This, one would have said, meant that member states should adopt legislation to give effect to the principle of equal pay.

However, in the famous case of *Defrenne v Sabena* the European Courts said there was no need to wait for national legislation, Article 119 was 'directly applicable' and national courts were obliged to uphold any claims justified by it.

There followed more European Court decisions. 'Equal work' was defined as 'work of equal value' and this was embodied into UK legislation. EEC directives extended the principle of equal pay to other conditions of employment and to social security provisions. The pioneers of sex equality went from victory to victory. But in a recent research paper the Equal Opportunities Commission, calls them Pyrrhic victories.[3]

There is a sense of disappointment with the actual results of applications made under the equal pay legislation to industrial tribunals. The applicants were successful in only 11 per cent of all sex discrimination claims and 10 per cent of all equal pay claims made between 1976 and 1983. Even in those successful cases the tribunals only rarely recommended a remedial action and the compensation they awarded was often desultory.

A substantial number of successful applicants had to go to the Employment Appeal Tribunal or to a higher court and many found the experience very stressful. In the four years 1980 to 1984 there were 151 successful applicants (a further 50 succeeded later after an appeal) and nearly half of them experienced difficulty or delay in getting an employer to pay the compensation or to take the action recommended by the tribunal. In a few cases employers were obstructive and the tribunal decision had to be enforced by a new procedure in the county court. Some applicants never received the money they had been awarded.

For some successful applicants the situation in their jobs became untenable and they had to leave. A number of applicants said they were dismissed or made redundant because they brought a case. Not one of the successful applicants who remained in their jobs felt that their working conditions and prospects had improved.

The difficulties which the Commission faces when trying to translate into reality some of the laudable objectives of the Treaty lead to the frustration of its officials and result in a bureaucratic bloodymindedness which makes things even worse. Since 1971, the Commission has invariably proposed that regulations introducing generalised tariff preferences be based on Article 113 of the Treaty. This provides for a majority decision of the Council of Ministers and is specific about the role of the Commission in the legislative process.

The Council however, always adopted such regulations citing only the

'Treaty', as it now explains, in order to embrance not only Article 113 but also Article 235 which requires unanimity. Its patience exhausted, the Commission took the Council to the European Court which solemnly annulled Council regulations 3599/85 and 3600/85 because they did not cite Article 113. The futility of the exercise is revealed by the court's postscript to its decision: the annulment will not deprive the regulations of their effects which are to be taken to be definitive!

Sometimes the Commission and the Court get themselves tangled up in a way which outsiders find unbelievable. For example, French books exported first to another EEC country and then re-imported to France can be sold at any price the bookseller wishes, while the same books placed directly on the French market by the French publisher are subject to the maximum 5 per cent discount rule. French courts asked whether this was not contrary to the Treaty principle of non-discrimination. The Court said no. Still in disbelief, the French courts sent a second reference with exactly the same question to Luxembourg. But the European Court would not be moved. It now gave an identical answer in Case 168/86.

Even more serious damage to the credibility of EEC law results from contradiction between the Commission's findings of fact and its legal conclusions.

Dealing with the proposed link between Philip Morris and the Rembrandt Group on the one side and BAT and Reynolds industries, their major competitors on the oligopolic cigarette market on the other, the Commission first found that it was infringing the EEC laws of competition and the second time gave it its blessing, though the changes adopted in the agreements hardly altered their effect.

I found it then difficult to understand the new rule enunciated by the Commission: that the acquisition of 30 per cent of equity in a competing enterprise was not anticompetitive; and its acceptance that a major tobacco company would put $350m into a competitor with no other objective than to obtain a good return on its capital.

It came to pass (in Cases 142 & 156/84) that Mr Advocate General Frederico Mancini shared my lack of sympathy for such reasoning: he proposed that the Court should annul the Commission's decision – but the court did not.

A more serious issue involving the relationship between Community law and national laws was raised by the Commission's attempt to search the Frankfurt premises of Hoechst. It is the practice of the Commission on such occasions to search desks and filing cabinets.

According to German interpretation of Regulation 17/62 it has no right to do such things. Further, as in other member states, no search and entry is allowed without a court warrant and none could be obtained at first by the German Cartel office because the Commission did not provide justification for its suspicion that Hoechst took part in a polyethylene cartel.

Several German courts got involved in the dispute as well as the European Court, first on the application of Hoechst for an injunction, and then on the complaint of the Commission that the German Government failed to do its duty to assist the investigation.

On the surface, the dispute appears to be about the supremacy of German fundamental law over investigatory powers claimed by the Commission. In substance the real problem may be how to overcome the contradiction between the far-reaching ambitions of Brussels with its distance from the places where things happen.

Can one expect the European Court, equipped mainly for solving issues of law, to authorise dawn raids in Frankfurt or in London? Will the future competition court of the Community be better equipped for such a job? Or should one rather look for a model to the dual legal system of the US where a hierarchy of federal courts exists side by side with state courts, and where, in spite of this facility, harmonisation of state laws is not given such a high priority as in the EEC?

Court tells Council to liberalise transport

In a landmark judgment of 22 May 1985, the European Court found the Council of Ministers, representing EEC governments, guilty of breaching the Treaty of Rome by failing to ensure freedom to provide transport services across the Community.

The judgment was the first delivered against the Council of Ministers on a complaint by the European Parliament, which was supported in this case by the European Commission. It establishes for the first time that the Parliament can take the Council to court and will be seen by parliamentarians as opening a new door to extending their influence over Community politics and policies.

The European Parliament cannot claim an unqualified victory. The court did not support the contention that the Council was at fault for failing to agree a common transport policy. It said that the Council had the discretion to organise its objectives on this front and that the Treaty did not lay a sufficiently specific duty on the Council for the court to determine whether it was failing to act.

The Council was at fault, the Court said, in not having established the freedom to provide transport services within the Community. To achieve this would mean eliminating discrimination against the provider of services on grounds of nationality or because of residence in another member state.

The Court said the Council had failed to take measures to comply with the Treaty of Rome, which stipulated that freedom of services should be established within the 12-year transitional period after its signature in 1957.

The Court did not adopt the Dutch Government's proposal that it should transform freedom of transport services from a Treaty objective into directly applicable law, enforceable in national courts. It has, therefore, stopped short of giving the European Parliament legislative powers by the back door.

The judgment is a moral victory for the Parliament but impossible to enforce. The Council has been told that it is its duty to agree but it can hardly be forced to do so.

The Council remains free to deal with most of the Commission's 14 pending specific training proposals as it pleases. The Court did not accept the view of Advocate General Lenz that the Council had a duty to reach a decision on such proposals as the weights and measurements of heavy goods vehicles, co-ordination of taxation of such vehicles, and harmonisation of social measures in inland shipping.

Transport, like agriculture, has its separate chapter in the EEC Treaty. But while the Treaty makes it abundantly clear that its purpose is the subsidising of farmers, it is extremely vague about the aim of any future transport policy.

On the continent, roads and railways have often been constructed and maintained with military rather than commercial needs in mind. This is one reason why there is a reluctance to leave it to the market forces to resolve the competing claims of railways, road transport and inland shipping. Another is the pressure generated by the railway unions and the motor industry.

It is, therefore, hardly surprising that the liberalisation of transport within the Community proceeds only very slowly. According to the Commission, only about 40 per cent of road haulage between member states has been liberalised, while domestic business remains the exclusive domain of local firms. No harmonisation of road taxes has been achieved, and that of the weights and dimensions of lorries causes great difficulties. A structural overcapacity of inland shipping is a barrier to the entry of foreign enterprises.

The conflict between the British desire for free competition on the air routes and the continental countries' desire to protect their national airways has not yet been solved, though it makes the UK appear to be speaking with two voices: fighting for more competition in Europe while defending the Iata cartel in the US. Some co-ordination has been achieved in the area of shipping conferences, but the results make no one happy except a few enterprising businessmen in Third World countries.

The evident inability of the member governments to reconcile their conflicting interests, often dictated by geographic location, as between mainly coastal and maily inland territories, did not deter the Commission from producing a stream of draft directives and regulations. Though some were approved, a pile of 14 proposals remains on the Council's table without any great hope of passage. Half of these concern liberalisation of road transport, including a measure for the equalisation of capacities.

The Commission takes the unrealistic view that the impossibility of reaching unanimity over deeply divisive issues does not absolve the Council from its 'legal' obligation to agree. Though there is no basis for this in the institutional or administrative law of member states, the Commission found an ally in the European Parliament, always keen on the publicity which comes from court proceedings.[4]

Community aid funds: a case for audit

A shrewd and honest manager views his auditors as friends from whom he can learn about his business. But the EC Court of Auditors is distinctly unloved and unwanted.

And yet, instead of viewing the auditors as nosey intruders, the institutions of the Communities could well use them to pursue EEC policies more effectively, confounded as these often are.

They need such help because of the weakness of their own internal audit. This follows the French model in which financial controllers are dispersed in the government departments as the eyes and ears of the powerful Ministry of Finance. The structural defect of the internal audit of the Community is the absence of a power centre equivalent to the French Ministry of Finance to which the financial controllers could refer. As things are, they spend their days by signing spending authorisations and can hardly be expected to carry out an audit of their own activities.

In the case of the Commission, the external audit is all the more important as the decision-making process is largely in the hands of officials without political accountability. The Commissioners who (in theory at least) can be sacked by the Parliament and have an informal responsibility towards the governments which nominate them, often have only the vaguest notion of decisions and other acts of the Commission emanating from departments other than their own. This is the result of a system called 'written procedure'. Proposals drafted for the Commission's approval are circulated to the Commissioners and if they do not protest within a specified time, their approval is assumed.

The real power rests, therefore, with the cabinets of the Commissioners, whose chiefs meet regularly to agree most of the proposals put up by the directors-general of the departments of the Commission. This explains why so many proposals of the Commission do not pass political scrutiny in the Council of Ministers. Such proposals are the product of bureaucrats and most Commissioners, presumably appointed for their political sense, have little chance of considering their likely impact.

The acts done in the name of the Commission can be still further removed from political scrutiny if the Commission delegates its power to another institution. This seems to be the case of aid granted by the Community to the Mediterranean and African countries. The Court of Auditors has tried hard but in vain to check on the use made of aid funds which at the end of 1982 amounted to ECU 5.7bn (£3.4bn).[5] Of this ECU 1.37bn was managed by the European Investment Bank (EIB) on a mandate from the Commission.

The auditors say that such delegation was contrary to the EEC Treaty which makes the Commission responsible for the administration of the Budget but the Commission contests its view and admits its validity only partly, where internal agreements did not yet receive formal approval because of the delays caused by the European Parliament.

Whatever the legal technicalities, the fact remains that the EIB is a closed book to the auditors. No records of the grounds on which aid projects were approved by it, or of their final evaluation, can be found on the files of the Commission. In contrast with other development banks, such as the World Bank the EIB publishes merely a list of projects which it is financing and nothing else.

The absence of information seems all the more serious as, according to its spokesmen, the EIB relies entirely on its own staff when evaluating the feasibility or results of individual projects. The bank seems to be proud of doing without the help of technical consultants.

Even if the promoter of a project is unable to furnish satisfactory information the bank insists that he should himself choose a consultant who will supplement the proposal or the feasibility study. Independent consultants are expensive, and the EIB may be saving some money in this way. However, more is lost by spending on undeserving projects or projects doomed to fail.

The auditors report only one example of a quite unsuitable project financed by the EIB: this was for a sugar refinery which would have absorbed all the water available in the region, leaving none for the population. One suspects that even if colossal blunders are rare, there must be many small errors which could be avoided by employing independent consultants.

Even without them the promoters of the projects and the staff of the EIB might proceed more prudently if they knew that a reasoned report would have to be submitted to the Commission for approval or evaluation. As things are, they can make mistakes without fear of being discovered. In a field where political lobbying combines with commercial interests of contractors, such freedom from scrutiny is bound to provide a fertile ground for undesirable practices.

The auditors' criticism pertains directly only to EIB operations which are financed from the EEC budget – not more than 10 per cent of their total activities. However, the interest differentials and commissions which EIB recieves from this part of its activities go a long way to finance its other activities.

Aid is not an altogether altruistic activity. Those who provide funds expect some business to result. However, the auditors complain that the projects financed by the EIB are not adequately publicised so that EEC companies often have no chance of taking part in the tenders which result from the aid.

Moreover, the bank makes available to Japanese and US suppliers tenders covering projects financed or subsidised from EEC funds, which according to the rules should be opened only to EEC suppliers. In smaller projects the EIB does not seem to ensure that all Common Market suppliers have an equal access. It is satisfied if the promoter submits three quotations for plant or equipment, of which one has to be from another country than his own. It is obvious that this gives the promoter practically a free hand in choosing the supplier. The bank has also renounced its control by ceasing to pay contractors directly and leaving it to the promoter to pre-finance supplies.

The EIB is a very special and influential animal. Right from its beginning it stood under the protection of the Ministers of Finance of the member states. This may explain the Commission's reticence: its bureaucrats may think it wiser not to insist on the letter of the law if this might incur the displeasure of those who hold the purse strings.

Agricultural fraud bleeds Community budget

Subsidies paid to traders when they export agricultural produce outside the Community represent some 25 per cent of the entire budget of the Community.

No one knows how much of this expenditure is due to fraud or abuse of the EEC regulations. If one could reduce the total by 10 per cent, by eliminating at least part of the fraud, a good deal of the community's budgetary problems would disappear.

The fraudulent inflation of EEC subsidies represents, therefore, a very big problem, and the Court of Auditors attempted to tackle it, albeit gently, in a special report[6] published on 26 August 1985.

No attempt was made to estimate the percentage of the expenditure due to fraud and abuse. Indeed, no such estimate is possible as the control of the expenditure is entirely in the hands of member states and, as vividly described in the report, their administrative arrangements for controlling this expenditure are so inadequate that they could not find out even if they wanted to.

The member states have no particular incentive to exercise strict control: it costs money, causes trouble with a valuable electorate, and whatever is spent on subsidies does not go out of their pockets but is charged to the Community. It is a curious division of labour. The Community pays but has no means of checking to whom and why. The member states should check but it costs them nothing if they do not.

The Court of Auditors does not deal with this basic fault in its report. It only analyses the inadequacies of the present system and recommends how it could be improved while retaining the absurd separation of financial interest and control.

The Community adopted no legislation which would ensure that exports for which subsidy has been paid had actually taken place. By contrast, regulations for the calculation of the subsidies abound. These contain now some thousand sections and there is little hope that even a small part of such verbose and detailed legislation could sink into the awareness of Customs Officers and of the clerical staff in the paying agencies. The more rules there are, the easier it is to avoid them. An unscrupulous trader can have a field day.

The methods used by such traders are now getting almost as numerous as the EEC regulations. Collating reports from member states, the Commission counted no less than 60 different types of fraud. One of them, the so-called 'round about operation', is thought by the Board of Auditors typical enough to be described in an annex to their report.

A trader employing this method exports a cargo of goods qualifying for the subsidy and then smuggles it back, either using a road without a customs checkpoint, or concealing the goods, or importing them under a false declaration. He may then sell the goods on the domestic market, benefiting from the high Community price in addition to the export subsidy, or repeat the 'export' transaction, possibly several times.

A physical check on the frontier cannot detect this sort of fraud. It may be discovered by checking the traders' accounts unless, of course, he falsifies them which a prudent fraudster would do.

Such hard fraud is not to everybody's taste, but even when preserving appearances money can be made by means of false declarations of tariff headings, of quality and sometimes even of weight. This is easy when the differences between goods which qualify for subsidy and those which do not is so small that it cannot be detected by a chemical analysis. Such is the case when the qualifying difference in quality is smaller than the degree of error to which analysis is subject.

Moreover, less and less use is made of physical checks – now carried out only in 0.82 per cent of cases – about one fifth of the checking rates, prescribed by EEC standards. Only one to three out of each 1,000 cargoes are subjected to chemical analysis, sometimes quite worthless because it is carried out during the production, possibly on a different batch of goods than those actually exported.

The 'innocent error' method of getting an extra income out of Community coffers is made possible, even encouraged, by the absence of any deterrents. The national agencies appear to prosecute and to impose severe penalties in the rare instances when they detect hard fraud involving large sums of money. They let off with a mere warning traders who made a habit of making erroneous but profitable declarations.

The Board of Auditors complains that no steps are taken in such cases to investigate or rectify previous false declarations and that this approach of national agencies constitutes an encouragement to commit fraud. The court believes that it would help if traders were to give a word of honour that their declarations are correct and risk heavy penalties if this was found not to be so.

Neither hard fraud nor 'habitual' false declarations of the Customs tariff position are necessary for milking the Community. This can be also achieved by sticking to the letter of the law.

The Court of Auditors gives the following example of a typical abuse of this sort.

A trader imports a product which contains n-1 per cent of oils and fats and for which the rate of levy is low, as the product contains less than n per cent of oils and fats. He pays the levy at the low rate. Once the product has been imported, he adds 1 per cent of oils and fats to it. He then re-exports the product and claims the refund, which is more or less equivalent to the levy rate for products containing more than n per cent of oils and fats. The trader has not committed any fraud, but, by adding a very small quantity of oils and fats, has caused the subsidised product to move into a higher refund bracket and has profited from the considerable difference between the low levy rate and the high refund rate.

The transaction may be repeated with the same goods by adding a small percentage of dry ingredients prior to reimportation, thus reducing the proportion of oils and fats once again.

While this sort of abuse is due entirely to the inadequacy of EEC regulations, the failure to detect fraud, whether hard or soft, is seen by the Court of Auditors as a consequence of the absence of EEC legislation which left the methods of surveillance entirely to the member states. Though these methods differ from one country to another, they all seem to have been developed primarily for customs checks on imports and are, therefore, inadequate for controlling exports.

The national systems are based on traditions which give priority either to physical and administrative inspections or to a scrutiny of the exporting firms accounts. The first method will not detect frauds of the roundabout type when an export on which a subsidy has been paid is followed by reimportation and possibly further export of the same product. The second method, by scrutiny of the exporter's accounts, risks that fictitious transactions, when no actual movements of goods take place, remain undiscovered. The court considers that best results could be achieved by combining the two methods of inspection.

In addition to the frauds and abuse made possible by inadequate inspection of either type, the Community also runs the risk that one and the same product will benefit from both a price support designed for the domestic market and an export subsidy. This has been the case, for example, for butter which benefits from a permanent subsidy if destined for consumption within the Common market. In theory it should not receive an additional export subsidy unless the domestic aid has been repaid, but in some member states the two subsidies are handled by different agencies, paid at different stages and no check is made at the time of exportation.

Inspections of accounts do not seem to pay attention to the possibility of double subsidy and though some cases were discovered, no prosecution was ever instituted. It seems that the authorities keep their eyes firmly closed.

Only a democratic lead can take Community out of its bureaucratic maze

---

To say, as some did, that Lord Cockfield, the Community Commissioner for the Internal market, was too big for his boots and unlikely to be reappointed was somehow besides the point. It requires exceptional self-control not to grow out of one's boots in the rarefied atmosphere of Berlaymont's 13th floor, with its vast and luxurious offices and devoted staff who have nothing much else to do but assure the commissioners that they are, or at least should be, ruling Europe. Little can be achieved by replacing a commissioner: his successor would succumb in no time to the snares of his physical surroundings. True, the selection of commissioners could be improved, but, above all, the Commission ought to be subject to the constitutional checks usual in democracies.

Through the legal service of the Commission, the bug of omnipotence and disdain for the letter of the Treaty of Rome spreads to the European Court in Luxembourg. It has also infected the staff of the Council of Ministers. No, I am not going to write about VAT on spectacles. In my view, the Court got that right. But there are other dangers and, given free rein, the Commission will find a pseudo-legal device to push up the price of children's clothes and push down that of cigarettes and alcoholic drinks.

Only recently, the Commission convinced many people that the European Court's judgment in *Morris* gave it the power to control mergers, denied to it by member governments. That move by the Commission at least had a clear, understandable objective even if it was a wrong one. The present, more trivial, pursuit of Lord Cockfield is to make the UK rewrite the State of Art clause of the Consumer Protection Act 1987 in words identical with the corresponding clause of the EEC Product Liability Directive.

The Directive reads:

> The producer shall not be liable . . . if he proves . . . that the state of scientific and technical knowledge of the time when he put the product into circulation was not such as to enable the existence of the defect to be discovered . . .

The Consumer Protection Act says that it will be a defence for the manufacturer to show

> that the state of scientific and technical knowledge at the relevant time was not such that a producer of products of the same description as the product in question might be expected to discover the defect if it had existed in his products while they were under his control.

This, though verbose, seems to be capable of the same effect as the directive. Even if there was some ambiguity in the Act, UK courts would choose from the possible interpretations the one which agrees with the directive. It is hard to say why the Commission makes so much fuss about so little.

Sometimes the fuss has a purpose: to entrench a procedure more favourable to Commission proposals. Thus, in Case 11/88, the Commission asked the Court to declare void a Council regulation defining the maximum permissible content of residual insecticides in animal feeding stuffs. The Commission has nothing against the contents of the regulation but complains that the Council had the temerity to base its decision not only on Article 43 of the Treaty as proposed by the Commission, but also on Article 100, thereby moving it from the category of acts requiring only majority decision to acts requiring unanimous decisions.

The contents of the regulation were also not in question when the Court recently annulled Council Regulation No. 85/469.

The UK was able to obtain its cancellation by the Court only because the Council did not discuss the proposal and adopted the Regulation by a written procedure, which, according to Council's rules should be, but was not, agreed unanimously. However, it was a pyrrhic victory for the UK: the Court also ruled that Article 43 provides a sufficient basis for the Regulation, and that there is no need to refer to Article 100 which requires unanimity. The Community will now go through the entire legislative rigmarole once again and re-adopt the Regulation, overruling British dissent.

A similarly worthless victory was achieved by the UK in Case 131/86. The Court cancelled a Council Directive of 25 March 1986 which provided minimum standards for the cages in which egg-laying battery hens should be kept, but confirmed again the Commission's claim that the Directive should be based only on Article 43, requiring majority voting and not jointly on Article 100, requiring unanimity.

Article 100 enables the Council to adopt by an unanimous decision a much wider spectrum of unspecified directives for the harmonisation of national laws directly affecting the operation of the Common Market. Measures taken for the benefit of animals can be brought under the wider scope of Article 100 but not under Article 43 which provides only for measures benefiting farmers.

This animal welfare aspect of the Directive was very evident from the text adopted by the Council.

However, these references disappeared from the text of the directive published in the Official Journal. The clever lawyers in the Council's secretariat deleted these references and replaced them by a reference to Article 42 of the Treaty which in their view supported their case for a majority decision under Article 43.

They fell into their own trap. The Court granted the UK's application and annulled the directive on the sole ground that the Secretariat is not entitled to change the text adopted by the Council, not even its preamble stating the reasons for, and the objectives of the legislation.

A little victory then against EC bureaucrats who rewrite their masters' decisions. No doubt, however, they will have no difficulty in making the Council adopt the 'improved' text of the directive.

There will be no real respect for the Treaty and the rights of member states unless the candidates for appointment to the Commission and the Court are subjected to the sort of parliamentary scrutiny to which candidates for posts of similar importance are subjected in the US; and unless the Commission is made fully answerable to a truly representative European Parliament.

Notes

1 *Klomps v Michel,* Case 166/80 [1982] CMLR 773.
2 HL236, External Competence of the European Communities, SO, £10.40.
3 Alice M. Leonard *Pyrrhic Victories*, SO, £4.95.
4 Case 13/83, *European Parliament supported by the EEC Commission v Council of Ministers supported by the Dutch Government.*
5 Special report on the management of CDA by the EIB, EC Publications Office, MX 40 84 690 EN C.
6 Special report of the Court of Auditors on the system for the payment of refunds on agricultural exports (Official Journal C 215 of 26 August 1985).

10 New European trade law

Pharmaceutical Society's Quixotic journey to Luxembourg

Ten years after the European Court's judgment in *De Peiper*,[1] believed to have been the last blow to trade mark barriers between member states of the Community, UK pharmacists could still complain – in 1986 – that they must not substitute for certain prescribed medicines the same product of the same manufacturer available more cheaply under a different trade mark in another EC country. It is even more remarkable that the Court of Appeal found it necessary to refer their complaint[2] to Luxembourg – though the Community law on the subject could not be clearer.

Those unfamiliar with the marketing of pharmaceutical products may ask why a company should wish to sell its products under different names in different countries. For the simple reason, of course, that in some countries it gets a better price than in others and that trade marks – as the present case shows – can still be used to prevent the product from being imported by an 'unauthorised' or 'parallel' importer from the low price country to the high price country.

The reasons why prices can differ very substantially between member states of the Community are varied: cartelisation in the Netherlands, price control in France, the National Health Service in the UK, all help to keep the prices high.

Perhaps the right course for the EC would have been to tackle the causes of these price differences. However, it took a different course, it attacked the use of patents and trade marks for the protection of high-price markets.

A series of European Court judgments established beyond any doubt that patent and trade mark rights are exhausted as soon as the product is placed by the manufacturer or with his approval on the market in any of the member countries. This opened the door to parallel importers, first in the audio industry and finally in the motor car industry, but in between the EC doctrine was firmly established and refined in a series of cases involving Sterling Drug and Winthrop, Hoffmann-La Roche, American Home Products, Merck Pfizer. These companies fought and lost seven cases altogether, each of which was a step in the gradual curtailment of patent and trade mark rights or of the registration advantage enjoyed under health and safety regulations in most countries by the research-based pharmaceutical industry. In each of these cases the real adversary was not the parallel importer but the EC Commission.

These judgments of the European Court, together with directives of the EC Council, led to the adoption throughout the Community of a system facilitating parallel imports. In the UK the Product Licence for Parallel Imports scheme (PLPI) was introduced by the DHSS in May 1984. Some 220 such licences were granted for products marketed at a lower price in another EC country by holders of a UK ordinary product licence. The only condition was that the therapeutic effect was identical. The result was that the parallel importers, often with their own distribution chain, made substantial profits out of the price difference.

Most of these products were marketed by the manufacturer under the same name abroad as in the UK but about 50, including 19 of the most commonly prescribed drugs, were trademarked differently. Pharmacists found it profitable to supply the foreign branded version even if the product was prescribed by the doctor under its UK name.

To put an end to this practice, the Pharmaceutical Society, with the backing of the DHSS, issued a statement on 12 June 1986, asserting that the chemists' obligation to follow doctors' prescriptions exactly precludes the substitution of differently named, PLPI licenced, imported products for the domestic brand of the same product. Any deviation from the rules exposes chemists to criminal charges. The effect of this statement of DHSS instructions was dramatic: the lucrative parallel imports of differently named drugs dried out almost instantly.

This prompted the Association of Pharmaceutical Importers (in fact parallel importers) to ask for a judicial review of the measures taken by the DHSS and the Pharmaceutical Society.[3] They argued that these measures were equivalent to quantitative restrictions on imports, prohibited by Article 30 of the EC Treaty.

This contention was rejected by a divisional court of Lord Justice May and Mr Justice Simon Brown. They held that the adverse effect of the measures on EC trade was not due to the infringement of Article 30 but to the doctor's reluctance to prescribe 'parallel imports'.

One may like it or not, but there is little doubt that this decision is grossly out of tune with the jurisprudence of the European Court.

First, the Divisional Court paid no attention to the very wide meaning given by the Luxembourg judges to Article 30. They held, in *Dassonville*, that this prohibits 'all trading rules enacted by member states which are capable of hindering, directly or indirectly, actually or potentially, intra-community trade . . . ! There is no way one can argue that the interpretation given by the DHSS and the Pharmaceutical Society to UK legislation does not fall within this definition.

Second, there is no fall back on the exemption provided for trade-mark rights in Article 36. In the *American Home Products*[4] judgment, the European Court went as far as to authorise the parallel importer to re-label the imported products with the domestic name whenever it could be proved that the manufacturer uses two different names or trade marks with the intention of separating national markets. It left it to the national judge to say whether such was the case. The Commission went even further: it encouraged the parallel importers to 'take the law into their hands'.

True to form, the Commission took the UK to the European Court, asking it to say that the DHSS instructions, confirmed by the Divisional Court, represent a failure on the part of the UK to abide by its Treaty obligations.

In the light of all this one would have said that the EC law applicable to this case was sufficiently clear for application by UK courts without reference to Luxembourg. However, instead of reversing the Divisional Court, the Appeal judges, LJJ Kerr, Ralph Gibson and Russell, sent it to Luxembourg for a prejudical opinion.

Reading the 38 pages of Sir Michael Kerr's judgment carefully, one can sense that he had little doubt about the outcome, though he believed the opposite to be arguable. He feared that because Lord Diplock sent to Luxembourg a case where he had no doubt about the meaning of EC law only because the Court of Appeal differed from his view *(Henn and*

Darby v DPP) the present case would have the same fate if appealed to the House of Lords.

One would hope, however, that their Lordships would not feel equally obliged to send the case to Luxembourg if they agreed with the decision of the Court of Appeal overruling a lower court. After all, if European law is part of UK domestic law, it should be as far as possible, applied by UK courts. The delay resulting from an unnecessary reference to Luxembourg may in fact serve only those who wish to frustrate the European law's effectiveness.

Protecting French hauliers against Belgian competition

Unbelievable as it sounds to someone attuned to a free market economy, there are countries where it is a criminal offence to sell goods or services for less than the amount determined by a cartel enjoying statutory blessing. Belgium is one such countries.

Criminal prosecution of Belgian haulage companies, which charged for their services less than they should, provided the European Court with an opportunity to tell a national judge to verify whether his country has satisfied its EEC obligations and, if not, to draw suitable consequences in respect of the criminal proceedings before him. This was the case in a ruling made on 30 November 1982, concerning the EEC regulation of tariffs for road transport between member states.

Regulation 1174/68 instituted a system of tariff bands providing that member states should agree bilaterally upper and lower limits of freight rates, keeping the lower limit 23 per cent below the upper limit. The manifest aim of this system was to avoid, by means of the upper limit, an abusive exploitation of any dominant position and, by the lower limit, ruinous competition. Member states might unilaterally increase the price limits as expressed in their currency to compensate for fluctuations of the rate of exchange but any lowering of these limits had to be agreed between them, and the EEC Commission might be called upon to arbitrate in cases of disagreement.

These provisions had a curious effect on transport between Belgium and France. The two countries fixed the limits in 1971. Subsequent devaluation of the French franc meant that the lower limit for French transport companies invoicing in French francs was well below the lower limit for Belgian companies invoicing in Belgian francs. The regulation led to unfair competition since the French could undercut the Belgians.

The Belgian companies could, of course, have cut their price to the level of the French, had they been allowed to invoice in French francs, but they were told they must not. To remain in the market, several Belgian companies invoiced transport below the lower limit of tariffs as expressed in Belgian francs.

When this case[5] reached the European Court, it held that member states had an inherent obligation to adjust the tariff band to fluctuations in the rate of exchange, though they had a certain discretion in deciding when an adjustment was necessary. By introducing a margin of discretion the court has, for all practical purposes, killed the obligation to adjust the tariff bands. It left it to the judges to stop criminal prosecutions in similar cases.

The court said nothing about the preposterous drafting of the regulation; it is anyone's guess whether the EEC institutions are unable to foresee the practical results of their legislation or whether they are determined to eliminate competition against the French.

Let the drinks flow freely – but only if of Community origin

While an Englishman will think nothing of starting with a Scotch, continuing with a Pils or even foreign wine with his meal, finishing off with a French brandy, no such broad view of the possibilities of alcoholic poisons offered by this world will be taken by the archetypal Frenchman. A French aperitif, followed by French wine with the meal, and a post-prandial French brandy to aid digestion, is the rule.

One suspects that this French self-denial is unnatural and, indeed, a little research reveals that the French are protected from temptation by ingenious legislation, known as the Code on the Sale of Beverages and Measures against Alcoholism. The Code prohibits the advertising of spirits distilled from grain, such as whisky and gin, but allows the promotion of rum and brandies distilled from wine and fruit which, according to the French authorities, are better for your health. Furthermore, natural, sweet wines of French origin may be freely publicised while the same type of imported wines are subject to restrictions.

The European Court held on 10 July 1980[6] that the discrimination in advertising between domestic and foreign wines and spirits was an indirect restriction of imports from other member states, and, as such, prohibited by Article 30 of the EEC Treaty.

Following this judgment, France was expected to amend its legislation. It did not. On the contrary, prosecutions of importers, journalists and publishers for engaging in prohibited publicity of foreign drinks continued. No fewer than four separate criminal prosecutions with a total of 30 accused were pending in 1982 before the Tribunal de Grande Instance of Paris.[7]

The accused submitted in their defence that the promotion of whisky, port and a particular French aperitif should no longer be regarded as an offence because the European Court had ruled that the relevant provisions of the Code were incompatible with the EEC Treaty. Moreover, they argued that the judgment had a 'global effect' and condemned the entire French Code. For this reason, French national products and products imported from non-member states, as Portugal then was, should also benefit from the judgment in the same way as the products of member states.

The French court referred the four prosecutions to Luxembourg, asking the European Court to determine the impact which its judgment of 10 July 1980, should have on the French national legal system. The court answered the questions at the end of 1982,[7] ruling that the judgment was binding both on the French legislature and on the French courts.

'The authorities participating in the exercise of legislative power are obliged to amend the offending provisions,' said the court, and 'French judges, in exercising their jurisdiction, are obliged to ensure that the judgment [of the European Court] is respected.' But the court was careful to stress that any individual rights – for example, to advertise freely imported beverages – did not derive from its judgment but from provisions of Community law which had a direct effect in the member states. The prohibition of quantitative restrictions on trade and of all equivalent measures contained in Article 30 of the EEC Treaty had such a direct effect.

The court was also careful to emphasise that its judgment protected only the freedom of trade guaranteed in the EEC Treaty and no more. It benefited only products imported from other member states and applied neither to Portuguese products nor to French domestic products. It did not abolish the French Code in its entirely, but only those effects which discriminated against products of other member states.

Beer and the German hangover

After a five-year struggle to uphold the purity of beer drunk in Germany, the German government had to concede defeat in the European Court on 12 March 1987.

German breweries will remain bound by the 470-year-old *Reinheitsgebot*, according to which beer must contain only malted barley, hops, yeast and water. But the German market will be opened to French, Dutch and Belgian breweries which use all sorts of additives.

The European Court may well be right that these additives do not seem to have caused much harm to the European beer drinkers. But this is not a judgment the European Court is called upon to make. The question it had to answer is solely a question of law: whether Germany is entitled to impose stricter quality requirements than other member states.

Reiterating its *Cassis de Dijon* decision, the court said that with some exceptions, member states must admit EEC products which satisfy the quality standards of their country of origin.

This goes too far: there is no justification for it in the EEC Treaty and it will be overruled by the Single Act which allows member states to apply stricter standards even when a Community standard has been agreed by a majority vote in the Council of Ministers.

The question of law may be arguable, but the politics of the decision are clearly wrong. For Germans, beer is an emotional subject. The breweries lobby is extremely influential. The present electorate is no longer willing to take EEC institutions on trust.

Moreover, it is no great problem for foreign breweries wishing to sell in the German market to observe the German standard of purity, at least in their export products, and many do.

To understand the change which German attitudes to community law are undergoing at present, it is necessary to realise that, like so many things in Germany, it is very much a generation problem. The generation which lived through 1918 and 1945 and learned that great schemes and ambitions may lead to a catastrophic bang has faded out from the scene.

For the past 20 years the world has got used to the generation of Germans who started their active life after 1945 – an optimistic generation, conditioned by the economic miracle and the new respectability gained by membership in the West European Community and Nato.

But the young people now crowding into the electoral register entered active life *after* the economic miracle. As they see it, the new German and European institutions are part of the establishment which they find either boring, square, suspect or, in any case, much too secure and snug. The extreme factions, whether green, red or brown, reflect in an exaggerated manner the generally more critical attitude of this generation.

Since it is this generation which will decide the next election, Bonn must take account of it.

This is the reason why one should not take Germany's past record of total support of EEC institutions for granted.

Germany not only took a major part in formulating Community law, it has also shown the greatest respect for it. According to the European Court, it failed in its Treaty obligations only 14 times out of the total of 181 such failures for all member states, in which Italy led with 81, followed by Belgium with 26.

Until recently, German courts were the most prolific source of requests for a binding interpretation of Community law by the European Court. Out of a total of 1,535 such references from national courts which reached Luxembourg by the end of 1986, more than one third came from Germany – more than twice as many than from France. But last year, the number of references from both these countries were halved compared with 1985.

The German courts also adopted a Community stance in cutting down trade mark rights in favour of 'parallel importers' in decisions which were sometimes very painful to German pharmaceutical industry. The Federal Supreme Court rejected the complaints of the pharmaceutical industry against an agreement between public health insurance bodies and the Association of Pharmacists, according to which patients will be supplied with German products bought cheaply on the price controlled Italian market and re-imported into Germany.

In October 1986, the German Federal Constitutional Court paid an even greater tribute to the Community's legal system. It overruled its 1974 decision (BVerf GE 37, 271), declaring that *as long as* the Community has no bill of rights and no democratically elected Parliament, the Court will protect German residents against the infringements of their fundamental rights by Community secondary legislation and administrative decisions.

In its 1986 decision, the Constitutional Court referred to the developments which have taken place in the Community since 1974 and held that 'as long as the Community and the European Court in particular provide effective protection of fundamental rights', it will not exercise its own jurisdiction in the area of Community law.

This second 'as long as' decision, representing the ultimate subordination of German law to that of the Community, was subjected to a severe test by the Commission's attempt to search the Frankfurt office of Hoechst without a court warrant, a severe provocation of the already upset beer-drinkers.

'What will you do if the European Court overrules your objections and takes the side of the Commission. Does not the latest decision of the Constitutional Court bind your hands?' I asked a leading German official. 'You overlook that it is only an 'as-long-as' decision. If the European Court ignores such a fundamental right, our Constitutional Court will again spring into action,' was the answer. The European Court is now on probation.

Good old Coxes destabilise the Common Market

In the 'apples and pears' judgment of 13 December 1983,[8] the European Court displayed great ingenuity in making nonsense out of an almost reasonable EEC legislation, without hardly any comment in the UK – so used has the public become to the vagaries of EEC law.

The key issue of that case was quality standards. These standards are usually imposed to protect the consumer against inferior or even dangerous products. In the case of the EEC Community standards are often laid down to prevent member states from restricting imports by imposing peculiar requirements, which are easily met by domestic producers but not by their foreign competitors.

Until the European Court handed down its apples and pears decision, I had never heard of standards imposed in order to prevent improvements in produce and to eliminate the risk that these might compete with inferior imported produce. We have had to wait for the European Court to hear that this is what the EEC is all about.

The trouble was, of course, started by the British Government which, in 1966, established an Apple and Pear Development Council. Producers cultivating at least 50 apple or pear trees on at least two hectares of land had to belong to it, paying a membership fee, which in 1983 stood at £40 per hectare.

However, a number of growers objected to the payment of this fee and argued that the creation of the Council was incompatible with the organisation of the common market in fruits. They claimed that it was equivalent to a quantitative restriction on trade and that the Council could not enforce the payment of dues for the financing of such illegal activities.

Tunbridge Wells county court found this matter to be somewhat outside its daily routine and referred it to the European Court in Luxembourg.

Once in Luxembourg, the dissident English apple growers discovered that they had a powerful friend in the EEC Commission. In its observations the Commission added to the growers' complaints by stating that the Council's activities, in fact, amounted to state aid, taking the form of obligatory membership fees and that the British Government erred greatly by reporting the recent increase in these dues only after it had been made.

However, Madame Simone Rozes (since promoted to the highest judicial office in France) who appeared in the case as Advocate General, thought that the increase in fees to keep in step with inflation was only of negligible importance. She said she would leave it to the Tunbridge Wells court to say whether the promotion by the Council of Coxes and Bramleys was on such a scale as to risk destabilisation of the EEC market. As far as the quality standards of the Council were concerned, she held that these were mere non-obligatory recommendations and, therefore, not contrary to EEC law.

The court rejected such a lenient view. It was contrary to the exhaustive nature of the EEC quality standards to exert pressure on producers and distributors to achieve higher quality products than those prescribed by the EEC. If the Council engaged in such illegal activities, producers were entitled to oppose membership and to refuse to pay their fees, or at least part of them.

Note well, then, a new commandment from the paper mountain: Thou shalt not produce better apples than Golden Delicious!

Free trade agreements given direct legal effect

It took some time before we got used to the idea that Community law may be directly effective and enforceable in the courts of member states. Even the court's ruling that directives can be directly effective if sufficiently clear and unconditional was ultimately accepted, though it clearly contradicts the EEC Treaty which provides that regulations are directly effective but directives only through implementing legislation or other measures adopted by member states. Few realise, however, that such direct force of law, which national courts must respect, has been granted by the court also to certain provisions of free trade agreements concluded by the Community with non-member states.

The Court performed this long jump on 26 October 1982, when considering the implications of the free trade agreement with Portugal, then not yet a member of the Community. The Luxembourg judges concluded that the prohibition of discriminatory taxation of imported products in the free trade agreement between the EEC and Portugal of 22 July 1972, is directly applicable law and national courts of the member states should ensure that it is observed.

This conclusion, reached when answering questions submitted by the German Federal Finance Court, will be applicable not only to similar provisions in other free trade agreements concluded by the EEC with numerous countries, but also to other provisions of those agreements which are sufficiently clear and definitive.[9]

The ruling is likely to restrict the flexibility of EEC trade relations and negotiations with non-Community countries. Equally, by introducing automatic performance of obligations on the part of the EEC alone, it may diminish the possibility of enforcing performance of its obligation by the other party, and deprive the EEC of the convenient and customary weapon of reciprocity.

The decision, taken in a relatively insignificant dispute between the main Customs Office in Mainz and C.A. Kupferberg & Cie, an importer of port wines, took most observers by surprise. The court's ruling runs contrary, not only to the views submitted by the Governments of West Germany, France and Denmark, but also against that of the Commission. Moreover, though its legal logic is impeccable, its practical effects and motivation seem to be totally opposed to the court's *Polydor* judgment.

The *Polydor* case,[10] which was referred to the European Court by the London Court of Appeal, concerned the same agreement between the EEC and Portugal. The dispute was about the rights of a copyright owner to stop imports from Portugal of gramophone records which were placed on the market there with his agreement.

The question was, first, whether the law developed by the European Court for the protection of parallel importers and prohibiting the use of intellectual property rights for compartmentalisation of national markets within the EEC can also be applied to imports from Portugal. The second question asked whether such judge-made law (known as the 'exhaustion doctrine') was directly applicable and enforceable by national courts.

Though the wording of Article 36 of the EEC Treaty and of the relevant provision of the agreement with Portugal is almost identical, the European Court held that the same words have an entirely different meaning in the two instances. It said, essentially, that Article 36 of the EEC Treaty must be interpreted in the light of the general aim of the Treaty to create an integrated market. This aim was absent in the treaty with Portugal.

Moreover, this treaty did not provide for the institutional and legal instruments which the Community has at its disposal for achieving the uniform application of law and the progressive abolishing of legislative disparities. The Court, therefore, ruled that the doctrine of exhaustion of intellectual property rights by the placing of the product on the market did not apply to trade with Portugal.

Having reached this conclusion, the Court felt it was unnecessary to deal with the question of direct applicability. The member governments and the Commission expressed in the course of the *Polydor* proceedings the opinion that the concept of direct effect, as developed in Community law, must not be transposed to the field of the Community's international relations. They argued that it was necessary to maintain in the context of free trade agreements a balance of the advantages and disadvantages which should exist between the parties to an international treaty.

Though the Court did not express any opinion on this, the general tenor of the judgment made one expect that it would have agreed with this view had it found it necessary to make a ruling.

This expectation proved wrong when in the port wine (Kupferberg) case, the Court could no longer avoid the question. It reached the unexpected conclusion that a free trade agreement may have a direct effect on the basis of a reasoning clearly intended to strengthen the role of Community institutions in the field of international trade relations. It held that the provisions of an agreement concluded by the organs of the Community with an outside country, imposed on member states not only obligations towards that country, but first and foremost obligations towards the Community, which had assumed responsibility for the proper realisation of such agreements.

Agreements so concluded were an integral part of Community law, and their legal effects must be the same, whether applied by institutions of the Community or by member states. In particular, the effects must not depend on the legal significance possibly different from country to country, which national laws accord to international agreements.

The Court said further that the fact that the law of one of the contracting parties accorded direct effect to the provision of an agreement, while the courts of the other parties might refuse it, did not in itself constitute a lack of reciprocity in the operation of the agreement. Also, the fact that the free trade agreements provided for mixed committees to supervise the operation of the agreements, was no obstacle to a direct effect of provisions creating an unconditional and unequivocal obligation which did not require the intervention of such a committee. The provision at issue, which prohibited discriminatory taxation of imported products, was unconditional and was expressed with sufficient lucidity to create a direct effect, and to be respected by courts of member states.

Having thus established an elegant doctrine of far-reaching and potentially harmful consequences, the Court proceeded to let the Mainz Customs Office off the hook. Though German legislation provides that fortified wine, such as port wine, would enjoy a lower rate of tax if produced by fruit co-operatives in Germany, no such wine was, in fact, produced by those co-operatives. And the 'might be' was not enough to establish discrimination.

The Kupperberg doctrine of the Court caused great alarm and within a year the member governments and the Commission succeeded in preventing its further extension to GATT. In a batch of judgments handed down on 16 March 1983 (166/81 and 267-69/81), the Court held that companies and private businessmen in the EEC cannot use their national courts to seek the enforcement of obligations taken on by their governments under the General Agreement on Tariffs and Trade (GATT).

However, the Court managed to keep its hand in the pie. According to previous rulings, the Court could interpret international agreements only if it was necessary for the determination of validity of Community Acts. In the judgments of 16 March, the Court expressly stated that it has the power to interpret the GATT for whatever purpose necessary.

It said it had this jurisdiction since 1 July 1968, when the Community took over the obligations undertaken by its individual members by assuming responsibility for external trade relations.

Public promotion of domestic products outlawed

It is good to hear from Luxembourg that neither Mrs Thatcher nor M Mitterrand would be sent to prison for saying 'buy British' or 'reconquer the domestic market', as the case may be, so long as they did not do anything about it. If, however, they should go so far as to sponsor a publicity campaign or, heaven forbid, introduce special labels or a complaints procedure to raise the quality of domestic products without also making such a procedure available to productts from other EC countries, they could be heading for serious trouble.

They have been warned. A judgment[11] handed down by the European Court, in time for the 1982 pre-Christmas shopping madness, declares, as the EC Commission requested, that the Irish Government failed in its EEC Treaty obligations by instituting such a 'buy Irish' campaign: the Government was also condemned to pay the legal costs.

The objective of the campaign was to increase the share of Irish products on the domestic consumer market by 3 per cent of the total sales and, in this way, to create 10,000 additional jobs in Irish industry.

This objective was to be achieved by four distinctive actions: (1) a 'Shoplink-Service' providing free information about Irish sources of supply; (2) an exhibition centre in Dublin; (3) promotion of a 'guaranteed Irish' label linked with a system of dealing with consumer complaints concerning products provided with such a label, and (4) the organisation of a publicity campaign for Irish products by the Irish Goods Council.

The Commission protested and when the Irish Government persisted with the 'guaranteed Irish' label and with the publicity campaign of the Irish Goods Council, the Commission took it to the European Court.

The Commission said it would be quite different if Ireland tried to promote its products abroad in other member states of the EC. That would be · compatible with Articles 30 and 34 of the EC Treaty. However, to promote them at home was contrary to letter k of paragraph 3 of Article 2 of Directive 70/50 which strictly prohibits measures promoting solely domestic products.

The Irish Government replied that, in adopting this Directive, the Commission abused its powers. There was no justification in Article 30 of the Treaty or anywhere in the Treaty prohibiting the promotion of domestic products. If the Commission objected to the financial aid granted by the Irish Government for this purpose, it should have taken action under Article 90 and 92 which deal with state aids to industry.

The famous Article 30 consists of a single sentence: 'Quantitative restrictions on imports and all measures having equivalent effect shall, without prejudice to the following provisions, be prohibited as between member states.' In all the relevant decisions of the court, the complaint concerned statutory measures and never mere persuasion. In its definition of 'equivalent measures',[12] the court spoke of commercial regulations (toute reglementation commerciale). It is, indeed, difficult to imagine that the fathers of the Treaty had in mind campaigns to bring domestic products to the attention of consumers when they spoke of 'quantitative restrictions on imports and all measures having equivalent effect'.

To the argument that persuasion was not a 'measure' meant by Article 30, the Commission simply insisted that incitement, even if purely of a moral character, was a measure in the meaning of Article 30 as soon as it was perpetrated by a public power and the fact that the European Court had so far not had an opportunity to pronounce on this was neither here nor there.

The Court first analysed the nature of the Irish Goods Council and, having found that its 10 members were appointed by the Minister and that the Government also subsidised its activity, concluded that the Irish Government could not claim that the 'buy Irish' campaign was carried out by a private organisation.

As to the objection that the subsidy which the Government provided fell under the rules established by Articles 92 and 93 of the Treaty, the Court said that this did not mean that the campaign could have escaped the prohibition contained in Article 30. The aim of the programme, said the Court, was to substitute certain imported products by national products and this could affect the level of inter-state trade in the Community.

The Court used the opportunity to make one of those sweeping pronouncements which are meant to re-appear on many different occasions and serve many different purposes still hidden in the future. It said:

> Even those acts of member governments which are unenforceable can influence the behaviour of traders and consumers . . . and can thus endanger the aims of the Community as stated in Article 2 and elaborated in Article 3 of the EEC Treaty.

A national programme devised by the Government, with the objective of putting the brakes on the exchange of goods by the promotion of national products by means of a publicity campaign and of special procedures applicable only to national products, was definitely forbidden.

We always knew that patriotism was not very effective in business – to make doubly sure, it is now also prohibited.

The EC's duty to take anti-dumping measures

What can companies threatened by imports of subsidised products do – only complain? Or can they take the EC Commission to court if it fails to take anti-dumping measures? In a surprisingly reassuring judgment[13] the European Court has held that companies have a right to protection and can ask for a judicial review of the Commission's acts or inaction.

Ever since the Community took over from member states the responsibility for anti-dumping measures in 1979, industry has been somewhat nervous, fearing that Brussels might take into account other considerations besides the harm caused by imports of subsidised products. In fact, the Commission has proved too hasty in some instances, as for example, in the Soviet nickel case. There it imposed an anti-dumping duty only to retreat completely when *Raznoimport*, the Soviet state export organisation, took it to the European Court and presented evidence that it was itself undercut by other cheap exporters to the Community.

Between 1980 and 1982 the number of annual investigations initiated by the Commission rose from 25 to 58. However, less than one-fifth of these led to imposition of countervailing duties. Some investigations were stopped even before they reached the formal stage, and this was the fate of a complaint made by Fediol, the Federation of the EEC Vegetable Oil Industry.

Fediol complained to the Commission in spring 1980 that Brazil's subsidies for soyabean oilcakes exported to the Community caused harm to the EEC industry. It asked for the opening of anti-dumping proceedings under Regulation 3017/79, and for a provisional countervailing duty. The Commission started informal investigations and obtained some concessions from the Brazilian Government, but not enough to satisfy Fediol which, in September 1981, sought an immediate opening of formal anti-dumping proceedings. Fediol warned the Commission that it might claim damages for the Community's failure to impose a countervailing duty.

About two months later the Commission telexed that it did not intend, for the time being, to open anti-dumping proceedings, and explained later that Brazil had withdrawn most of the subsidies. Consequently it did not appear 'opportune' to the Commission to open proceedings.

As the Commission said, it had to bear in mind not only the interests of the European industry but also those of consumers. Its informal communications were concluded by a letter to Fediol stating that the Commission would not open anti-dumping proceedings, although it was not happy about the advantage received by Brazilian exporters in the form of credits. Against this decision Fediol appealed to the European Court, asking for its annulment.

The court, which, in most cases follows the Commission's legal opinion, this time decided in favour of Fediol. It also used the opportunity to lay down rules to be followed by all participants in the Community anti-dumping game.

Enterprises or trade associations, said the court, may complain of dumping either to the Commission or to a member state, which would then be obliged to transmit the complaint to Brussels. The Commission should consult with member governments to establish whether the exports are subsidised and cause real prejudice to a Community industry and, if so, what measures should be taken.

If the Commission concludes that there is insufficient evidence to open proceedings, it must inform the plaintiffs. If, however, it is of the view that such evidence exists, it is obliged to announce the opening of proceedings in the Official Journal and continue investigations, either directly or in co-operation with member states. The plaintiff should be kept informed and given an opportunity of meeting other parties to the investigation. At this stage the Community institutions can take preliminary decisions or promptly apply provisional measures.

These measures can include obtaining assurances from the exporting country or imposing a provisional countervailing duty. A definitive countervailing duty may be imposed by the Council when proposed by the Commission.

The Court concluded that Community producers not only have a legitimate interest in the institution of anti-dumping measures but that Regulation 3017/79 also gives them a right to be informed if the Commission decides not to take anti-dumping measures. The plaintiff should receive at least an outline of the conclusions and of the grounds on which these were reached by the Commission.

The Court said that the Commission is obliged to make objective findings about alleged subsidies and the harm they might cause, but has a wide discretion when it comes to deciding on protective measures. It followed that, in addition to appealing against infringements of the rules, Fediol could also ask for a judicial review of the use made by the Commission of its discretionary powers.

It could appeal to the Court not only because the Commission did not observe the procedure prescribed by Regulation 3017/79, but also on the grounds that it misjudged the facts, ignored signs pointing to the existence of an export subsidy, or abused its power by reaching its conclusions improperly.

Do not do to others . . .

From initial hesitation, the EC Commission soon moved to the other extreme, wielding the anti-dumping weapon in a way which turns it into a boomerang. In this it received full backing from the European Court in its judgments of 7 May 1987 (Cases 240, 255, 256 and 259/84) rejecting appeals by a number of Japanese manufacturers of small ballbearings against an anti-dumping duty instituted by Council Regulation 2089/84.

The main complaint in all these appeals – as well as in those in the pipeline and now likely to be abandoned – concerned the method of calculating the dumping margin by the Commission. This should be the difference between the 'normal value' charged on the exporter's domestic market and his lower export prices. The anti-dumping regulation gives the Commission a choice of methods of calculation – transaction prices, averages, mean prices, most frequently encountered prices. According to Article 2/9 of regulation 3017 'in order to establish a valid comparison, the export price and the normal value should be assessed on a comparable basis in respect of physical characteristic of the product, quantities and sales conditions'.

The Commission used a weighted average for calculating the 'normal' domestic price in Japan but compared it with an average of only that part of the export prices which was under the level of the 'normal' price. The excess of export prices which were higher than the domestic price in Japan was cut off and these prices appeared in the calculation as equal to the 'normal price'. The Japanese companies may have been guilty of dumping but such an arbitrary method of calculation seems to ignore the reality of the market where individual transactions are at different prices to meet marginal demand.

The Japanese companies complained that the Commission obtained in this way a lower average of the export prices than corresponded to reality and that the use of the two different methods made the figures incomparable and the result unfair. The Court said the Regulation said nothing about the need to use identical methods and rejected the complaint of unfairness, reasoning that the Japanese charged higher prices in some transactions only to achieve an average which would obscure the dumping effect of other transactions. One can only pray that a similar treatment should not be applied by others to the subsidised exports of the Community.

Notes

1 *De Peiper* [1976] ECR 613.
2 *R v The Pharmaceutical Society of Great Britain, ex p The Association of Pharmaceutical Importers* FT Law Report, 20 October 1987.
3 Case 8/7, *Procureur du Roi v Dassonville* [1974] CMLR 436.
4 *Home Products* [1979] CMLR 326.
5 Case 32/82, *Public Prosecutor v Patrus Suys,* 30 November 1982.
6 Case 152/78; judgment 10 July 1980, Rec. p. 299.
7 Cases 314-6/81, 83/82, 14 December.
8 Case 222/82, *K. & J. Lewis Ltd and others v The Apple and Pear Development Council,* FT Business Law Brief, January 1984.
9 Case 104/8i, *Hauptzollamt Mainz v C. A. Kupferberg & Cie,* judgment of 26 October 1982, unreported.
10 Case 270/80, *Polydor and RSO Records Inc v Harlequin Record Shops,* judgment 9 February 1982, FT European Law Letter, March 1982.
11 Case 249/81, *EEC Commission v Ireland,* judgment 24 November 1982, unreported.
12 *Dassonville,* Case 8/74, Rec. p. 837.
13 Case 191/82, judgment 4 October 1983.

11 Competition, mergers and takeovers in a shrinking world

The need for a world-wide competition policy

The competition enforcement policies of the Western world have largely outlived their usefulness. Both the EEC and the German systems have their roots in the US anti-trust laws conceived early after the Civil War between the North and the South at a time when the federal government as well as the small businesses of the victorious North were afraid of the strength and power of the newly emerging trusts.

Since those days both the US trusts, now better known as 'transnationals', and the economies of the European countries have spilled over their national frontiers. For a time the fear of the political power of big business was reinforced by the backing which Hitler received from it on his way to despotic power. This, too, now seems to be only history.

The UK system – if one can call a system the confusing multitude of rules whose unpredictability is unimportant only because they are so ineffective – differs from the US, EEC and German concept by its lack of all religious fervour; it is largely agnostic when it comes to weighing the advantages of competition against other interests.

The present form of all these systems has its origin in the 1950s. Much has changed since then and there seems to be a universal agreement that the rules now need to be revised. What a pity that no one seems to see this as a great opportunity for harmonising competition policies internationally and reducing the conflicts in which the US became involved by trying to apply its anti-trust laws to behaviour taking place outside its frontiers.

Looking back at the history of the UK's restrictive practices legislation, one can see that its only real effect has been to drive the cartels underground. The Office of Fair Trading can act only where it has firm evidence that a price-fixing cartel exists. It cannot actively seek evidence of such price-fixing agreements. Companies forming a cartel are obliged to register it and to volunteer details of their agreements but if they do not, the penalties are, according to Sir Gordon Borrie, Director General of Fair Trading, 'neither immediate nor serious'.

The Government is well advanced in its review of competition policy and Sir Gordon is pressing for a radical change in the system which would amount to prohibition of certain categories of restrictive agreements and which would give his office the power to search for such prohibited restrictive agreements and bring them to book.

He seems to be much happier with the present control of mergers which the Government can, for most practical purposes, stop by allowing them to be referred to the Monopolies Commission. The Government professes to be guided by the Tebbit rule that references should be made 'primarily' on competition grounds and that competition should be considered in an international and not simply a UK context.

The international context of mergers and acquisitions is now also the dominant consideration in the US. Indeed, only about 10 mergers were stopped in the US over the two years 1986 and 1987 compared with much higher figures in the 1970s. New legislation proposed by the Administration to Congress would prohibit only those mergers in which the domestic anticompetitive effect is not offset by a potentially greater competitive capability of the merged companies on international markets. Industries threatened by foreign competition on the US market should be able to apply for anti-trust exemption of up to five years.

Even before the Reagan era, the Chicago school had brought about a radical change in the thinking of US anti-trusters. It achieved a much more relaxed view of vertical restraints of trade such as exclusive or selective distributorships, licensing of different sorts and franchising. It is now recognised that such practices can be often procompetitive. They are seen as anticompetitive in certain cases only on the basis of economic analysis and not on the basis of a 'per se' legal doctrine.

By contrast the EC Commission religiously sticks to a legal doctrine acquired from a previous generation of US anti-trusters, and does so with disastrous effects. Article 85 of the EEC Treaty was modelled on the prohibition of business 'conspiracies' by the Sherman Act of 1890. It is so widely worded that it can be applied both to horizontal agreements – price fixing and market sharing – and to vertical agreements concerning distribution, licensing and franchising. Worst of all, Article 85 provides for a complete and automatic nullity of all agreements which it prohibits; its application by the Court and the Commission has succeeded in depriving of validity a vast number of agreements which are completely innocent in the sense that the restrictions which they impose on the parties are not anticompetitive in any real sense of the word. They may even be, and often are, procompetitive.

The Commission and the European Court brought within the prohibition of Article 85 agreements or terms which only restrict the grants of rights, which the grantor could have exercised alone and by the granting of which he increased competition either immediately or for the future. This includes patent and know-how licensing agreements, franchising and many, though not all, distribution agreements. The Commission, which pondered thousands of notified patent licensing agreements for years and then perpetuated the state of uncertainty by a vague block exemption regulation, is now poised to administer a similar blow to know-how and franchising agreements. It is assisted in this destructive policy by the European Court.

The EEC Treaty rules do not provide for merger control but joint ventures are caught by Article 85. The Commission, while professing a full understanding of the potential contribution of joint ventures, has done little so far to make them safe from illegality under EEC rules.

The German Federal Cartel Office (FCO) seems rather proud that out of 40 joint ventures for research and development which it investigated, it disapproved of only three. Merger control is now wielded in Germany with a light hand. Only seven mergers were formally prohibited, though 25 were given up, during discussions with the FCO in the two years 1983 and 1984 when 1,130 mergers were notified. In 75 per cent of cases, the merger was approved within a month of notification though the law gives the FCO four months to decide.

Not all prohibitions made by the FCO prove to be the last word. In the 11 years from 1973–1984, 62 mergers were prohibited by the office but only 25 prohibitions stuck. In three instances the companies avoided the prohibition by modifying their projects, in 18 cases the prohibitions were lifted in appeal procedure, and in 15 cases appeals are still pending.

On the whole, the FCO now accepts the new US doctrine that some mergers and restrictive agreements may not only be harmless but even procompetitive. Regarding possible abuse of market power by means of vertical restraints the FCO seems to be mainly worried about the weak bargaining position of small and medium-size manufacturers facing the great buying power of retail chains. The FCO has also received new powers to counteract predatory pricing by such organisations, aiming at the elimination of weaker competitors from the market.

To sum up, a more relaxed and more pragmatic approach to competition enforcement seems to be evident both in the US and in Germany, while in the UK Sir Gordon Borrie pleads for new powers to toughen up the ineffectual restrictive practices legislation. The three systems, therefore, move closer together.

As for the EEC Commission, that has tied itself in knots by a combination of bigotry and inefficiency. The need for a revision of the competition rules of the Treaty and the establishment of an EEC court of the first instance – from which there would be a further appeal to the European Court – has now been approved by member states.

Though no improvement can be achieved without a change of heart (and of some heads) a revision of the Treaty could make it easier by removing automatic invalidity of prohibited agreements, by confining the Commission to the role of prosecutor and by leaving the adjudication to the competition benches of the new court of the first instance. This should be constituted so as to decide quickly in an informal process, very much like the decision-making units of the FCO in Germany. This might be also a suitable model for the reform demanded by Sir Gordon in the UK.

An international harmonisation of competition enforcement should also provide for measures against the sovereign villains. Opec, the cartel of oil-producing countries, bears a heavy responsibility for the inflationary recession after 1973; the 'recirculation' of the exorbitant profits of the oil producers has led to an unhealthy expansion of credit and unmanageable indebtedness of less-developed countries.

Still with us are the Government-sponsored or protected air transport and shipping cartels, and the national cartels of insurers closing the market to interstate competition within the EC, and these, too, need to be curbed with greater rigour.

A tall order for anti-trusters, but then, they were not constituted to make life difficult to distributors of bridal gowns and inventors of windsurfing boards, but to tackle dangerous combinations.

Competition: the different concerns of the UK, FRG and EC

Though France has been edging forward in recent years, Europe – the whole of it – has still only three competition enforcement agencies worthy of that name, in London, Berlin and Brussels.

The problems which these three agencies face could not be more different: while the EC one is now mainly concerned about state aids, and the West German about deregulation, Sir Gordon Borrie, UK's long-lasting and increasingly radical Director General of Fair Trading, is worried about extra work caused by private attempts to frustrate competition opened up by deregulation and privatisation.

It says something not altogether pleasant about the state of the UK, that a large part, perhaps a quarter, of Office of Fair Trading (OFT) resources is absorbed by regulation of consumer credit. There was an 11 per cent rise in the number of applications for money lending and debt collecting licences – by July 1986, the total number had reached 200,000. At one end of the scale are the shady money lenders exploiting those who cannot make ends meet; at the other, large reputable institutions which constantly fill my letter box with unsolicited offers of credit.

The first category is despicable, the second is respectable but probably more damaging to the economy. The 20–23 per cent per annum interest may add to production costs through pressure on the wage bill, not to speak of the effects such a boom in consumer credit has on inflation and the balance of trade.

The effects of consumer credit inflation are probably made worse by the near impotence of the OFT to proceed against cartels. This is how Sir Gordon describes his position: 'With almost Gilbertian absurdity, I find myself having to possess sufficient evidence of a cartel's existence to convince a court, before I can issue a formal notice to the parties inquiring if they have a cartel agreement between them.'

In 1986, the OFT considered 313 mergers compared with 192 in 1985. These 313 takeover bids were aimed at targets with total assets of £123bn.

Mergers in banking and finance topped the list. The 38 bids in this category, 11 by foreign institutions, aimed at £47bn of assets – an average of £1,236m per bid. The same number of bids in food, drink and tobacco sectors aimed at assets worth £23bn. Other active areas were distribution (30 bids: £7bn), business services (26: 93bn), ancilliary financial services (25: £6.3bn) and mechanical engineering (20: £5.6bn). These were the statistics of the Big Bang. Was such pace of concentration good or bad? How often did it improve efficiency and competitiveness in the world markets?

Two years later and the 1986 figures are history. But they indicate a trend. Bigger and more dramatic takeover bids followed. As there is not much the OFT can do against consumer credit expansion, cartels and mergers, it turns its attention to restrictive practices in the professions and all sorts of unfair trading. Indeed its reports lead one to the conclusion that an act against unfair trading would not come amiss.

The report of the Federal Cartel Office (FCO), for the years 1985 and 1986, underlines that the internationalisation of competition makes it increasingly subject to trade policy. 'Actual or potential foreign competition can prevent market dominant situations at home only when the foreign competition is not restricted by protectionist measures.'

As in the UK, the number of mergers in West Germany reached a new peak, with 802 completed in 1986. However, more than 70 per cent of the mergers notified in 1985 and 1986 were acquisitions of small and medium-sized enterprises with a turnover of no more than DM 50m (£17m). Only 3 per cent of mergers concerned the acquisition of enterprises with a turnover of DM 2bn and these 52 cases were mainly a West German offshoot of mergers taking place abroad, particularly in the US. Within the reported period falls, of course, the biggest West German merger so far, between Daimler-Benz and AEG.

The FCO stated that the effect of mergers on competition was in most cases slight because of the small turnovers involved and because many of the mergers were really acts of financial reorganisation. A number of mergers was viewed by the FCO as benefiting competition, when the merger enabled a foreign competitor to enter the West German market. This explains why the FCO prohibited only seven mergers in 1985 and two in 1986.

A quarter of all notified mergers took place between trading organisations. Of the 347 trading enterprises taken over in 1985 and 1986, 68 were engaged in food retailing and had a turnover potential of more than DM 6bn. The merger control provided an effective barrier against takeovers by leading enterprises, but the FCO fears that this barrier has been dismantled by the latest decisions of the West German courts which practically reduce the ground for prohibition to market domination by a single enterprise.

The FCO reports that there were 50 mergers in the press sector and that it is trying hard to preserve the remaining independent papers battling against the regional newspaper monopolies.

The competition department of the EC Commission, much smaller than either the OFT or the FCO, concentrates on three issues, described by Mr Peter Sutherland, the Competition Commissioner, as 'current and practical': state aid, civil aviation and merger control.

The attempt to evaluate state aid from a Community rather than a national perspective is a tall order. As the Commission says, aid to shore up the lame duck industry in one member state may put a viable competitor in another member state out of business. The issues are, therefore, highly political and the Commission relies on support from the European Court, which recently ruled that aid for which the Commission's approval was not obtained has to be repaid. However, Mr Sutherland assures that state aid for small and medium-sized companies, particularly in the field of research and development, are generally regarded as beneficial.

The attempts to introduce competition into European air transport appears to be even more of an uphill task. The Commission faces resistance from both governments and airlines. It launched a series of proposals for liberalising government controls over fares, capacity and market access. It started direct actions against airlines for infringement of the competition rules. But it is the European Court where the most radical moves for introducing competition into air transport take place.

Finally, the merger mania has encouraged the Commission to revive one of its most cherished projects: the 1973 proposal for Community-wide merger control. It has been twice amended, in 1981 and 1986. Though objections were directed mostly against details, it seemed that some member states were opposed to the very principle of a Community-wide system of merger control. However, the relentless offensive of Mr Sutherland seems to be having some effect.

As merger control (or its absence) is so much a matter of economic policy and transatlantic relations, a harmonisation of national objectives on merger policy might be an indispensable prelude to a Community-wide procedure.

Why the EC, US and German models of competition enforcement may not work in the UK

There is a danger in the dominant role economists have in the great debate about the future of the UK's competition policy: while a competent lawyer will keep his fees within the limits of his client's earning capacity, so as not to kill the goose, an economist has no personal stake to restrain him. In his selfless endeavour to convince other economists of the correctness of his particular theory, he may destroy the wealth of nations in total innocence.

It is not enough to view competition policy as part and parcel of a broader economic policy. It is also necessary to consider its practical effect on the industrial, social and legal infrastructure, which will differ from one country or region to another.

There seems to be considerable impatience with the results of the UK's competition policy and law, and a tendency to think that a version of the US Sherman and Clayton Acts, in the guise of Articles 85 and 86 of the EEC Treaty, should be adopted in the UK to give competition enforcement the necessary bite.

Though the restrictive practices legislation has achieved quite a lot in various fields, often without much publicity when companies modified their agreements and practices to avoid being taken to the Restrictive Practices Court by the Fair Trading Office, the dissatisfaction is justified. Many cartels have simply been driven underground and the present merger mania needs little comment. It is also true that the Director-General of Fair Trading is in a Catch 22 situation, as he cannot start investigations unless he has reason to believe that some specific infringement is taking place.

Private actions by those who suffer damage from anticompetitive behaviour might be more efficient than public prosecutions. However, though such actions are feasible in the UK in respect of infringements of statutory duties imposed by the UK or EEC legislation, no one seems to be very keen to go this way. Indeed, there is only one example when damages were paid: the Post Office obtained £9m in compensation in the case of the cable cartel but this resulted from a settlement rather than a court judgment.

One reason why companies seem to be so diffident may be that those who live in glass houses do not like to throw stones. Another, no doubt, is the enormous cost of litigating an issue uncertain as to facts and to law. In the US, the temptation is greater, because of the possibility of obtaining treble damages, and the risk is mitigated: the plaintiff can agree contingency fees with his lawyers, and in any case will not have to pay the other party's costs if his complaint is rejected.

It should be also borne in mind that in recent years, competition enforcement in the US has undergone a profound change. Under the influence of the Chicago school, vertical restrictive agreements between suppliers and their distributors or between patent owners and their licensees are not automatically prosecuted. Indeed, it is recognised that many such restrictions help to establish new products on the market and are, therefore, procompetitive.

By contrast, the EC Commission sticks to the formalistic notion that every restrictive agreement must by its very nature distort competition and is prohibited unless exempted by the Commission. Supported by the European Court, it restricts in this way the transfer of technology by licensing, puts in question the legality of franchising agreements and attacks distribution agreements even if these are for branded products for which there is sufficient competition from other brands on the market.

The greatest damage done by the EEC competition policy, however, springs from the contradiction between the enormity of its ambition to root out every conceivable restrictive agreement right from its beginning, and the inability of the relatively small staff of the Competition Department to master such a gigantic task. While UK legislation provides that restrictive clauses of agreements which should have been registered with the Fair Trading Office, but were not, are void and can be attacked as such by the parties in court, the EEC rules go much further. Paragraph 2 of Article 85 declares null and void all prohibited agreements.

Initially, the European Court held that, as in the UK, notification of such agreements to the Commission gives them provisional validity. This concession to the demands of legal certainty were withdrawn many years ago, so that all suspect agreements can now be attacked in courts as invalid by a party which is reluctant to pay or perform.

The 'comfort letters' which the Commission now sends to firms whose notification have been placed on the 'dead file' mean only that the Commission has no immediate intention to investigate. The European Court held that these letters have no legal effect. It may be practical policy to rely on them when the stakes are not too high. But in the case of major projects, or even small projects opening the possibility of further development of EEC competition law, one should beware of the possibility that the Commission may reopen the file at any time, to the great embarrassment of the parties who in the meantime might have become heavily involved in the project.

It would be very bad if the automatic invalidity of suspect agreements became part of UK law. Indeed, no effort should be spared to convince the European Court that it should revert to its earlier concept of provisional validity.

The uncertainty created by the automatic invalidity of prohibited agreements particularly affects small and medium-sized firms which have not the means to defend their agreements in courts and to have them referred, if necessary, to the European Court. The Commission does not decide more than a dozen cases or so each year, so that the notification of suspect agreements piles up and firms which do not want to bear the risk for an unforeseeable future have to give up promising projects, which could not bear the burden of a provisional, but practically perpetual invalidity.

Another aspect of EEC competition which cannot be ignored is that it applies only to one sector of the economy. Manufacturing industry and its distributors are required to abstain from all measures protecting market shares and price levels. But the prices of their raw materials, of energy, of transport and of communication are kept artificially high.

The high prices of food and transport lead to much higher wage bills for industry.

The EEC was designed as a gigantic cartel for agriculture, steel and the coal industry. It tolerates the air transport and shipping cartels and deals very gently with the oil companies. This basic imbalance, discriminating against manufacturing industry, should be in the forefront of the competition debate. German competition enforcement which, like the EEC rules, is modelled on American anti-trust, is sometimes viewed as an effective way of protecting competition. But rigorous application of competition rules does not interfere with the real planning and co-ordination system of German industry, which is operated by the big banks. Unlike UK banks, German universal banks have for 100 years had an important stake in industry, expanding their empires with each recession by a series of 'rescues'. Not only their own equity but also the shares they hold on behalf of their customers give them a decisive say on the supervisory boards of major German companies. Their investment and marketing policies are co-ordinated by the banks with the help of hundreds of backroom boys – probably more numerous than the staffs of the central planning commissions in communist countries.

To apply EEC or German methods in the different conditions of the UK might put British industry at a great disadvantage.

Competition rules which may hamper competition

The economic approach to law – a fashion arriving from the US – leads sometimes to the conclusion that both justice and law have or should have as their overriding aim the maximisation of the wealth of society.[1] Far be it for me to subscribe to such a dangerous philosophy, which is no better than the old-fashioned utilitarianism, in the name of which all things good and evil can be equally justified.

However, if there is one branch of law in which economic analysis should precede and justify legislation, it is the field of competition, anti-trust, restrictive practices or whatever name is given to the government's efforts to preserve the freedom and possibility to compete, often against the will of the most important potential competitors, and almost always against the will of the professions. Even in this field, however, a note of caution is necessary. The freedom to compete may be instrumental to the maximisation of wealth but even where it is not, it may still be justified by the need to prevent monopoly turning into a dictatorship.

For a long time this objective, which one may call ideological, dominated the thinking of anti-trusters in the US, in Germany and in the EC. A turn towards an economic evaluation was signalled by the US Supreme Court's decision in *Continental T.V. v G.T.E. Sylvania*.[2] In this judgment the court abandoned its earlier ideological stance, according to which certain restrictive agreements were anticompetitive and prohibited per se.

Instead, the court held that it was necessary to analyse the market in order to see whether distribution agreements did, in reality, restrict competition. It recognised that it might sometimes be necessary to restrict competition between dealers selling a certain brand of a product in order to improve and promote competition between different brands of the same product. This way of thinking, taken up and developed by the Chicago school of anti-trust economists led to a substantial relaxation of anti-trust enforcement in the US.

Unfortunately, this new thinking has not yet penetrated the EEC fortress in Brussels. The two regulations on distribution agreements, much the same as that on patent licensing, are dirigistic exercises which, under the guise of an exemption, try to tell businessmen what they should do.

* * *

The result is, as Dr Valentine Korah, says in her penetrating study of the two new regulations

> that . . . all the trouble taken by the Commission to open up markets, most of which were already subject to substantial inter-brand competition, all the trouble that will now have to be taken by legal advisers to understand the new legislation, and the cost to businessmen in having to rethink and renegotiate their distribution agreements have done little to increase competition and may well have reduced both efficiency and flexibility.[3]

The Commission's main concern has always been to prevent distribution agreements from creating an exclusivity: there should always be the possibility for dealers who are not appointed to obtain supplies through 'parallel imports' across the state frontiers within the Community. This is the way the Commission wants to protect the Common Market against partitioning. In many sectors this is about as real as wanting to protect pie in the sky against mice. In drinks, for example, there is no Common Market for the simple reason that the member states still continue to protect national markets in different ways, ranging from price fixing to health and safety regulations.

The Commission is not strong enough to remove the real barriers to inter-state trade put up by governments but it can facilitate the life of free-riding parallel importers.

There is certainly some truth in Dr Korah's view that if a brand owner has to compete against other brands he will not be able to afford to give his distributors unnecessary protection from competition, and he will do better if they compete with each other. However, when it is the supplier who is collecting the higher price in a protected market, as happens in motor cars and pharmaceuticals, the argument does not apply, but even in these sectors parallel imports will hardly do the trick. A global solution is needed, taking into account the factors which led to differential price levels in the first instance.

*   *   *

The Chicago school makes much of the 'barriers to entry', ie, the cost to the supplier of establishing himself on a new market. Unless this is exceptionally high, new suppliers will be attracted to the market by increased profit margins. This may be so, but it is of little interest when all the potential suppliers are already represented on the market and when enormous investment is required to start a new production. Both these conditions exist in the motor car and in the research-based pharmaceutical industries. However, these arguments hardly justify numerous petty and unnecessary restrictions which the Commission has built into its two regulations.

Why should the exemption apply only when the exclusivity is granted to re-sellers and not when it is granted to re-processors? And in exclusive procurement agreements, such as between oil companies and petrol stations and breweries and tied houses, why is it important for the Commission that the supplier provides special commercial and financial advantages – the tied house or the petrol station may be better off if it obtained finance and equipment elsewhere?

Powerful suppliers who think it is vital to prevent competitors from reaching the market, will try to acquire their distributors or to establish their own distribution networks by growth. Where the supplier has no great market power and has no hope of closing the market to competition, a distribution agreement would not infringe the competition rules. In these two extreme cases the block exemptions, therefore, will be either ineffective or unnecessary.

The blurred divide between competition laws of the EC and of the member states

Most crimes of violence happen in families. Disputes about a fence can, not surprisingly, take place only between neighbours. So far, there has been little interference between UK restrictive practices legislation and the EEC rules of competition, mainly because the two systems are miles apart.

If the Government's 1988 Green Paper can tell us anything about the future UK anti-trust enforcement, it will come much closer to the prohibition of cartels and restrictive practices of Article 85 of the EEC Treaty and to the prohibition of abuse of a dominant position of Article 86. The future

UK rules may cover the same anticompetitive behaviour by procedures which will be very similar.

In short, the two systems may come so close together that collisions will be unavoidable – unless care is taken to avoid them when drafting the new UK legislation or the EEC Commission starts to exercise a restraint, which is most unlikely.

The West German competition law has been fairly close to the EEC rules, partly because both systems were modelled on the US anti-trust law and because in the competition department of the Commission, German officials traditionally held the leading role. As a result of this closeness there is greater awareness of the potential conflicts in Germany than in other member states. And it may, therefore, be useful to study the German experience.

Professor Kurt Markert of the Federal Cartel Office in Berlin drew some conclusions from this experience.[4] His starting point was the European Court judgment of 27 January 1987 rejecting the German fire insurers'appeal against a Commission decision that their association's recommendation of premium rates was infringing Article 85 of the EEC Treaty. The Court said this was a case of prohibited price-fixing because the recommendation was concerned not only with the net premium necessitated by the risk alone but also with the mark-up for the insurers' overheads and profit.

The Court used this occasion to say not only that the competition rules of the Treaty as well as the procedural Regulation No. 17/62 have unrestricted application to the insurance sector but made also a statement of great general importance. It said that the application of Articles 85 and 86 is independent of the manner in which a member state exercises supervision over certain economic sectors. In any case, the Court added, the appellants have not shown that the application of the EC rules could frustrate the national supervision of the insurance business in Germany.

Insurance matters seem to be very close to the hearts of governments of most states. The gentle treatment of restrictive practices at Lloyds of London is still in fresh memory. In Germany, the application of national competition rules to the insurance industry is restricted by section 102 of their Competition Act (GWB). The general provisions of this Act, prohibiting horizontal cartels as well as vertical agreements on prices and terms and such recommendations of trade associations which restrict competition, do not apply to the insurance industry if connected with operations subject to the supervision of the Federal Insurance Office.

This exemption of the insurance industry from the competition rules is, however, not unconditional. Individual behaviour falling under the exemption can still attract prohibition if the exempted agreements or recommendations are abused or are likely to be abused.

The requirement of registration of such agreements and recommendations gives the Federal Cartel Office three months in which to investigate the proposed measures before these become operative. In practice, the Federal Cartel Office used this power only in agreement with the Federal Insurance Office in Berlin, though the law provides that if the two institutions disagree, the matter has to be settled by the Ministers of Finance and of Economy.

The German anti-trusters were for some years rather unhappy about this partial exemption of the insurance industry from their reach. The proposal that the next review of the competition law should remove this exemption was widely discussed. The European Court's decision in the fire insurance case seemed to have pre-empted the proposed change. Because of the doctrine of supremacy of community law, German anti-trusters cannot approve or exempt behaviour prohibited under EC rules nor prohibit behaviour expressly approved by the EC Commission or the European Court. In as far as the European Court's decision proclaimed that the insurance industry is subject to EEC competition rules without any restrictions, it removed the need for the revision of the German competition rules urged by the German anti-trusters.

The same seems to apply very much in the field of patent and know-how licensing where the EEC rules are stricter than the German rules and much stricter than the UK rules.

As all this applies only to behaviour affecting trade between member states one could, in theory, arrive at two sets of rules and decisions applicable to the same behaviour: it could be prohibited for interstate business and allowed for domestic business or vice-versa. This is only an academic issue in cases of nationwide agreements as the European institutions interpret the interstate trade clause so widely that it embraces all agreements of national importance even if their effect on interstate trade cannot be visualised in the ordinary way of reasoning. In matters of smaller importance which will not attract the attention of European institutions, the practice may differ.

However, as Prof. Markert points out, an EEC decision exempting a certain agreement, concerted practice or decision of trade associations, from the prohibition of Article 85/1 need not necessarily imply that there are not other aspects and effects not considered by EC institutions but still prohibited under national laws.

This may well be so under the fairly strict German competition law though not under the fairly lax UK law. The situation may change if the policy outlined in the Green Paper becomes law. UK companies may then be put in the unpleasant situation of having to clear their potentially restrictive agreements twice, with the EC and the UK anti-trusters. This duality of competition enforcement has been expressly confirmed in block exemption number 123/85 dealing with distribution of motor cars.

The national competition laws remain unrestricted as long as there is no block exemption or exemption of a particular behaviour by an individual decision. Such exemptions made by the EC institutions subsequently could be retroactive and the national anti-trusters must take this possibility into account when arriving at their decisions. The Federal Cartel Office, as Professor Markert states, already takes the precaution of informing the EC Commission in such cases. Should the UK law take the shape outlined in the Green Paper, UK anti-trusters will be in the same position.

All this points clearly to a much greater muddle and uncertainty than we have at present. To avoid it, it would be necessary to draw a line dividing clearly the scope of the EC rules and the national rules. It is becoming even more urgent that the restrictive agreements notified to the Commission should have provisional validity until condemned by the Commission. Otherwise, an approval of the agreement by the national authorities would remain insecure for the many years it takes the Commission to deal with notifications.

It becomes evident, too, that the Commission should in the future see its main role in the harmonisation of national competition laws, either by legislative measures or by decisions obtained from the European Court on matters of exceptional importance. Better still, the competition enforcement throughout the EC should be left mainly to private actions of those hurt by the anticompetitive behaviour, with anti-trust agencies intervening only against major infringements of general importance.

Regulation v anti-trust in US

The sweet sound of reason heard in the early 1980s from several US courts dealing with issues of the extraterritorial application of anti-trust laws was mightily reinforced on 27 March 1985, by the Supreme Court of the US.

The court dealt[5] with the constantly reappearing question, whether a state policy or direction can provide immunity to a private company accused of price-fixing or another conspiracy prohibited by the Sherman Act. The court abandoned the settled view, highlighted by a long series of leading cases, that a private party is not entitled to state action immunity unless the state *compelled* it to act in violation of the federal anti-trust law.

From now on, to use the words of the dissenting Justice Stevens,

a state may exempt price-fixing from the federal anti-trust laws if it clearly articulates its intention to supplant competition with regulation in the relevant market, and if it actively supervises the unlawful conduct by evaluating the reasonableness of the prices charged.

The majority justified this reversal of law by saying that it is more consistent with the principle of federalism, and that it also better serves the objectives of anti-trust laws because to recognise as defence only such acts of state which *compel* the party to act anticompetitively means to invite the states to make mandatory rules when otherwise they might be satisfied to issue non-compulsory guidelines.

The Supreme Court's decision concerns price fixing by 'rate bureaux' of motor carriers operating in four states of the US under the supervision and with the approval of the Public Service Commission in each state.

The collective rate-making by these bureaux is authorised but not compelled by the respective states. Common carriers are required to submit proposed rates to the appropriate Public Service Commission for approval, and the rate becomes effective if this state agency takes no action within a specified period of time. If a hearing is scheduled, however, a rate will become effective only after agency approval. The State Public Service Commission' thus have and exercise ultimate authority and control over all intrastate rates – in a manner not altogether different from that exercised by the UK and US aviation authorities over private agreements between airlines.

The act of state which the Supreme Court considered here was therefore the act of a state within the Union, providing immunity against federal anti-trust laws.

Nevertheless, the doctrine which the US courts apply to truly extraterritorial issues was originally developed when courts dealt with domestic issues of the sort which were referred to the Supreme Court in the present case. Any decision of the Supreme Court which modified the act of state doctrine in a domestic dispute can be therefore expected to influence decisions dealing with acts of a foreign state.

It is also not entirely clear whether the present decision would provide complete immunity, for example against an accusation of predatory pricing designed to annihilate a competitor. As the Supreme Court requires that there is not only an approval of price fixing but also an active supervision and evaluation of reasonableness of the prices by the state, one could argue that the decision does not provide protection for any sort of price fixing and particularly not for such price fixing which is predatory, coercive or discriminatory.[6]

It is questionable whether, in view of the latest Supreme Court decision, the US courts can go any further than to consider whether there was an 'active supervision' of the anticompetitive conduct and evaluation of the 'reasonableness of the prices charged', and substitute their own decision as to reasonableness, etc, for that made by the state authorities.

That much for the possible wider implications of the Supreme Court's decision. Those interested in the US judges' technique of law-making may like to hear a little more about the case. It was brought as a criminal prosecution against the Southern Motor Carriers Rate Conference and North Carolina Motor Carriers Association, operating as rate bureaux and composed of common carriers in North Carolina, Georgia, Tennessee and Mississippi.

The two rate bureaux were charged in November 1976 of violation of the Sherman Act. Their defence was that their conduct was exempt from the federal anti-trust laws by virtue of the act of state doctrine as defined by the Supreme Court in *Parker v Brown*.[7] On that occasion the Supreme Court held that the Sherman Act was not intended to prohibit states from imposing restraints on competition. The Parker decision has been interpreted in a number of subsequent cases as making the state action immune only where the anticompetitive conduct was 'directed' by the state.

The accused rate bureaux argued, therefore, that the rates were ultimately determined by the appropriate state agencies. The District Court found this argument without merit in a summary judgment in favour of the Government and was confirmed by the Court of Appeals for the Fifth Circuit sitting *en banc*, the majority of which held that the conduct was not entitled to *Parker* immunity because it was not compelled but only approved by the state.

The Supreme Court did not reverse its *Parker* decision but said it should be understood differently. It held that the federal anti-trust laws do not forbid the states to adopt policies that permit but do not compel anticompetitive conduct by *regulated* private parties.

There were only two conditions expressed by the Supreme Court earlier.[8] First, the challenged restraint of competition must be 'clearly articulated and affirmatively expressed as state policy' and second, 'the state must supervise actively any private anticompetitive conduct'.

When other evidence conclusively shows that a state intends to adopt a permissive policy, the absence of compulsion should not prove fatal to a claim of *Parker* immunity concluded the court. This opinion, written by Justice Powell on behalf of the majority, found no favour with the dissenting Justices Stevens and White. But it will probably be welcomed by foreign trading partners of the United States.

Breaking down barriers in airspace

The dream which holds that all products and services will flow freely through the European Community by 1992, can be given a touch of realism by looking at the present national barriers to services such as air transport and television broadcasts – services which are international by their very nature.

Take air transport first. After the International Air Transport Association (Iata) cartel disintegrated, prices of seats on scheduled lines started to diverge. The differences between prices in different countries were further increased by the movement of exchange rates. West German prices rocketed in comparison with those charged for the same journey in other Community countries. This was exploited for the benefit of German air passengers by Ahmed Saeed Flugreisen, an admirably enterprising bucket-shop operator.

According to the German Air Transport Act, all journeys beginning on German territory must be charged at D-Mark prices approved by the German authorities. In practice, this means that the price of all scheduled flights, domestic or foreign, which start in Germany are tied to those of Lufthansa.

However, some foreign flights starting and ending outside Germany have a stopover at a German airport. Let us say that a Milan/Stockholm flight has a stopover in Frankfurt. By buying the Frankfurt/Stockholm tranche of the ticket abroad, Ahmed Saeed was able to offer passengers starting their journey in Frankfurt a ticket substantially below the price approved by the German authorities. In fact, the discounts sometimes amounted to as much as 60 per cent.

Ahmed Saeed's operations were attacked by the German Association against Unfair Competition. On appeal, the Federal Supreme Court (BGH) decided that, though Ahmed Saeed could be prohibited from doing what he did under German law, the law itself might be in conflict with EEC Rules of Competition, and therefore invalid. They referred the matter to the European Court in Luxembourg, as case No. 352/85

From that moment on, Ahmed Saeed's operations assumed European importance: similar price-fixing by, or with the blessing of, governmental authorities, exists not only in Germany but in Denmark, France, Greece, Ireland, Italy and, last but not least, the UK. If the conclusions delivered by the Advocate General, Carl Otto Lenz, on 28 April 1988 are upheld, the price-fixing practices of the member states will have to go – unless the Commission moves quickly and makes a block exemption, as it seems intent on doing.

Mr Lenz said that the Commission's intention of granting such a block exemption to the attacked price-fixing agreements had no effect on the present state of the law. The agreements concerning internal flights within the Community were, in his view, clearly contrary to Article 85 of the

EEC Treaty; there was no need for a finding by the Commission or by a national authority to make them null and void and to prohibit such anti-competitive tariffs.

Flights between an airport within the Community and another outside it, could also fall under the prohibition, but only when either the Commission or a national authority found an infringement. This condition was due, the Advocate General said, to a judgment of the European Court (in Cases 209–213) of 30 April 1986.

However, such previous findings of illegality by the Commission or national authorities were not necessary if the operation of the tariff agreements could be seen as an abuse of dominant position prohibited by Article 86 of the EEC Treaty. In the present case the national cartel of airlines could be seen as having a dominant position.

One way or another, the price-fixing is, according to the Advocate General, prohibited without further ado, both for internal flights in the Community and flights starting at a non-Community airport. To drive his point home with even greater force, the Advocate General also concluded that by authorising such cartel prices, member governments are failing in their duties under the EEC Treaty.

*   *   *

The other essentially international service where member governments are tempted to exclude foreign providers as far as possible, is, of course, radio and television broadcasting. This crosses frontiers not only by means of terrestial radio waves and cables but also by satellite transmissions.

As with other trans-border services, these broadcasts fall under the freedom of provision of cross-border services guaranteed by Article 59 of the EEC Treaty. However, in view of the absence of harmonisation of the national rules applicable to radio and television broadcasts, the European Court held in 1980 (Case 52/79) that each member state can regulate, restrict or even completely prohibit television broadcasts on its territory for reasons of public interest, as long as all such broadcasts are treated alike, irrespective of the nationality and location of the broadcaster or supplier of programmes.

A severe restriction of foreign programmes, aimed at Dutch audiences through the medium of cable networks, was achieved in the Netherlands by a ministerial order of 26 July 1984, known as *Kabelregeling*. This has now been found by the Court to lack the virtue of non-discrimination and condemned. This took some time. The Dutch Association of Advertisers first approached Dutch courts which then passed the buck to Luxembourg in October 1985. The European Court came round to saying what it thinks of it only on 26 April (Case No. 352/85).

The impact of *Kabelregeling*, prohibiting public cable retransmission in the Netherlands of all radio or television programmes received from abroad on the waves, by cable or by satellite, can be understood only against the background of *Omroepwet*, the Dutch Broadcasting Act of 1967. This aimed at securing a pluralist and non-commercial operation of the two Dutch broadcasting channels.

Omroepwet prohibits the broadcasting of publicity or advertising material by the two channels. Such material may be handled exclusively by *Stichting Etherreclame* (STER), a non profit-making organisation, which sells advertising time to commercial programme-makers and allocates commercials to the two channels and, in a lesser degree, also to the press. In this way, the broadcasting channels, as well as the government-approved programme makers, representing major currents of opinion, are thought to be insulated from the influence of advertisers. The money received by STER from advertisers is handed over to the government and used to subsidise the approved programme makers. The subsidies amount to 30 per cent of total receipts of the programme makers, the rest coming from licence fees.

This system restricts advertising time severely and advertisers and their agents are keen to buy foreign broadcasts aimed at the Dutch market to supplement the airtime which they can buy from STER.

The European Court said in its judgment that the *Kabelregeling* obstructs the trans-border provision of two kinds of service: first, that provided by cable operators established in one member state to broadcasters in another; secondly, that provided by the foreign originators of advertising programmes to advertisers in the country of reception.

In this way, the prohibition of foreign commercials in the Dutch market represents a double restriction of the freedom to provide services. If one compared the position of the entirety of Dutch broadcasters with foreign broadcasters, said the court, then one could immediately see the discriminatory nature of *Kabelregeling*, which the Dutch Government had denied. The prohibition of Dutch sub-titles, which had the purpose of eliminating publicity content of foreign feature programmes, reinforced the prohibition of foreign advertising and was therefore also a contravention of Article 59 of the Treaty.

Having said that much, the Court did not find it necessary to consider a further complaint by the advertisers, namely that *Kabelregeling* violated the freedom of the press, guaranteed by the European Human Rights Convention.

However, the Court added a sweetener for the Dutch Government and others in its position: it would be within the EEC Treaty rules if foreign broadcasters were given the choice of conforming with 'objective' restrictions of advertising, such as prohibition of advertising of certain products, on certain days, or a limitation of the time and frequency of commercials.

Even without waiting for 1992, competitors for the ITV and Channel Four advertising service are getting ready to enter British airspace. English commercials producers can of course reciprocate, provided that they learn Dutch, French, German and all the other languages of the Community.

EC Commission adopts the effects doctrine to fight foreign export cartels

'Europe without frontiers', the catchword for the *really* common market promised for 1992, has been given a new meaning in the course of hearings concluded in the European Court in Luxembourg in January 1988.

The occasion was an appeal by 41 leading wood pulp producers, fined by the Commission in 1984 for alleged price-fixing. The hearing concerned the preliminary issue of the Commission's jurisdiction over foreign cartels.

Put simply, the Commission's case is that these 41 suppliers of US, Canadian, Swedish, Finnish, Norwegian, Portuguese and Spanish wood pulp, as well as three of their associations, exchanged information about prices, and between 1973 to 1981 followed a concerted practice of charging higher prices than they could have obtained if they had competed between themselves.

The Commission based its decision on the 'effects doctrine', created by US anti-trusters, and opposed by the UK.

The alleged concertation of prices and terms clearly took place outside the Community. But there is little doubt that it had an effect inside the Community, where paper mills had to pay more for the pulp.

One cannot help being reminded of an even more consequential price-fixing exercise – the OPEC cartel. Why did the Commission fine the 41 pulp producers while leaving the oil sheiks in peace? This illustrates better than anything that the effects doctrine has little to do with law and everything with politics and trade policy. As Mr Joel Davidow, then Director of Policy Planning in the US Department of Justice said in 1981:

the US applies its anti-trust law to restrictive business practices involved in foreign conduct not to test abstract theories of jurisdiction . . . but because prosecution under a national law is the only practical way to punish, remedy and deter international offences which cause direct and substantial injury to important economic and legal interests of [the US].[9]

In the course of time the US has used the effects doctrine against British shipping, airlines and uranium producers and also against Australian, Canadian and European companies – to the dismay of the governments concerned which felt obliged to enact 'blocking statutes' to protect their business interests.

The European Court has never confirmed the Commission's claim that the EEC rules of competition imply the effects doctrine. It went as far as to enable the Commission to proceed against cartels of multinational companies with subsidiaries within the Community which could be said to act as an extended arm of their parents, so that the anticompetitive conduct could be said to have taken place within the Community.

Most of the member states are indifferent to these problems but two take a clear stand: Germany's competition law explicitly adheres to the effects doctrine, though German courts apply it only sparingly when the foreign anticompetitive behaviour has direct and important effects in Germany. The UK, by contrast, has always been opposed to the effects doctrine and in its Aide-Memoire of 20 October 1969 to the EC Commission said: 'a State should not exercise jurisdiction against a foreigner who, or a foreign company which, has committed no act within its territory.'

Of course it is not in the UK's interest to pay more for wood pulp than is necessary. For this reason, it supports the Commission in the appeal case before the European Court. However, the UK's government lawyers showed great ingenuity in trying to support the Commission without endorsing the effects doctrine.

In its submission to the Court, the UK concludes that the effects doctrine has never been accepted as such by the international community. For that reason it considers that the Commission has infringed the principles of international law by applying community rules of competition to KEA, an association of US suppliers which has a one-man office in the US and never operated directly in the Community.

However, the UK supports the Commission's case against the individual suppliers of wood pulp, relying on the European Court's ruling that in certain circumstances, companies situated outside the Community may be held liable for the conduct of their EC subsidiaries for prohibited acts done or implemented within its territory. Most of the pulp suppliers however, do not have a subsidiary within the Community and sell their products either with the help of visiting salesmen or through agents. The UK proposes therefore, that the Court's ruling should extend the possibility of making foreign companies liable also when they have no subsidiary in the Community and only employ an agent there. However, the UK considers that the exercise of the EC jurisdiction is not justified where the foreign suppliers have been selling into the Community without using agents.

Taking a look around, one can see that very few exporters operate without a local agent, so that the UK submission seems to open the back door to the effects doctrine which it threw out of the window. Of course, the relationship between a principal and agent can take many forms. This may be the reason why the court asked the appellants to submit texts of their standard agency contracts.

As the UK states in its submission, the Commission did not make clear the basis on which it intends to exercise its jurisdiction. This obliged the court to ask the Commission the following question:

> Does the Commission maintain that it has jurisdiction in these cases by reason of conduct which has taken place within the Community and, if so, what is that conduct? Or does it base its jurisdiction on the effects within the Community of conduct which took place outside the Community and, if so, what is that conduct and what are its effects?

The Commission's answer is a masterpiece of obfuscation. It confesses that it finds it difficult to distinguish between the effects of a conduct and the conduct itself. It states that the place where the agreement was made is of little relevance. The relevant conduct is not only that of the principals but also that of their agents and others whose acts they direct. The Commission concludes that in this case the penalised conduct did indeed take place in the Community because the prices were announced and charged in the Community by the producers or their subsidiaries, branches, agents or employees.

If the court accepts this very wide concept of what constitutes conduct taking place within jurisdiction, the consequences for world trade would be far reaching. Most countries approve, and some even support export cartels of companies based within their jurisdiction. The competition laws of Germany, the UK and US, provide specific exemption for such export cartels. In Communist countries and many developing countries, the export cartels are institutionalised or there is even a monopoly of foreign trade.

An attempt by the US or the EC to penalise such cartels would affect the entire trade of the exporting countries and not only that directed towards the complaining state.

Moreover, the effects doctrine, or the same by any other name, cannot be applied equally to all: state trading countries and powerful groups like OPEC would be immune while others would bear the consequences.

And though we all know that this is not a legal issue but a matter of trade policy, if the Commission's arguments are endorsed by the Court, they are likely to deprive Community exporters of an important defence should they be prosecuted in a similar case in a US court.

Post script. On 27 September 1988 the European Court rejected the appeals of the wood pulp suppliers and adopted an 'effects doctrine' in terms more radical than ever heard in a US court; it held that in competition matters the EC jurisdiction reaches foreign firms trading with the Community even if they have no presence on its territory—not even a visiting representative.

UK courts ignore rules of competition

If a reluctant rescuer agrees to save a shipwrecked man only against a promise of a 21-year servitude, it will be fairly obvious that the promise should not be enforced.

Substitute into this pattern an oil company, a near bankrupt petrol station owner and the promise not to sell for 21 years other petrol than supplied by the rescuer.

Add that in 1968 the Monopolies Commission concluded that it was against the public interest if oil companies avoided competition by tying petrol retailers for periods longer than five years and that this conclusion was embodied into the law by the Esso judgment[10] of the House of Lords.

Until 8 November 1984 one could expect that an oil company would not be allowed to enforce a 21-year tie agreed by a retailer in distress. But on that day, reversing the trial judge, the Court of Appeal unanimously decided[11] that Total Oil Great Britain Ltd held a monopoly, good and valid for 21 years, over the supply of petrol to Alec Lobb (Garages) Ltd. The monopoly was obtained by Total when Lobb fell into financial difficulties and had to lease the forecourt to Total for 51 years for nothing, in order to secure its financial existence. In reaching this decision, the court not only opened the door to restrictive practices and abuse of monopoly power but also departed radically from the accepted meaning of 'unequal bargaining power' and 'public interest'. In short, the Court of Appeal seems to signal a reversal of the world-wide tendency which puts human and social considerations, including competition policy, above the contract between two parties.

The Esso decision has been generally taken as laying down the rule that it is an unreasonable and invalid restraint of trade to tie retailers with previous ownership or tenancy of a petrol station to an oil company for longer than five years, except when the oil company can prove that a longer period is an economic necessity.

Total did not offer any evidence showing that it was an economic necessity for it to tie the Lobbs for 21 years and the trial judge therefore declared it to be void in accordance with the *Esso* rule.

The Court of Appeal, however, set out to show that the case did not fall under the Esso rule as the 21-year tie could be seen as 'reasonable' even if it was not an economic necessity for Total. They based their reasoning on Lord Reid's dictum in Esso that a restraint of trade must be justified to be enforceable; and that the only justification is that it is reasonable in reference to the interest of the parties concerned and also reasonable in reference to the interest of the public.

There was no difficulty in showing that the tie was a reasonable proposition for Total. It was not equally easy to show that it was also reasonable for the retailer. Here the appeal judges had to overcome the formidable objection – which applied to the entire deal and not only to the tie – that the bargain was not only between two unequal parties but that one of the parties, the Lobbs, had no other choice than to reach an agreement with Total or to go bankrupt. The deal was so bad that their solicitor advised against it. They acted against his advice.

The appeal judges brushed this objection aside. Most deals are between unequal parties, they said. Total did not use its greater bargaining power unconscientiously and oppressively and the acceptance of the deal enabled the Lobbs to continue trading – hence it was reasonable for them.

The biggest surprise, however, is how the Appeal Court dealt with the second limb of Lord Reid's justification of the tie, namely that it should be 'reasonable in reference to the interests of the public'. Instead of referring to the price competition between the oil companies and to the interest of the consumer, or motorist, the appeal judges merely said that it was clearly in the public interest that a petrol pump operator should be enabled to survive and that the oil company should preserve its outlet. It is clearly in the shipwrecked man's interest to be rescued, one can add, and he should not question the price demanded by the rescuer.

After decades of restrictive practices legislation and an incessant stream of Monopoly Commission's reports, one can be excused for believing that the public interest in these matters has something to do with competition policy. But this is not even mentioned in any of the three judgments delivered by Lord Justices Dillon, Dunn and Waller.

EC Commission's quest for merger control

For the past 14 years the EC Commission has been trying to obtain powers to control mergers and acquisitions. The EEC Treaty does not provide for it, and the member states have been reluctant to approve a merger control regulation proposed by the Commission.

In an attempt to break this resistance, Mr Peter Sutherland, the

Commissioner for Competition, threatened that, if denied the merger regulation, he will have to proceed against mergers of European size 'by means available to the Commission'.

By this he means the powers founded, or believed to be founded, on two judgments of the European Court. The first was made in 1972 in the case of Continental Can, when it held that an acquisition increasing further the market power of a dominant company may constitute an abuse prohibited by Article 86 of the Treaty. The Commission has so far wisely refrained from relying on the strength of this maverick judgment.

In 1988 Mr Sutherland added to his arsenal a new and no less controversial judgment. In this, the 6th Chamber of the Court rejected a complaint by BAT and R. J. Reynolds[12] that the Commission should not have approved agreements concluded between Philip Morris and Rembrandt. These established the two groups' joint ownership of Rothman International and – as the plaintiffs alleged – an anticompetitive sharing of the European cigarette market. Mr Sutherland claims that this judgment gives him the power to control mergers and acquisitions under the other competition rule of the Treaty, Article 85, which aims against cartels and other restrictive agreements.

Although Mr Sutherland's interpretation appears to go much too far, it has to be conceded that his view is at least arguable. This, however, raises a constitutional issue of real gravity. There would be surely something very wrong with the Community if a junior bench of the European Court had the power to legislate in a way that would throw the law into confusion and uncertainty. And it is hardly proper for the Commission to threaten the Council that it would apply such controversial judgments, with ominous consequences for business, if it did not first obtain the member states' approval of its merger regulation.

It is unthinkable that the Commission would really enter such an adventurist path, putting its own authority at risk. Nor can the Council's attitude be wholly negative, since there is a need for some common European Community merger policy in the long term, especially in the light of the programme to complete the internal market.

However, as long as an agreement has not been reached, the Commission is likely to make much of the rather unimportant Morris judgment. The court itself was obviously quite unaware of any general and far-reaching importance of the case, otherwise it would deal with it by its full bench and not in a chamber of five judges, none of which had any experience of French, UK or Italian law and two of which joined the court only recently.

The 6th Chamber defined the issue rather modestly: it was whether, and in what circumstance, the acquisition of minority shareholding in a competing company, agreed between companies which have remained independent, might constitute an infringement of Article 85. It held that the acquisition of an equity interest in a competitor does not in itself restrict competition but may serve as an instrument to such end.

The Court continued (in point 38):

> That will be true in particular where, by the acquisition of a shareholding or through subsidiary clauses in the agreement, the investing company obtains legal or de facto control of the commercial conduct of the other company or where the agreement provides for commercial co-operation between the companies or

creates a structure likely to be used for such co-operation. That may also be the case where the agreement gives the investing company the possibility of reinforcing its position at a later stage and taking effective control of the other company.

The Court dismissed the application of Article 86 in four brief sentences. Abuse of dominant position, it said, can only arise where the shareholding results in effective control or at least some influence on the commercial policy of the target company and it was not established that the 1984 agreements had any such effect.

There is nothing new in saying that acquisition of shares in a subsidiary or the creation of a joint venture may be an instrument – one of many possible – of an anticompetitive agreement between two competitors who remain independent. The court emphatically denied that it is anticompetitive in itself. The only novelty of the judgment is, on the contrary, in its tacit confirmation of the Commission's new rule that acquisitions of less than 25 per cent of voting rights by an oligopolist in a competing company does not in itself create the presumption of influence likely to restrict or distort competition.

Some UK lawyers do, however, take point 38 of the judgment as if it was a clause in an English statute. This leads them to conclude that any acquisition of equity leading to 'legal or actual control' may be contrary to Article 85. Indeed, one complaint against such an acquisition has been made to Brussels as soon as the news of the judgment was received in London.

However, the rulings given in an European Court's judgment must not be interpreted as clauses in an English statute. They must always be understood in the context of the entire judgment, which in this case is about creating a joint subsidiary by two out of four leading companies, allegedly to share the market. Moreover, as the European Court never tires of reminding us, EC judgments, decisions, directives and regulations, and even specific provisions of the Community treaties, must be interpreted in harmony with the overall system of Community law. This system provides for the control of mergers and acquisitions only in the Steel and Coal Community Treaty but not in the EC Treaty. The EC competition rules are addressed only to the behaviour of companies not to structural changes in industry.

One cannot assume that the court wanted to rewrite the Treaty in such a fundamental way. And one can be certain that if it did want it, it would have had the courtesy to do so with the authority of its full bench.

US anti-trust sheds 'economic perversity'

One of the objectives of President Reagan's competition policy was to overcome what Mr William F. Baxter, his Assistant Attorney General, called 'the economic perversity' of the populist anti-trust doctrine developed by the US courts. One of Mr Baxter's first moves after taking charge of the Anti-trust Division of the Department of Justice was to introduce an economic course for the department's lawyers: he says they think it is 'great fun' and enjoy it.

In contrast with the decisiveness of his views and the upheaval these must have caused in the anti-trust community, Mr Baxter is soft-spoken, unassuming and prefers the language of sweet reason and persuasion to forceful declarations. One has to keep reminding oneself that he is now a politician and no longer a disinterested academic. He has lost no time in making the department's brain-force recant. There are no fewer than 1,300 old decrees on record – many, he thinks, wrong from the beginning and others which have ceased to have the desired effect with the lapse of time. Mr Baxter wants them revoked.

The new line was to prefer a hard look at the business reality of each case to legalistic screening of commercial behaviour against the absolute *per se* prohibitions.

However, the impact of a new policy will be necessarily limited. Prosecution by federal agencies, the Department of Justice and the Federal Trade Commission, represents only a small fraction of anti-trust enforcement. Ninety per cent of cases are private actions aiming at treble damages; Mr Baxter's second major programme established a systematic monitoring of these private litigations to enable the anti-trust division to intervene by an *amicus curiae* brief at the right moment.

Amicus curiae briefs have been tried before with little success. The US judges are rarely willing to listen, jealously guarding the separation of the judiciary from the executive power. The Department of Justice neither appoints nor feeds them. Any political influences worth consideration are likely to come from the territorial proximity of the courts or from the Supreme Court. The numerous *per se* prohibitions developed by courts will hardly be removed without legislation.

Another move heralding the Reagan era was the revision of the 1968 merger guidelines, though in Baxter's view 'these were less economically perverse than the judicial doctrine', but still much too destructive.

As a broad rule, Mr Baxter would rather eliminate friendly mergers than unfriendly takeovers. In Wall Street quoted companies, the shareholders of acquired firms do very well – better than the shareholders of the acquiring firms – and this is seen as evidence that either the target company has been badly managed or that there was an important advantage in combining capacities. The fact that the shareholders of the acquiring companies do less well can be explained by the existence of several potential acquirers who push up the price paid for the target company.

Also, institutional shareholders seem to view the danger of a takeover as an excellent means for concentrating the mind of the management. In several instances when the companies wanted to include anti-takeover clauses in their articles of association, the institutional shareholders stepped in, threatening that they would sell their shares and that, consequently, the company would have to pay more for its capital.

As always, one of the most difficult problems of merger control is the definition of the market. Mr Baxter suggested that the proper definition of the relevant market, both territorially and in terms of products, should be such, that an imaginary monopoly supplier should be able in such a market to increase prices profitably. The Anti-trust Division has also replaced the conventional consideration of market shares by a more sophisticated calculation.

The new method obtains the concentration ratio of a given market by adding up the squares of market shares of all competitors. If there is only one company which controls 100 per cent of the market, the concentration ratio will be 10,000. If there are 100 competitors, each with a 1 per cent share, the concentration ratio will be 100. The Anti-trust Division is not troubled much about markets with a post-merger concentration ratio of less than 1,000. When it is between 1,000 and 1,800 any merger which increases the concentration ratio by 100 is likely to be challenged. If the ratio is over 1,800, an increase of 50 might lead to a challenge.

In Mr Baxter's now somewhat dated view the Anti-trust Division would investigate such a merger taking also other factors into consideration. One of these would be the ease of entry into a market.

But as Caesar was *supra gramaticos*, so politics might prevail over econometricians.

Management takeover and minority shareholders

The impotence of minority shareholders to restrain management brought on a dangerous path by its takeover mania, and their difficulty in recovering whatever losses may have been caused by this to the company, has been highlighted by the Guinness scandal.

The courts are, of course, enabled by the Wallerstein decision of the Denning Court of Appeal, to make the company bear the legal costs of the individual shareholders suing the management for fraud or for overstepping its powers, but, like with so many Denning innovations, the courts are now reluctant to make use of this power. In 1986 the petitioners were refused such assistance in *Smith and others v Croft and others* by Mr Justice Walton on the grounds that the accountant's report refuted their allegations in a case[13] in which Mr Justice Knox later ended his judgment with these words:

> ... I believe that it would be helpful for there to be specific procedure laid down, whether by way or Rules of Court or Practice Direction I know not, for the initiation and prosecution actions by minority shareholders to recover on behalf of a company.[14]

The case represented a fairly typical conflict between a minority, whose trusted chairman was dislodged with the help of a financial institution, and the reconstituted board backed by this institution. It raised not only some issues of procedure, as pointed out by the judge, but also points to vast uncharted areas of relations between minority shareholders and a group controlling the company.

The minority shareholders, holding 42 per cent of the equity, complained that management provided company funds to associated companies for these to buy the company's own shares – a contravention of section 42 of the Companies Act 1981, and criticised as excessive salaries which the directors paid themselves.

The case has brought to light many curious aspects of the court's attitude to these problems.

First the refusal of legal costs to the plaintiffs was based on an accountant's report though this severely criticised the laxity of approval and recording procedures for directors' fees and expenses and found that payments to associated companies, for the purchase of the company's own shares were not disclosed to the then chairman and not approved by the board.

The plaintiffs fared even worse the next year when the case came to trial before Mr Justice Knox. Though his last words, quoted earlier, made it clear that he regretted the plight of the minority, he felt obliged to conclude – after 17 days of argument! – that they had no arguable case and had to bear legal costs approaching £1m. He struck the action out mainly on the ground that the parent company (which commanded the majority vote after the share manipulations infringing section 42, appointed the new chairman and backed the board when the 42 per cent minority complained) declared to be happy with the board and did not want it to be prosecuted.

Still more curiously, the judge said that the controlling company formed a majority within the 'independent minority' and concluded that even if the management does a wrong which cannot be healed by subsequent approval by the majority of shareholders, such as an infringement of section 42, a minority shareholder, who forms a majority within the minority of independent shareholders, can stop the prosecution of the board.

A commonsensical reading of the law would have one lead to believe that it was the minority shareholder's personal right to seek recovery of loss caused by illegal action of the board, independent of whatever other minority shareholders think (even real ones, and not those who nominated the chairman). And Mr Justice Knox *did* find that there was a *prima facie* case of infringement of section 42 by financing the purchase of company's own shares.

However, Mr Justice Knox rejected, albeit with bleeding heart, such commmon sense as contrary to English company law, praying for remedy from on high. In case the powers which decide about sense and nonsense wish to answer his plea, they will find plenty of ready-made solutions abroad.

Turning up the Austrian Companies Act 1965 one finds the perfect solution in section 122: a 10 per cent minority can sue members of the board for mismanagement and 5 per cent is enough if they base their claim on facts reported by the auditors. How simple it can be! But then there would not be much to talk about for 17 days.

In Switzerland any shareholder may challenge in court the validity of any resolution of the general meeting if it is contrary to law or articles of association. In Denmark the minority which opposes the approval of accounts may sue in their own name, recovering legal costs from any award made to the company.

English courts seem to be resigned to the 'impossible position' (in the words of Lord Denning), of those who sit simultaneously on the board of the holding company and of a subsidiary, where their interests clash. In France, academic lawyers insist that the duty of a director is only to his company and not to the group, but courts think otherwise. They approve actions taken in the interests of the group.

Germany is the only country with a statutory regulation of the relationship. This makes the directors of a company controlling a public company liable for careless or unskilled instructions to the dependent company, which, of course, is not bound by illegal instructions.

The EEC Commission, inspired by the German legislation, proposed a harmonisation of law applicable to groups in its Ninth Company Law Directive. This somewhat clumsy attempt has been sharply criticised by the Institute of Directors. Some radical changes may be needed to improve it, but it would be a pity to throw out the baby with the bathwater.

Management v shareholders in US, France and UK courts

Should judges try to second-guess the decisions of managements? It seems to be a generally accepted principle of common law, both in the UK and overseas, that they should not. The reason for this is that if judges try to predict the future effect of decisions, they are in no better, and possibly in a worse, position than the managers who, through long experience, can make a better educated guess and benefit from accumulated intuitive knowledge.

As to decisions which have already proved to be wrong or unlucky, it would not be fair to criticise the managers with benefit of hindsight so long as their intentions were beyond reproach.

This principle of judicial non-interference in business decisions, usually termed the 'business judgment rule', served well for a long time but its foundations have been undermined because the interests of managements and those of shareholders in large companies no longer necessarily coincide. In takeover battles and buy-outs the interests of the management may be in conflict with those of shareholders, employees and creditors.

US

In the US the future of the 'business judgment rule' has been recently called into question by a series of decisions taken by the courts of Delaware, that Mecca of company lawyers, where managements have traditionally felt free to do almost anything they liked. However, leveraged takeover bids, management buyouts and poison pills have obliged the courts to redefine the 'business judgment rule' in a way which has alarmed the company Bar who fear that Delaware may cease to be multinationals' favourite place of registration.

US law does not differ in principle from the English treatment of business judgment, but elaborates it in greater detail. According to the Principles of Corporate Governance at present being considered by the American Law Institute, the duty of a director or officer to perform his functions in good faith, and in what he believes to be the best interest of the corporation, is further qualified: he should perform his functions with the care that can be expected from an ordinarily prudent person; he is obliged to make such inquiries as he reasonably believes to be appropriate. The Principles further define when a business judgment is made in good faith: when the director is not personally interested, is properly informed, and rationally believes that his decision is in the best interest of the corporation.

In a 1981 decision,[15] the Supreme Court of Delaware said that when the interest of the board clashed with that of a shareholder who required it to bring an action, the board's refusal to do so was covered by the 'business judgment rule' if it was based on the advice of an independent and informed committee.

However, this may merely shift the court's attention to whether the committee was really independent and whether its advice was given in good faith. Though it must have been obvious that the court can reverse the directors' business judgment, by finding that they were not properly advised, it caused great consternation when Supreme Court of Delaware actually did so in *Smith v van Gorkham*.

Mr van Gorkham, faced with the financial difficulties of a company of which he was chief executive, arranged a leveraged buy-out in which the price offered for the shares was substantially higher than the average share price in the preceding five years. The offer was accepted by the board and subsequently by shareholders representing 70 per cent of the equity. A 7 per cent minority opposed the deal, asking for $100m in damages. The Court of Chancery rejected the complaint on the grounds that the acceptance of the offer fell within the protection of the 'business judgment rule'. The Delaware Supreme Court, however, reversed this decision; it concluded that the board's decision had been hasty and not sufficiently informed.

In the case of *Continental Illinois*, where the senior management team was sued for managing the bank imprudently as well as failing to disclose its problems promptly and violating security laws, nine executives, including the former chief executive, denied liability but agreed to pay $28m to shareholders, who also received $25m from the bank. It seems that the protection of the 'business judgment rule' is not what it used to be in the US.

The problems faced by the Delaware courts are essentially the same as may be faced by English courts as similar takeover defences come for scrutiny before them. The same problems may soon appear in France.

FRANCE

After a long absence, hostile takeover bids have arrived on the French scene in 1986. New rules[16] facilitate takeover bids by laying down time limits within which the executive board of the stockbrokers' association must give its approval and the COB (stock exchange commission) certify the information which must be published by the bidder and the target company. French authorities seem to have a much more active part to play than is usual in London.

In contrast with the relaxed attitude of common law courts, French law makes managements liable for their errors. In his 1986 Blackstone lecture,[17] Professor Alphonse Tunc, the eminent French commercialist, expressed the view that the time is ripe for the French and English systems to come closer together.

Professor Tunc said that in no case so far had a French court declined to judge a business decision made by the directors of a company. French company law expressly provided that the directors were liable to the company and to others for any breach of the rules or for any fault in their management. Judge-made law extended this liability to mistakes and errors even if not committed directly by members of the board. Every fault which caused damage led to the liability of the management.

The French Companies Act encourages and facilitates shareholders' suits against members of the board. In the case of liquidation, when the assets are not sufficient to meet debts, the court may order the directors and executive officers to pay up to the extent the deficit was due to their own fault. In only one respect does French law treat management more leniently than English law: defying legislation, the courts do not inquire into the fairness of dismissals of employees. They accept any significant reasons stated by the employer.

UK

By contrast, English courts, which do inquire into the fairness of dismissals, tend to leave other managerial decisions well alone, and certainly do not make directors liable for mere errors of judgment. According to Lord Wilberforce,[18] when the actions of directors are challenged, the court should first consider the nature of the power which they exercised and whether they did so for a proper purpose; and respect their judgment as to matters of management if it finds that they acted in good faith.

Trying to frustrate a hostile takeover bid by Argyll, the Distillers board, supported by some institutional shareholders, agreed to reimburse Guinness for the £40m cost of launching a friendly takeover. The Takeover Panel rejected Argyll's complaint, though the move had been criticised by a number of leading City institutions.

Argyll brought an action in the High Court under section 151 of the Companies Act 1985 – which prohibits financing the purchase of own shares – but decided against suing the directors individually. After the bid was referred to the Monopolies and Mergers Commission, the court action was not pursued, but the Stock Exchange passed a rule that, in future, such 'poison pills' would have to be approved by shareholders if they exceeded 25 per cent of the past three years' profits in value or if their value was unlimited.

Thus, even in the UK it is now recognised that the freedom to exercise business judgment in normal circumstances cannot be left uncurtailed in takeover battles. If not the courts, the authorities feel obliged to put up at least token limits to management's deviation from the interests of the shareholders, Professor Tunc's invitation to close the gap between the French and the common law approach may be brought about by necessity, the supreme taskmaster of law-makers.

Notes

1 This philosophy is expounded in *The Economics of Justice* by Richard A. Posner, Harvard University Press.

2 433 US 36, 53 L Ed 2d 568.
3 *Exclusive Dealing Agreements in the EEC,* European Law Centre, 1984.
4 Kurt Markert 'Die Anwendung des Paragraph 102 GWB auf die Versicherungswirtschaft vor dem Hintergrund des EuGH – Urteils im Fall "Feuerversicherung"' (1988) Versicherungsrecht 5, pp 101–104.
5 In *Southern Motor Carriers Rate Conference Inc et al v United States,* No. 82-1922, decided 27 March 1985.
6 *US v Baltimore and Ohio Railroad et al* 1982-1 CCH Trade Cases 164,692 (DDC, 15 April 1982).
7 317 US 341 (1943).
8 *California Retail Liquor Dealers Association v Midcal Aluminium Inc* 445, US 97 (1980).
9 Mr J Davidov at the ICC conference in Paris, 12 March 1981.
10 *Esso Petroleum Co Ltd v Harper's Garage (Stoutport) Ltd* [1969] AC 269.
11 FT Comm LR, 21 November 1984.
12 Joined Cases 142 and 156/84, *British American Tobacco and RJ Reynolds Industries v EC Commission supported by Philip Morris Inc and Rembrandt Group Ltd,* judgment (sixth Chamber) of 17 November 1987.
13 FT Comm LR, 11 February 1987.
14 *Smith and others v Croft and others* [1986] FT Comm LR 1 at 410-423.
15 *Zapat Corpn v Maldonado.*
16 Decision of the Stockbrokers' Association, March 1986, Official Journal, 13 March 1986, p 3,848; Commission des Opérations des Bourse, Regulation No. 86-01 of 13 March 1986, Official Journal, 16 March 1986, p 4,285.
17 Delivered at Pembroke College, Oxford.
18 *Howard Smith Ltd v Ampol Petroleum Ltd* [1974] AC 821, PC.

12 How to prevent disputes and what to expect if one does not succeed

Disputes for the love of them

The propensity of first year law students to scrutinise all sorts of daily trivia in the light of their freshly acquired knowledge serves a useful purpose: in this way they are able to remember what they have heard at the last lecture. Unfortunately, some of them never grow up. They love legal trivialities, particularly if they can get some publicity from bringing them before an international court; and even more so if they can find a sponsor willing to pay the costs.

In this way we were treated to the unedifying spectacle of the European judges in Luxembourg solemnly pontificating about a complaint by two French prostitutes that a Belgium measure preventing them exposing themselves in a shop window was a contravention of the EC principle of free movement of workers. We also followed with utter amazement the Duke of Westminster's complaint to the European Court of Human Rights against UK legislation giving leaseholders the right to purchase the freehold – a complaint which seemed quite hopeless in the light of previous jurisprudence of the court.

We are now promised more such legalistic entertainment with the suggestion that London buskers ask the Human Rights Court to say that they have the freedom to fill public places with song and music – a petition I would support only on condition that they play Mozart, and play it well.

And then there are the Irish 'homeless' who have a home in the Republic but are threatening to take Camden Borough Council to Luxembourg for refusing to pay their hotel bills. They seem to overlook the fact that once the Community is viewed as a single market, a person can make himself no less 'intentionally homeless' by giving up his home in Dublin than by giving up one in Birmingham. In addition, skipping legal niceties, it would be quite impractical to expect Camden to house every Greek, Italian, Spanish, Portugese and Irish worker who came to look for a job in London.

Disputes: how to avoid them

Business disputes can be resolved by a variety of methods: by direct negotiations between the two parties in dispute, by the intervention of a third party acting as a conciliator, mediator, adjudicator or arbitrator – or by leaving it to the courts and entering the path of litigation. Various new forms and combinations of the conventional methods have been recently designed to reduce costs and to prevent a deterioration or a rupture in the business relationship between the two parties.

Though some of these methods will be more suitable and more economical than others, there will always be aggravation, loss of time, waste of managerial effort and considerable expense. For these reasons, prevention of disputes is probably the best safeguard of contract profitability.

If disputes cannot be prevented, their resolution will at least be facilitated if at the time when an agreement is made the parties are fully aware of each other's interests and capabilities and express their intentions in ordinary language, avoiding obscure terms, market-related idioms and lawyers' gibberish.

One always thinks that one knows one's own mind, though that is not always the case, but what the other party has in mind is sometimes thought to be less important than the written contract it has signed. Yet it is seldom enough to rely on the other party's good financial standing and production capability. Both may be meaningless without knowledge of the limits imposed on a company by the group to which it belongs, the legal, economic and political regime in which it operates, and the constraints and vicissitudes of the market to which it is subject.

A contract easily and quickly agreed is seldom a good contract, for the simple reason that the parties did not have time and opportunity to gain a proper insight into the economic, technological and legal problems involved. Nothing is more dangerous than to take one or more old contracts, cut out the clauses which seem suitable, and paste them together.

Good contracts are always tailor-made and that means to take the measurements of the case before you start to think of drafting. The man in charge of the negotiations need not and seldom will be, familiar with all technological, legal and local aspects, but he must give those who know an opportunity to brief him.

Nor is it enough just to brief the lawyer, and leave the drafting to him, and to sign the long, mostly incomprehensible document which he produces. A good negotiator will insist that the contract is drafted so as to be understandable without a lawyer's explanations.

My father used to say that one should not make contracts with people one cannot trust without a contract. However, when dealing with large business organisations or public agencies, the man negotiating the contract may have little to do with its performance. Even if he has, he may be overruled or replaced. The bigger the organisation one deals with and the longer the time required for performance of the contract, the greater is the need for a good contract with a built-in 'learning mechanism'.

If the performance of the contract is likely to take time, it will be necessary to provide for its adjustment by agreement or by reference to a third party. English law does not provide judges and arbitrators with an automatic authority to fill in the gaps in the contract.

At the very least, the contract should provide for an independent survey and factual report to be made at the time when the trouble occurred. As arbitration or litigation may take place years after the completion of the work when witnesses are no longer available, such an objective report can eliminate the need for long, fruitless hearings before an arbitration tribunal or in court.

In the building and construction industry, the monitoring of contract performance and its adjustment to changing circumstances are often left to the architect or consulting engineer.

More elaborate precautions are advisable in large international deals.

Site managers and suppliers' representatives should have the final authority to agree minor variations of the contract on the spot, thus eliminating pretexts for later claims. A contract management committee can be established to deal with more important issues, and there should be a procedure for appeals against its decisions to top management, designating which executives have the authority to agree changes that have become necessary.

There is a tendency on the part of many business executives to believe that once they have agreed the 'what, when and where' of a sale, and clinched the price and the conditions of payments, the rest can be safely left to lawyers. This is compounded by the dangerous habit lawyers have of 'drafting' contracts by using the texts of previous contracts on their files or a combination of time-honoured contract clauses. The advent of the word-processor has put a premium on mental laziness.

However, no adequate substitute has yet been invented for thinking, though a computer can help a little by providing a checklist. If future disputes are to be avoided, it is necessary to think before you sign a contract of the possible impact of the many laws and regulations for the control of business, either existing at the time or which could be adopted before the performance of the contract is completed. This will be particularly difficult when trading with a country, where new regulations come as a surprise without any previous public discussion or parliamentary process.

Rules of competition may invalidate your contract and the failure to notify a restrictive agreement may expose the parties to fines. And beware of customers or suppliers who want an 'official' invoice to differ from the real one: in countries which signed the Bretton Woods Agreement of 1944, courts will not enforce any contract offending against exchange regulations enacted in any other country that is a signatory to the agreement.

The worry about exchange controls, trade embargoes and sequestrations should not overshadow the need for ensuring the simple things; for example, that the other party will let you know (really and not merely by satisfying a local formality) when it wants to start action against you in foreign courts: under the 1968 European Judgments Convention, courts are obliged to execute default judgments of foreign courts, without allowing an appeal against them.

All these matters and many others should be considered before your lawyer sits down to draft the contract; and if he tells you that the other party – perchance a state trader – may only use a standard and unvariable form of contract, try to pack into schedules and technical specifications what you want, but cannot have in the main text of the contract.

Big projects: solving problems as they appear

The task of drafting major international contracts is probably one of the most challenging tasks of a business lawyer: the general rules applying to the sale of goods are hardly suitable for complex deals which have a life of their own, in which the original contract, like a marriage contract, is about things future and largely unforeseeable.

The task of those drafting the contract is to get away from the unsuitable general rules or, at least, to revise them. There is no adequate standard solution, and to use standard clauses out of their original context may lead to surprising and undesired results.

One of the frequent omissions seems to be the lack of provision for a 'break-in period' between delivery of the plant and the time it functions properly. Good contracts provide for such a commissioning period during which any bugs in the system can be removed, but sometimes the marketing man believes his own sales talk and prevails with the help of an over-optimistic engineer. The result is that the guarantee period starts from the date of actual delivery, which may be bad for both parties. If the buyers then asks for a performance test during the actual but unrecognised break-in period, the seller can be in real trouble.

The traditional industrial guarantee clauses – for repairing or replacing faulty parts of plant during the guarantee period – do not take into account that in large projects of this type the buyer often takes an important part in developing the technology. The guarantee clause should, therefore, exclude the seller's responsibility for things done at the request of the buyer.

Both the industrial and the performance guarantees require many more procedural provisions than are usual in standard contracts, and this applies with even greater force when the deal involves novel technology. There is need for detailed assignment of responsibilities during the break-in period, for detailed provisions for the test run and for a precise description of the measuring and weighing procedures and instruments. It is, apparently, not always realised how even a very widely formulated guarantee can be narrowed down by the technical conditions of the test. This is particularly important when dealing with state traders whose officials are not allowed or willing to depart from the authorised text of the main contract. Most guarantee clauses in current use are inadequate and risky.

Consulting engineers are willing to admit the usefulness of lawyers when drafting the contract but tend to consider them as quite useless in the many disputes, small and big, potential or actual, which emerge during the life of the contract, often as a result of unforeseen circumstances – geological or political, bad weather or human error, or simply resulting from the 'quite normal' delays.

One of the novel devices for smoothing the performance of the contract is the institution of a claims review board. The seller and the buyer each appoint one member, but this also has to have the approval of the other party. The two members agree on a chairman. All three members of the board are expected to serve for at least a year and to give three months' notice if they do not wish to continue beyond that.

The review board receives complete documentation of the project and visits the site at regular intervals, say three times a year for a week. As its arrival is not necessarily the sign of a major dispute, it does not create the same sort of tension said to be produced by arbitration. On the contrary, those who believe in this method insist that it has a beneficial pyschological effect as the people on the spot try to settle their problems and disagreements before the board arrives.

When it arrives, the board first inspects the active sections of the project site, and then holds hearings. Its decisions do not bind anybody but are disregarded only if quite unacceptable to one of the parties. The disregarded decision can, however, be used as evidence in subsequent arbitration. It seems that a claims review board of this type may help the parties to adjust to difficulties and prevent small disagreements from accumulating and growing into major conflicts.

The one sore point of international contracts which neither an individual engineer nor lawyer can overcome concerns performance bonds, particularly the 'on demand' type under which the buyer may demand payment from the bank without giving any reason, not to speak of any evidence of breach of contract on the part of the seller. A fraudulent, or at least unjustified calling of such bonds, is becoming more frequent and little help can be expected from courts, particularly in common law countries where the unconditional obligation of the bank is considered sacrosanct and quite divorced from the underlying transaction. The situation is slightly better in those civil law countries where courts give protection against 'abuse of the law'.

The acceptance of such an unequal and onerous condition of contract, as represented by a performance bond payable on demand, is a consequence of the competition for contracts. The EC has been guilty of many unnecessary harmonisation projects. The elimination of unfair performance bonds might well be a suitable case for harmonisation treatment.

Keep disputes within your budget

Before going on to discuss methods of dispute resolution, one may as well pause a little to consider ways and means of reducing the legal costs.

The first thing, of course, is to attempt a settlement. Indeed, the great majority of legal proceedings never come to trial. Even so, the cost may be very high – and irrecoverable. Such costs can be avoided, or at least kept within reasonable limits by refusing to be involved in legal issues at an early stage of the dispute. Solicitors love to impress their clients and to frighten the other party by starting their letters, 'We are advised by leading counsel.'

Do not be impressed or frightened. The two leading counsels on either side of the dispute tend to have opposed views about the rights of the case – and one of them is bound to be wrong. It may happen that both are proved wrong by the judge. Before getting entangled in the legal web, one should seek a businesslike solution, keeping in mind that second-best achieved by agreement is better than the best resulting from litigation.

When behind the wheel of a car, most business executives behave reasonably and give way rather than be killed while insisting on their rights. Behind their desks, however, they can be led into ruining their business by unsuccessful litigation.

Lawyers being only human, they cannot be expected to put over the entrance of their door a big warning: 'You can lose even if you win.' For this reason, it may pay to turn first to a wise man who can neither gain nor lose by the advice he gives you. This may be a person with business experience, an arbitrator, a retired judge perchance, or even a practising lawyer, as long as it is made clear to him that he will not be asked to represent you in any litigation or arbitration.

In a big company, with its own legal department, it should be the task of the in-house lawyer to assess the likely outcome of litigation against the expected legal business and costs. Under the heading of business costs include not only managerial time but, in the first place, the likely disruption of business relations with the other party to the dispute and with third parties who may be deterred from doing business with someone who appears to be unnecessarily litigious.

In short: to act 'on legal advice' may safeguard your legal position but still be bad for business. In the end, the executive has to make his own decision, bearing in mind that only part of the legal costs can be recovered in successful litigation or arbitration.

If all other avenues seem to be closed and litigation becomes inevitable, one should apply to it the ordinary criteria of cost-effectiveness.

Are the solicitors normally looking after your company affairs also the best to handle litigation? They know you and your business better and are more interested in its prosperity than someone who approaches the case on a one-off basis. On the other hand, they may not have the expertise and will be running to counsel with every single letter, causing delays and costs.

Different criteria apply to the choice of counsel. Some solicitors tend to go for 'the best', that is the most expensive they think they can afford. This may not be good for you. If the legal issues are fairly simple, there is no need to pay the astronomical fees commanded by the leaders of the profession. A less famous barrister, whose diary is not so overcrowded, will be able to give your affairs more thought and bring the litigation to a conclusion faster.

Whoever you choose as your lawyers, try to subject them to budget discipline. 'No cost spared to win' may be an expression of grandeur, or of a rather vulnerable ego, but it transgresses the fiduciary duties of a company director. When planning a legal action with your solicitors, ask for a list of persons who will be involved, the time they are likely to spend on your case, and the rate at which their fees are calculated. Insist on a budget for the separate stages: pre-trial, trial and appeal. Treat litigation as any other speculative venture – set to the risk a limit beyond which you will not go, and on the reaching of which you are prepared to cut your losses. If you are refused a budget, try another law firm.

Settling disputes by conciliation

'The first thing to do,' said Dick the Butcher, 'let's kill all the lawyers.'[2] This is obviously a counsel of despair with which one need not agree, not entirely anyhow. There is some hope that lawyers can be re-educated, at least some of them. The first point of the re-education programme should be that for most people justice matters more than law. And the second point is that when it comes to justice, money does matter. As Lord Devlin said: 'The trouble at the root of our legal system is that we have allowed it to grow up in an atmosphere in which, where justice is concerned, money is hardly an object.'

The cost of litigation in the UK is such that most people are frightened of the judicial system – and the cost of arbitration is sometimes even greater. And it is even worse in the US. Judicial statistics reveal that the proportion of actions settled before they come to trial is rapidly growing. In a minority of cases, the settlement is brought about by genuine agreement. In most cases, the fear of the enormous costs of the trial obliges the financially weaker party to give up. This is a very unsatisfactory solution which has nothing to do with the pursuit of justice.

A reaction against the mounting cost of litigation and arbitration – sometimes greater than the award to the winning party – leads to a proliferation of non-judicial methods of dispute resolution. All sorts of UK complaints procedures fall into this category. Some are operated by trade or professional organisations – the Insurance Ombudsman Bureau and the Banking Ombudsman, for example. If you think your solicitor's bill is bigger than it should be, you can ask him – within a month – to obtain a Law Society remuneration certificate, and if you are still dissatisfied, you can go further and ask for taxation of the costs by the court, if these are related to litigation.

There is also a proliferation of independent, quasi-judicial dispute determinators, often operating in a two-instance system. Thus, trading standards officers can refer serious consumer complaints to the Office of Fair Trading; the Lay Observer supervises and reports on the way the Law Society deals with complaints against solicitors; there are the Local Administration Commissioners to be approached through local councillors and the Parliamentary Ombudsman to be approached through Members of Parliament in his capacity of Commissioner for Administration and directly when he wears the hat of the Health Service Commissioner.

All these and many other complaints and arbitration schemes serve the consumer or private individual facing a big trading organisation, a profession or a government department. However, there is a remarkable lack of quick and cost-efficient methods of resolving disputes between businessmen. Conciliation is still a dirty word for most English lawyers and the conciliation procedure made available by the Chartered Institute of Arbitrators is rarely used.

This contrasts sharply with the US attitude expressed by Robert Coulson, president of the American Arbitration Association:

> The process of managing business disputes has changed. Business executives no longer think of controversies as discrete adversarial transactions. Every disagreement with an outside entity resonates throughout the corporate structure, sending pangs of apprehension through the various levels of the organisation and to its constituents.

The association has adopted a much broader objective than European arbitrators. It is its policy to encourage not only arbitration but also negotiation, mediation, conciliation and other procedures of dispute resolution which are now emerging.

A conciliator does not resolve the dispute by a binding and enforceable decision as an arbitrator does, but by helping the parties to agree – and their agreement is, of course, binding and enforceable as any other contract. Conciliation can, and often does, proceed without formality, but the parties can also adopt rules formulated for this purpose by several institutions. These include the conciliation rules of the International Chamber of Commerce, of the UN Commission for International Trade Law (Uncitral), published in 1981 and of the International Centre for Settlement of Investment Disputes, published in January 1985.

A pre-trial or a pre-hearing conference called to determine what is common ground between the parties and to define the disputed issues can sometimes lead to conciliation and US judges are known sometimes to take an informal and beneficial initiative towards that end. In Europe both judges and arbitrators have to be more careful not to get involved to a point which would make them seem biased in favour of a solution which they had suggested in their effort to help the parties to settle their dispute.

Some of the new schemes are derived from old-established 'adjudication' functions of the architect or consulting engineers. Independent teams consisting of technical experts, arbitrators and lawyers offer their services extending from contract management, fact finding, conciliation to arbitration producing binding awards. One of such new organisations is Polycon Endispute Management Services, whose founder, Ron Baden Hellard, claims: 'We resist lawyers' strong inclination to treat arbitrators as High Court judges, which they are not, and seek the just resolution of disputes as one businessman helping another.'

To reduce the legal costs of US corporations – estimated at $80bn a year – the Federal Bar Council has devised a scheme to eliminate or reduce the burden of discovery and of other pre-trial procedures. The parties using the scheme agree on an experienced trial lawyer to serve either as 'special counsel', a mediator in effect, or as 'adjudicator' making an award on the merits of the case. They agree further on a fixed time schedule and on the fee to be paid to the lawyer. Whether acting as special counsel or as adjudicator, the lawyer appointed by the parties has complete control over the procedure, and it is understood that he will not adopt the conventional US adversary procedure with its discovery clashes and numerous interlocutory motions and other diversions.

Consultation and contract re-negotiating, old established methods of dispute resolution between reasonable people, are becoming unavoidable and more structured to respond to the requirements of high finance and of big business. They can succeed where litigation and arbitration are bound to fail because neither the judge nor the arbitrator can rewrite the contract to meet new developments and unforeseen circumstances. 'Renegotiation' is the word when defaults of sovereign borrowers have to be papered over, 'consultation' when the International Monetary Fund and the World Bank step in.

On a less august level, we have now the 'mini-trial' – a misnomer, as it is no trial but a carefully prepared session designed to clarify the claims and possibilities of the parties and to arrive at a solution which would not harm an ongoing business relationship. It can be strictly 'off the record' and 'without prejudice' to any future litigation or arbitration; or parties can agree that certain disclosures or partial agreements can be carried forward to the next stage. It may be that a party which rejects the chairman's recommendations will have to pay the costs of subsequent litigation unless it thereby obtains a substantially better result.

Though the scheme is of US origin, the Zurich Chamber of Commerce has also introduced a 'mini-trial' designed for international commercial disputes. A panel consisting of two senior corporate officers of the disputant concerns and a neutral chairman of equivalent standing hears the issues and aims to achieve a settlement. Written submissions are limited to 25 typed pages and time limits of 30 days are imposed. Lawyers are not discouraged. If no agreed settlement is reached by the deadline, the panel submits a settlement recommendation, unanimous if possible, otherwise from the chairman.

The mini-trial can be often a faster procedure than suggested by the Zurich scheme – it can be concentrated into one or two days, during which executives of the parties in dispute hear, often for the first time, what the real issues are and how they appear to the other side. There is time for only brief oral submissions by lawyers, a free-for-all question session and the chairman's estimate of the probable outcome, duration and costs of litigation. And after a lunch, taken by the two parties and their advisers separately, an agreement – or so one must hope.

Lawyer-dominated arbitration

The establishment in London of the European Users Council is the latest step in the efforts of the London Court of International Arbitration (LCIA) to improve its image and to attract to London the arbitration of 'heavy' international disputes mainly concerning industrial development projects, civil engineering works and large-scale public building construction.

Similar councils are planned for the North American and Pacific users, or potential users, of London Arbitration. The fund created from the council members' contribution should enable the court to spread the good news about improvements achieved by the 1979 Arbitration Act and the LCIA's 1985 rule for international commercial arbitration.

The improvements are considerable. The 1979 Act replaced the greatly abused 'case stated' procedure with the judicial review of points of law which should be admitted by a judge only when real interest of parties – and not only abstract legal problems – is at issue. The 1985 rules of the LCIA, drafted under the influence of United Nations Commission for International Trade Law (UNCITRAL), are flexible enough to allow their use in any part of the world and not only for resolution of disputes governed by English law.

Unfortunately, these improvements are not enough to equip London for successful competition with the newly emerging arbitration centres and for coping with the great opportunities opened to arbitration, particularly by the recent decision of US Supreme Court to allow arbitration of antitrust claims in the context of international disputes (see p 280). One would hope that the Users Council will be employed by the LCIA not only as a vehicle of publicity but as a real marketing instrument: the feedback from these councils should lead to a better product. Another revision of the Arbitration Act may be necessary but not sufficient. Also, the practice and attitude of London lawyers will have to change and, above all, London arbitrators will have to free themselves from their dependence on the legal profession.

In spite of the 1979 reform, the fear of a judicial review still looms large over most cases of London arbitration. Though the parties can now exclude judicial review of international arbitration in contracts concerning industrial and other one-off projects, the possibility of appeals to the Commercial Court cannot be removed by the agreement of the parties in maritime, commodity and insurance contracts. The Government could easily remedy this by an order made under the 1979 Act, but is deterred by the combined opposition of judges and the legal profession.

As a result, the tendency to treat arbitration as a rehearsal for litigation survives. In spite of Lord Donaldson's, the Master of the Rolls, campaign for greater brevity and a more rational procedure in courts, the old habits of long oral submissions die hard and are nurtured by the method of paying the lawyers for real or fictious time spent on the case. Arbitrators, who are paid similarly but would often gladly move on to another case waiting for them, do not dare to cut the long speeches and procedural maze for fear of antagonising the legal profession. A reform of the way lawyers are paid seems, therefore, to be one of the main paths towards a more efficient and more attractive London arbitration.

Some observers seem to be concerned about the High Court's statutory power to set aside an award for arbitrators' 'misconduct'. This provision of the 1950 Arbitration Act was not removed by the 1979 Act, and the interpretation of the term is certainly in need of revision, either by statute or by the House of Lords. Its interpretations as 'procedural errors and omissions by arbitrators who may otherwise be doing their best to uphold the highest standards' is definitely too wide. A simplified procedure should be the hallmark of arbitration and, as long as it is fair to both parties, it should not be open to attack in courts.

It is, of course, true that other countries provide alarming possibilities of appeal to courts, some creating considerable uncertainty. US courts can set aside an award for 'manifest disregard of the law'. In France, the courts are able to deny recognition to an award because it is contrary to 'international public policy' which may be all things to all people. In Switzerland, the judges have the power to set aside awards which violate law or equity or are based on findings manifestly contrary to the facts, which could go much further than the judicial review of the 1979 Arbitration Act in the UK. However, because of history and practitioners' attitudes, even smaller opportunities to delay by appeal loom larger in the UK.

The removal of this psychological barrier would enable London to have the full benefit of the unique experience accumulated by its arbitrators and lawyers as well as of their high reputation for impartiality. While the Paris-based International Chamber of Commerce finds it necessary to select arbitrators from a third country to eliminate any suspicion that they may favour one of the parties on nationalistic grounds, I have not yet heard such suspicion addressed to a London arbitrator. A strict impartiality and freedom from national bias is an essential requirement for operating in the context of world-wide trade. Indeed, London arbitrators and English courts can often be reproached for bending over backwards, treating foreign state trading organisations as if they were sovereigns.

Judges urge a restatement of the English law of arbitration

English arbitration law should be clarified and made certain by an explicit and comprehensive statutory restatement, possibly on the basis of the UNCITRAL Model Law[3] if this succeeds. But the possibility of judicial review of issues of law should be retained, except when the parties agree to opt out and indicate this in a positive and unambiguous way.

This was the conclusion reached by Lord Justice Kerr, president of the Chartered Institute of Arbitrators, when delivering the 1984 Alexander Lecture.

The 1979 Arbitration Act was a compromise solution, little loved and understood even less, as the unedifying battle between the Commercial Court, on the one hand, and the higher courts on the other, has shown.

The Commercial Court judges did not wish to reduce substantially input of appeals from arbitration tribunals – the bread and butter of their court. The Court of Appeal and the House of Lords interpreted the 1979 Act so as to restrict this flow and eliminate appeals which were of no great importance and often served only to delay the enforcement of the award. The battle ended with an uneasy stalemate and the call for clarification of the law is one of its symptoms.

The need of a restatement can hardly be doubted, and no one is better qualified to start the ball rolling than Sir Michael Kerr, who as judge, judge-arbitrator, writer and lecturer, has contributed much to the development of international arbitration and to international co-operation in this field.

A review of the English law of arbitration and its linkage with an international harmonisation project is a matter of great practical importance. Arbitration is a great industry and London has all pre-requisites for its further development. Some 10,000 arbitrations take place in London each year, generated by the activity of the London markets and attracted by the availability of specialised arbitrators and commercial lawyers, and the fact that English is still the lingua franca of the commercial community.

Responding to the need, the Institute has expanded the volume of its services, not only by providing guidance and its own arbitration rules where needed, but by helping with the logistics of the process: it provides a complex of court rooms, conference rooms, a library, catering facilities and all the services necessary for the conduct of arbitrations.

The Institute's membership is now drawn from 72 countries and, out of its 5,900 members, 1,300 are fellows manning panels specialised in various fields from which the membership is drawn.

However, great as the advantages of London as an arbitration centre are, many parties are deterred from using them by the very close and somewhat uncertain relationship between arbitrators and English courts, causing some appeals to go as high as the House of Lords, and producing much delay and formidable legal costs to the parties.

Sir Michael argued convincingly that in this respect things are not worse in London than in any other arbitration centre but are only made to appear worse by the profusion of legal reports which are indispensable for the development of English law but are rare and receiving much less attention in civil law countries.

Nevertheless, he had to admit that some of the fears are well founded. In the first place the power of English courts to intervene in arbitrations by orders for discovery of documents and other evidence should be abolished as arbitrators already have the power to make such orders themselves. While arbitrators should be given greater autonomy, the courts should be equipped with the power to consolidate arbitrations involving the same or overlapping issues, and to terminate stale arbitrations. To this end it would be necessary to reverse the much criticised[4] decisions of the House of Lords in *Bremer Vulkan* and *The Hannah Blumenthal* (see p 279).

The UK Arbitration Acts lay down the powers of the courts in relation to arbitrations but provide virtually no information about the circumstances in which these powers are, in fact, exercised by the courts. Nor can such information be easily obtained by ploughing through textbooks which give a bewildering array of reported decisions.

Even without the opportunity provided by the reception of the model law, there is, in Sir Michael's view, an urgent need of a restatement of the English law setting out the principles governing rights of appeal on issues of law so as to state explicitly how English law actually operates in practice.

Sir Michael argues that this could also take much of the horror out of the powers which courts have to set aside or to remit awards on the grounds of 'misconduct of the arbitrator', which in practice is directed only against arbitrators who would deny a party a full and proper opportunity of presenting its case. Also, the power to intervene in the course of arbitration is in practice used only when the arbitrator has shown actual or potential bias or has given serious grounds for the loss of confidence in his ability to conduct the dispute judicially and competently.

While Sir Michael favours the acceptance of the model law by the UK if its trading partners do the same, and clearly looks forward to the opportunity of using it as a basis for an explicit restatement of English arbitration law which would apply to all arbitrations held in the UK (and not only international arbitrations), he warns that when it comes to the relationship between arbitrations and the courts, the model law must undergo radical changes. It must leave room for a judicial review in cases of necessity and at least in the extent to which it is possible to obtain judicial review of the legally binding acts or decisions of all tribunals, authorities or individuals in the UK, with the exception of the Sovereign and the judicial committees of the House of Lords and the Privy Council.

This requirement, that no one should be left at the mercy of an unscrupulous, biased or incompetent arbitrator, is included, as far as I know, in the laws of most civilised countries concerned with arbitration, and is opposed only by the diminishing band of those who believe in the possibility of a 'floating arbitration' divorced from any national machinery of justice.

Another question is the courts' power to revise awards on issues of law. The 1979 Arbitration Act allows parties to exclude such a revision of international awards, except in the case of marine, commodity and insurance arbitrations. 'If the model law gained general acceptance,' Sir Michael said.

> a logical modification would be to allow exclusion agreements in all cases, but not as terms which may be incorporated automatically by printed clauses in standard forms of contract. The parties should be given a real choice in each case.

This proposition is, of course, biased in favour in judicial review. The parties may not be even aware of the reviewability of English awards and of the possibility of making them final by means of an exclusion clause. The arbitration clause ought to be so drafted as to offer a real choice.

UNCITRAL – the not-quite-perfect Model Law of Arbitration

After many years of ardent discussions between delegations of 61 governments taking part in the projects, UNCITRAL, the Vienna-based UN Commission of International Trade Law, adopted in 1985 a Model Law of Arbitration. Ever since the member states have been pondering what use to make of it.

Some may reject it altogether. Countries with a developed system of arbitration law are unlikely to adopt the model law as it stands without modification. To do so may be more attractive for countries where arbitration is a novelty, not thought of before.

The argument of harmonisation is an important one. It would greatly facilitate business if arbitration were subject to the same rules everywhere. Unfortunately, there is no chance that this will happen. Belgium and France have only recently adopted new legislation and it is improbable that they would be ready to change it. The European communist countries seem to favour adoption of the Model Law by others, but not by themselves. They can hardly adopt it since their state arbitration Commissions are more akin to commercial courts, which they superseded, than to the concept of private arbitration as practised in the West.

The burning issue in arbitration is its relationship with the law and that between arbitrators and courts. The Model Law follows the tendency to leave the parties or the arbitrator free to choose their rules of procedure and applicable law and gives the award a far-reaching freedom from judicial interference, excluding appeals to the courts on points of fact and law.

English judges favour using the Model Law as a basis for the much needed restatement of English law of arbitration but cannot visualise its adoption as it stands, eliminating judicial review of arbitral awards on issues of facts and law. Lord Wilberforce differs from the Commercial Court and Court of Appeal judges: he thinks that insistence on judicial review, beyond the scope provided by the Model Law, in countries where the courts are trusted and experienced, could encourage a similar modification of the Model Law in countries where the same conditions did not exist. The result would be that international arbitration in those countries would become less, rather than more safe.

The contradictory decisions of courts and the number of appeals from courts of first instance indicate that judges are no less prone than arbitrators to misinterpret the law. When they do, it is often because judges attach greater importance to the letter of the law than to the practicalities of the case. When an arbitrator errs in law, it is more often because he prefers a pragmatic, business-like solution to the letter of the law.

In the end, one must balance the risk of an erroneous decision against the risk of a long, costly and arduous journey through the courts with a delay which will deprive the winning party of the fruits of victory.

On balance, it seems advisable to relax still further the control which English courts have over arbitration by extending the possibility to opt out of judicial review to marine, insurance and commodity arbitrations.

A relaxation of the judicial review should be compensated by stricter and more precise provisions concerning the choice of law and procedure than those offered by the Model Law. In the view of Dr Francis Mann, an authority on conflicts of law, the Model Law puts the parties and their advisers into an impossible situation as they would have to decide whether to arbitrate or not without knowing what evidence they could obtain and which law would be applicable.

Another danger inherent in the Model Law is that appeals will be lodged not where the awards are made, but only in the countries of enforcement so that instead of one appeal procedure, there will be several, possibly with contraditory results.

In short, the much-needed harmonisation of arbitration laws is unlikely to be achieved by the UNCITRAL product; there were too many cooks and the ingredients they put in do not always blend. But it may come useful in countries desperate for a ready-made legislation.

A tale of two cities

The Court of Arbitration of the International Chamber of Commerce (ICC) in Paris celebrated its sixtieth anniversary in 1983.

More than 600 arbitrators and lawyers attended the conference, chaired on the first day by Sheikh Ahmed Zaki Yamani and on the last day by Sir John Donaldson (now Lord Donaldson), the Master of the Rolls. In between these two great practitioners of law and business, a number of eminent academics delivered their lectures and answered questions.

Fortunately, there was much to distract the visitors, their wives or sweethearts: warm rain and autumnal sun made Paris look exactly as it should according to Utrillo and other French Impressionists. The view of magnificent thorough-fares, arcs, and palaces, could be enjoyed at leisure because traffic jams made fast progress impossible. And at the great dinners given at the Conciergerie of the Palace of Justice, and at the Palace of Versailles itself, the torture by seemingly interminable speeches was soon forgotten when battalions of waiters invaded the great and venerable halls, bringing superlative wine and food.

One quickly became aware how much, not only arbitration but also the discussion of its problems, is a matter of style. Although attaching great importance to being an international organisation, the ICC and its Court of Arbitration appeared to the foreign visitor as being very French. Not only was there much intoxication with the sheer beauty of the language with which dignitaries delivered their solemn speeches, but also in the working sessions one had to listen carefully for coded messages to detect any particular problems or difficulties of what, in deference to the occasion, all speakers described as the best possible arbitration system.

There is no doubt that in the 60 years of its existence ICC arbitration developed from very small beginnings into an important international system playing a very specialised role in disputes arising from large industrial projects, particularly when one party to the dispute is a government or a state trading agency. So far the ICC arbitration clause has been acceptable to many Communist and developing countries when signing contracts with companies from western industrialised countries.

Between 250 and 300 arbitrations are now initiated in the ICC each year and, although this seems little when compared with the 10,000 or so arbitration awards made each year in London, one has to keep in mind that the ICC proceedings concern some of the biggest international disputes – so important that the London International Arbitration Trust was created especially to facilitate and attract this sort of business.

Both France and the UK recently adopted legislation designed to facilitate international arbitration and to give awards greater finality and security of enforcement. In the UK the 1979 Arbitration Act enabled parties to opt out of the possibility of judicial review when concluding an international deal.

The way for giving up the formalism, meticulousness and long oral submissions, characteristic of English civil procedure, has been paved by the International Arbitration Rules adopted by the London Court of Arbitration from 1 January 1981.

These new rules give the arbitrator or the parties complete freedom to choose such procedure as they think fits best the needs of the particular case, and leave it to the arbitrator to determine which law is applicable to the agreement in dispute. Very little seems to be known in Paris, not only about these changes but also about the unique advantage which the 1979 Act gives to London arbitrators, where orders are flouted by one of the parties. The arbitrator can apply to the High Court and obtain powers to continue with the proceedings 'in like manner as a judge of the High Court may continue with proceedings in that court where a party fails to comply with an order of that court or a requirement of rules of court'.

Compared with the London procedure, the ICC system enables less professional arbitrators to exercise their function under the watchful eye of the Court of Arbitration and its expert staff. Arbitrators have to submit terms of reference and, no doubt, have them trimmed when necessary; even more importantly the arbitrators have to submit a draft of their award to the ICC court which will correct formal deficiences and point out shortcomings concerning the merits of the case. This is sometimes criticised as causing delay and uncertainty, and such a procedure is certainly not necessary in the highly professional ambience of London arbitration.

Continuing the tale of the two cities, one can see that, like the 1979 UK Act, the French Decree of 14 May 1981 freed international arbitration from rules applying to domestic arbitration, and strengthened the finality of awards by reducing to four statutory grounds their voidability in courts. Unfortunately, one of these grounds enables annulment of the award if it is contrary to 'international public policy'.

As a result, French courts will take into account requirements of French foreign policy. Together with Sheikh Yamani's insistence on the application of Islamic law and the Libyan 'administrative contracts' which the Government can modify or abandon unilaterally, this may leave arbitration without a leg to stand on.

This could deflect some big arbitrations between private parties and governments to London – if only English courts did not cling to the notions of absolute sovereign immunity in spite of it having been discarded by Parliament.

The interminable threat of a pending arbitration

The ghost of the *Bremer Vulcan* decision, better known as '*The Sleeping Dogs*' case, is up and about, and doing much damage. This decision concerned an arbitration conducted with such inordinate delays that after some 11 years the respondents applied to the High Court to have it stopped; witnesses were not longer available and a fair decision could not be reached.

Sir John Donaldson, then sitting as a judge in the High Court, granted their application, which was confirmed by a unanimous Court of Appeal. But on further appeal to the House of Lords, he was reversed by a majority of 3-2. Lord Diplock found that the respondents did not do anything to prod the plaintiffs into action. He said: 'Respondents in private arbitrations are not entitled to let sleeping dogs lie and then complain that they did not bark.'

This decision made in January 1981, has had disastrous effects. It has resulted in the revival of references to arbitration which were thought to be long dead. It is causing the greatest concern, not only in the UK but also abroad; it puts at risk the numerous foreign parties who bring their disputes to London for arbitration.

The decision was based on an utterly unrealistic argument of Lord Diplock. He said that far from being able to treat the other party's failure to proceed as repudiation, the defendant was himself in breach of contract if he did not prod the plaintiff to greater activity.

Imagine that someone brings a claim against you which you consider worthless; he starts arbitration proceedings in the hope that he will win some concessions from you, but you remain firm and he leaves you in peace. Would you, under such circumstances, insist that the arbitration must go on? No one does such a thing. Yet, after the *Bremer Vulcan* judgment, the sword of Damocles dangles interminably over the respondent's head.

It was another seven years before this piece of common sense was voiced in the House of Lords by Lord Goff. Speaking on the appeal of Food Corporation of India, he said that the doctrine of mutual obligation of the two parties to arbitration contradicted commercial reality.

However, the facts of the case did not reveal a lack of prosecution and Lord Goff thought that the case was not appropriate for a reversal of the 'sleeping dogs' doctrine. Instead he concluded: 'The sooner the matter is brought before the legislature for consideration the better.'

Their Lordships, always happy to let the sleeping dogs lie, agreed. They recognised they made a terrible blunder in 1981 and left it at that.

This will not help. Lower courts remain bound by the 1981 decision which the Law Lords could have reversed even when dismissing the appeal on facts. Parties can hope to succeed with another appeal – if the composition of their Lordships' bench remains the same, and they have not changed their minds again.

There is, of course, a strong argument in favour of leaving it to Parliament: a legislation would not have a retroactive effect. A Lords' reversal would leave all those who, relying on the 1981 decision, used arbitration as a time bomb, high and dry. Because English courts, unlike those of the US and European Community do not limit the retroactive effect of their decisions.

What a way to dispense law!

Arbitration of US anti-trust disputes

On 2 July 1985, the Supreme Court of the United States held that anti-trust claims raised in the context of international disputes could be decided by arbitrators, and that as long as they respected American anti-trust laws, their awards would be enforced by US courts. But they need not respect the provisions concerning treble damages; simple damages will do.

The judgment, by a majority of 5-2, came as a big surprise after a series of previous decisions that anti-trust claims were so much a matter of public interest and public policy that they could not be entrusted to arbitrators.

As a new interpretation of the US Arbitration Act, and the Convention on the Recognition and Enforcement of Arbitral Awards (the New York Convention), it is bound to become a powerful influence on legal developments in Europe and in Japan, and wherever the US anti-trust law serves as a model. Above all, it opens up to parties engaged in international deals the possibility of ensuring, by means of an arbitration clause, against the hazards of US treble damage suits for real or imagined anti-trust violations.

One party in the dispute was Mitsubishi Motors Corporation,[5] a joint venture of Chrysler International and of the Japanese corporation, created for the purpose of distributing through Chrysler dealers outside the continental United States, motor cars made in Japan. It sued one of its dealers, Soler Chrysler Plymouth Inc, a Puerto Rican corporation.

In 1981 the new car market slackened, and Soler attempted to arrange for the transhipment to the continental US and to Latin America of a quantity of the vehicles it had received earlier.

Mitsubishi refused permission, and brought an action in the US District Court for the District of Puerto Rico under the Federal Arbitration Act and the New York Convention. It asked the court to compel Soler to agree to arbitration in accordance with the clause of the sales agreement which provided for arbitration in Japan in accordance with the rules and regulations of the Japan Commercial Arbitration Association.

Soler countered by claiming that Mitsubishi and Chrysler had conspired to prevent the transhipment of some 966 surplus vehicles from Puerto Rico to other dealers in the American market, thus violating Section 1 of the Sherman Act. Soler argued that arbitration of anti-trust claims could not be compelled and that such claims could be brought only to US district courts.

The district court ordered arbitration of most of the issues raised in the complaint and counterclaims. It also said that the federal anti-trust issues might be resolved by arbitration, but on this point was reversed by the US Court of Appeals for the First Circuit.

Mitsubishi then appealed to the Supreme Court on this single point. It was supported by the International Chamber of Commerce which filed an *amicus curiae* brief urging the court to approve arbitration as a suitable means for settling anti-trust disputes. Soler had a more powerful supporter: the US Government filed another *amicus curiae* brief urging the court to confirm the ruling of the Court of Appeal that anti-trust laws and treble damage policy and public interest must not be left for arbitrators to decide.

The fact that the Supreme Court rejected the views expressed by the US Government, as well as the impassioned and very convincing arguments of Justice Stevens – suggests that the court had in mind the increasing frequency of conflicts with its closest allies into which unrestricted application of US anti-trust laws and their burdensome pre-trial procedures, treble damage suits, has brought the US government. It quoted from one of its previous decisions: 'The expansion of American business and industry will hardly be encouraged if, notwithstanding solemn contracts, we insist on a parochial concept that all disputes must be resolved under our laws and in our courts . . . .'

It had been thought that the US Arbitration Act provided for the enforcement of arbitral disputes only if these arose out of contracts and that it created a presumption against arbitration of statutory claims. The Supreme Court has now said that was wrong. The Act simply created a duty to honour an agreement to arbitrate, and this duty should be rigorously enforced. Questions of arbitrability 'must be addressed with a healthy regard for the federal policy favouring arbitration'. Any doubt should be resolved in favour of arbitration. Having made the bargain to arbitrate, the party should be held to it unless Congress itself provided that any statutory rights at issue must be left for the courts to decide.

The appeal court decision rejecting arbitration of anti-trust issues was based on the doctrine established by the Supreme Court in *American Safety*.[6]

The first point of this doctrine was the importance for the enforcement of anti-trust laws of private actions for treble damages.

The court has now said in effect that it is not indispensable. No citizen was under an obligation to bring an anti-trust suit, and the private anti-trust plaintiff needed no executive or judicial approval before settling one. It followed at least in the context of international disputes that the prospective litigant may provide in advance for arbitration or for another mutually agreeable procedure for the settling of his anti-trust claims.

The court also rejected the *American Safety* doctrine, where it asserts that anti-trust issues require sophisticated legal and economic analysis unobtainable in arbitration. Adaptability and access to expertise, said the court were hallmarks of arbitration.

It was also wrong to assume, as the doctrine did, that there was a danger of innate hostility to anti-trust law on the part of foreign arbitrators who are businessmen. As in the present case, where the tribunal consisted of three eminent Japanese lawyers, one of whom was an expert in American and Japanese anti-trust law, arbitrators were often drawn from legal circles.

Finally, the court dealt with the objection that anti-trust laws were designed to promote national interests and to preserve democracy in the US, and that it could not be left to foreign arbitrators deciding under foreign law – Swiss law was stipulated in the agreement under dispute – to ignore such fundamental public interest. It said that, though the international arbitration tribunal owed no prior allegiance to statutory dictates of particular states, it was bound to decide disputes in accordance with the national la., giving rise to a particular claim – in this case the US anti-trust law. Whether they did or not would be considered when Mitsubishi asked for the enforcement of an award.

> We merely know that in the event the choice of forum and choice of law clauses operated in tandem (to exclude anti-trust remedies), we would have little hesitation in condemning the agreement as against public policy.

Justice Stevens pointed out in his dissenting opinion that the New York Convention did not require the recognition of awards in disputes which were not capable of settlement by arbitration under the domestic law of the country in which enforcement was sought. The majority assumed that anti-trust issues would not be arbitrable in a purely domestic dispute, and without paying detailed attention to the New York Convention held that concern for international implications required the admittance of arbitration when such disputes had an international character. What their decision lacks in legal logic, it makes up by its practical and political wisdom.

English litigation could be improved

> The judge or arbitrator who sits back and says nothing when the parties or counsel are labouring a point he fully understands and may indeed accept, is not helping the parties. He is just increasing the cost of settling the dispute.

This pronouncement by Lord Donaldson, the Master of the Rolls, made in 1985, is still viewed as revolutionary by the Bar. Are we not moving towards the continental system, labelled 'inquisitorial' to bring to mind the horrors of the Spanish inquisition? The English judge, and his wigless *alter ego*, the arbitrator, exist, according to the accepted wisdom of the profession, merely to hold the rope at which the two parties pull in opposite directions. Any curtailment of the long speeches (lawyers are on time rate) is against natural justice. But the red light which stops American lawyers after 30 minutes of speech-making is not against natural justice (especially when the American lawyer is not paid according to the time spent on his feet but receives a share in the award).

There are other possibilities, well tested elsewhere, such as scales of fees proportionate to the amount in dispute. A system of flat fees for certain standard litigations and arbitrations would do wonders in shortening the proceedings – we might be even faced with the problem of judicial redundancy.

There are thousands of arbitrations taking place in London each year which are about the quality of the delivered goods and are settled quickly by sniffing, tasting or touching. These have little in common with the other type of arbitration concerned with the interpretation of contracts. That is considered to be an issue of law and, as such, exposed to the possibility of judicial review.

The first requirement for making arbitration work, therefore, is the removal of the judicial review of points of law. Once this is done, parties in dispute will have no need of barristers to represent them, and arbitration will be faster and cheaper.

The second question concerns the method of channelling to arbitration disputes which now go straight to courts. One can adopt either the methods used in some federal circuits in the US, where the courts can order arbitration whenever the amount in dispute is under a certain limit, or one can go the French way. This is to establish regional commercial courts composed of lay judges elected by the business community. These commercial courts decide mainly on the basis of an opinion by an expert appointed by them from a semi-permanent panel. The more legally difficult cases are usually steered to the first bench of the court with more experienced lay judges who may have some legal training.

This system has very much the same function as English arbitration but is less formal, faster and cheaper than 'big' arbitration when parties come with lawyers. It has two serious disadvantages. First, in a provincial town all the businessmen know each other and have intertwined interests, so that the impartiality of elected judges can be questioned. Second, the panels of experts, who play a crucial role, are often out-of-date and inadequately specialised, so that it may happen that an electrical contractor is invited to give an expert opinion on a computer or another electronic device.

Unsolved issues of international litigation in London

London markets attract international litigation. In numerous disputes heard by the Commercial Court in London both parties are foreign. In 90 per cent of disputes heard by that court at least one of the parties is foreign.

The Commercial Court is a department of Queen's Bench of the High Court. It consists of five judges specialised in commercial matters. It is therefore a purely British court by its constitution, yet by its function it is truly an international court. Some judges, including the Master of the Rolls, Lord Donaldson, attach greater weight to the courts function and would say it is an international court. The Law Lords disagree: they emphasise the court's constitution.

The diparity of views came to light in the case of *Amin Rasheed Shipping Corp v Kuwait Insurance Co.*[7] This case also raised a possibly more interesting and certainly more practical question: Can one say that a standard Lloyd's policy has become 'internationalised' – and with it a big chunk of English commercial law – because that policy is widely used all over the world?

The view that a Lloyd's policy is a sort of floating contract, unattached to any system of law, was adopted by Commercial Court judges but overruled by the majority of the Court of Appeal and in the House of Lords.

These issues may seem rather theoretical but have far-reaching consequences for parties to a Lloyds policy or a similarly 'internationalised' London commodity contract or charter party. The answer given to the two questions will decide whether English courts will accept jurisdiction and how they will interpret the contract if they do. It is therefore essential to anticipate the answer before starting litigation in English courts.

Unfortunately, it is almost impossible to predict which line an English court will take, as the *Amin Rasheed* case illustrates.

The events which gave eminent English judges the opportunity for disparate answers to such fundamental questions took place far away, in the Arabian Gulf. The Al Wahab, a small cargo vessel of the landing craft type, was arrested by Saudi Arabian authorities on charges of smuggling. The crew and the master were imprisoned and after some time released and repatriated to their home countries in India and Bangladesh. The vessel remained in the Saudi port, apparently confiscated. Its owners, a shipping company incorporated in Liberia but with its head office and business in Dubai, claimed compensation for 'constructive total loss' from their insurers, the Kuwait Insurance Company.

The insurance policy, underwritten on the insurer's standard printed form, was in English, and with minor and immaterial omissions its text was identical with Lloyd's SG policy, subject to the 'Institute War and Strikes Clauses Hulls'. Under these clauses the insurers were exempt from responsibility if the ship was arrested because of infringement of customs regulations. The insurers denied responsibility, relying on the official reason given by the Saudi authorities for the detention of the ship. The assured denied however, that the vessel was engaged in smuggling. This was the principal issue of the dispute which the assured wanted to have decided by an English court.

On their first attempt they obtained an *ex parte* leave to serve the writ abroad from Mr Justice Robert Goff. However, after hearing both parties, Mr Justice Bingham set it aside. He took the view, later adopted by Lord Justice Robert Goff (who in the meantime had been promoted to the Court of Appeal), that the policy was internationalised and became a sort of floating contract unattached to any system of law.

In consequence, the jurisdiction of an English court could not be justified under the rules of the Supreme Court which give the judge discretion to deal with the dispute if the contract is, by its terms, or by implication, governed by English law. Moreover, he said that even if he had discretion he would not use it in favour of the assured because the Kuwaiti court was better able to decide whether the vessel was engaged in smuggling.

When the case came before the Court of Appeal, Lord Justice Robert Goff was overruled on the jurisdictional point by the Master of the Rolls and Lord Justice May, who both held that the contract was governed by English law. Sir John Donaldson rejected the view that there was a supranational or transnational body of marine insurance law: the law with which the transaction had the closest and most real connection was English law.

As to whether the court should accept jurisdiction he found in favour of the assured, holding that Mr Justice Bingham erred by overlooking the special position held by the commercial court. This court he said, was the *curia franca* of international commerce, in so far as that commerce is based upon the concepts of English law . . . . It is far more than a national or domestic court; it is an international commercial court, the overwhelming majority of whose judgments are concerned with the rights and obligations of foreign nationals.

When the case reached the House of Lords, all the Law Lords agreed that the obsolete and unintelligible language of the Lloyd's SG form of policy made it impossible to discover the mutual rights and obligations of the parties without reference to the Marine Insurance Act 1906, which codified the English law relating to marine insurance. The absence of an indigenous law of marine insurance in Kuwait before 1980, in Lord Diplock's view, made the English law the proper law of the contract and allowed the assumption of jurisdiction by an English court.

Lord Wilberforce, however, did not go that far. Disagreeing with the view that the policy was an internationalised floating contract unattached to any system of law, he said that it had been taken into a great number of legal systems either by statute or as a matter of commercial practice. Though it made sense only in the context of the 1906 Act many other circumstances had to be considered when deciding which system of law had the closest and real connection with the policy. He reached the conclusion 'with no great confidence and reluctantly' that in this case it was English law.

What should one make of such a diversity of judicial opinion? First that the majority of the highest judges, including the Law Lords and the Master of the Rolls, were leaning towards a universalist view of English law, tending to impose English law and jurisdiction on reluctant defendants in situations which were not believed to justify it in the past.

Would the Law Lords still hold this view now that the protaganist of the 'internationalised policy' defeated in Court of Appeal has been once more promoted, to become as Lord Goff the intellectual leader of Lords' Judicial Committee, at least on issues of commercial law?

There seems to be a need for formalising the *de facto* 'internationalisation' of English marine insurance law by a convention leading to the adoption of uniform statutes. It would still not be a real internationalisation. The uniform statutes would still have the force of law of individual countries, but the convention could help to decide both jurisdictional and material issues. Until that is done the more restrained approach of Lord Wilberforce to the determination of the 'proper law of contract' is probably safer if one wishes to avoid conflict with the courts of other countries.

Finally, the clash of judicial opinion about the nature of the London commercial court – whether it is English or international – reflects a contradiction inherent in what it does: it stands in for a badly needed court dealing with the rapidly emerging international law of contract. Accordingly, its jurisdiction in reviewing arbitration awards has been restricted to issues of law. But where it operates as a trial court, it also deals with issues of fact, an impossible task for an international commercial court. It would be good if the detention of the Al Wahab triggered off developments which would make the words of Sir John Donaldson come true.

Beware of US 'bad faith' litigation

Faced with a claim of doubtful legal strength, prudent managements tend to reject it and to wait and see whether the claimant will have the courage to take them to court: then they may be in a better position to decide whether to settle or to go the whole way of litigation. This may no longer be a prudent policy with regard to claims which can be litigated in the US.[8]

By unreasonably or negligently refusing to settle a claim right away, an insurer, or another strong party to a contract, would run the danger of additional or punitive damages if found guilty of a breach of contract.

Though developed in insurance cases, the 'bad faith' litigation is now also applicable in banking, employment, real estate and ordinary contract disputes. Considering the insurer, the bank, or the employer to be the stronger party, the US courts imply in the contract an obligation to treat the insured, the bank customer or the employee fairly. If the stronger party unreasonably refuses or delays the settlement of a claim, the courts will award, in addition to damages for the breach of contract, additional damages for 'bad faith' and punitive damages if there was any 'malice' or intention to harm the weaker party. While in the ordinary breach of contract suit the plaintiff can only claim compensation for damage foreseeable by the defendant at the time when the contract was made, in the case of a 'tortified' contract – where performance was unreasonably refused – it is possible to claim compensation for a greater damage foreseeable only at the time when the performance was refused. In addition, it is possible to claim also compensation for emotional stress, attorneys fees and other legal costs.

There is no sign yet that English courts will adopt this model. However, the US judicial practice already has its effect on UK insurers and may later influence the behaviour of other non-US enterprises doing business in the US: they will have to take into account that by rejecting a doubtful claim they risk the US courts making them pay substantially more than would be necessary for settling the claim right away.

The principle that corporate bullying – violating standards of 'good faith and fair dealing' – should be punished, was developed primarily in California but gradually adopted by other sun-belt states down to Texas. There was a string of 'bad faith' cases against insurance companies who were accused of doing less than they should in investigating and handling the claims of the insured or of the third parties.

The failure to deal fairly came to be considered as a civil wrong. Along with this expansion of tort liability came the imposition of punitive damages against insurance companies. In 44 jury verdicts between January 1983 and March 1985, Californian courts made punitive awards in excess of $165m (£101m). The highest single award was for $44 million. Early in 1985 the Shell Oil Company was found to have caused a loss of $75,000 to a service station operator by obstructing his sale of the franchise. On top of the $75,000 of actual damages, Shell was made to pay a further $5 million in punitive damages and a further $42,000 for emotional distress. In March of the same year, an Oakland court awarded $125 million in punitive damages to 55 investors in Computer Land Corporation, claiming that the firm violated the terms of a $250,000 loan agreement; and in May 1985, a San Jose jury awarded a former sales representative of NEC Electronics $53.3 million in punitive damages for wrongful termination of employment, breach of contract and defamation.

The US courts derive the duty of good faith and fair dealing from the existence of a special relationship between the parties to a contract. In the case of the insurance contract, the relationship is characterised not only by the unequal bargaining power of the two parties but also by the insured's expectation that his insurance company will not wrongfully deprive him of the security which he attempted to obtain by taking out an insurance policy. In a number of cases dealing with third party claims, when the insured was covered only for part of the claim and had to bear the excess himself, the Californian courts held the insurer responsible for the entire claim, including the excess, if it refused a settlement offered by the claimant and which in the view of the court, a 'prudent insurer' would have accepted. The insurer may be held liable for the excess judgment if he failed to settle at or below the policy limits, even if he acted in good faith and was sincerely, though erroneously, convinced that the claim is not covered by the policy.

This doctrine of strict liability was brought a step further when the California Supreme Court held that a third party can sue an insurer directly for the mishandling of a claim and that the insurer owes a duty, to manage properly settlement negotiations, both to its insured and to third party claimants. He will be held liable for any additional losses occurring after a failure to accept or make reasonable offers of settlement.

The tort concept, leading to extra-contractual damages was well established by 1974 but since then the judge-made law has been further refined. As a result, Californian courts seem to be ready to find that the implied covenant of good faith and fair dealing was breached whenever the insurer withheld a settlement unreasonably and without proper cause. This would be so, for example, when he failed in his duty to investigate thoroughly the insured or the third party's claim. The Californian Unfair Practices Act provides further that the insurer must 'attempt in good faith to effect a prompt, fair and equitable settlement' when liability has 'become reasonably clear'.

While in California these duties of the insurer can be enforced by private action, the Arizona insurance code as well as Indiana law reserve these matters to public prosecution. To establish 'bad faith' conduct, it is enough to show that there was an unreasonable withholding of benefits by under-payment, delay or a wrongful refusal to pay altogether. In such cases extra-contractual compensatory damages are assessed on the basis of actual, proven, losses. However, if the claimant can show that the insurer's conduct was malicious, fraudulent or oppressive, he has a chance of obtaining punitive damages assessed not on actual losses, but on the basis of the defendant's wealth or company assets.

Even if an insurance company obtained an independent lawyer's opinion before refusing a claim, the courts may not accept this as proof of good faith, but will investigate any allegation that the lawyer was acting in collusion with the company. The courts also introduced a number of measures designed to protect the defendant. These may take the form of a requirement of a higher standard of evidence or of telling the jury that the defendant is entitled to a presumption of innocence, or requiring a unanimous verdict.

A constitutional attack on the abuse of punitive damages litigation has been made in the case of *Bankers Life and Casualty Company v Crenshaw*. In this case the Supreme Court was invited to say that the Mississippi law, which gives a jury unfettered discretion to award punitive damages on vague grounds, violates the 'Excessive Fines Clause' of the Eighth Amendment of the US Constitution and the 'Contract Clause' and 'New Process Clause' of the Fourteenth Amendment.

The US law enabling the awards of punitive damages by which UK firms now feel threatened, has its roots in Anglo-Saxon England where the wrongdoer was required, in addition to compensatory damages to the victim, to pay a further fine to the community on the ground that every evil deed is also a public offence. These fines, called amercements after the Norman conquest, became an important source of Crown revenue and escalated accordingly.

In an attempt to contain the escalation of these punitive damages, the Magna Carta introduced the principle of proportionality between the amercement and the wrong done to the Lord or the court. The US Supreme Court has been reminded of this by the appellant in the *Greenshaw* case. The insurance barons, as well as others, hoped that the Court will be impressed by King John's example.

Notes

1 Organised by Oyez Conferences, Copenhagen.
2 Henry VI, Part 2.
3 United Nations Commission on International Trade Law: Draft model law on international commercial arbitration.
4 FT 23 April 1981 and FT 16 December 1982.
5 *Mitsubishi Motors Corpn v Soler Chrysler-Plymouth Inc*, No. 83–1509, decided 2 July 1985.
6 *American Safety Equipment Corpn v J. P. Meguire & Co* 391 F 2d 821 (CA2).
7 *Amin Rasheed Shipping Corpn v Kuwait Insurance Co*, judgment 8 July 1983, FT European Law Letter, September 1983.
8 I am indebted for information on these developments to Mr Guy Kornblum, the senior partner in Kornblum, Kelly and Herlihy, and founder of the Hastings National College of Advocacy.

Index